STEAM TITANS

STEAM TITANS

*Cunard, Collins, and the Epic Battle for
Commerce on the North Atlantic*

WILLIAM M. FOWLER JR.

B L O O M S B U R Y
NEW YORK · LONDON · OXFORD · NEW DELHI · SYDNEY

Bloomsbury USA
An imprint of Bloomsbury Publishing Plc

1385 Broadway   50 Bedford Square
New York   London
NY 10018   WC1B 3DP
USA   UK

www.bloomsbury.com

BLOOMSBURY and the Diana logo are trademarks of Bloomsbury Publishing Plc

First published 2017

© William M. Fowler Jr., 2017

ISBN: HB: 978-1-62040-908-4
     ePub: 978-1-62040-909-1

Library of Congress Cataloging-in-Publication Data is available.

2 4 6 8 10 9 7 5 3 1

Typeset by Westchester Publishing Services
Printed and bound in the U.S.A. by Berryville Graphics Inc., Berryville, Virginia

To find out more about our authors and books visit www.bloomsbury.com.
Here you will find extracts, author interviews, details of forthcoming events and
the option to sign up for our newsletters.

Bloomsbury books may be purchased for business or promotional use.
For information on bulk purchases please contact Macmillan Corporate and
Premium Sales Department at specialmarkets@macmillan.com.

To: Olivia

CONTENTS

INTRODUCTION

IN 1492, CHRISTOPHER COLUMBUS CROSSED the Atlantic in thirty-five days; three centuries later, passage from Europe to America took just as long. During the early nineteenth century, Atlantic voyagers still sailed aboard wooden vessels powered by the natural energies of man and nature, muscle and wind. Between 1815 and the American Civil War, however, there was a sea change in oceanic transportation, delivered by the greatest invention of the Industrial Revolution, the steam engine. "Vulcan now rides in Neptune's barge," and the Atlantic was transformed into a pulsating highway over which steamships ferried people, supplies, money, and information with astounding speed and regularity.[1]

Ashore, steam-powered factories consumed vast quantities of raw materials, turning them into a stunning array of goods. Mass production, in lowering prices, spurred mass consumption. Decreasing the costs and increasing the momentum of transportation, steam at sea, linked in turn to rails on land, overwhelmed the traditional world of sail. In a single year, for example, one steamship could easily complete more than a dozen round-trips between New York and Liverpool, whereas masters of sailing vessels were fortunate if they managed three. Between 1820 and 1860, cargo clearing the port of New York increased more than fifteen-fold. American raw materials and foodstuffs flowed into England and Europe, satisfying the demands of industrialization and feeding millions of workers, while westbound vessels carried manufactured goods and immigrants to an emerging American empire. Because it allowed for a rapid and reliable exchange of information, steam passage reduced uncertainty about price and supply, which created a stable economic environment. Thanks to the steamship, the Atlantic world grew interdependent and prosperous.

Two ports, Liverpool and New York, the Atlantic antipodes, gained dominance. Each was blessed by geography, but only when their citizens brought entrepreneurial talent to nature's gifts did the ports thrive. Steamships demanded new services—coal, repair facilities, larger docks, sizeable warehouses, and links (rail, canal, rivers, coastwise) to distant markets. Guided by skilled management and funded with deep capital reserves, the ports developed a level of efficiency unmatched in the Atlantic world.

Liverpool entered the fray with a distinct advantage. Given its ready access to the English midlands—heartland of the Industrial Revolution—Liverpool enjoyed a well-ordered port system. Her merchants and bankers had extensive experience in Atlantic shipping. Moreover, they benefited from the support of an imperial government determined to strengthen the sinews of empire, and they had long drawn upon the rich resources of London's private-money market as well as of the Bank of England.

In 1838, the British steamship *Sirius* made its maiden voyage across the Atlantic from Liverpool to New York. That same year, a rebellion in Upper Canada stirred rumors that America had instigated the uprising and might be planning to invade. Appealing to the Colonial Office, Canadian officials argued that security depended upon establishing "a line of rapid communication by steam." The ministry agreed; it invited tenders, with the enticement of a generous subsidy for anyone who would guarantee regular steamship service between Halifax, Nova Scotia, and Liverpool. Samuel Cunard, a Canadian familiar with both ports, submitted the successful bid. He christened his enterprise the British and North American Royal Mail Steam Packet Company. Everyone called it the Cunard Line.

Americans were flabbergasted. For years, Liverpudlian shipowners had lamented the loss of business to the Yankee sailing packets, but the rules of the game were shifting and the United States was unprepared. American shipowners, unlike their English counterparts, suffered from a shortage of capital, aggravated by a parsimonious national government unwilling to proffer aid. The demise of the Bank of the United States (1836) threw American markets into disarray, as capital was dispersed among hundreds of loosely regulated state banks. Credit was limited, and compared to London, interest rates were high. The costs of building and operating steamships far exceeded the capacity of traditional partnerships, while the mounting complexities of international finance baffled the clerks tallying accounts in waterfront counting houses.

In 1825 James Brown, one of four sons of Alexander Brown, a successful Baltimore merchant and banker, arrived in New York to set up a branch office. Thanks to another brother, William, who had moved to Liverpool, the Brown Brothers forged a strong transatlantic network. Within a few years, they were America's most influential players in currency exchange and international banking. When Edward Knight Collins, a Cape Codder transplanted to New York, stepped forward to challenge Cunard's domination of transatlantic steam travel, the Browns were behind him. An indefatigable promoter and shipowner, Collins also successfully lobbied Congress. Like the British, the U.S. government extracted a political and military quid pro quo for its support: Collins's vessels must be readily convertible to warships. His commitments in place and optimism his watchword, Collins built a series of magnificent steamships. The first, the *Atlantic*, steamed out of New York Harbor, bound for Liverpool, in April 1850.

For nearly a decade, in a quintessential Anglo-American rivalry, Cunard and Collins mounted a colorful, pitched battle to wrest control of the globe's most lucrative trade route: the North Atlantic. Through their lives and through the ports they represented, New York and Liverpool, these two fierce competitors sent to sea the fastest, biggest, and most elegant ships in the world, hoping that each in turn might earn the distinction of being known as "the only way to cross." In their clash for supremacy, Collins and Cunard employed every weapon available to them—technology, money, secret deals, bribery, government influence—while at the same time coping with the inevitable, sometimes crushing, perils of the sea. In the midst of this spectacle—and in no small part because of it—New York rose to take her place among the greatest ports and cities of the world.

As the icons of their respective country's merchant marines, Collins and Cunard embodied and reflected their nation's goals and commitments. For Great Britain, an island state in possession of a vast empire, the sea was a primary and indispensable conduit for transferring knowledge and values as well as goods or, in times of war, armies and supplies. For the United States, with its immense hinterland, much of it still to be claimed, settled, and rendered productive, the merchant marine was less attractive to capitalists and legislators than were railroads and canals. Great Britain kept a steady hand on the throttle, while America was always peering over the horizon to the next best opportunity. Neither fortitude nor enterprise prevailed in the long run. By the early twenty-first century, among the world's seafaring nations, the United States ranked a lowly 26th in the number of her merchant vessels, while her old rival Great Britain did little better at 22nd.

CHAPTER ONE

The New Nation

T HE AMERICAN REPUBLIC WAS BORN into a hostile mercantilist world that did not wish her well. Heavily dependent upon export of raw materials, the new nation's trade suffered a series of blows as European nations, including her former ally France, imposed duties on salted fish, tobacco, whale oil, and other commodities. Spain and Portugal banned American tobacco. England closed the lucrative West Indies trade. In the face of these melancholy events, many Americans concluded that their affairs had fallen into a very disagreeable condition of "hard times." Ever optimistic, the octogenarian Benjamin Franklin saw matters differently and advised his countrymen "to take a cool view" for matters were "less gloomy than imagined."[1] Franklin was right, for while postwar adjustment was difficult, nearly a century and a half of prosperity and growth within the protective embrace of the British Empire had left a legacy of entrepreneurial spirit, a strong commercial base, growing population, a large merchant marine, vibrant ship building, and several bustling urban centers—all ports. What the new nation lacked was a strong central government that could bring thirteen fractious states into a firm union to provide for the common defense, secure its own revenue, and regulate trade. In the aftermath of a successful revolution against authority the centrifugal forces of local autonomy, expressed in a weak central government under the Article of Confederation, held sway. The spectacle of a dithering government in Philadelphia, unable to deal with issues of national concern, convinced some states to take action on their own.

In March 1785 delegates from Virginia and Maryland met at Mount Vernon to discuss issues concerning navigation rights on rivers that the two states shared. The meeting resolved the issues. Success at Mount Vernon caused the Virginia Assembly to call for a national meeting at Annapolis, "to remedy the defects of the federal government" and "to take into consideration the trade of the United States," and "to consider how far a uniform system in their commercial relations may be necessary to their common interest and permanent harmony."[2] Only five states answered the call (New York, Virginia, Delaware, Pennsylvania, and New Jersey). Although disappointed by the sparse turnout, the delegates present, including Alexander Hamilton from New York and James Madison of Virginia, seized the opportunity to draw up an address to the Confederation Congress recommending that it summon the states to a meeting in Philadelphia "to take into consideration the condition of the United States, and to devise such further provisions as shall appear to them necessary to render the constitution of the federal government adequate to the exigencies of the Union."[3]

The report from Annapolis was read in Congress on September 20, 1786. In its usual dilatory manner, Congress delayed action until February 21, 1787, when agreeing "entirely . . . as to the inefficiency of the federal government," Congress called for a "convention of delegates" to meet "on the second Monday of May next . . . for the sole and express purpose of revising the Articles of Confederation."[4] One week later, the New York Assembly elected three men to represent the state at Philadelphia, with Alexander Hamilton among them.

As Hamilton's biographer Ron Chernow has noted, "With the possible exception of James Madison, nobody had exerted more influence than Hamilton in bringing about the convention or a greater influence afterward in securing passage of its sterling product."[5] After sitting silently in the chamber for three weeks, on June 18 Hamilton rose to speak. In a six-hour speech, he revealed himself as an Anglophile, a quasi-monarchist deeply distrustful of democracy and in favor of granting complete sovereignty to the federal government with elites holding power. It was one of the greatest blunders of his life. Thrust to the edge by his extreme views, Hamilton complained that the people were not yet ripe for his plan, and returned to New York. His retreat was temporary. Back in Philadelphia in early August, he was pleased to discover that to a great extent the Convention had fashioned an energetic document, particularly in those areas about which he cared deeply—the power of the federal government to regulate commerce and to secure an independent revenue. Article I, Sections 8, 9, and 10, granted wide and exclusive authority to Congress to "lay and collect Taxes, Duties, Imposts and Excises," insuring that they "shall be uniform throughout the United States." These same sections, however, also placed limits on Congress. Congress could not lay any direct taxation, nor impose any tax on exports. To ensure equality among the states Section 9 provided that "no preference shall be given by any regulation of Commerce or Revenue to the Ports of one State over those of another: nor shall vessels bound to, or from, one State, be obliged to enter, clear, or pay Duties in another."[6]

The contest for ratification was fierce. *The Federalist Papers*, authored by James Madison, John Jay, and Hamilton, first published in three New York newspapers as a series of eighty-five essays in the fall-winter of 1787–88, proved critical in securing ratification. In Federalist numbers 11, 12, and 13, "The Utility of the Union in respect to Commerce and a Navy," "The Utility of the Union in respect to Revenue," and "The Same Subject continued, with a View to Economy," Hamilton drove home the importance of foreign commerce to the survival of the new nation. Commerce, he noted, "is one of those points, about which there is the least room to entertain a difference of opinion." He wrote that "an active commerce, an extensive navigation, a flourishing marine" were essential for the success of the new republic and warned that to remain passive would be to allow "the profits of our trade [to be] snatched from us, to enrich our enemies and persecutors."[7]

Since "no Capitation, or other direct, Tax shall be laid" to secure a national revenue, the only means were excise taxes and tariffs. The first, according to Hamilton, "the people will ill brook" since it would likely hit individuals, particularly rural distillers. "In America it is evident," he concluded, "that we must a long time depend for the means of revenue, chiefly on duties."[8]

Thanks to a well-organized campaign including the *Federalist Papers*, the Constitution was ratified.[9] Election returns for Congress and the Presidency confirmed that the new government was safely in the hands of friends. By April 1, 1789, the House had sufficient members to begin business, and five days later the Senate counted a quorum allowing both chambers to meet, count the electoral votes, and declare that "George Washington, Esq. was unanimously elected president, and John Adams, Esq. was duly elected Vice President, of the United States of America."[10]

William Penn once remarked that "governments, like clocks, go from the motion men give them."[11] With a constitution to guide them, the President and Congress put the machine in motion. In their first session (March 4, 1789–September 29, 1789) the House and Senate passed, and the President approved, twenty-six Acts. Eight of those measures, including the establishment of the Department of the Treasury, put in place a system aimed at raising revenue, regulating trade, and offering protection and support for the American merchant marine through a system of licensing, enrolling, and registering vessels.[12] The new nation's policies, granting favorable treatment for the American merchant marine while discriminating harshly against foreign-owned vessels, reflected a mercantilist world.[13] The agency responsible for implementing these measures was the Treasury Department. On September 11, Washington nominated Hamilton to be Secretary of the Department. The Senate approved him the same day.[14]

Although the United States now had a strong central government, change in political status had not altered the basic tenets of the Atlantic economy. Old ties were hard to break, and although Great Britain denied Americans access to her West Indian islands, she was generous in permitting trade across the Atlantic. Between 1783 and 1788 British imports from her former colonies increased fourfold, representing nearly 25 percent of total American exports.[15] Under these circumstances, Hamilton was anxious to assuage any ill feelings between the two nations. He revealed his sentiments in a confidential conversation with British agent George Beckwith. "I have always preferred a Connexion with you, to that of any other country," and hope to "form a Commercial treaty with you."[16] Outstanding differences, however—including compensation for Loyalists, British occupation of western posts, and American exclusion from the West Indian trade—foiled negotiations. In the meantime, under Hamilton's leadership the administration charted "a policy by which the federal government took direct responsibility for encouraging the growth and prosperity of the nation's maritime interests, and used the duties levied to finance the operations of the federal government." By the end of the first year of the republic, and notwithstanding the challenges, "America's seaborne trade was greater than it had been at any time in history"[17] under the benevolent eye of the federal government.

While most American merchants continued to sail in familiar waters, some turned their eyes far eastward. Within the empire, the colonies had been banned from trade with China; independence freed Americans to venture east. In December 1783 *Harriet*, a small fifty-five-ton sloop from Boston, loaded a cargo of ginseng—a medicinal herb much in demand in China—and sailed for Canton. Upon arriving at the Cape of Good Hope agents of the East India Company, anxious to thwart any competition, offered to purchase her cargo at twice its value in exchange for Hyson tea. *Harriet*'s captain took the offer and returned home.[18] *Harriet*'s success encouraged others; in the following year a more substantial vessel, the *Empress of China*, left New York and completed the first voyage of an American ship to China. Between 1784 and 1790, forty-one American vessels called at Canton. In volume, the trade was minor compared to Great Britain and Europe, but despite the substantial expense and highly unpredictable outcome, the profits were considerable.[19]

Success at sea reverberated at home. Shipbuilding benefitted from both Congress's protective measures, and the availability of ample supplies of timber, which pushed costs of construction 50 percent lower in American yards than in Great Britain or Europe. Between 1789 and 1795 American tonnage, all built in American yards, doubled. By 1795, 92 percent of all imports and 86 percent of the exports were carried in American vessels—a proportion never since equaled.[20] Earnings from shipping services provided a vital source of income that helped offset the chronic imbalance of payments as the value of imports exceeded exports.[21]

Sailmaking, ropewalks, warehousemen, teamsters, and other trades reveled in the prosperity. America's largest cities were all bustling

Balance of merchandise trade and international freight and interest
payments of the United States (annual averages: millions of dollars)

	Merchandise	Freight	Interest
1790–1798	−11.1	13.3	−4.7
1799–1808	−18.8	27.9	−4.8
1809–1818	−21.2	21.2	−4.9
1819–1828	−5.7	10.0	−5.0
1829–1838	−20.8	8.2	−6.5
1839–1848	−1.9	11.4	−9.5
1849–1858	−10.6	11.8	−16.3
1859–1868	−9.5	6.3	−38.8
1869–1878	52.7	2.7	−87.7
1879–1888	132.4	−6.0	−89.2
1889–1899	240.8	−8.0	−127.6
1900[a]	640.0	−7.0	−114.0
1900[b]	754.0	−36.0	−99.0
1901–1913	570.2	−39.2	−71.5

[a]Comparable with earlier years. [b]Comparable with later years.
Source: Bureau of the Census *Historical Statistics*. Series U2, 3, 5, 9, 10, 13.

seaports. Between 1790 and 1800 Boston's population grew by more than one third, Philadelphia increased by nearly 50 percent, while New York and Baltimore almost doubled.[22] The rise of the port of New York was particularly notable. In 1790 the port accounted for 10 percent of American foreign trade, a number that rose to nearly 30 percent by 1800, while tonnage registered in the port between 1790 and 1794 grew at an even faster rate.[23]

While Americans enjoyed their prosperity, across the Atlantic trouble was brewing. Great Britain and France were on the precipice of war.

On February 1, 1793, the Revolutionary government of France declared war on Great Britain and plunged Europe into a conflagration that, with only brief respites, engulfed the world until 1815. Washington, fearful that America might be sucked into the vortex of war, issued a proclamation advising the citizens of the United States to be "impartial towards the belligerent powers."[24]

While Washington tried to steer a safe course between warring parties, he was also anxious to resolve outstanding disputes with Great Britain, particularly the continued occupation of the western forts and the ban on West Indian trade. In April 1794 Washington, with backing from Hamilton, dispatched John Jay, Chief Justice of the Supreme Court, to London to negotiate a settlement. Jay returned with a treaty that satisfied almost no one, especially the French, who condemned it as a wanton betrayal of the 1778 Treaty of Amity and Commerce.[25] "Washington," according to a writer in the French journal *Decade philosophique*, "has concluded with our most implacable enemies a treaty wholly inimical to our interests."[26] Nonetheless, concerned that an open breech with the United States might force her into the arms of Britain, the government in Paris refrained from an open declaration of war while giving a quiet nod to French privateers, encouraging them to attack American vessels and permitting their navy to seize ships engaged in ill-defined "illegal" trade. It was a reckless path, and affairs deteriorated into crisis in 1798 when corrupt French officials demanded a bribe from a diplomatic delegation sent by President John Adams to mend relations. Never an official war, hostilities in the Quasi-War were confined principally to the waters of the West Indies, where a string of American victories offered bright moments for the fledgling American navy to display its prowess. Ended by a "Convention" in 1800, the war had little impact on transatlantic trade.[27] However nettlesome, France's vexations on American trade were minor. Great Britain's depredations were far more damaging.

In this long war, the massive armies of France were often dominant on land, while the wooden walls of the Royal Navy granted Great Britain supremacy at sea.[28] It was the tiger versus the shark. In a series of spectacular victories, Britain defeated the French navy and swept the enemy's merchant marine from the oceans. Having seized control of the sea lanes, and eager to implement additional tactics to strangle commerce and starve the enemy, the Royal Navy laid a tight blockade along the coasts of Europe.

With their own merchant marine in disarray, France, conveniently rejecting traditional mercantilist doctrine, threw open her ports to all comers. Loath to miss opportunities for profit, American shipowners, taking the broadest interpretation possible, took refuge behind the cry of neutrality, and sailed into the West Indies taking on cargo at French ports and carrying it across the Atlantic to the Continent, thereby boldly defying the British blockade.[29] American profits soared as British anger boiled.

Elected president in 1800, Thomas Jefferson sought to answer the British and keep his nation out of war by asserting an extreme view of American rights, arguing that "free ships should make free goods." He instructed Robert R. Livingston, the American Minister to Great Britain, to remind the British government that "no nation ever pretended a right to govern by their laws the ship of another nation navigating the ocean. By what law then can it enter that ship while in peaceable and orderly use of the common element? We recognize no natural precept for submission to such a right."[30] In response, the British ministry drew from its archives the Rule of 1756—trade not allowed by a nation in time of peace could not be opened in time of war.[31] American merchants found a clever answer to this in the doctrine of the broken voyage, by instructing their captains to load cargo at French or other foreign ports and then carry it to an American port.[32] By landing the goods at an American port and filling in the proper customs forms, when the cargo was reshipped—usually destined for a port under British blockade—the manifest listed the goods as "American." Despite continued harassment by both the French and (mostly) British, the fiction of the "broken voyage" worked. Between 1797 and 1807 American foreign trade more than doubled.[33] The years between 1793 and 1807 were extraordinarily prosperous.[34] In proportion to her size, the United States had become one of the world's principal trading nations. Her exports were nearly 3 percent of the world's and 5 percent of Europe's, while in comparison, her population was barely 0.5 percent of the world's and only 2.5 of Europe's. In terms of exports on a per capita basis, the new nation was twice as trade-oriented as Europe and more than five times the world.[35] To accommodate this enormous growth, by 1807 the American merchant marine numbered nearly 1,300 vessels and employed 20,000 seamen, the largest wage-earning class in the country.

Wrapped tightly in the economic strands of the British Empire, and facing the might of the Royal Navy, Jefferson's diplomatic approach made sense, and for the time at least his policies kept peace and prosperity. In the Mediterranean, however, the president faced a more direct challenge—one to which he responded with force.

For generations, the Barbary States along the North Coast of Africa— Morocco, Algiers, Tunis, and Tripoli—had demanded tribute from nations sailing in waters they claimed to be their own. European nations generally paid their due, including Great Britain whose payments before 1776 also bought protection for the American colonies. Once outside the Empire, the United States was on its own. On May 14, 1801, unhappy that the Americans had not paid him tribute, Tripoli's ruler, Pasha Yusuf Karamanli, declared war on the United States.[36] Jefferson responded by sending naval forces to attack Tripoli and protect American commerce. After some initial lackluster performances, a force under the command of Commodore Edward Preble managed to inflict sufficient harm that on June 3, 1805, the Tripolitans signed a treaty ending the war and permitting American vessels peaceful passage.[37]

At the very moment when American warships were pummeling Tripoli and driving the Pasha to the peace table, a far more important development was under way in a British Vice Admiralty Court, convened in Nassau, where lawyers were arguing a case brought against the Salem vessel *Essex* that carried profound implications for the American merchant marine.

America's maritime prosperity angered British nationalists who viewed the "broken voyage" as a charade. Lord Sheffield, a British politician and essayist, noted that the Americans had done nothing but follow "the natural policy of nations" (i.e., self-interest), but lamented that his country, through "weakness," had lost a good deal of the Atlantic-carrying trade to the Yankees by adopting "false notions of liberality or conciliation."[38]

Those false notions were at the heart of the case against the Salem brig *Essex*. On June 22, 1805, the court swept away the legitimacy of the "broken voyage." *Essex*, carrying goods of Spanish origin that had been landed in an American port and there declared American, was taken by a British cruiser. After hearing arguments, the court declared

Essex to be involved in a "fraudulently circuitous voyage."[39] Freed from legal shackles, British cruisers swooped down on suspicious American vessels, seizing ships and cargo.

On December 3, 1805, in his fifth annual message to Congress, Thomas Jefferson drew Congress's attention to the increasingly hostile environment at sea. "Under pretense of legal adjudication" employing "new principles . . . founded in neither justice nor in the usage of acknowledgement of nations," Great Britain was plundering American trade.[40] Worse, however, than crimes against property were the impressment of American seamen. Sailing warships were huge consumers of manpower; a single ship of the line manned for combat might require upward of 700 crew. The long war with France had exhausted Great Britain's pool of volunteers available for sea service. Left with little recourse, the Royal Navy turned to impressment.

An early form of the "draft," the King's right to impress his subjects for service was unchallenged, and had officers of the Royal Navy confined the practice to their own shores and ships, Americans would not have been affected. However, the navy's desperate need for men pushed officers to stretch their authority. Rotten food, harsh discipline, long stays at sea, and the risks of battle persuaded large numbers of British seamen to "run." Not a few of those deserters ended up in the forecastles of American merchantmen. When stopped and boarded at sea, officers of the Royal Navy ordered American masters to muster their crew. They then went down the line looking for deserters or subjects of the King. Not wanting to return to the ship empty-handed, the officers' examinations were imprecise, and it was a rare merchantmen who did not lose crewmen. Between 1796 and 1812 nearly ten thousand seamen were taken forcibly off American ships, the majority after 1805.[41]

Believing American trade to be essential to Great Britain, Jefferson, harkening back to the heady days before the Revolution when the colonies imposed a variety of boycotts, called for a ban on British imports. Congress complied, and on April 18, 1806, approved an act "to prohibit the importation of certain goods, wares and merchandise." It was a feckless effort, and eight months later, December 19, 1806, it was repealed.[42]

British provocation reached an explosive high in June 1807 when Captain Salusbury Humphreys, commander of HMS *Leopard*, ordered the American frigate *Chesapeake* to heave to so that a press gang might board to seize British deserters. When *Chesapeake*'s captain Samuel Barron refused, *Leopard* fired into the frigate, killing four crewmen and wounding eight others. *Chesapeake* struck her flag, and several seamen were removed.[43]

Chesapeake-Leopard pushed America to the brink of war, but Jefferson, wary of the disastrous consequences of open hostilities with Great Britain—which Sheffield warned would unleash Britain's "whole power of reaction and retaliation"—stepped back, and instead renewed his efforts at economic warfare and persuaded Congress (December 22, 1807) to "lay an embargo on all ships and vessels in the ports and harbors of the United States."[44] The act prohibited all foreign commerce, land and sea. Intended to pressure the British toward relaxing their relentless harassment of American trade and cease impressing seamen, the law was poorly crafted, vague, and laced with loopholes that in subsequent sessions Congress attempted to close. The measure was harsh and punitive, and came, unfortunately, at a moment when American foreign trade was at an all-time high and profits from freight were climbing. Despite British seizures, according to the prominent Salem merchant George Cabot, "a successful voyage by just one vessel out of three was sufficient to make a comfortable profit."[45] At a time when 60 to 70 percent of imported manufactured goods came from British factories, the measure proved a political and economic disaster.[46] It not only "brought merchants to bankruptcy, but affected every other part of the economy: it threw seamen and laborers out of work, impoverished farmers, who could not market their produce abroad, and inflated the price of imported goods."[47]

American trade plummeted. In the embargo's first year the value of imports fell from $139 million to $57 million while exports collapsed from $108 million to $22 million.[48] Customs receipts, representing 95 percent of the federal government's income, tanked from $16,364,000 to $7,296,000.[49] As embarrassing as the plunge in income was, it was the inability of the federal government to enforce the embargo that proved even more distressing. Stretched far beyond their limited capabilities, neither the revenue service nor naval gunboats could adequately surveil every harbor, river mouth, bay, and inlet along a two-thousand-mile coast. The embargo was a sieve. Recognizing the failure of a general embargo, three days before leaving office, March 1, 1809, Jefferson signed the Non-Intercourse Act, which repealed the embargo on all trade except that to Great Britain and France.[50]

Jefferson's successor James Madison had no better luck. Non-Intercourse proved unworkable. To it Madison signed an equally ineffective measure, Macon's Bill No. 2, which opened trade with Britain and France on condition that if neither of them agreed to respect American rights, then trade with the other would be suspended.[51] Had the problems at sea been the only disrupter between the United States and Great Britain, a fragile peace might have been preserved, but British activities in the west—such as inciting Indian attacks on American settlements—and a rising spirit of nationalism and honor drove American passion to a fever pitch.

In a run-up to a war that most Americans believed was inevitable, on April 12, 1812, Madison approved an "embargo for the term of ninety days from and after the passing of this act."[52] News of the measure set off panic as shipowners rushed to get their vessels to sea before federal agents could close their ports. "Had the city been in flames," wrote one New York merchant, "property could not have been moved off with greater expedition."[53] On June 1, 1812, Madison sent a war message to Congress asserting that while Great Britain was "in a state of war against the United States," on the other hand the "United States [was] in a state of peace towards Great Britain." As the Constitution required, he informed the members, he was placing the solemn question of war or peace in their hands.[54] On June 18, 1812, by a close vote, 79 to 49 in the House and 17 to 13 in the Senate, the United States declared war on Great Britain. Madison signed the declaration the next day.[55]

Having spent a hectic spring getting their ships to sea, owners confronted the challenge of getting the scattered sheep home once war was declared. Fortunately, it took more than a month for the news of war to arrive in London and several months thereafter before the Admiralty dispatched ships to blockade the American coast.

In its early stages the war at sea went well for the Americans, as a few "fir built frigates" thrashed the enemy, and plucky privateers sortied.[56]

Other Americans, however, made profits by avoiding fighting and colluding with the enemy.

Since the beginning of the republic, American farmers had been shipping considerable quantities of wheat to Europe. The outbreak of the Anglo-French wars fueled even higher demand as production on the Continent fell while the demand to feed huge armies rose. The Duke of Wellington's army in Spain was in particular need of food supplies. To the British the war with America was a nuisance. Napoleon was the real enemy. Winning the peninsula campaign was far more important than damaging the Yankees, so in spite of being at war with America, the ministry issued more than 500 licenses guaranteeing safe passage to American ships carrying foodstuffs to Wellington via Portugal.[57] Profit trumped patriotism as farmers and shipowners in New York, Philadelphia, and Baltimore rushed to fill orders. Gradually, as the tide turned against the French, other food sources became more available closer and cheaper, lessening British dependence upon American farmers. No longer dependent upon American supplies, the Royal Navy turned its attention to their lesser enemy, and in November 1813 declared a blockade of the entire Atlantic coast from Rhode Island to New Orleans—noticeably excluding the area north of Cape Cod in order to accommodate a brisk illegal trade across the Gulf of Maine between New England, New Brunswick, and Nova Scotia.[58]

Whatever quick gains might have been garnered through licenses or outright smuggling, they could never equal the steady profits of peace. As the war dragged on, weary merchants in London and elsewhere lamented the loss of American trade and yearned for a return to the halcyon days before the war. While the war in America might be pursued, what was the cost? Napoleon's abdication in April 1814 stirred the appetite for peace. The Tory Prime Minister, Robert Banks Jenkinson, Lord Liverpool, told his colleagues in Parliament that while "we might certainly land in different parts of their coast, and destroy some of their towns, or put them under contribution; but in the present state of the public mind in America it would be in vain to expect any permanent good effects from operations of this nature." Taking into account the restive mood in Parliament, he said, he believed it impossible "to continue [wartime taxes for the purpose of carrying on an American war]"; better, he thought, "to conclude peace at the present moment."[59] Similar sentiments in America persuaded President Madison to seek peace as well, and in August 1814 negotiations began in Ghent, Belgium, ending on Christmas Eve with both parties agreeing to end the war "which has unhappily subsisted between the two Countries" with an end to "restoring upon principles of perfect reciprocity, Peace, Friendship, and good understanding between His Britannic Majesty and the United States."[60] Two days later the treaty arrived in London.[61] It would take six weeks to reach America.

CHAPTER TWO

From Cape Cod to New York City

O N THE BITTERLY COLD EVENING of February 11, 1815, His Majesty's sloop of war *Favourite* passed the Narrows, entered New York Harbor, and came to off the Battery. Before the anchor had touched bottom and the crew furled the sails, *Favourite*'s captain ordered a boat lowered to be sent ashore carrying the King's messenger bearing glorious news. The war was over. New York went wild with cries of "Peace, Peace, Peace." "Oh, what a scene!" noted one observer. "In a few minutes thousands and tens of thousands of people were marching about, making the jubilant street appear like a gay and gorgeous procession."[1] Among them would likely have been thirty-nine-year-old Israel Collins, recently married, and tired of the seafaring life, who had forsaken his native Cape Cod to settle in New York as a merchant and shipping agent.

Collins hailed from Truro, a small town on the lower part of Cape Cod's "beckoning arm," a place described by Henry David Thoreau as "long, and lank and brown."[2] In his rambles along the Cape Thoreau stopped often to admire "the glassy surface of the herring ponds," and he relished evenings spent in gray shingled cottages sharing hospitality with fishermen, farmers, lighthouse keepers, and oystermen. He admired these "hardy" folk, possessed of "bold daring, hard common sense and bluff independence," struggling to scratch a living from "desolate hills worthy to have been the birthplace of Ossian." For all of its charm, however, Thoreau concluded wistfully, the Cape "will never be agreeable to the fashionable world."[3]

Collins's Truro stretched across the narrow Cape between Cape Cod Bay and the Atlantic. On the ocean side, steep sand dune cliffs rose up overlooking a "voracious beach," pounded by breaking waves and marked by shifting sandbars, a graveyard for ships.[4] On the bay side, a gentle shore, salt marshes, and tidal flats provided access to abundant shellfish and places to shelter small boats. In the midst of this kindly shore the Pamet River emptied into Cape Cod Bay. The Pamet was more an estuary than a river.[5] At its mouth, offering a depth of not more than twelve feet at high tide and less than half that at low, the water was barely sufficient to accommodate small fishing craft.

In its early days Truro was a raucous "resort of a wild undisciplined crew of traders and fishermen. Drinking, gambling, and bacchanalian carousals were continued sometimes for weeks with unchained license."[6] As more respectable folks arrived, the town evolved into a peaceable place. At first the Collinses and their neighbors did well. Farming was a precarious enterprise on the Cape, where thin topsail was always vulnerable to assault by wind and creeping sand.[7] Unlike native peoples who inhabited the Cape for thousands of years and did little harm to the environment, Europeans, in their greater numbers and with advanced skills and tools, devastated it. Quickly and savagely they cut away trees and low growth shrubs to build and fuel their homes. Stripped of natural cover that had held the soil in place, glacial sands swept unfettered across the emptiness, and formed into large shifting dunes. With growing families and less arable land, the people of Truro turned to the sea. According to Thoreau, "Only a few men stay at home to till the sand. The farmers are fishermen-farmers and understand better to plough the sea than the sand."[8]

The American Revolution hit Truro hard. In the war's early days the town's young men marched with the militia; as the struggle dragged on, however, enthusiasm waned. Truro men served in the Continental army and navy, and a few, out of motives of patriotism and profit, signed aboard privateers in hopes of reaping the rewards of a rich capture. Those who were left at home, fearful of being taken by British cruisers prowling the coast, either kept their boats on the beach or confined themselves to the safer world of clamming, oystering, and inshore fishing.[9]

So critical was fishing to the well-being of New England that John Adams, one of the American commissioners negotiating peace in Paris, stood boldly against any treaty that did not guarantee American fishing rights. His perseverance paid off. Article three of the Treaty of Paris (1783) guaranteed that

> the people of the United States shall continue to enjoy unmolested the right to take fish of every kind on the Grand Bank, and on the other banks of Newfoundland; also in the Gulph of Saint Lawrence, and at all other places in the sea where the inhabitants of both countries used at any time heretofore to fish.[10]

For Cape Cod fishermen, however, words on paper meant little. Catching fish was one thing; selling it was another matter. Barely had the treaty been ratified than the King issued Orders in Council that made it all but impossible for Americans to market their fish in the empire. Even as they recoiled from the loss of markets, a global war broke out between Great Britain and France (1793–1815), during which both belligerents did all they could to harm American commerce. Cape Codders were beset by a world that seemed intent on destroying their livelihoods.

So dire was the "wretched condition" of the New England fisheries that Congressman Fisher Ames of Massachusetts warned his colleagues of its ruin. "I shudder for the consequences. They [fishermen] are poor; they are in a sinking state; they carry on their business in despair. Why, then, do they not quit the profession? I answer in the words that are often used in the eastern country respecting the inhabitants of Cape Cod—they are too poor to live there, and are too poor to remove."[11] But the Cape did have "some determined sailors, who, as soon as they could get their bearings did go to sea again." Among those who took new "bearings" was Israel Collins.[12] Born in the year of American independence, 1776, Collins left Truro and went to sea in the early days of the republic. By 1800 he was owner and master of a small coasting vessel sailing between New York City and Charleston.

A city known for its charms, its churches, and a hint of "French culture," Charleston was a far cry from Truro. Collins enjoyed his visits, and during one of his pleasant interludes ashore he met and fell in love with Mary Ann Allan. Born in England about 1780, she was reputed to be the niece of a British admiral, Sir Edward Knight. In 1801 they were married in Grace Church on Sullivan's Island.[13]

Israel brought Mary Ann home to Truro. Her accent and genteel manners charmed the local Cape Codders, who described her as "a beautiful and accomplished lady, a clever performer on the spinet an instrument she brought with her."[14] On August 5, 1802, Mary Ann gave birth to her only child, Edward Knight Collins. Five months later, having struggled through a harsh New England winter unlike any she had endured in Charleston, and weakened by the complications of childbirth, she died. A widowed father, Israel faced the dilemma of remaining at home to eke out a living farming and fishing, or returning to the sea. He chose the wider world and returned to New York. For the next several years he shipped from that city, voyaging to southern ports and leaving his infant son at Truro in the care of his aunt, Elizabeth Small.[15]

For ten years Collins remained a widower. During that time, he kept close ties with Charleston, visiting often in the course of his business. Among the men with whom he dealt was a local merchant, John Mathews. His daughter Mary drew Collins's attention, and in June 1813, in the Independent Congregational Church of Charleston, they married.[16]

The nation was one year into a second war with Great Britain. For Israel and other shipowners, the war provided opportunity. The threat of British cruisers off the American coast sent freight rates spiraling up. Lucky enough to avoid capture in his coastwise business, Collins did well. He reaped handsome profits, and with them he and Mary bought property in New York City. Middle-aged by then, Israel grew tired of the sea and was ready to come ashore. He gave up seafaring and took up life as a merchant and shipping agent. Israel and Mary could not have picked a better time to settle in New York. The war was winding down and the port, freed of wartime shackles, was about to release years of pent-up energy and burst into the Atlantic.

Geography had blessed the port, located at the tip of Manhattan. On its western side, the Hudson River (North River) flowed down from

Albany and was navigable for nearly 150 miles. Farmers along the river's shore loaded huge quantities of fruits and vegetables onto sloops, which sailed easily down to the city to fill ships bound to ports along the coast or across the Atlantic to distant foreign markets. On Manhattan's opposite shore, the East River (a misnomer since it is really a tidal strait) provided a protected, albeit difficult to navigate, winding passage between the harbor and Long Island Sound. Joining at the tip of the island (the Battery), the two rivers formed one of the greatest natural harbors in the world, exiting to the Atlantic via the Narrows, a two-mile stretch of water between Brooklyn and Staten Island that at one point is less than a mile wide. Once clear of the Narrows, outbound vessels might lay a course northeast to bring them onto the great circle route toward Europe or take a more northerly direction, making their way toward southern New England sailing the sheltered waters of Long Island Sound.[17] A third option was to starboard, heading along the Jersey coast toward the southern states, Latin America, the Caribbean, or Mexico. In every case the prudent captain followed the sage advice of *Blount's American Coast Pilot* to always keep "distance from the beach."[18]

Nowhere in the city did the news of peace cause more rejoicing than along the East River's waterfront, where Israel Collins kept his place of work at 73 South Street. Shipyards bustled to the rhythmic sound of mallets striking caulking irons and the cutting noise of saws. With a quick step, riggers and sailmakers went back to practicing their skills, reeving tackle and bending sail. From slip to slip, seamen made their way along the river front seeking berths, while on the opposite side of the street merchants reopened their offices, and clerks awaited messengers bringing evidence of renewed business—manifests, customs clearances, bills of lading, correspondence, and piles of other documents.

Scarce during the war, American products were fetching a high price in Liverpool. The best prices would go to the early arrivals. Collins's neighbor, the firm of Rutgers and Seaman at 79 Pearl Street, was the first to get a vessel off. On March 6 *Othello* left her East River slip, fell into the stream, and set a course for Liverpool via Belfast carrying a cargo of flaxseed. Unfortunately, she proved to be a sluggish sailor, and although she had a six-day head start, the ship *Milo*, under Captain Stephen Glover and hailing from Boston, was the first American to pass Holyhead and come up the Mersey River. She received a rousing welcome. According to a writer for the *Liverpool Mercury*, Thursday, March 30, was a "remarkably fine" spring day. Just after noon thousands of Liverpudlians, hearing news of *Milo*'s arrival, rushed "the piers and shore" to catch a glimpse of "the first ship belonging to the United States [to] arrive here since the peace. [S]he came up the river in very fine style, with the British flag flying at her mainmast head; the American colours at her mizzen mast. This first effect of the restoration of amity between two countries designed by nature, habits and mutual interest, to maintain uninterrupted the relations of peace, was hailed with great delight." *Othello* arrived a few days later to a similar, if more subdued, welcome.[19]

Glover wasted no time in the Liverpool dock. He knew that the first ship home would fetch premium prices for English goods not seen in New York or Boston for years. He brought back "Nine cases of Scotch Muslins . . . sixty seven trunks and cases, light cambric prints," a variety of other textiles accompanied by "13 casks and cases of hardware," all to be sold at Frederick Cabot's shop at 28 Broad Street, Boston. Consigned to Rutgers and Seaman, *Othello* landed similar freight at New York, a "full cargo of dry-goods, hardware, etc."[20]

While Americans scurried off to Liverpool, British merchants launched a mercantile invasion aimed at New York. During the spring and early summer of 1815, dozens of American and British vessels departed Liverpool, their manifests listing goods similar to those stowed aboard *Othello* and *Milo*—textiles, hardware, and manufactured goods. For nearly three years warehouses in Liverpool and Manchester had been bulging with unsold goods held captive by the war. To rid themselves of heavy inventories and regain the American market, British merchants resorted to "dumping" their product at almost any price.

British merchants were wise to choose New York. Only that port had the capacity to absorb such a surge of cheap goods. Trying to sell into a glutted market was risky, but New York offered the promise of quick sales through its auction system, that is, "selling property, in open competition to the highest bidder."[21] Used in the city since the late seventeenth century, the system expanded dramatically after 1815. By previous custom it had often been the practice for English manufacturers to sell their goods to a Liverpool exporter, who in turn sold them to a New York merchant. The merchant, essentially a wholesaler/retailer, then undertook distribution and marketing. While the system functioned when supply and demand balanced, it was slow, allowed for little competition, and was too cranky and inflexible to adjust to the price volatility brought on by postwar dumping. Auctions, on the other hand, were quick and flexible. Instead of consigning cargoes for sale to particular merchants, British agents sold to licensed New York auction houses, offering them long credit periods (twelve to eighteen months); the auction houses then arranged public sale. In 1817, local taxes on auction sales were reduced dramatically (East India goods 1 percent, textiles 1.5 percent). Even more importantly, new regulations required that regardless of price "every piece of goods offered at auction should positively be sold." Sales were to be held "between sunrise and sunset to prevent poor lighting from misleading buyers," and fees could not exceed 2.5 percent.[22]

Traditional merchants, fearing rightly that they might lose their hold on the market, raised a hue and cry against the system, but to no avail. At other ports, however—particularly New York's chief competitors Boston and Philadelphia—merchant lobbies successfully thwarted change. In Philadelphia, for example, "goods were allowed to be offered and withdrawn . . . and the purchaser went to the auction rooms of that city with no certainty of making his purchases."[23] Competitive prices and guaranteed sales combined to create a powerful vortex that drew rural shopkeepers to New York City seeking bargains. "Retailers flocked in from all over the country to replenish their stocks."[24] Since many shopkeepers came to the city rarely, and even those who made regular trips needed assistance, local intermediaries played a key role as brokers, purchasing goods at the best prices and offering buyers long-term credit. The flood of arrivals in the city created demand for housing, food, and transportation. With more vessels calling at the port, New York also became a place for travelers going abroad to congregate awaiting passage. Ships tying up on the East River not only deposited their cargo, but also brought the latest news and information in the form of mail, including letters, books, magazines, newspapers; New York was the center for commerce and "intelligence." The goal, boasted Abraham Thompson, one of the city's leading merchants, was nothing less than to "cause all the Atlantic cities to become tributary to New York."[25]

New York could not have achieved her place as the nation's chief importer had she not also been able to offer shippers exports to fill the holds of eastbound ships. Along the East River piers dockworkers loaded boxes, bales, and barrels containing a variety of products, including flaxseed for Ireland; salted meats, vegetables, and flour for England's hungry urban population; and tobacco for addictive pleasures. Much of what they stowed had been brought to New York by coastwise vessels, including those owned by Israel Collins. However, one cargo stood out from all the others. No American export was more important than cotton, and despite its location far from the vast cotton plantations of the south, no American port was more vital to the trade than New York.

New York's rise in the cotton trade began in the spring of 1794, when Robert Bolton of Savannah sent a bag of cotton to Isaac Hicks, a Quaker merchant in New York, as payment for a shipment of goods he had recently received. Bolton feared that Hicks was likely to frown on the arrangement, since, as he wrote Hicks, everyone knew that cotton was "a dull article in New York."[26] Bolton's fears were misplaced. The year before, only a few miles distant from him at Mulberry Grove, a Georgia plantation owned by the widow of the Revolutionary War hero Nathanael Greene, Eli Whitney had built a cotton gin. He was a nineteen-year-old Yale College graduate who had been hired as a tutor for the Greene children. It was a simple machine that separated cotton fibers from their seeds. Whitney's invention revolutionized southern agriculture. Even though Whitney managed to secure a patent on his machine, unhappily for him, the gin was so easily replicable that no law could prevent its spread. Within a short time, southern cotton went from being a minor crop to becoming America's most important export, making the American south the world's first agricultural superpower. Exports of Bolton's "dull article" went from 189,000 pounds in 1791 to nearly 100 million pounds in less than a decade. No longer loosely stuffing bags of various sizes, slaves "screwed cotton" into tight four-hundred-pound bales, which by their regular shape could be stowed easily and efficiently in a ship's hold.[27]

Cotton arrived in New York via southern ports, most importantly New Orleans. By the hundreds, crude wooden rafts (later steamboats),

with bales stacked high, floated down the "huge and turbid" Mississippi
to the Crescent City.[28] Along the city's levees gangs of slaves, often
chanting songs "to regulate and beguile their labor," toted bales across
the wharves and into warehouses to await the next leg of the journey to
New York, and thence across to Liverpool.[29] From that port a system of
rivers and canals carried bales to the English midlands, particularly the
monster Cottonopolis—Manchester—to feed the insatiable demands
of textile mills gorging on huge quantities of American cotton.

Slightly more than a hundred miles upriver from the Gulf of Mexico,
New Orleans, the South's only major city, was "regularly laid out, the
streets running at right angles, very narrow and but few of them paved."[30]
It was a rough town that had "little to gratify the eye of taste."[31] At the
edge of the river, the busy waterfront gave the appearance of prosperity,
with people bustling about, vessels, increasingly steam-propelled,
arriving from upriver while sailing ships deeply laden with cotton
departed downriver, hoping to pass safely over the treacherous bars at
the Mississippi's mouth. New Orleans's apparent prosperity, however,
disguised the reality of the South's darker side: a deeply flawed economic
system. Unlike the North, where fast-growing cities, factories, and an
expanding free population fed by immigration created demand for
imported and domestic manufactures, the American South offered a
dismal scene. While wealthy planters and a few city dwellers were active
consumers, the majority of the population was made up of poor white
farmers and slaves, who worked hard and bought little.

The South's monoculture economy presented challenges. Cotton
flowed out like a river, but given a lack of customers for manufactured
goods, only a trickle of goods returned. Shipowners had little incentive
to put their vessels in a trade where half the time they sailed with near-
empty holds. At the same time, however, planters, anxious to grow
more cotton for expanding domestic and foreign markets, invested
heavily to acquire land and slaves for which they needed financing. The
astonishing increase in cotton production placed profound demands
on planters for an array of services—banking, insurance, marketing,
transportation—most of which the south, with its undiversified economy,
could not provide. Northern—and to some extent British—interests

grasped the misfortune of their southern customers and seized an opportunity for profit.

Northern mercantile houses dispatched agents to southern ports (New Orleans, Charleston, and Savannah) to buy up cotton and arrange for shipment, either by a direct route overseas or via New York. Navigating through a dizzying swirl of cash, commodity bartering, bills of exchange, and letters of credit, the planter and the merchant joined in an intricate dance of international trade dubbed the "cotton triangle." Cotton moved from the south to New York or directly to Liverpool. Liverpool shipped back manufactured goods to New York, some portion of which was reshipped south on vessels that would return north with cotton. New York shipowners and merchants had developed an early version of the hub-and-spoke system, with Liverpool their principal eastern terminus. The trade had a variety of tracks; nonetheless, on every line northern merchants took payment in the form of fees, commissions, and charges for freight.[32]

As the web of relations between north and south grew more tangled planters became increasingly dependent upon their northern partners, not only for shipping and financial services like insurance and banking, but for other matters as well. If the planter could not come to New York, his agent might select and purchase goods for him, including personal items such as clothes, wine, and furniture. He might even oversee the well-being of a child sent north for school or arrange for him to take a grand tour of Europe. At every turn, and for every service, New York took its tribute. Through clever manipulation, New York "took over a large share of the South's commercial activity. The combined income from interest, commissions, freight, insurance, and other profits was so great that, when the southerners finally awoke to their thralldom, New Yorkers were already scooping forty cents of every dollar paid for southern cotton." Pointedly, the historian Robert G. Albion concluded that it was "the uncommercial attitude of the southerners" that "gave New York port its opportunity."[33] Thanks to the cotton business, by the mid-1830s New York had outpaced every other American port, controlling nearly one-quarter of all American trade.[34]

Israel Collins's marriage to Mary Ann Mathews provided special links to Charleston, and when her father died he left his daughter $8,000,

her share of the proceeds from the sale of his slaves. In 1820, successful
as an importer, well-established, and permanently settled, Israel invited
seventeen-year-old Edward, from whom he had been separated for more
than half a decade, to join him and his stepmother in the city. His aunt's
death in 1816 and his own graduation from the local Sandwich Academy
left him with few ties to Truro, and so, ready to embark on a career,
Edward Knight Collins headed for New York.[35]

Israel apprenticed him to the firm of McCrea and Slidell, cotton brokers
who specialized in the New Orleans trade. Much to his advantage,
Collins's apprenticeship took him beyond the counting house at 41
South Street. He sailed to New Orleans, learning firsthand the business
of shipping and trading. Unfortunately, McCrea and Slidell soon went
bankrupt; then Israel persuaded his New York neighbor in business
on South Street, John F. Delaplaine, to take Edward. Like Israel's,
Delaplaine's business focused on southern trade; but unlike Israel, whose
vessels kept to coastwise voyages, Delaplaine sent his ships to the West
Indies.[36] Although not yet out of his teens, Edward convinced Delaplaine
that he was ready to take on significant responsibility. The merchant
sent the young man to the West Indies as his super cargo, the owner's
personal representative charged with managing the ship's business affairs.
For Collins the assignment turned out to be far more adventurous than
haggling with merchants and tallying accounts. Delaplaine specialized
in the coffee trade, which drew his vessels toward the dangerous shores
around the island of Hispaniola, where uncharted waters hid sharp reefs
and sandy shallows. It was also a lawless haven for gangs of pirates, who
lurked in remote bays and inlets ready to pounce on unsuspecting
merchantmen, seize their cargoes, and murder their crews. According
to family lore, Collins was twice shipwrecked in these waters and, on
one occasion, helped fight off a pirate attack.[37]

While Edward was surviving shipwrecks and fighting off pirates, his
father was doing well on South Street, in a neighborhood alive with
activity. An 1828 guide to New York for "Strangers" described its bustle:[38]

> South-street, in its whole extent, is exclusively occupied by the
> merchants owning ships, and by those connected with that line of
> business, and it forms a range of warehouses, four and five stories

in height, extending from the Battery to Roosevelt-street, facing the East River. Front-street and Water-street, together with the various slips intersecting them from South-street, are occupied by wholesale grocer and commission merchants, iron dealers, or as warehouses for the storage of merchandise and produce of every description.

South Street owed much of its success to a bold venture undertaken by a group of New York merchants in the fall of 1817.

On Monday, October 27, 1817, New York's Tontine Coffee House at the corner of Wall and Water Streets, a favorite gathering place for merchants, was abuzz with the usual rumors about events abroad, the price of cotton at New Orleans, and political activities in Albany and Washington. This morning, however, these seasoned veterans of commerce and politics read an item that startled them. In bold type, the New York *Commercial Advertiser* announced a "Line of Packets Between N. York and Liverpool." The story went on to promise "regular conveyance for GOODS and PASSENGERS, between NEW-YORK and LIVERPOOL [caps in original] to sail from each place on a certain day of every month throughout the year." Four ships—*Amity*, *Courier*, *Pacific*, and *James Monroe*—were to "sail from New-York on the 5th and from Liverpool on the 1st of every month."[39] On January 5, 1818, a snowy Monday morning, at 10 A.M., precisely as promised, *James Monroe*, with a cargo of apples, cotton, flour, and wool slipped down the East River, passed through the Narrows, and at four in the afternoon dropped the pilot off at Sandy Hook and headed to sea, bound to Liverpool. Four days before, her sister packet *Courier* had departed Liverpool for New York, on time.

Five New York shipowners were responsible for this bold venture: Isaac Wright, his son William, Francis Thompson, Benjamin Marshall, and Jeremiah Thompson. It had long been the custom for New York owners to ignore any fixed schedule, avoid winter crossings, and only send their ships off when their holds were full. Contrary to these practices, Wright and his partners promised to sail on time, full hold or not, every month of the year. At first the line lacked a name, but as *James Monroe* slid away from her East River pier and her crew loosed the gaskets to unfurl her foretopsail, the canvas cracked down to reveal a huge painted black ball. Thereafter the line would be known as the Black Ball Line.[40]

Three and a half months after bidding farewell to *James Monroe*, the coffeehouse clique rejoiced at more good news for the port. After years of political wrangling and failed attempts to secure federal assistance, the New York state legislature decided to go it alone, and on April 17, 1817, authorized a "Canal Fund" to finance the construction of a canal from Albany to Buffalo. Completed in 1825 at a cost of $7 million, the Erie Canal, linking America's agricultural hinterland with the Atlantic world, was a bonanza for the state and the port of New York. Shipping costs from Lake Erie to New York City plummeted from $100 per ton to less than $10, while the time for transit was cut by weeks. Within a few years the canal was carrying a volume of freight twice the value of movements down the Mississippi. Between 1820 and 1830, while export tonnage at the rival ports of Boston and Philadelphia actually declined, New York's figures increased by nearly 50 percent. Shipments of flour from Buffalo, one of the principal cargoes coming to New York via the canal, increased nearly fourfold. At the same time that inland freight rates were declining as a result of the Canal, so too were ocean rates pushing lower as service regularized and increased along with tonnage. No port in America benefitted more from this combination of circumstances than New York.[41]

Maintaining scheduled service year-round in all weather was expensive. Westbound winter crossings were the worst. Howling westerly winds, biting temperatures, rain, snow, and constant sea spray coming over the rail coated lines with ice and froze sails into stiff slabs of canvas. Hard-driving captains and "bully mates," with their brass knuckles and belaying pins at the ready, drove packet ships and their crews mercilessly. It was dangerous work, but for owners and masters, it was worth a man's life to arrive on time. Ships and men wore out quickly.

At first no one rushed to compete with the Black Ball, but as the business grew and profits rolled in, competition emerged. In January 1822, New York's Red Star Line inaugurated regular service to Liverpool. Seven months later the Swallowtail Line followed. One-upping the Black Ball, these companies offered weekly sailings to Liverpool. Every merchant along South Street watched and wondered how they could profit from these square-riggers running on schedule. Edward Knight Collins was among them. In 1824 he left Delaplaine, walked next door, and at barely twenty-two, became a full partner in the newly named firm of I. G. Collins and Son. Edward stood out in South Street, cultivating the image of a wily, plucky, if somewhat eccentric New England character. A showman, he was dubbed by his mercantile colleagues "the short man in the tall hat."[42] In the winter of 1825, "the short man" made a dramatic move that proved his mettle and drew attention to him.

Of all the cargo the Black Ballers delivered to New York, nothing was more anticipated and valued than information. Being the first to know current prices of commodities in distant markets, cotton most importantly, gave merchants and shipowners a huge advantage. Low prices in Liverpool made it advantageous for New York merchants to hold bales in their warehouses, suspend purchasing more, and wait for better times. High prices abroad, on the other hand, sent a signal to buy and ship. Timing was key. For a buyer in New York to know before a southern seller that Liverpool prices had risen gave the northerner insider information to exploit.

On the evening of January 30, 1825, the Black Ball packet *Canada* hauled alongside her East River pier bringing important news. Cotton inventories in Liverpool were at record lows. Desperate for material, English mill owners were bidding up prices. Liverpool was in an "orgy [of] cotton speculation."[43] The news energized South Street. Dealers rushed to buy up existing cotton stocks. According to one contemporary, "several merchants, also seized with a similar purpose, determined to send an agent to Charleston, South Carolina," to buy up cotton from planters yet unaware of the Liverpool boom. No time could be wasted, and even though it was a Sunday and the street was quiet, a group of merchants gathered at the Collins office "and asked the junior member of the firm" to set out for Charleston. Edward willingly agreed and confidently asserted he could be ready quickly. "As soon as I can charter a pilot-boat and ship provisions and crew—about three hours. I will be ready to sail at four o'clock this afternoon." The men in the room were uneasy knowing that the regular Charleston packet would leave at that hour. Collins dismissed their concerns. "At precisely four o'clock, from the pier at Burling Slip," across the street from the Collins office, "the pilot boat, under the command of E. K. Collins, cast loose her moorings" and headed down the East River. "Speculators aboard the Charleston packet hooted and hollered mocking the 'boy' for his temerity in undertaking to beat them." But Collins arrived at Charleston ahead of the packet and hurried ashore, buying "all the cotton in that city and on the Cooper and Ashley Rivers," and then set sail "in his saucy little craft" bound home to New York. Collins and his associates reaped huge profits. It was a "splendid start for a young business man of twenty-three years."[44] With pluck and profits, and cutting a figure "of fine physical proportions, muscular and compact," Edward Knight Collins had earned his place as a rising figure in New York's maritime community.[45] On January 4, 1826, he furthered his business and social standing by marrying Mary Ann Woodruff, the daughter of Thomas Tyson Woodruff, a prominent contractor and alderman for the Fourteenth Ward whose family enjoyed connections to the city's Knickerbocker aristocracy.[46]

While Collins's personal reputation was on the rise, unknown to him the firm of I. G. Collins and Son was sailing in troubled waters, headed toward the rocks. In New York, both as a port and city, few services were more important than marine and fire insurance. Profits were plentiful but so too were risks, and with investors focused on the former, an environment ripe with "innumerable cases of frauds" was created. Israel Collins got caught up in this cyclone of corruption. In 1824 he invested in the Mohawk Insurance Company, a firm underwriting coverage for both marine and inland concerns. Three years later, the directors elected him president. Undercapitalized and unable to satisfy claims, the company collapsed under his leadership.[47] Collins took a heavy hit. He owed more than $8,000. His creditors sought and obtained a judgment against him that imperiled the solvency of the firm.

For three years Edward did his best to save the firm, but the stress took a toll on his father's health and mental state. Edward had Israel declared insane and committed to an asylum. With his father "insane" and "insolvent," Edward moved quickly to distance himself from this jumble of trouble. In 1830 he dissolved I. G. Collins and Son and created a new firm—E. K. Collins Co. The following year Israel died, still in the asylum, leaving Edward to straighten out his father's lingering financial mess.[48]

Now working on his own, Edward grew increasingly bold. Undeterred by his father's failure, he plunged into the cotton triangle. Although America's export of raw materials, cotton principally, burgeoned, the value of exports never balanced the more costly imports of manufactured goods. New York merchants sought numerous ways to right the imbalance and cover the deficit owed to their English suppliers.[49] One means of payment, always acceptable since its value was certain, was specie (gold and silver). The United States, however, in the days before the California Gold Rush, was in short supply of precious metals.

Through his contacts in the Caribbean and Gulf of Mexico, however, Collins was well aware of one of the world's chief sources of silver—Mexico. That country was in chaos. Since the first uprising for independence from Spain in 1810, the nation had struggled through a kaleidoscopic succession of rebellions and leaders—a long, drawn-out, bloody, and costly effort. Finally, in 1825 Royalist forces abandoned the last bastion of Spanish rule, the fortress of San Juan de Ulua at Vera Cruz. Since the days of the Spanish conquest, Vera Cruz had been Mexico's principal port. "It was the funnel through which passed three-fourths of all the silver bound for Spain."[50] According to Jedidiah Morse's *American Gazetteer*, Vera Cruz was "the grand port of Mexico . . . one of the most considerable places for trade in the world, being the natural centre of the American treasure and the magazine for all the merchandise sent from New Spain or that is transported thither from Europe."[51] Deep in debt and desperate for revenue, Mexico's bankrupt revolutionary governments threw open its doors to trade. The market for imported goods, mainly textiles, grew.[52] The only export of consequence available to pay for these imports was silver. Vera Cruz offered "a vault for specie destined to grease the wheels of trade . . . in the Atlantic world."[53] Early in 1826 the *New Bedford Mercury* reported tantalizing news that "our merchants appear to be drawing pretty freely from the rich mines of Mexico . . . Several vessels have arrived with heavy sums in the precious metal."[54] Among those "drawing pretty freely" was the firm of I. G. Collins and Son.

Collins had done well in the Mexican trade. He and Mary lived with their three children—Thomas, born in 1831; Edward Knight, born in 1833; and Mary, born in 1836—in their home at 413 Houston Street, a fashionable neighborhood whose "resident[s] were among the wealthiest and most renowned in the city." The street was "lined with shops and elegant three and four story houses, most built of red brick in the Greek revival and Federal styles."[55] Nonetheless, running a line of "Mexican Packets"—small schooners carrying silver north and "flour, furniture and textiles south"—lacked prestige along the New York waterfront and failed to satisfy Edward's growing ambition. Collins understood that better money was to be made in the New Orleans to New York cotton packets. That trade, however, required large vessels capable of carrying bulk cargoes of cotton, sugar, and tobacco. His small schooners of 100 tons were totally inadequate. He sold his interest in the Mexican trade and, with additional financial help from his father-in-law, sought better vessels, buying out the Louisiana and New York Packet line.[56]

CHAPTER THREE

Liverpool

ALTHOUGH THE PURCHASE of the Louisiana and New York line boosted Collins up a few notches on South Street's merchant hierarchy, he was fully aware that in the competitive world of New York packets great attention was paid to the reputation of the line's ships—distinctions connected to their size, elegance, and the fame of the builder. To attract attention to his lesser-known line, Collins announced that he had engaged the firm of Brown and Bell—located at the foot of Houston Street, which had built more packets than any other yard in the city—to launch a new ship for him named *Congress*. On Saturday, October 1, 1831, Collins stood proudly watching *Congress* launch into the East River.[1] At 376 tons she was the largest vessel Collins had ever owned. With *Congress* and her sisters the line was able to provide service twice monthly from each port carrying cotton, sugar, and tobacco north, and manufactured goods south. Quickly earning a reputation for luxury and speed, Collins's ships garnered the passenger trade—wealthy planters who were willing to pay a premium fare of $80.00 to sail in comfort between New York and New Orleans. In 1835, Collins decided to make an ever bigger splash. He would build a ship more than twice the size of *Congress*, larger than any packet in service.[2]

Most New York shipowners named their vessels after historic figures or places; Collins, playing on the literary pretentions of the city's Anglophile elite, announced that his new ship, to be built by Brown and Bell, would be christened *Shakespeare*. Her name drew attention, but Collins was keen to make an even bigger impression. In a stunning move, he persuaded an American hero to take command of his new ship.

Readers in antebellum America were enthralled with romantic images of the sea.[3] Bookstores stocked the works of the British author Frederick Marryat, creator of *Mr. Midshipman Easy*, and James Fenimore Cooper's numerous swashbuckling yarns. Richard Henry Dana's classic *Two Years Before the Mast* would shortly appear in 1840. Newspapers, particularly the *New York Herald*, owned by Collins's good friend and maritime enthusiast James Gordon Bennett, gave wide coverage to shipping news, announcing the arrival and departure of ships and mentioning in every notice the ship's master. "At the apex of the little floating world," Herman Melville's "oaken box," stood the captain, the undisputed sovereign. The public devoured stories of these high flyers who braved ferocious seas, put down mutinies, and survived shipwrecks, all to bring their ships safely to port. New York packet captains, who drove themselves, their crews, and their ships to the edge of disaster and sometimes beyond, were the elite of this seagoing fraternity. "With them, there was none of the anonymity, which hung over the seamen and the mates . . . Captain and ship were inseparately linked."[4] For passengers, sailing with such stalwarts afforded one of the few fringe benefits of an otherwise unpleasant Atlantic crossing. Standing on deck, they witnessed the master scan the horizon for signs of changing weather or bark orders to the mates while all the time keeping an eye on the compass and the sails aloft. No experience ashore came close to the extraordinary spectacle of a sea voyage. At dinner the "autocrat" of the deck took his place at the head of the table, casting off his stern, brawny character to become a "courteous gentleman with a rough sort of amiability," charming his guests with rollicking tales from the sea.[5] Once ashore, passengers eagerly shared their experiences with their landlubber friends and relatives. Travelers often made their choice of passage on the basis of a captain's reputation. Collins understood the value of a name when he announced that America's most famous seaman, Nathaniel B. Palmer, would design and supervise the construction of *Shakespeare*.

A native of Stonington, Connecticut, where he grew up working in his father's shipyard, Palmer went to sea in the business for which the town was famous—sealing in the South Atlantic. In 1821 the Stonington fleet set off for its annual expedition to the sealing grounds on the South Shetlands Islands, 600 miles south of the Falkland Islands. Palmer, barely twenty-two years old, sailed in command of the tiny sloop *Hero*.[6] Shortly after the sealers reached their base at Deception Island, Palmer separated from the company and headed further south to investigate some unusual sightings that he took to be land. After a few days sail, passing close by icebergs and cavorting penguins, Palmer came up on a rugged coastline that he incorrectly identified as an island, but was instead a peninsula connected to Antarctica. For a few days he jogged along the coast, but when a heavy fog rolled in, he decided to lie to and await better weather.

As the fog lifted, Palmer looked about to find himself in the company of two Russian vessels, *Mimy* and *Vostok*, under the command of the famed Russian explorer Admiral Fabian Gottlieb von Bellingshausen. As surprised as Palmer to encounter company in such a remote place, the Admiral invited the American aboard. Impressed that the young man commanded a small sloop, ten thousand miles from home, Bellingshausen toasted Palmer: "We must surrender the palm of enterprise to you Americans," he said, adding, "Wear your laurels with my sincere prayers for your welfare." In a gesture of fellowship, while maintaining his own status and authority, Bellingshausen announced, "I name the land you have discovered in honor of yourself, noble boy, Palmer's Land."[7] The following year, on a second sealing voyage, commanding a larger vessel, *James Madison*, Palmer revisited "Palmer's Land." Finding "not the least appearance of vegetation . . . only a few Sea-Leopards, beautifully spotted," Palmer returned home to a hero's reception. Newspapers hailed him as the man who had proved that "Southern Thule" actually exists.[8]

Palmer's reputation for boldness and fine seamanship attracted Collins's attention, and early in 1834 he recruited him to help solve a dilemma: was *Shakespeare*'s hull to be V-shaped or flat-floored? It was a critical question and one that had been hotly debated for many years. Travel by sea to New Orleans was tricky; the Mississippi's powerful down current made progress upstream difficult, while numerous shifting sandbars and twisting channels offered a constant hazard of running aground. The typical East River–built vessel was particularly ill-suited for the river passage. New York builders favored hulls with a deep V shape, which gave their ships a greater capacity to resist sideways motion, a characteristic useful for ocean sailing. Unfortunately, the V's extreme draft was an invitation to grounding, and it was not unusual for one of these ocean sailors to find her keel stuck in the Mississippi's mud. Vessels with long, flat bottoms and shallower draft fared better on the river, but according to the opinion of conservative New York shipbuilders, that hull shape was slow at sea and offered little resistance to being easily blown off-course. When Collins consulted Brown and Bell on the issue, they gave him a conventional response: a flat-floored hull would not be able to grip the water properly, leaving the ship sliding to leeward, particularly when she had the breeze on her beam or was tacking into the wind.[9] Not one to follow "conventional wisdom," Collins had his doubts. He told Brown and Bell that over his years in the trade, he had "learned a thing or two from the old cotton droughers."[10] To win the argument, he needed evidence, and so he ordered Palmer to take command of *Huntsville*, a flat-floored packet that had a reputation for being one of the fastest ships on the New Orleans route. After two voyages, Palmer reported that in his opinion, *Huntville*'s flat-floor design was superior and eminently suitable for the North Atlantic.[11]

Palmer's testimony persuaded Collins, and he insisted that Brown and Bell lay down *Shakespeare* with a flat floor. To guarantee that construction went ahead according to his instructions, Collins asked Palmer to give up command of *Huntsville* and stay with him in New York to supervise *Shakespeare*'s construction. Palmer agreed "enthusiastically." The popular press christened him "Commodore" of the Collins Line.[12]

Late in 1834, to cheers of a crowd amply supplied with libations, *Shakespeare* slid down the ways into the East River. For the next few weeks, under Palmer's careful eye, she sat alongside the fitting-out dock as a swarm of workers came aboard. First her masts were stepped so that riggers might climb aloft to reeve miles of running and standing rigging. Sailmakers carted heavy canvas from nearby lofts and then went aloft to bend the sail onto spars. Carpenters and joiners were busy finishing off areas belowdeck as painters touched up the hull. Work went quickly, and on January 27, 1835, *Shakespeare* fell down the East River on her maiden voyage to New Orleans.[13]

The captain who superintended a ship's construction customarily had the privilege of first command, particularly for a ship like *Shakespeare*, whose progress on the ways had been so closely followed, but Collins the showman had other plans. Nathaniel Palmer was not standing on the quarterdeck as *Shakespeare* headed to sea; instead she sailed under the command of Collins's uncle John, his father's younger brother.[14] A blockade runner and privateersman during the War of 1812, Collins had been captured by the British and imprisoned in the notorious Dartmoor Prison. Unlike many of his fellow prisoners, he survived the ordeal. After the war, he commanded a number of vessels, mostly in the coastal trade. Described as "muscular and compact," he was known for his "loud voice and hot temper," useful qualities for a captain.[15]

It had never been Collins's intention to keep *Shakespeare* on the New Orleans run; he had a more ambitious plan in mind. He had sent her to New Orleans under his uncle as a means to test her sailing qualities. She performed well, and after a few voyages, Collins revealed his true intentions and announced that *Shakespeare* was leaving the New Orleans trade to begin service to Liverpool. Collins was entering the booming business of the Atlantic packets.[16]

Over the seventeen years between the first Black Baller's departure in 1818 and the launching of *Shakespeare*, American cotton exports had more than quadrupled.[17] In the business of carrying cotton across the Atlantic, according to her former mayor Philip Hone, New York held "unrivaled eminence," due, he claimed, "more than any other cause," to the "regularity" of the packets. By the mid-1830s, nearly fifty packets were crossing between London, Liverpool, Le Havre, and New York.[18] On any day, Collins might gaze out from his South Street office or walk along the piers to admire these splendid "floating palaces," each one "superior to the last."[19] Crowds rushed to catch a glimpse of a packet breezing up the harbor, her sails billowing and lines taught. As the ship neared her berth, onlookers could often hear the crew singing a deep sea chanty as the men walked around the capstan hauling in lines—it was a magical and romantic scene. As he watched these festive scenes, Collins could only lament the scant attention given to the arrival of one of his cotton droghers. He was hungry for profit, but he was also driven by the spur of fame. Regardless of his success in the cotton trade to New Orleans, to rank among New York's maritime grandees he would have to stride the North Atlantic stage.

At 747 tons, *Shakespeare* was big enough to match the competition, and her sailing record on the New Orleans route gave promise that she would be a stiff contender in passage time as well. To avoid a dangerous winter crossing, Collins waited until the spring of 1836 to dispatch her to Liverpool under the command of his uncle, with a full cargo of cotton.[20]

One-third of the foreign tonnage entering New York originated from Liverpool.[21] It was New York's most important trading partner. Nature gifted New York with a spacious harbor and easy access to a vast interior. She was less generous to Liverpool. Located on the Mersey River, "an insignificant stream, navigable for not more than 20 miles the town sat upon slopes of several hills that reached down the south-eastern shores of the Mersey."[22] Made hazardous by the presence of extreme tides, swirling currents, and confounding sandbars, mariners found navigation on the Mersey dangerous and difficult. Poor holding ground and strong winds blowing in "from the flat Cheshire shores on the west and high lands of Lancashire on the east" made anchoring chancy. A wise captain posted a double anchor watch to guard against being driven upon a "shallow and deceitful shore."[23] Wary of the river's hazards, referring to it as a rocky creek, the early Romans opted to supply their posts in the west via a more southerly route up the Dee River to Chester. In the eighth century Vikings coasted the area, but they too showed little interest.[24] When William the Conqueror ordered a survey of his realm (Domesday Book) this "little fishing village" was deemed too insignificant to be included.[25] A century and a half later in 1207, however, the hamlet had grown sufficiently to attract the attention of King John, who saw the political and commercial advantages of having "a new free borough on the sea" and granted "to all our faithful subjects, who are in the occupation of burgage tenures at Lyrpul all the liberties and free customs in the town of Lyrpul which any other free borough upon the sea has in our territories."[26] Succeeding monarchs, pressed hard by the townsmen of Liverpool who lobbied for greater autonomy, added to the immunities and privileges of the Corporation, creating a body politic powerful enough to exercise considerable political and fiscal authority. Enhanced legal status, however, brought little change to the port's economy, and even as trade along the coast and across the Irish Sea increased, the little creek of Liverpool remained long in the shadows of her more prosperous neighbors.[27] Beginning in the years of Queen Elizabeth (1558–1603), as English "sea dogs" sailed forth to plunge into the fray of competing world empires, Liverpool's pulse began to beat faster. It was salt, Liverpool's "Nursing Mother," that excited the port.[28]

Left behind by retreating seas, salt deposits dotted the environs of Liverpool's neighbor Cheshire. Since Roman times, workers had extracted the salt by digging shallow pits and drawing brine to the surface; the liquid was then boiled in open pans to remove the scum, and the concentrated residue was thereafter poured into troughs where it was allowed to cool and harden. Although the resource seemed unlimited, the market for salt was not very extensive, and so by a "long tradition of ordered restraint and gentlemanly calm," local brinemen worked carefully to control their output by regulating the number of pans employed and by confining their work to a few days a year.[29] Despite Cheshire producers' best efforts to control their industry, by the early 1600s the old order was breaking down. As demand for salt both domestically and abroad increased, forests, heretofore the source for firing heating pans, became exhausted, and "coal, the herald of change, replaced wood as fuel at the salt works."[30] Compared to wood, coal was expensive. It took one and a half tons of coal, all of which arrived from mines in southeastern Lancashire, to produce a ton of salt. Although the distance to be traveled was only a few miles, carrying coal by either pack horse or crude wagons over rutted, muddy, poorly maintained roads proved to be difficult and costly. By the time the Lancashire coal reached the Cheshire pans, its cost had doubled.

In 1670 the brinemen suffered a second sad blow when John Halton, a prospector searching for coal in Cheshire, dug a pit and instead of coal he discovered a rich bed of solid rock salt thirty feet below the surface.

Unlike brine, which needed lengthy processing at its source before it could be transported, Halton's superior salt could be removed directly from the salt mine, conveyed, and refined elsewhere.[31] By the early eighteenth century, a three-cornered trade linking the salt fields of Cheshire, the coal mines of Lancashire, and the port of Liverpool had developed. Even though salt exports from Liverpool increased dramatically, the business was constrained by reliance upon a primitive and inefficient system of transport that could barely move coal to the refineries and salt to customers. Searching for improvements, merchants, mine owners, and others settled on the cheapest method of transport—water—and proceeded to invest large sums to improve river navigation and construct canals that would ease congestion and cut costs. Relentless in their pursuit to better organize the industry, "the men of Liverpool brought the coal and salt trade to a high degree of economic organization."[32]

Built with "art and labour," the same system that moved salt and coal to Liverpool carried other products as well, from the increasingly industrialized midlands including textiles, refined sugar, metal products, leather goods, glass, pottery, and coal.[33] Their quays now stacked with goods, enterprising Liverpool merchants turned their attention toward emerging Atlantic markets, and especially the empire's expanding settlements in North America: New England, the middle colonies, and the tobacco, rice, and indigo regions of the plantation south—as well as the rich sugar islands of the West Indies. Under the protectionist umbrella of a complex and effective mercantilist system directed at excluding foreign competitors, Liverpool ships carried salt, coal, and manufactured goods west and returned with cargoes of foodstuffs, tobacco, and sugar, processed and sold through the city's increasingly sophisticated business network.[34] The imperial system worked marvelously well for Liverpool. In the first decades of the eighteenth century tobacco imports tripled, sugar increased by 50 percent, and the population grew from five thousand to twenty thousand. On visiting Liverpool in 1724 an observant Daniel Defoe marveled at what he saw:

> The town has now an opulent, flourishing and encreasing trade, not rivalling Bristol, in the trade to Virginia, and the English island

colonies in America only, but is in a fair way to exceed and eclipse it, by encreasing every way in wealth and shipping. They trade round the whole island, send ships to Norway, to Hamburgh, and to the Baltick, as also to Holland and Flanders; so that, in a word, they are almost become like the Londoners, universal merchants.[35]

Profits accumulated as Liverpool shipowners acquired the vast array of skills needed to manage long, perilous, and costly voyages to exotic destinations. They learned what goods were likely to find ready markets. In a global market largely devoid of cash, they mastered the tortuous task of buying and selling goods through complex remittances, paying through bills of exchange whose value depended upon the signer's reputation. Most important, sitting at their nexus point on the Mersey, and with vessels arriving each day from distant ports in the Atlantic and beyond, Liverpool merchants, through their extensive overseas contacts, garnered vital, timely market intelligence that gave them a decided edge over their less well-informed competitors. Wisely seeking to spread their risks, profits not ploughed back into voyaging found their way toward investments in real estate, banking, insurance, shipbuilding, coal mining, salt and sugar refining, and pottery manufacturing, as well as the construction of canals. Looming over this good fortune, however, was the grim specter of Liverpool's most infamous business—the slave trade.[36]

Initially, by virtue of a monopoly granted in 1672, the London-based Royal African Company had exclusive rights to the British slave trade. Although opponents sought their share of the lucrative business and "interlopers" defied the law and traded on their own, the company managed to retain its privileged status thanks to royal favor. In the aftermath of the bloodless Glorious Revolution and the departure of James II, however, the political winds shifted; Parliament abolished the Company's monopoly in 1698 and opened the trade to all comers. The rush was on. Among the first ships to get under way was the *Liverpool Merchant*, laden with trade goods bound for West Africa to purchase a cargo of slaves, and thence to Barbados.[37]

Slave trade voyages, which required significant capital and carried high risks, often lasted as long as eighteen months. The African coast was a dangerous destination. Tropical diseases, the threat of being cut off by angry natives, pirates, and wrecking in uncharted, shark-infested waters took a heavy toll. Casting a critical eye over the legendary profits associated with Liverpool's slave trade, the economic historian Francis Hyde analyzed the papers of one firm and concluded that "losses on venturing seem to have been as frequent as gains."[38] Hyde's critique notwithstanding, and whatever the true profitability of the business might have been (the records are unclear), the slave trade was undoubtedly the backbone of the town's prosperity.[39] By the mid-1730s, at least fifteen ships per year were leaving the Mersey for Africa, a number that grew to fifty in the 1750s, when the port surpassed Bristol and London in the slave trade and import of sugar and rum.[40] Nearly every Liverpool merchant with ready money ventured into the business. In a memorable moment in 1772, after being hissed off the stage of the Theatre Royal in Liverpool for a poor performance in *Richard III*, the erratic and alcoholic George Frederick Cooke returned to face his audience, laying bare their sin as he declared, "There is not a brick in your nasty town but is cemented with the blood of an African."[41] Cooke fled Liverpool, later ending up in New York to enjoy tremendous success on the American stage.

Liverpool's dominant position in the slave trade was a direct result of her efficient connections to the increasingly industrialized midlands, which provided access to a wide variety of manufactures important to the African trade including textiles (from Lancashire and Yorkshire) as well as copper and brass items from the foundries and shops of Staffordshire, Warrington, and Cheshire. Knives, bells, and personal ornaments were particularly popular along the coast. Carried from Birmingham— a center for gun manufacturing—muskets by the thousands flowed through Liverpool to the shores of Africa, where they were used to secure traders' violent business. Not all goods shipped to Africa bore the stamp of local manufacture, however. West African slave dealers had a special fondness for lightweight East Indian cloth. British trade with the East was in the exclusive domain of the behemoth East India Company. Chartered in 1600 and headquartered in London, the company enjoyed a monopoly on all trade to the East between the Cape of Good Hope to the straits of Magellan.

Excluded from the East, Liverpool merchants had little choice but to buy textiles from the middlemen of the East India Company or, on occasion, if they could avoid detection, obtain similar goods from the company's Dutch competitors, including the Vereeniging Oost-Indishe Companie. In either case, buyers paid a premium to middlemen. The same was true for another article popular in the African trade—decorative glass beads. For these low-in-bulk/high-in-demand decorations, Liverpool's slave traders depended upon the glass factories of Venice.[42]

As a result of her role in the slave trade, eighteenth-century Liverpool stood at the center of a violent explosion of European hegemony across the Atlantic world and beyond, termed "war capitalism" by the historian Sven Becker. This global phenomenon, which made possible Europe's rise to economic dominance, was based on "slavery, the expropriation of indigenous peoples, imperial expansion, armed trade and the assertion of sovereignty over people and land by entrepreneurs," who drew their strength from powerful institutions and states.[43] By the mid-eighteenth century Liverpool controlled one-fourth of the kingdom's foreign trade.

Although the slave trade was a key economic driver in Liverpool, slavery was never embedded in the fabric of English society as it came to be in the American colonies, where slavery permeated nearly every part of the community. Still, in eighteenth-century England, a rising abolitionist chorus, led initially by English Quakers and joined later by religious reformers such as John Wesley and powerful politicians including William Wilberforce, proclaimed the horrors of the trade. Encouraged by the 1772 *Somerset* decision, which did not abolish slavery but declared it unsupported by English and Welsh common law, reformers persisted in their campaign to abolish the trade and slavery itself.[44]

While not necessarily prescient, Liverpool slave traders, who for generations had been nimble enough to navigate through the hazards of their sleazy business, sensed change.[45] As early as 1795 they began to hedge their bets by seeking new markets and investments.[46] Their concern was purely fiscal, not moral, for among their newfound alliances were the cotton planters of the American slaveocracy.

Lancashire had long been the center of English wool production. In the fourteenth century, the Crown encouraged Flemish weavers to settle there. Although initially shunned by local weavers, the aliens were eventually admitted into the guilds. The industry grew, and in the seventeenth century, Huguenot refugees, fleeing persecution in France, introduced cotton weaving into Lancashire. Merchants-employers "put-out" cotton imported from the eastern Mediterranean and the West Indies to local peasant families, who in the evenings and agricultural off-season spun and weaved at home, producing cloth for local sale or export. While not yet the cotton cloth of a later century, these early pieces were instead a mix of cotton and linen famous since the sixteenth century. As the export market for cotton cloth expanded, "spinning and weaving became ever more important to smallholding peasants, and some of them eventually gave up their traditional crops and became entirely dependent on the industry."[47] Despite the increased number of workers, the cumbersome toil of hand production and limited supplies of cotton hampered growth. To satisfy customer demand, merchants opted to buck the prevailing doctrine of mercantilism, which dictated protectionism and self-sufficiency, and to import Indian cloth. Reaction from the fledgling cotton industry to this competition was swift and effective, prompting Parliament to enact numerous laws discouraging, and in some instances banning, the domestic sale of Indian imports.

While politically expedient, and popular in the countryside, these laws failed to give the English cotton industry the wherewithal to compete with less expensive Indian products.[48] With production dispersed across the countryside, English entrepreneurs faced the challenges of poor quality control, unpredictable rates of output, and high costs of transportation. These factors alone were sufficient to stifle the industry, but wage differential was the fatal blow. Workers in England earned six times the rates paid their Indian counterparts. The interests of part-time rural workers, who were contentedly employed at home and earned reasonable wages, clashed with those of merchants, who persistently pursued new sources of raw materials, higher production rates, and lower costs. During the eighteenth century, a stunning confluence of economic, social, and technological forces radically altered the English countryside in favor of those merchants who were eager to secure their place in a growing world economy.

In 1733 John Kay introduced his flying shuttle, a hand-powered device that enabled weavers to triple production. The shuttle's speed created an insatiable appetite for yarn, but production could be increased only by increasing the number of spinning wheels employed. That advance arrived in 1764, when James Hargreaves patented his spinning jenney— which turned eight spindles (later versions turned as many as one hundred and twenty) instead of the one found on the spinning wheel—which more than tripled output. Other inventions, including Richard Arkwright's water frame and Edmund Cartwright's power loom, also boosted progress. Mill owners embraced the new machines. Because they were too large and complicated to be housed in cottages or powered by human hands, mill owners installed them under one roof, where they tapped a single source of power—water and especially steam—to turn wheels and drive the belts. In this new industrial model, workers, previously accustomed to working at home governed by their own clocks, were now crowded into factories where owners pushed production under regimes of rigid control.

Although at great human cost, the new system worked marvelously well. Where Indian spinners "required 50,000 hours to spin a hundred pounds of raw cotton, their cohorts in 1790s Britain could spin the same amount in 1,000 hours."[49] As production increased, costs fell, profits rose, and the boom was under way. "Between 1780 and 1800, output grew at an annual rate of 10.8 percent, while textile exports expanded at an astonishing 14.0 per cent per annum."[50] Such extraordinary growth would have been impossible without additional supplies of cotton and expanding global markets to absorb rising production. Liverpool was at the center of this phenomenon.[51] The vast bulk of raw cotton destined to feed the mills of Lancashire arrived at the port to be carried inland, and on return the products of the midland manufacturers spread over the globe through the docks of Liverpool.

That the port of Liverpool, whose harbor had few natural advantages, could manage this huge flow of raw materials and manufactured goods across its docks was due almost completely to nearly two centuries of imaginative engineering and huge financial investments, aimed at combating nature to create a haven for shipping. Extreme tides left only a few short hours for a vessel to enter the river, come alongside a pier, and land cargo before a fast ebb dropped the hull more than twenty feet to wedge in the mud. To avoid stranding, some masters opted to anchor in the deep stream, hoping that their anchors would hold as small lighters, at great expense and difficulty, came alongside to ferry goods back and forth to shore. Although "spasmodic efforts were made from time to time" to improve port facilities, the city's entrenched leadership, under the control of landed manorial families with little interest in commerce, did "nothing very noteworthy to accommodate the small traffic of the day."[52] Notwithstanding the elite's lack of interest, the traffic of the day did increase, and along with it the fortunes of a rising merchant class—men with enterprise and initiative who leveraged their economic influence to edge their way toward political power.[53] They envisioned Liverpool as a great port, but unless they found a way to mitigate the harsh environment of the Mersey, their ambitions were doomed.

By the early eighteenth century, realizing that the financial scope of the challenge was likely to be beyond even the ample "revenues of the Corporation Estate," Liverpool authorities launched a political arm-twisting campaign aimed at engineering support from Parliament.[54] On November 3, 1708, Liverpool's mayor John Seacome "order'd that S. Thomas Johnson and Richard Norris Esq, the representatives in Parliam for this Corporation (being now goeing to Parliam) be desir'd and impower'd to treat with and agree for a proper person to come to this town, and view the ground, and draw a plan of the intended Dock."[55] Two well-known civil engineers, George Sorocold and Henry Huss, prepared a plan. Johnson and Norris laid it before Parliament and explained the city's plight:

> In the harbor of Liverpool the sea or tide flows about five hours and a half, and ebbs about six hours and a half; and that in spring tides it rises about thirty feet, and at the lowest neaps fifteen feet. The distance between high and low water mark against the town side, it is stated, is between three and four hundred yards, the

shipping which trades to the port, to take in or deliver out their merchandise, either lie on the ground between high and low water mark, which is rock covered with a thin sand, or else ride afloat in the channel or current of the tide, where they often suffer great damage, either by beating on the rocks by an extraordinary wear and tear of their cables and rigging, or by being driven from their moorings and wrecked against the town side.[56]

To answer the dangers the Corporation proposed to build "a dock covering four acres of ground, capable of containing one hundred ships at a time." Even "at the lowest neap tides" there would always be at least "fourteen feet of water; and at spring tides enough for a fourth or fifth rate man-of-war." By this arrangement, they noted, "shipping will always have three hours every tide, that is, every twelve hours, for going in and coming out of the dock." All around the dock the town planned to build quays and wharfs as well as warehouses. The estimated cost was £6,000 to be collected by a complex scheme of fees collected from vessels using the port.[57]

It was a daring plan, and notwithstanding opposition from some quarters—the cheesemongers of London, for example, whose trade in cheese would be taxed, wanted no part of paying for costly docks— nearly everyone recognized that this work would improve navigation.[58] What could not be agreed upon was whether the construction of the largest commercial wet dock in the kingdom was practicable. Debate went on for nearly a year until finally on October 5, 1709, Parliament enacted legislation permitting the construction of a "Wet Bason" to be located "in or near a certain place called the Pool, on the south side of the said town of Liverpool."[59] When Sorocold and Huss declined to oversee construction, the city employed Thomas Steers.

Steers faced a series of steep challenges. While enclosed docks—whose construction created areas where water levels could be controlled—had been built since ancient times, Liverpool's extreme tides, the Mersey's fast current, and a muddy bottom that needed to be penetrated deeply in order to set foundations on firm footing posed work of a special nature.[60] Not surprisingly, construction took longer and cost more than estimated, but the dock finally opened on August 31, 1715.[61] Although it proved a success, Defoe referring to it as the "greatest benefit," given the considerable expense of building and ongoing operating costs, Liverpool waited twenty-seven years before opening a second dock.[62] A third dock opened in 1771, and before the end of the century Liverpool boasted six active docks. By 1850 that number had nearly quadrupled to twenty-three. From the shore the docks pushed the edge of the river out into the stream.[63] Around them clustered a bevy of buildings and activities—warehouses, counting houses, forges, cooperages, glassworks, sugar refineries, and iron foundries.

In 1839, on his first voyage, Herman Melville—a twenty-year-old foremast hand sailing aboard the New York packet *St. Lawrence*—arrived in Liverpool. For six weeks the packet lay in Prince's Dock adjacent to Bath Street not far from the Exchange. Melville took the time to explore the area, recounting that "having only seen the miserable wooden wharves, and slip-shod, shambling piers of New York, the sight of these mighty docks filled my young mind with wonder and delight."[64] Once ashore, he walked along the "river-side, passing dock after dock, like a chain of immense fortresses; Prince's, George's, Salt-House, Clarence, Brunswick, Trafalgar, King's, Queen's and many more."

He gave a particular description of Prince's dock (1821):

From the river, Prince's Dock is protected by a long pier of masonry, surmounted by a massive wall; and on the side next the town, it is bounded by similar walls, one of which runs along a thoroughfare [Bath Street]. The whole space thus enclosed forms an oblong, and may, at a guess, be presumed to comprise about fifteen or twenty acres.

The area of the dock itself, exclusive of the enclosed quays surrounding it, may be estimated at, say, ten acres. Access to the interior from the streets is had through several gateways; so that, upon their being closed, the whole dock is shut up like a house. From the river, the entrance is through a Watergate, and ingress to ships is only to be had, when the level of the dock coincides with that of the river; that is, about the time of high tide, as the level of the dock is always at that mark. So that when it is low tide in the river, the keels of the ships enclosed by the quays are elevated more than twenty feet above those of the vessels in the stream.

The operation of the dock was a complex matter. All movement was carefully managed:

> The Dock-master, whose authority is declared by tin signs worn conspicuously over their hats, mount the poops and forecastles of the various vessels, and hail the surrounding strangers in all directions: *"Highlander ahoy! Cast off your bow-line, and sheer alongside the Neptune!" "Neptune ahoy! Get out a stern-line, and sheer alongside the Trident!" Trident ahoy! "Get out as bow-line, and drop astern of the Undaunted!"*

Laid out between the edge of the dock and a high brick wall,

> a paved area, very wide which was lined with ranges of iron sheds, intended as a temporary shelter for the goods unladen from the shipping. Nothing can exceed the bustle and activity displayed along these quays during the day: bales, crates, boxes and cases are being tumbled about by thousands of laborers; trucks are coming and going; dock masters are shouting; sailors of all nations are singing out at the ropes.[65]

These "long China walls" enclosed "a small archipelago, an epitome of the world, where all the nations of Christendom, and even those of Heathendom, are represented." Melville's long China walls might well have been built of cotton bales.

CHAPTER FOUR

Dramatic Line

LIVERPOOL GAVE *SHAKESPEARE* a warm welcome, and although she was not a record-setter, her average of thirty-six days on west-bound crossings was respectable.[1] *Shakespeare*'s success spurred Collins the following fall to announce a new line of packet ships leaving New York "on the 30th of each month, and from Liverpool on the 12th."[2] *Shakespeare* would be joined by four sisters, all to be built by Brown and Bell under the careful eye of Nathaniel Palmer.[3] Collins grabbed more publicity for his line when, unlike his New York competitors whose ship names often bore no relation to one another, he pursued a theatrical theme for his line of packets.[4] *Garrick* was named for the inimitable David Garrick, one of eighteenth-century England's best known actors and manager of London's famed Drury Lane Theater.[5] Richard Sheridan, the playwright, was likewise connected to that theatre, and so Collins named a ship for him—*Sheridan*. The third packet, *Siddons*, celebrated Sarah Siddons, an actress who won acclaim while performing under Sheridan at Drury Lane. The fourth and largest vessel of the quartet, 167 feet in length, 1,130 tons, bore the name *Roscius*, recalling Quintus Roscius Gallus, a Roman actor whose name, according to one of Collins's contemporaries, was "given to every performer of transcendent merit."[6] Collins's dramatic touch played well in New York and received rave reviews in England, where the *Liverpool Mercury* celebrated the establishment of "The *Shakespeare* Line to Liverpool."[7] Taking their cue from the ships' names, New Yorkers called it the Dramatic Line. Calling up historic literary names and engaging celebrity captains such as Nathaniel Palmer and John Collins gave the line panache, but that was only one part of Collins's strategy.

In their early days packets carried few cabin passengers, not more than ten to twenty per trip. As transatlantic business picked up in the 1820s and '30s, however, that number grew. In 1829 the Swallowtail Line's *Napoleon* boasted "forty-four cabins." For these "spacious rooms, extensive and elegant" travelers were willing to pay a high fare. By the 1830s New York's packets were reaping considerable profits from their first-class cabin passenger business.[8]

To attract the well-heeled "gloves and cane" crowd, Collins touted his vessels as superior to all others.[9] As the ships took shape, Collins, accompanied by Palmer, checked on their progress. On occasion he brought along his wife and young children Thomas, Edward, and Mary Ann.[10] Each launching was a grand public event. "Whenever one of these leviathans slid down the ways, thousands of spectators converged on the scene to watch and applaud."[11] While *Siddons*, impressive at 890 tons, 157 feet, was still on the stocks, and leaving no opportunity for publicity to chance, Collins took out a newspaper advertisement inviting "persons who are curious in such matters" to come and inspect the vessel. New Yorkers came to gawk.[12] One admiring visitor gave a report:

> We stepped down to the wharf at the foot of Wall Street, to take a look at this paragon of aquatic beauty. From the size of the ship, and the manner in which she is painted, a person would be excused in mistaking her for a frigate instead of a packet ship. The cabin is intended for the accommodation of thirty-six passengers, and is an elegant room, richly furnished and decorated with the most consummate taste. The stern window's ornamented glass has a peculiarly fine effect, and sheds a rich and mellow light over the after part of the cabin. The staterooms are of considerable size, fitted up with two berths and neatly carpeted and furnished.[13]

Lest anyone mistake *Siddons*'s namesake, Collins arranged with the city's best-known ship carvers, the father-son firm of Jeremiah and Charles Dodge, to ornament her with an impressive figurehead, "a carved representation of Mrs. Siddons in the character of [Henry VIII's wife] Queen Catherine."[14] In the saloon the royal image appeared on a sunlit, stained glass window.

Roscius, the queen of the fleet, was the last to launch. Named for the ancient Roman actor about whom the poet Catullus wrote "though he is human he seems more beautiful than a god," she embodied what Collins valued in life and work—grand performances, admiring audiences, beauty, and elegance. *Roscius* did not disappoint. As the *New York Spectator* proclaimed:

> The cabin is thought to surpass in finish and elegance that of any craft afloat, either in this or any other country. The stern lights are of stained glass, exceedingly beautiful, with a painting of Neptune in his car drawn by sea horses. The cabinet work of the cabin is rose-wood, satin and zebra-woods, highly polished and of most beautiful shading, with pilasters of imitation porcelain.[15]

Roscius and her sisters set new standards for comfort on the Atlantic crossing. Ships of the Dramatic Line were bigger and often faster than their competitors. "*Roscius* made her westward crossings in an average of 26 days in 1840—a record that stood until 1853." A year later, *Garrick* made an eastward passage in fifteen days and four hours.[16] In addition to quick passages, Collins offered shipboard amenities not seen before. Instead of being jammed below in dark, damp, and often foul-smelling spaces, Collins put first-class cabins on "the level of the quarterdeck . . . airy and spacious."[17]

By moving cabins up a deck, Collins also managed to open up lower decks for additional cargo. These were spaces where, in later years, grasping owners squeezed in hundreds of steerage passengers, but for the moment the Dramatic Line ignored steerage passengers, finding greater profit carrying cabin passengers and high-value cargo between New York and Liverpool and leaving the "huddled masses" to book passage on cheaper and far less luxurious vessels.

Able to carry nearly twice the number of cabin passengers sailing on other American packets, *Roscius*'s main saloon could "accommodate forty ladies and gentlemen." Collins's packets carried the most fashionable members of American society.[18] The line drew particular attention when the American artist George Catlin announced that at the invitation of the British Lords of the Treasury, he was taking his extensive collection of Indian paintings and artifacts to England for exhibit. He chose to sail on *Roscius*.[19] As was his wont, Collins's friend James Gordon Bennett at the *Herald* seized the moment to publish a paean for the Dramatic Line.

> It is now a well ascertained fact, that in proportion to the number of passengers carried in them, for the last twenty years, fewer lives have been lost than by any other known means of conveyance, but exempting transportation on railroads, and in steamers on our noble rivers. And as to comfort and living, why what on earth can exceed that to be found on board either the *Roscius*, the *Garrick*, the *Siddons*, the *Sheridan*? They make the quickest trips, have the best accommodations, and, are the safest vessels that ever walked the waters.[20]

Although the competition for passengers and freight was fierce, Collins entered the packet contest at a propitious moment. While the "most consistent packet travelers" remained businessmen, government bureaucrats, diplomats and their entourages, an increasing number of people on both sides of the Atlantic opted to cross for the pleasures of touring Europe and America.[21] By the 1830s and '40s, in both the United States and Great Britain, a rising middle class was embracing the notion of cultural travel. To come home after a grand tour and be able to chat with friends about London, Rome, Paris, and other foreign sights enhanced an individual's social status. In addition, an increasing number of young men traveled to Europe to burnish their professional credentials by attending prestigious universities. Seventy-five to 90 percent of all American travelers booked passage on American packets.[22] Collins's ships were especially popular. Even Liverpudlians, persistent baiters of all things American, confessed that Collins's *Siddons*, for "elegance" and "capacity," was "not surpassed by any ship sailing out of our port."[23]

Once at sea, however, not even the plush surroundings of rosewood paneling, stained glass, fine tableware, and Wilton carpets could mask the stress of an ocean packet crossing. Ralph Waldo Emerson made the point:

> I find sea-life an acquired taste, like that for tomatoes and olives. The confinement, cold, motion, noise and odor are not to be dispensed with. The floor of your room is sloped at an angle on twenty or thirty degrees, and I waked every morning with the belief that someone was tipping up my berth. Nobody likes to be treated ignominiously, upset, shoved against the side of the house, rolled over, suffocated with bilge, mephitis, and stewing oil. We get used to these annoyances at last, but the dread of the sea remains longer.[24]

While storms, particularly on westbound winter crossings, brought a special form of terror, the passenger's more common state of mind was boredom. On good days, with a fair wind blowing, men and women strolled the deck and chatted, mindful to secure their hats and bonnets against the breeze. It was the captain's prerogative as to whether they might be permitted to walk the quarterdeck, a part of the ship ordinarily reserved for officers. If invited aft, they might converse with the officer of the deck but never with the helmsman, whose attention to the compass and sails could suffer no distraction. Conversation with any of the forecastle crew was discouraged.

Under the unrelenting sun of summer crossings, shade was at a premium and could be found only in places where sails or deckhouses blocked the rays. Women sought shelter in the saloon, settling into over-stuffed sofas and chairs, while men congregated in the smoking room or, in fair weather, near the leeward rail. Seasickness was a constant companion for which a plethora of folk remedies were offered—drink more water, look at the horizon, go up on deck, stay below, eat dry crackers, drink dill pickle juice, drink peppermint tea. Those struck down by relentless motion caused by heavy seas might take slight solace that at least the ship was making progress toward port and health. On doldrum days, however, when the ship wallowed listlessly, sails flapping, making no progress, passengers lying ill in their stifling cabins feared that they might never come to port. Commenting about his packet's progress on one such day Emerson noted that "a nimble Indian would have swum as far."[25]

For those able to keep their meals down, American packet owners proved they were up to the challenge. Food aboard was plentiful, and some of it even fresh. Cows and chickens were kept on board for milk and eggs. Beer, wine, and alcohol flowed. As with modern cruise ships, eating was the chief pastime of the voyage. Harriet Martineau, the English essayist and a keen observer, described food's centrality as she crossed in 1834 aboard *United States* of the Red Star Line. When the bell summoned passengers to dine, "the tables were filled in five minutes." According to her, "the best hours of the day [were devoted] to dinner and dessert."[26]

"Thirty guineas, wine included" was the standard fare among the packet lines.[27] At that price, a typical voyage of twenty-five to thirty days, the steward's department might show a profit. On longer voyages, with more time to eat and drink, it was otherwise. As passengers and crew supped, the ship's profits dwindled. Owners grumbled about the costs incurred and were particularly galled by the outrageous waste of wine and food by callous passengers. For Collins the problem was especially acute since his ships, larger than the others, carried more passengers and thus required a larger pantry. In the face of stiff competition, Collins could not raise fares; indeed the entire trend of transatlantic fares for the period was down. Collins advertised new rates, "$140 with wines or $120 without."[28] Teetotaling passengers approved.

Although passengers often socialized with the ship's officers, they had very little contact with the ordinary crew. In the early days of the packet service, young men, mostly from New York and New England, filled American forecastles. As more and bigger ships took to the Atlantic, however, demand for foremast hands sapped that supply of labor, while at the same time fewer Americans felt that "drizzly November" in their "souls" calling them to work upon the sea, as had Melville's Ishmael.[29]

The dangers and harsh conditions of the seafarer's life could not compete with the enticements of expanding cities, western lands, and rapidly growing industries that promised better pay and more comforts.

To fill out their crews, captains often turned to brutal and unsavory methods, which included employing crimps, who, for a price and with no questions asked, prowled the waterfront recruiting men of uncertain character, many of them impoverished Liverpool Irish and rowdy "packet rats." Some crimps went so far as to shanghai men, kidnapping them to fill the forecastle of a departing ship.[30] Unable to find men even by these means, and facing strong competition and declining profits, owners cut costs by short-handing crews, leaving the captain and his mates to command men overworked, unhappy, and often insolent.[31] Undermanned vessels were dangerous. In nasty weather, particularly on winter crossings, the crew often answered to the call "all hands on deck." Standing "watch on watch," having no time for rest, exhausted and bleary-eyed men were prone to accidents such as falling from the rigging or being swept over the side. In extreme situations a worn-out crew might lose their ship.[32] One in six packet ships "was totally wrecked in service."[33]

Nonetheless, fear of the bosun and the "bucko mates" largely kept the men from complaining. In song, however, through their chanties, they voiced their lament.

> "Lay aft," is the cry, "to the break of the poop,
> Or I'll help you along with the toe of my boot."
> 'Tis larboard and starboard on deck you will sprawl,
> For Kicking Jack Williams commands that Black Ball![34]

Not surprisingly, given his origins, Collins favored New Englanders in selecting his captains. However, he was hardly alone in his preferences, for in the glory days of the packets "New England [was] the greatest breeder of good seamen."[35] His uncle John served him the longest, and in 1839 Collins promoted John to command *Roscius*.[36] While master of the packet, John Collins became an international hero. About midway on a blustery eastbound December crossing in 1839, *Roscius* "fell in with the wreck of the *Scotia*, bound from Quebec to Glasgow, loaded with timber." Collins bore down on her, and as he came within hailing distance the desperate captain pleaded, "We are water logged, seventeen feet in the hold." Among the ninety-one passengers aboard *Roscius* was Richard Robert Madden. A noted travel writer, Madden was also an ardent abolitionist who was on his way home from superintending the freeing of slaves in the British West Indies.[37] In an essay that he wrote later for a popular boys' book, *The New Excitement; or a Book to Induce Young People to Read*, Madden recounted his adventure. As *Roscius* drew near, "a cheer from the people of the sinking vessel followed . . . every hat and cap was seen waving on the crowded poop." *Scotia* "pitched heavily," and "the sea swept over her." Collins called over, "Put out your boats," but steep seas made launching impossible. Night came and *Roscius* stood by. "We must stay by the poor wretches at all events till morning," Collins told his passengers and crew; "we can't leave them to perish there." In the morning, once the seas calmed, *Scotia*'s crew managed to launch their boats. With help from *Roscius*, the exhausted officers, seamen, and passengers came to safety aboard *Roscius*. Once ashore, *Scotia*'s captain wrote a public letter to Collins thanking him for rescuing the crew of *Scotia* from "certain death." The passengers of *Roscius* offered similar laurels, while the underwriters of Liverpool "awarded the freedom of their rooms to Capt. Collins," and the Humane Society of London presented him with a medal. Tributes accumulated in New York as well. When Madden wrote a poetic paean titled "To Captain Collins of the *Roscius*," James Gordon Bennett published it in the *Herald*.[38]

Two years later John Collins made the news again with a second dramatic rescue during another boisterous winter passage. *Erin-go-Bragh*, bound from Montreal to Liverpool with a load of timber, hit heavy seas. Her hatches broke open, water poured in, and she soon began to founder. *Roscius* came to the rescue, taking off the crew. Peter Sumpton, master of the vessel, published a letter offering "heartfelt and most gracious thanks for [Collins's] humanity." For "his noble behavior and eminent services," the vessel's owners, Fisher and Sons of Liverpool, presented the captain with a "handsome snuff-box."[39]

Thanks to well-built ships, able captains, and fast passages, by the early 1840s the Dramatic Line was riding a swell of international renown that brought Collins fame and profits, ranking him one of New York's most renowned packet-ship operators and a wealthy man.

Collins's success was set against the larger tableau of New York's prosperity. Since his arrival twenty years before, the city's population had tripled. So too had personal fortunes, prompting the diarist and lawyer George Templeton Strong to note that "wealth is rushing upon us like a freshet."[40] In addition to prosperous shipowners along South Street, Collins's New York "teemed with bankers, brokers, importers, exporters, manufacturers, insurance tycoons, blueblood professionals, real estate moguls, department store lords, railroad barons, and publishing magnates."[41] The well-to-do, however, were a minority. In this sprawling urban giant, most of the population growth came from immigration. By the end of the decade nearly half of New York City's population was foreign-born. Cheap housing was in short supply. As the poor pressed into neighborhoods in lower Manhattan economically mobile natives moved out. Speculators purchased and carved the properties left behind them into tiny pre-tenement style apartments.[42]

While many affluent New Yorkers escaped uptown to Washington Square and Gramercy Park, some of the disaffected fled the city entirely. Distancing themselves "from the too great bustle and excitement of our commercial cities," they sought the tranquility of an ideal portrayed by writers such as Emerson and William Cullen Bryant and by romantic painters including Frederick Edwin Church, Thomas Cole, and Asher Durand of the Hudson River School, who captured the countryside's mysteries of light and color.[43] From these influences they imagined, in short, a bucolic existence modeled in the style of the English country gentleman.

This romantic connection between nature and the home captured the imagination of Andrew Jackson Downing, a young landscape architect from Newburgh, New York, who wrote a series of widely popular books on domestic architecture. In language that swelled with popular romanticism, Downing presented plans for "well proportioned" country homes and villas. Living in such country homes reflected the character of those who sought an "intelligent and cultivated life" that led to a higher "moral, social and intellectual existence."[44]

Watching unhappily as his neighborhood changed, Collins made his own attempt at rusticating. He sold his property on Houston Street in the summer of 1845 and moved to Mamaroneck, Westchester County, alongside Long Island Sound, where at auction he purchased the home and estate of Peter Jay Munro for $30,000, nearly three times the amount for what he had sold his Houston Street property. Munro was the nephew of the American revolutionary diplomat, and the republic's first chief justice, John Jay. A New York City lawyer in partnership with Aaron Burr, Munro had built a traditional Federal-style home on 300 acres in 1797. Although his property overlooked the Sound, in an age more concerned with commerce than nature, Munro turned his home away from the grand vista over the water and instead laid out his house to front the nearby heavily trafficked Boston Post Road. That siting was completely unacceptable to Collins. An endless procession of rattling wagons and carriages spewing up clouds of dust was too reminiscent of the city from which he had escaped. Collins rejected the home's old-fashioned, stiff Federal style. He spun the orientation of the house 180 degrees, redoing the interiors so that the main rooms faced east toward a view of the Sound and the sunrise. At each level these light, airy chambers opened onto a two-story ornate Classical-style veranda with a graceful central staircase. Collins paid particular notice to the landscape. He made it into a place where "the entire property is finely shaded, and the extensive lawns around the mansion have arches and avenues of superb trees, native and imported." Among the most beautiful of the "superb trees" were the larches for which Collins christened his estate "Larchmont."[45]

The mansion was large enough to accommodate the entire family—Collins, his wife, and their four children, Edward, Mary Ann, Thomas, and the youngest, Henry.[46] Joining them were Collins's three half sisters, Ann, Sexta, and Mary, who chose not to live with their mother with whom they and Collins, since the death of his father, had long been estranged.[47] Collins, the aspiring country gentleman and a sailor, joined other neighboring New York City businessmen with country homes along the Sound to form the Tautog Club, named for a very good table fish abundant along the shores of the Sound from late April through October, a season that coincided nicely with the arrival of the New York summer folk.[48] To accommodate himself and his fellow Tautog Club members, Collins built a cottage-style boathouse with a landing dock and small derrick to lift boats.[49]

Edward Knight Collins, shipowner and country squire, was at the head of his profession. The Dramatic Line had made him wealthy and famous, and with his shoreside estate in Westchester he was clearly trying to elbow his way into New York society. Collins might easily have slid into the casual ways of a rich New York businessman, satisfied to collect dividends and profits from an established and stable business, avoiding all risk; however, he was restless, and had caught "steam fever."

It originally struck him on a spring afternoon in 1838 when, at the height of his fame and still living in New York City, he rode down from Houston Street to the Battery to join thousands of other New Yorkers who thronged on the shoreline to catch a glimpse of two British steamers, *Sirius* and *Great Western*, that had arrived within hours of one another, promising a "new era in the history of Atlantic navigation."[50] Collins, gazing out, proclaimed prophetically: "There is no longer chance for enterprise with sails; it is steam that must win the day." The reaction of his South Street neighbors to this heresy, uttered by one of their own, is unrecorded, but like most prophets he was ignored. Finding neither interest nor investors, Collins stayed with his packets, but steam was on his mind, as it was for a shipowner in Halifax, Nova Scotia.

CHAPTER FIVE

Samuel Cunard

O N TUESDAY, JULY 24, 1683, Thones Kunder and his family stood silently on the deck of the ship *Concord* as it prepared to sail for America. They were bound across the Atlantic to the colony of Pennsylvania, a religious refuge where, according to its founder, William Penn, "the air is sweet and clear, the Heavens serene."[1] The Kunders were among thirteen Mennonite-Quaker families from the village of Krefeld, a small German community in the lower Rhine Valley. Wishing to settle his "Holy Experiment" with people who shared his religious views, Penn had dispatched agents to eastern Germany to recruit settlers among the Mennonites, "sober people [who] will neither swear nor fight."[2] One of Penn's emissaries, the pietistic poet and lawyer Franz Daniel Pastorius, visited Krefeld where, armed with promises of good land and religious tolerance, he persuaded the Kunders and a dozen other Krefeld families to join the company sailing on *Concord*.[3]

The journey from Krefeld had been difficult. Having come down the Rhine to Rotterdam, the Krefelders expected a quick crossing to England. Unfortunately, Penn's agents had failed to make the necessary arrangements, and the emigrants were forced to wait weeks for passage. Finally, James Claypoole, a prominent London merchant and close associate of Penn's, straightened matters out and could finally report happily to his patron that "the Crevill ffriends are coming."[4] The summer trip across the Atlantic was pleasant, with Claypoole noting that "the blessings of the Lord did attend us so that we had a very comfortable passage, and had our health all the way."[5] Waiting to greet them was Pastorius, who quickly arranged for the Krefeld families to draw lots for sections of land in an area northwest of the newly laid out city of Philadelphia, a neighborhood christened, appropriately, Germantown. The Kunders did well in the new world. Thones's neighbors elected him one of the community's first burgesses and a justice of the peace. His descendants remained in Germantown, but over the generations, family members drifted away from their faith, and in the process, anglicized their name. By the eve of the American Revolution Kunder had become Cunard.[6]

When the British army occupied Philadelphia in the fall of 1777 the Cunards, like so many other families caught in the Revolution, suffered divided loyalties. Most of the family supported the patriot cause, although Thones's twenty-one-year-old great-great-grandson Abraham, a carpenter, favored the King, but like many others he did so in silence. His cousin Robert, also a carpenter, was less judicious and joined the King's army. For his treason, the Pennsylvania Assembly listed his name in a Bill of Attainder and confiscated all his property.[7] After the British abandoned Philadelphia in the spring of 1778, Abraham and Robert, fearing retribution at the hands of their patriot neighbors, joined the exodus of the "King's Friends" and fled across New Jersey, seeking refuge in British-occupied New York City.

It was a melancholy time for American Loyalists. The war had not gone well for the British. For Abraham and Robert, New York City was as much a prison as a refuge. Having abandoned any hope of subduing New England and the Middle Colonies, the British ministry had decided to hold New York as its principal base while dispatching forces to conquer the South. The strategy failed. The South proved to be a quagmire for the King's forces, culminating in the disastrous defeat of Lord Cornwallis at Yorktown in October 1781. By early 1782, it was clear that the war in America was lost. In May, Sir Guy Carleton, His Majesty's newly appointed commander in chief, arrived in New York. Carleton's appearance sparked hope among the thousands of refugees that the general had been sent to launch a new campaign to restore the authority of the King. When Carleton announced that His Majesty had consented to the "independency of America," they fell into "fits of despair." Those Loyalists who had joined the King's Army "rendered their facings from their uniforms, plucking out their cockades and uttering execrations."[8] Instead of a military commander, Carleton confessed to being a "mere Inspector of Embarkations."[9]

As the news spread quickly, thousands of frightened, displaced, and disgruntled Loyalists outside the city abandoned their homes and crowded into New York. Carrying nothing but their clothes and a few household belongings, they were dependent entirely upon the King's largesse. Carleton's instructions from his London superior, Lord Shelburne, were to treat the Loyalists "with the tenderest and most honourable care giving them every assistance and prudent assurance of attention in whatever other parts of America in His Majesty's possession they chuse to settle."[10]

His Lordship, however, made it abundantly clear that under no circumstances were the Loyalists to become an impediment to peace. "A part must be wounded that the whole of the Empire may not perish." The Loyalists were to "be considered rather as collateral and incidental than as principals to the present dispute." Carleton was troubled by Shelburne's callous instructions. Thomas Jones, a prominent New York Loyalist, noted that as the refugee numbers grew and their conditions worsened, Carleton grew increasingly sympathetic. It became for the general, Jones recalled, a matter of honor, and he "determined not to sacrifice the loyalists, nor leave the country, till every one of them who chose to go should be sent off."[11] As "His Majesty's Commander in Chief in North America," Carleton's authority extended north to Canada. With Shelburne's instructions in hand, and pushing his own authority to the extreme, Carleton launched a massive effort to transport and resettle refugees in the King's Province of Nova Scotia.

Ceded by France to Great Britain in the 1713 Treaty of Utrecht, Nova Scotia had long enjoyed a close association with her neighboring colonies to the south, particularly New England. Although fertile land in the province was limited, confined mostly to areas on the western shore abutting the Bay of Fundy, Nova Scotia had abundant timber, and its ports on the Atlantic coast stood close to rich fishing grounds. The province's largest settlement, Halifax, established in 1749 as a naval base, possessed one of the finest harbors in the world. Sparsely populated, the province had vast areas of unsettled land belonging to the Crown.[12] In late summer of 1782, Carleton dispatched orders to Nova Scotia's governor, Andrew Snape Hamond, to prepare to "reserve as much land as possible in his province to answer demands" of Loyalist resettlement.[13] Carleton alerted Hamond to expect "upwards of 600 people." The final number would exceed twenty-five thousand. Hamond, however, was not in office long enough to witness the mass arrival. On October 8, 1782, John Parr, a man of "small slight stature, withered in face," but whose personality earned him the nickname "Cock Robin," arrived as his replacement. In December the first transports entered the harbor.[14]

Abraham and Robert Cunard were among the first to leave New York, but they did not do so together. Robert boarded a vessel bound for Saint John, New Brunswick (set off as a separate province in 1784). Abraham took passage for Halifax. His ship reached Nova Scotia in a few days. As it passed Sambro Light at the mouth of Halifax harbor, Abraham saw off the port side the wooded promontory of Point Pleasant jutting out between the harbor and the northwest arm.[15] Over the tall pines, he spied the looming outline of a huge glacial drumlin rising up abruptly from the shore. Further west, but hidden by the curve of the shore, was the Royal Naval Dockyard. The harbor was alive with activity as small boats shuttled back and forth from transports to land the refugees. The lucky and the rich brought with them trunks of clothes and perhaps bits of furniture and other household goods. Most, however, Abraham included, had few possessions. Compared to Philadelphia or New York, even with all of their wartime discomforts, Halifax looked to be a miserable place. Looking over the bulwark, Abraham's eye was drawn up a steep hill terraced by rough unpaved streets. The town of barely 1,200 was overwhelmed with the swell of migrants.[16] "Every shed, outhouse, store and shelter was crowded with people." Thousands of refugees sought protection under hastily erected canvas shelters. Halifax's two churches, St. Paul's and St. Matthew's, sheltered hundreds, while nearby neighborhoods were dotted with temporary shacks scattered along the hillside. Food was scarce. "The flour mills at Sackville were kept at work night and day, to provide bread," while sailors "brought cabooses and cook-houses ashore" to prepare food for starving people, but all that was available was "codfish, molasses and hard biscuit." Overcrowding resulted in poor sanitary conditions, leading to sickness and death.[17] "Caught between righteous Loyalist demands and growing British parsimony," Governor Parr was not ready for the deluge of the displaced.[18]

While civilian authorities muddled about, military and naval officers took action. Ships of the Royal Navy opened their stores and shared food supplies with the Loyalists. The army behaved with equal energy. General Walter Patterson, longtime governor of Prince Edward Island, reported that he had "given every kind of assistance" to the refugees. Abraham Cunard received particular aid from the army. Many of those coming ashore were rural people with experience and skills connected to farming. For them Halifax was a waypoint on a journey that would take them inland to live on lands promised to them by the Crown. Cunard, on the other hand, was an urban carpenter. Caught in a building boom, Halifax was in desperate need of his talents. The Army offered him a job as foreman carpenter.[19] He accepted quickly, and settled in the city.

Among other refugees at Halifax were a number of Scots-Irish farmers who had fled from the western regions of South Carolina. Led initially by the Reverend William Martin, a Reformed Presbyterian minister from County Antrim, they had come to America in 1772. Drawn west by the promise of good, cheap land, they settled in District Ninety-Six. When the Revolution exploded, they opted to support the crown. Their choice cost them dearly. In the spring and summer of 1781, after an unsuccessful attempt to subdue the interior of the Carolinas, British forces, weakened by repeated encounters with the Americans, began a retreat to the safety of Charleston. The violent struggle in the back-country had taken on the dark character of a vicious civil war. The Scots-Irish Loyalists of Ninety-Six knew what tender mercies the Rebels had in store for them should they decide to remain behind. Hastily loading onto wagons the few possessions they could carry, they joined the retreat. It was a bitter upheaval. "Melancholy was the spectacle that followed; trooping slowly and gloomily in the van and rear of the British Army, went the families of the unhappy faction. For days the roads from Ninety-Six were crowded with this wretched cavalcade."[20] Among the wretched was the family of John Murphy.[21]

For months the Loyalists from Ninety-Six bided their time in Charleston waiting for news of their fate. A city known for its stifling summer heat, and at that point surrounded by the enemy, Charleston turned into a squalid jail. For nearly a year the evacuees holed up behind British lines. The meager resources the refugees brought with them were quickly consumed. Supplies from New York came only intermittently, forcing the British commander, Major General Alexander Leslie, to order dangerous foraging expeditions into enemy-held country. Finally, in the late fall of 1782, Carleton informed Leslie that he was dispatching transports to evacuate the garrison and the Loyalists. On December 13 and 14, nine thousand civilians and slaves boarded dozens of ships anchored in Charleston Harbor.[22] Patriot forces had granted a truce to allow the King's forces to debark; nonetheless, fear and tensions rose as rumors circulated of the terrible fate visited on the King's friends who remained behind, many of whom were beaten and even murdered. Anxious to leave, officials hustled Loyalists onto transports. With their few belongings, mostly consisting of only what they could carry, families from Ninety-Six filed onto vessels "crammed like a sheep-pen," bound for Nova Scotia, a distant place about which they knew virtually nothing.[23] When they landed at Halifax, even the hardened Parr was shocked at their woeful condition. It was winter. "Those from Charlestown," he wrote to his London superiors, "are in a much more miserable situation than those from New York, coming almost naked from the burning sands of South Carolina to the frozen coast of Nova Scotia destitute of every necessity of life."[24]

The sad band from Ninety-Six wintered over in Halifax. Living off government rations, they struggled to keep warm in drafty, ramshackle huts. It may have been during this dismal season that John Murphy's daughter Margaret met the army carpenter Abraham Cunard.

In the spring, after mud season had ended and the roads had become passable, the Murphys and several other South Carolina families moved thirty miles west of Halifax and settled on land granted them by the

King. They called their new home Rawdon, after Lieutenant Colonel Francis Lord Rawdon, the British officer who had escorted them safely to Charleston.

Abraham followed Margaret to Rawdon.[25] The courtship was brief and in 1783 they married. Soon after the wedding, the couple moved to Halifax, where they built a home in the north end of the city not far from the Naval Dockyard where Abraham, having moved on from his job with the army, was now working for the Royal Navy.

Margaret, Abraham and Margaret's first child, was born in 1784; Samuel, their second, arrived on November 1, 1787, followed by seven more siblings. Although activity at the dockyard slacked off after the American war, it provided Abraham with steady employment to support his growing family. Peace was short-lived, however, and in 1793, with the outbreak of England's war with France, Halifax's prospects, and those of Cunard, improved dramatically.

From 1793 to 1815, with only one major interruption lasting barely fourteen months, Great Britain was at war.[26] As the Royal Navy's principal base in North America, Halifax prospered as it refitted and resupplied the fleet. In addition to the King's money, profits from privateering were also substantial. Hoping to prey on the French, Halifax shipowners rushed to obtain privateering commissions, arm their vessels, and descend on the enemy. Captures were plentiful, and soon local prize courts were convening to condemn captures. Halifax warehouses were crammed with captured cargoes, and along the bustling waterfront, auctioneers offered an array of plunder for sale, including sugar, molasses, manufactured goods, and the seized vessels themselves.

In the midst of the port's revival, a distinguished visitor arrived. Prince Edward, Duke of Kent, son of George III and Queen Charlotte, fourth in line to the throne (and future father of Queen Victoria), was appointed commander of the King's forces in Nova Scotia and New Brunswick. Although known for advocating high moral standards and imposing stern discipline on his troops, Edward was less observant in his personal life. He brought with him to Halifax his mistress Julie Saint-Laurent. The prince and his mistress "dazzled" the city.[27]

Edward, however, did more than bring romantic intrigue to Halifax. With access to the public purse, he launched an ambitious program of new building, improving the city's defenses as well as sponsoring construction of two iconic structures, the Round Church and the Garrison Clock. "Alive to the charms of music and society," Edward never missed a major event in the city. Haligonians revered him. "He gained the hearts of the civilians by his affability, benevolence and liberality. His generosity was displayed in many ways. He gave employment to workmen of every kind, laborers, masons, carpenters, etc."[28] Among those who fell under the Prince's patronage was Abraham Cunard. The Prince promoted him to Master Carpenter to the Contingent Department of the Royal Engineers at the Halifax garrison. In a city bursting with possibilities, particularly for those who had cash to invest, Cunard's steady and secure income from his government post provided opportunity. Abraham chose wisely. Unlike many Haligonians, instead of sinking money into wild speculations, he focused on the city's rising real estate market, purchasing valuable properties along the waterfront. Abraham was a provident man, a trait he passed onto his eldest son.

Abraham and Margaret likely enrolled Samuel at the Halifax Grammar school, where he sat for a basic education—reading, writing, math—a prosaic curriculum but one his parents thought quite sufficient.[29] That early experience shaped Samuel's attitude toward education, whose purpose he always viewed to be not a liberal introduction to the world but a road to employment. Later, when planning his own sons' education, he decided against sending them to King's College in Windsor, the oldest and most prestigious college in the province that aimed to prepare "candidates for the ministry of the church." Seeking a more practical education, Samuel sent his sons to Pictou Academy to study under the "talented and irascible" Presbyterian minister Thomas McCulloch, whose watch words were "thrift, sobriety and hard work."[30] When McCulloch strayed from his own strict path and suggested to Samuel that his boys study Latin, the father shot back that there was no need for such instruction for his sons for "they are intended for business and a plain English Education answers the purpose." He admitted to McCulloch that he had "very contracted ideas," but that was simply the way of it.[31]

Samuel did not limit his "contracted ideas" to education. In business too he trod a cautious path. With his father as a partner (it seems clear that, as the eldest, Samuel was first among the sons) he bought real estate, built ships, and invested in land and timber, all secure investments. Even during the War of 1812, when more than 500 American vessels were taken by local privateers and brought into Halifax, the Cunards resisted investing heavily in such risky business.[32] Let others take chances at sea; they preferred to stand patiently on the wharf waiting for their chance to bid on captured cargo.[33]

In an ironic twist, many of the same patriotic Halifax merchants eager to plunder American vessels were also involved in the less admirable (but decidedly profitable) activity of dealing with the enemy. Profit and patriotism lived side by side along the weakly patrolled border between New Brunswick, Nova Scotia, and New England. Business between the two, which had been sizeable before the war, continued during the war and was made legal by British authorities, who issued "licenses." The cross-border traffic reached new heights in 1814, when forces under the command of Nova Scotia's lieutenant governor, Sir John Sherbrooke, swarmed over the border, surged down the coast, and overran most of Maine's eastern shore. Commerce flourished during the occupation, leading the British to establish a customs house in Penobscot Bay at Castine to levy duties on American imports.[34] The Cunard family happily took part in this trade. In spite of threats from American privateers, they also continued voyages to the West Indies. Prowling Yankee privateers made the route dangerous, but exorbitant freight rates and high demand for cargoes made successful ventures profitable enough to offset losses. The family was fortunate, for only one vessel, *Margaret*, was lost. To the relief of the family, however, a sympathetic prize court later returned *Margaret* to her owners.[35]

After more than two decades of war, peace descended on the Atlantic world in 1815. In February that year Susan Duffus and Samuel Cunard married. Eight years younger than Samuel, Susan was the daughter of William Duffus, a Scot immigrant from Banff and a well-known Halifax merchant, one of many who had profited from privateering in the late war. On January 1, 1816, Edward, the first of Samuel and Susan's nine children, was born.[36]

Peace was a mixed blessing for the newlyweds, as it was for all Haligonians.[37] The dangers of war were over, but the perils of peace loomed darkly. For his entire adult life Samuel had lived and prospered in a world at war. Halifax had hummed with activity, war contracts abounded, new buildings went up to house the growing garrison, ships were built and repaired, and thousands of soldiers and sailors fed and supplied. From 1791 to 1816, the city's population doubled and jobs increased.[38] "Soon after the peace," however, as regiments left and warships returned home, "the prosperity of Halifax began to wane."[39]

Postwar readjustment was difficult, and not all the merchants of Halifax survived the transition. Samuel's father-in-law, William Duffus, was among those who failed. The Cunards, however, having acted cautiously, managed to avoid the rocks and shoals upon which their neighbors wrecked. Rising from virtually nothing, Abraham Cunard, the first-generation immigrant, had done well, but his hard work had left him little time for civic engagement, nor had his humble origins positioned him to advance in Halifax's rigid social hierarchy. His children fared better. During the war years, thanks to his father's influence, Samuel held employment as First Clerk in the office of the Royal Engineers. He also secured a variety of posts, including serving in the city militia and working as a fire warden. All of those, however, were minor sinecures, until in 1816 a more substantial honor befell Samuel, as the governor appointed him to the key provincial post of commissioner of lighthouses.[40]

Cunard relished his appointment, not simply for the duties or the prestige, but for the cash. Living in a minor imperial outpost, far distant from London, source of power and money, Cunard and his fellow Haligonians struggled to compete in an emerging Atlantic economy where peace had brought a new pace to trade. Across the Atlantic, merchants danced about in an endless series of complex exchanges with numerous partners. Insufficient quantities of hard money—gold and silver—meant credit was the principal medium of reconciling accounts. Merchants bartered with one another and paid for goods with swarms of paper—promissory notes, bills of exchange, letters of credit, and on occasion a simple handshake. Caught up in the frenzy of exchanges, the Cunards, like Collins in New York, searched for ways to finance their operations. Family holdings in timber and real estate that they had bought from their shipping profits held value, but they were illiquid. To pay for the goods brought to their wharf from the West Indies, America, England, or Europe, the Cunards offered returns in local products, mostly timber and fish, or perhaps a bill of exchange they had received from a corresponding merchant. Rarely did they have cash. It was a precarious business, subject to the perils of war, shipwrecks, bankruptcies, or any number of unforeseen hazards that could easily disrupt the flow of trade and payment. Merchants lived on the edge, constantly concerned that anxious creditors might make claims on them that they could not meet. With margins so small and risks high, the daily demands of business made accumulating capital for investment nearly impossible. In such a financially constrained world, the one place to look for capital was the King's treasury, and while the stipend for lighthouses commissioner was small, it was sure, and it earned hard money. Having grown up in a refugee family that from its first arrival in the province was supported by the government purse, Samuel Cunard understood the value of official favor and looked for more opportunities. They were not long in coming.

While the 1815 Treaty of Ghent ended hostilities between the United States and Great Britain, its vague terms left unanswered a number of pestering problems between the two nations, among them an uncertain border and the question of fishing rights off Nova Scotia. As New England fishermen returned to rich grounds, tensions between the two nations rose, and in the summer of 1815 Governor Sherbrooke, concerned to ward off "Yankee trespassers," called for an armed vessel "for the protection of the Trade and Fisheries of the Province."[41] A number of tenders were submitted, with the contract awarded to the lowest bidder, A. Cunard and Son, which provided the sloop *Earl of Bathurst*. A small sloop unable to keep to the sea for long periods and endure the harsh weather offshore, *Bathurst* proved inadequate, and so Samuel Cunard, who by this time had taken charge of the firm, negotiated to furnish a larger vessel. Finding none available in the province, he "sent a Person to England expressly to purchase or build one." The agent returned with the brig *Chebucto*, for which Cunard paid £2,960. Forced, he complained, to sell *Bathurst* to raise funds for *Chebucto*, Cunard let the smaller vessel go for only £375, "by which," he reported, "I lost a considerable sum."[42] Keen to make up for the loss, Cunard aimed his sights at another, even more lucrative government contract—carrying the Royal Mail.

Canada's only regular communication with England was via the monthly Post Office Mail Packets—small, fast vessels, sometimes referred to as "coffin brigs" for their propensity to come to disaster.[43] Unfortunately for Canadians, during the winter months these fragile vessels could not risk a North Atlantic crossing, and so they diverted to Bermuda, from whence British officials forwarded the mail to New York to await transfer to Halifax. It was a time-consuming, uncertain arrangement further complicated by the fear that while awaiting transfer in New York, American agents might secretly inspect confidential correspondence. By prior arrangement, the Royal Navy was charged with moving the mail from Bermuda to New York and on to Halifax. Station commanders, however, balked at assigning scarce warships to what they viewed as a civilian responsibility. As a result, Halifax mail often sat neglected for weeks in Hamilton and New York, with a letter from London taking as long as three months to reach Halifax.

Desperate to establish better overseas communication, provincial authorities in Nova Scotia took matters into their own hands. Late in 1819, Nova Scotia's recently appointed lieutenant governor, Sir James Kempt, a veteran of the Napoleonic wars known for having a "passion for road making and pretty women," entered into a private agreement with the navy that allowed the province to establish its own mail service to New York. In an unusual move, the governor awarded the contract to Samuel Cunard's *Chebucto* at the enormous compensation of nearly £2,000 per year—a figure, according to local critics, nearly three times the normal cost.[44] Howls went up over the corrupt and "useless expenditure." Cunard might have weathered the storm had he not defied his opponents by telling them that their efforts to challenge him were of no avail since he held the contract "by Parliamentary interest."[45]

Cunard's haughty response set off a firestorm. When complaints reached the Colonial Secretary, Lord Bathurst admitted that they were "deserving of Inquiry." Upon further examination Bathurst found good reason to question the contract, and he instructed Kempt to terminate it.[46] Not surprisingly, Cunard complained bitterly to Kempt that he was a "great sufferer" in this matter. He offered to reduce his contract by £400 and "cheerfully submit to the loss." Embarrassed by his association with Cunard, Kempt rejected the offer and asked for bids. The provincial government placed advertisements in Halifax newspapers and Cunard's was the winning bid at £1,500. In Cunard's calculation, keeping a steady flow of income trumped reduced income. Cunard provided regular and trustworthy service.[47] He had learned his lesson: in the tangled web of the Colonial Office, "interest" was best sustained in person. Visiting offices and recruiting "friends" was essential. It was the *modus vivendi* of imperial government.[48]

While Cunard brought the mail up from New York, official transatlantic mail service remained with the Falmouth packets. By the mid-1820s, however, their unreliable and infrequent arrivals compared poorly to the regular, fast, and inexpensive service offered by the New York packets, which ultimately captured the bulk of British mail and passengers bound to America. Correspondence destined for "America from the commercial and industrial centers of England was [now] sent to Liverpool, [not Falmouth] where forwarding agents put it in the Black Ball, Red Star, or Swallowtail mail bags hanging conveniently in one or other of the coffee-houses."[49] By 1825, the once famed Falmouth packets carried only "such official correspondence as the British government deemed should not be subject" to prying American eyes.[50]

In an impracticable and futile attempt to compete with the Americans, the Admiralty offered Cunard a contract to carry the mail from Bermuda to Halifax. Cunard, like "virtually everyone," knew that this system, which added cost and time, was "unworkable." It lasted barely nine months and simply proved "the inefficiency of the administrative process of that era."[51] New York remained the communication nexus between England and Canada, a fact that stirred considerable uneasiness in Halifax and London.

On January 10, 1824, Abraham Cunard died at his country home in Rawdon, to which he and Margaret had retired. Samuel was his principal heir. After a decent time for mourning had passed, on July 14, 1824, a notice appeared in the Nova Scotia *Royal Gazette* announcing that the firm of A. Cunard and Son no longer existed; it was to be succeeded by Samuel Cunard and Co.[52] The news came at a moment when Samuel was about to set out on his most ambitious, and potentially profitable, enterprise yet.

Haligonians loved their tea, but like Bostonians in the years before the Revolution, they preferred to buy it cheap, which often meant, ironically, that they smuggled chests in from the United States. Legal tea could only arrive at Halifax via the East India Company, whose longstanding monopoly and complex marketing rules drove prices up. To undercut smugglers, the Company announced in 1824 that they were abandoning the practice of shipping tea to Canada via London and would instead route ships directly from Canton to Halifax. To manage affairs in Canada, the Company needed a local agent. When Cunard heard the news, he wasted no time booking passage to London to launch his campaign for the post in person.

Shortly after arriving in the metropolis Cunard met with John Bainbridge, who was serving as the colonial agent for both Nova Scotia and New Brunswick. A skilled lobbyist who kept close to government ministers and members of Parliament, Bainbridge provided important advice and contacts for colonial merchants trying to navigate London's corridors. The firm of A. Cunard and Son was well acquainted with Bainbridge's services.[53] With his help, Cunard presented his petition to the directors of the company. "Our pretentions," he wrote, "are grounded upon our long residence in the Provinces and a thorough knowledge of the Trade and People, we possess every convenience in Fireproof Warehouses and means to effect the intended object . . . you may rely upon our zeal and attention."[54] Cunard managed to elbow his way through the East India Company bureaucracy and return home with the grand prize—the exclusive right to market tea in the British Atlantic colonies. A few months later, when the first tea ship arrived at Cunard's wharf, a large crowd gathered to welcome her. "She smelt like a tea pot" was the onlookers' general consensus. Similar to the *Chebucto* contract, the tea agency gave Cunard a steady and secure income. It made him, according to the Halifax lawyer Lewis Bliss, "rich."[55]

While expanding his business across the Atlantic, Cunard was careful to keep a wise eye on business at home, where he had spread his investments widely into shipping, timber, tea distribution, and land speculation. To one degree or another, however, in nearly all of his ventures, the hand of government was present, directly or indirectly.[56] Not every adventure turned profitable. Taking advantage of a provincial bounty, Samuel invested in whaling voyages, including at least one long trip to the Pacific. Because voyages stretched over long periods of time, whaling tied up capital without return for extended periods. The business required deeper pockets and more expertise than might be found along the Halifax waterfront. When the provincial treasury, short of money, defaulted on the bounty, Cunard counted his losses, and by the late 1830s he had abandoned whaling.

Among all his investments, building and selling vessels and operating them on various routes across the Atlantic brought Cunard his greatest return. This interest drew him to a new venture—coal mining on Cape Breton Island.

In 1788, King George III had granted to his improvident son, the Duke of York, rights to a wide range of minerals—not including coal—in Nova Scotia. The arrangement sat dormant until the mid-1820s, by which time the wastrel duke had incurred a heavy debt to the jewelry firm Rundell, Bridge, Bigge and Rundell.[57] Getting an improvident royal to pay was no easy task for the shop, but the duke's mineral rights in Nova Scotia offered a possible source of funds, and after some conversation with the duke, the partners dispatched a Cornish mining engineer to the province. Although coal deposits were long known to exist on the island, the jewelers hoped that a survey would reveal other rich mineral deposits, particularly copper. The engineer's report fell far short of expectations: there was only coal. With steam power making its way forward, the demand for coal was increasing rapidly—especially in Great Britain; but, with its own considerable coal mining industry, the mother country had little need for Cape Breton's, nor was there any significant Canadian market.

However, coal was in demand in the United States, and until railroads breeched the Appalachians, the vast coal reserves in western Pennsylvania, Virginia, and Ohio were completely inaccessible. Eastern coal deposits, particularly along Virginia's James River, were "small" and "mediocre." High-quality British coal was available, but an eleven-shilling export duty made it very expensive. Nova Scotian coal, on the other hand, incurred no export duty and was easy to extract, and the principal mines were within a few miles of the ports of Sidney and

Pictou, where it could be easily and cheaply shipped to the States. With this in mind, in 1826 Rundell and his partners managed to revise the duke's lease to include coal, and then enticed him into a deal by which they obtained a sublease guaranteeing them 25 percent of the profits. With a new lease in hand, the duke and his jewelers invited other investors into the scheme, forming the General Mining Association (GMA), a company owned entirely by British interests.[58]

When news of this scheme spread across the Atlantic to Halifax, Nova Scotians were outraged at the secrecy and heavy-handedness of the plan. The company was, they cried, "an agent of colonization."[59] As the province's largest shipowner, Cunard joined the protest, but he also saw an opportunity, and laid a plan to outflank the GMA. Early in January 1826, when the GMA was still working to secure its claim, Cunard approached Lieutenant Governor Kempt. He offered to assume a thirty-year operating lease on the mines, for which he would pay an annual rent and royalties on the coal. If Kempt agreed, Cunard would be the most powerful man in Nova Scotia.[60]

Kempt had just returned from a year's leave at home, and he likely knew a good deal about the duke's financial plight and leases in Cape Breton. When weighing the duke's interests against Cunard's, the governor had no doubt about his decision. Samuel Cunard, for all of his accomplishments, was a merchant in a colony that remained a distant outpost of empire; he rejected Cunard's bid as "too low." Cunard, however, was too powerful in the province to be summarily rejected. At the governor's urging, the GMA appointed Cunard as their resident agent, "thus compensating him for his lost opportunity in coal mining and transforming a potential enemy into a strong ally." It was a clever move, but also an uncomfortable reminder of how dependent the province was upon imperial largesse. Thomas Chandler Haliburton, a prominent politician and the province's most famous author, noted that English money "flowing in a thousand streams" sustained the province.[61] Cunard floated along in the streams nicely.

In the midst of this business Cunard suffered a terrible personal loss. On January 23, 1828, his wife, Susan, gave birth to their ninth child—a daughter, Elizabeth. Elizabeth survived, but ten days later, weakened from the ordeal of childbirth, Susan died. Devastated, Cunard fortunately had the financial resources as well as the help of his mother-in-law, Susannah Duffus, to care for the children.[62] Samuel never remarried.

Cunard continued to pursue new interests. Since 1825 he had been a partner, with seven other wealthy Haligonians, in a private bank: the Halifax Banking Company. By 1831 the bank held more than one-third of the entire provincial debt. Such a concentration of wealth in the hands of only seven men raised furious charges of monopoly.[63] Intending to challenge the bank on the last day of December 1831, a group of competing merchants met at Halifax's Merchant Exchange Coffee House and laid plans for a publicly chartered bank. On March 30, 1832, the royal assent was given to a bill incorporating the Bank of Nova Scotia. Although Cunard retained his partnership in the controversial Halifax Bank until 1836, he was astute enough to appreciate the growing power of the competition and its likely usefulness. A stable source of credit was essential to his growing businesses. Toward that end, to assuage ill feelings and curry favor, Cunard used his authority as the agent for the GMA to direct the company's considerable financial business to the new bank.[64]

Not surprisingly, as a person tied intimately into the imperial network, Samuel Cunard was a staunch Tory. He distrusted the liberal reformers led by Joseph Howe who were pushing for greater autonomy. Howe was a fierce critic of the status quo, and his sharp pen cut deeply. "The government is like an ancient Egyptian mummy, wrapped up in narrow and antique prejudices—dead and inanimate, but yet likely to last forever."[65] Like his Tory colleagues in England, who were suffering similar popular attacks, Cunard was wary of the rising voice of the people. In 1826 a group of his Tory friends, "merchants and other respectable inhabitants" of Halifax, had cajoled him to run for a seat in the Assembly. Reluctantly, he issued an election card and launched his campaign.

Nova Scotia society was divided into upper and lower classes. Samuel Cunard had moved decisively into the former. Completely unaccustomed to the provincial world of popular politics, however, in the province where "carousing and gambling with the men or dancing with the girls" was a requirement for electioneering, Cunard was a failure.[66] His first and only speech fell flat. His foray into electoral politics was brief.

Complaining that time spent on the campaign trail was a waste, he withdrew.[67] Rather than making stump speeches, at which he was terrible, Cunard preferred walking through Province House's corridors of power among more decorous and genial surroundings. He had, for example, no qualms about accepting the favor of an appointment by the royal governor to the Council of Twelve, a body with extensive legislative, administrative, and judicial authority. Composed of an elite clique of Haligonian merchants, it was derided by reformers as "twelve old women," and held by the people in "no good odor."[68]

Cunard could afford to ignore criticism from the masses. With a fortune estimated at more than £200,000, he stood near the pinnacle of Nova Scotia's colonial elite. Through the breadth of his investments on land and sea that stretched across the province and across the Atlantic, Samuel Cunard had accumulated great wealth, but more importantly he had established a reputation as an international entrepreneur with strong links to influential people on both sides of the ocean.[69] Those links to power and money would prove invaluable as he envisioned his next and boldest venture—steamships across the Atlantic.

Cunard's interest in steam began modestly with an investment in a steam ferry, the *Sir Charles Ogle*, which made its first trip across Halifax harbor to Dartmouth on January 1, 1830. His next venture, on a much larger scale, came three months later when the legislature of Lower Canada (Quebec), anxious to establish "an easy direct intercourse by means of steam vessels between this Province and the Province of Nova Scotia," offered a subsidy of £3,000.[70] Encouraged by the promise of a subsidy, on March 11, Cunard and more than seventy-five other Haligonians gathered at a Halifax coffee house to subscribe their names and purchase shares in the Quebec and Halifax Steam Navigation Company. The Halifax investors elected Cunard to represent them as their agent. Launched from Wolfe's Cove at Quebec City, the new vessel, *Royal William*, 364 tons, 160 feet in length, arrived at Halifax on August 31, 1831.[71]

In her first year of operation *Royal William* fulfilled her promise of connecting Quebec and Halifax. Her second year, however, was a disaster. Cholera struck along the Saint Lawrence, and officials, fearing that passengers would spread the disease, placed the ship in quarantine.

Revenues collapsed, and without necessary funds for proper maintenance *Royal William*'s machinery deteriorated. In the spring of 1833 she
was sold to a group who put her in service along the Saint Lawrence as
an excursion boat, and even sent her to Boston. Their efforts came to
nothing. After failing to sell her at home, and looking for a better market,
the owners sent *Royal William* to England, where she eventually ended
up in the Spanish navy. *Royal William* taught Samuel Cunard a number
of lessons: steamships were far more expensive to build and operate than
sailing vessels; good engines and proper maintenance were essential;
and without a substantial government subsidy, these costs would doom
the enterprise.

CHAPTER SIX

Steam

DESPITE BEING RAISED in sail, both Edward Knight Collins and Samuel Cunard recognized the advent of steam. To some, however, steam at sea was like a sudden gale sweeping down unannounced, but in fact, it was a storm that had been making up for some time. The power of steam had been understood for centuries. Hero of Alexandria invented a steam device in the first century C.E. Called an aeolipile, it was a "temple wonder," a machine meant to entertain, unconnected to any mechanical device. Not until many centuries later did the first commercially successful application of steam power emerge. The Scottish engineer Thomas Newcomen invented the atmospheric engine in 1712, a machine powered by steam that was used to pump water from mines. A few years later, James Watt, another Scot, improved upon Newcomen's design while working at the University of Glasgow. Other engineers and inventors fiddled and tweaked until by 1822, "a stock of 10,000 engines producing at least 200,000 horsepower" were powering Britain's Industrial Revolution. The vast majority of these engines, however, were stationary, land-based behemoths.[1] Some entrepreneurs fancied using engines to pull carriages or propel boats, but such applications were often dismissed as too complex and costly. Steam engines were too large and cumbersome for the narrow confines of wooden vessels, and their vibrations threatened to shake hulls apart. Down below, the space needed for supplies of wood or coal to fuel the grossly inefficient engines left little capacity to carry cargo, while the sheer size and weight of the engine threatened the vessel's stability.

Despite these challenges, a few innovators did attempt to put steam power on the water. Among them was an American, John Fitch, who in 1787 ran a steamboat, *Perseverance*, on the Delaware River. He demonstrated his invention to the members of the Constitutional Convention, then meeting in Philadelphia. Clumsily propelled by a row of paddles, her pistons leaked, and she was unable to gain adequate speed.[2] *Perseverance*'s performance was disappointing. Three years later Fitch returned to the Delaware River with a more practical design, but it too failed for lack of investors.

In 1807, Robert Fulton launched the *Clermont*. An accomplished artist, Fulton had left the United States in 1786 to spend several years in London studying under the noted painter Benjamin West. He traveled widely in England and Europe. Fascinated by developments in mechanics and steam power, Fulton set aside art and focused on invention. During a long stay in France, he invented and built a working submarine, and in Paris met Robert R. Livingston, a wealthy New Yorker. Fulton returned to the United States in 1806 and settled in New York, where he married Livingston's daughter. With his father-in-law's financial backing, Fulton built the *North River Steamboat*, better known as *Clermont*.[3]

Powered with an engine built by the English firm Boulton and Watt, the steamer left New York City bound upriver for Albany on the afternoon of August 17, 1807. With Fulton at the tiller, *Clermont* "[moved] into the stream, the ponderous machinery thumping and groaning, the wheel frantically splashing, and the stack belching like a volcano." Like most early steamboats, *Clermont* had an ungainly appearance. The weight of her boilers and machinery sat the hull low in the water. Her "side wheels were a clumsy affair, uncovered with twelve huge paddles . . . that sent water splashing upon the deck with every revolution." As the crew of *Clermont* took in her lines, from the shore critics hurled "sneers, jibes, and cat-calls—'Fulton's folly,' 'God help you Bobby.' " To the surprise of many, though not Fulton, *Clermont* made the upstream run of 150 miles to Albany "in thirty-two hours—nearly five miles an hour."[4] *Clermont*'s triumph silenced her carping critics.

Clermont's success pointed to vast possibilities. Beyond the Hudson River Valley, America's expansive network of rivers and lakes, shallow and protected, was perfectly suited for steam navigation. At Pittsburgh in 1811, Nicholas Roosevelt, following plans supplied to him by Fulton, launched *New Orleans*, the first steamboat on western waters. Fulton's design—side wheels mounted on a conventional deep draft hull— proved, however, to be poorly suited for navigation on the twisting, shallow rivers of the west, where dangerous snags lay in wait to tear hulls apart, and sandbars promised groundings. Recognizing the problem, Henry Miller Shreve, a New Jersey inventor transplanted to the banks of the Monongahela River, proposed a radical new boat. The hull was flat-bottomed, in the manner of a barge, and instead of side wheels, Shreve mounted a single large wheel at the stern, driven by an engine mounted on the main deck. Since the engines and stacks of wood used for fuel occupied so much area, Shreve added a second upper deck for passengers and cargo. The draft of Shreve's boats were measured in inches, prompting him to boast that his steamers could "navigate on heavy dew."[5]

In the east, *Clermont*'s success prompted the launching of other steamboats and gave rise to dreams of an even more ambitious project— regular steamboat service to New England. The shortest route north from New York City was via the East River, but traversing that waterway, however, involved passing through the treacherous narrows of Hell Gate, a slender curving slit peppered with jagged rocks at the junction of the East and Harlem Rivers. Sailing vessels bold enough to venture through had to wait for perfect tides and wind, and even then, transit was dangerous and often denied. Hell Gate was strewn with wrecks. Notwithstanding the challenge, on Tuesday, March 21, 1815, the steamboat *Fulton*, commanded by the devil-may-care captain Elihu Bunker, departed Beekman Slip for New Haven, heading north to defy Hell Gate. Three times a strong tide forced him back, but on the fourth attempt he won, which "surprised everyone on board, and satisfied them that no vessel can be so well calculated to navigate the dangerous channel as the steamboat." She made the trip in eleven hours. It was, announced the *New York Evening Post*, "a proud triumph of human ingenuity."[6]

To accommodate this potentially lucrative business, Bunker added a new and more powerful boat, *Connecticut*. By 1817 "the success of the *Fulton* and the *Connecticut* opened up a new chapter of water transportation. Regular steamship service with two weekly round trips, soon to be extended to three, serving New York on one hand and New Haven and New London on the other."[7] Offering fast, scheduled service and the comfort of fine food and plush cabins, steamboats skimmed the choicest and best-paying cargo—passengers and mail—from less reliable and painfully slow passages on sailing packets or bone-racking trips by stagecoach.[8]

Fulton, Shreve, and Bunker set a fast pace, and within a few years steamboats were a regular sight on America's rivers, lakes, and coastal waters. By 1820 nearly seventy-one steamboats plied western water, and fifty-two steamboats operated on the Atlantic coast. Ten years later, in 1830, those numbers had increased fourfold.[9]

Believing that Fulton's genius made them the inventors of the steamboat, Americans proudly hailed their "sublime" machine. The *American Journal of Science* grandiloquently stated that these "floating palaces transcend[ed] the wildest dreams of which the builder of the gigantic Pyramids or even Archimedes himself might be supposed capable."[10] What they were not capable of, however, was transoceanic travel.

With the premium on regular, fast service, for which passengers were willing to pay, American shipbuilders laid down steamboat hulls that were designed for speed—long, narrow, and lightly built, with a considerable superstructure above the main deck. It was a well conceived form that followed function, allowing the steamer to glide easily across shallow, protected waters. It was a shape, however, unsuited for rough, deepwater sailing, where towering waves were likely to sweep over the vessel decks, while the high superstructure and shallow draft exposed the vessel to a dangerous propensity for excessive roll.

Hull design was not the only issue. Until coal became more generally available, wood was the chief fuel. Given wood's low caloric value, operators on the western rivers faced a choice, either to stack huge piles of wood on board, giving up valuable space that could accommodate paying cargo and passengers, or take less aboard and refuel more often. Since most American rivers and lakes were lined with deep stands of timber, the choice was easy; frequent landings were the answer. Steamers on Long Island Sound had access to more efficient coal and needed only to ship enough for voyages of less than 200 miles. Long ocean voyages, in contrast, would require ships to carry enormous amounts of fuel onboard.

Aside from the question of design and fuel, seagoing steamers would face an additional problem. Boilers required a constant supply of water to produce steam. On rivers and lakes, through intakes in the hull, boats drew from the water around them. Even freshwater, however, was fouled with a variety of impurities, and "cleaning the boilers of mud was a daily occurrence."[11] The intake of saltwater caused worse problems, and despite primitive condensers and frequent cleaning, incrustations scaled the inner wall of the boilers, producing a coating of unwanted insulation that decreased their already low efficiency, while clogging connecting pipes and valves.[12] The danger, however, went beyond loss of efficiency. Western boats depended upon light, compact high-pressure engines. Struggling to maintain adequate steam pressure to ensure their schedules, engineers all too often pushed boilers to their limits and beyond. Lack of—or deliberately disabled—safety valves, and operators' primitive knowledge of the consequences of metal fatigue, resulted in catastrophic failures. Between 1807 and 1840 more than 200 boiler explosions on American steamboats killed 1,330 passengers and crew.[13]

Despite the headwinds impeding oceanic steam travel, a group of businessmen from Savannah, Georgia, led by Moses Rogers, a Connecticut Yankee and former captain of the steamer *Fulton*, organized a company in 1817 "to attach, either as auxiliary or principal, the propulsion of steam to sea vessels, for the purpose of navigating the Atlantic and other oceans."[14] The speculators' aim was to outfit a vessel with steam, sail her to Europe, and then, by capitalizing on the euphoria they were convinced her arrival would generate, sell her at a nifty profit. During a visit to New York in the summer of 1818, Rogers found a suitable vessel under construction as a conventional sailing packet destined for trade between New York and Liverpool, on the ways at the East River yard of Crocker and Fickett. Rogers and his partners decided to purchase and add steam machinery to her. On Saturday, August 22, christened *Savannah*, she slid into the river. Once she was alongside the pier, carpenters, caulkers, sailmakers, painters, and riggers climbed aboard to fit *Savannah* out as a sailing vessel. Nearby on Cherry Street, at the marine engine building works of James Allaire, the largest such facility in the United States, workers were preparing to cast the cylinder— "the heart and soul of the engine." Jacob Abbott, a writer for *Harpers New Monthly Magazine*, explained the importance of the cylinder:[15]

> The steam is generated in the boilers, but while it remains there it remains quiescent and inert. The action in which its mighty power is expended, and by means of which all subsequent effects are produced, is the lifting and bringing down of the enormous piston which plays within the cylinder. This piston is a massive metallic disc or plate, fitting the interior of the cylinder by its edges, and rising or falling by the expansive force of the steam, as it is admitted alternatively above and below it.

The cylinder was cast in a deep pit dug into the foundry's floor. The sides of the pit were secured by iron plates and then filled with moulding sand, "a composition of a damp and tenacious character. The mould is made and lowered into the pit; the pit is filled up, the sand being rammed as hard as possible all around it." As some men prepared the pit, others stood by the furnace ready to carry tons of molten metal in huge ladles to a reservoir that flowed into the mould. It was a "magnificent spectacle. The vast mass of molten iron in the reservoir, the streams flowing down the conduit, throwing out the most brilliant coruscations, the gaseous flames issuing from the upper portions of the mould, and the currents of melted iron which sometimes overflow and spread, like mimic streams of lava." The work was dangerous. Gas bubbles might form in the molten mass and burst, "scattering the burning and scintillating metal in every direction around."[16]

Once the hot iron had cooled and solidified, the mold was dug up and opened "to reveal a solid iron cylinder inside, about six feet in height and 3½ feet in diameter." By an elaborate system of block and tackle, the solid cylinder, weighing 23,600 pounds, was hauled out of the pit.[17] The next step in the job was to bore the cylinder. At this point in his company's history, Allaire did not have the capacity for such precise work, and so he shipped the cylinder across the harbor to the Speedwell Iron Works in Morristown, New Jersey, where proprietor Stephen Vail undertook the delicate process of boring a circular cavity into the cylinder that would create the "internal space where steam would move the piston up and down."[18] Precision was key: "The boring had to be both perfectly round and straight down." It was imperative that the piston fit snugly to form an airtight seal. Any space left between the piston and the cylinder's surface would cause erratic motion, which would damage the wall of the cylinder, break the piston, and likely cause catastrophic engine failure. Unfortunately, Vail's first attempt proved bad, and he had to rebore the cylinder.[19]

As Vail bored the cylinder, other shops fabricated boilers, piston rods, shafts, piping, braces, and a heavy iron floor bed on which to sit the engine. The work was complicated and required extraordinary over-sight on the part of Rogers and others to ensure that the hundreds of parts being cast were properly made and fitted well. Compared to later oceangoing steamships, *Savannah*'s power plant was small, generating barely ninety horsepower, but aside from scale, the methods for casting and building steam engines employed by Allaire and Vail changed very little until the 1860s.[20]

Work went slowly. Crocker and Fickett took two months to complete *Savannah*'s fitting-out as a sailing vessel. In late October she left the East River and made the short trip, under sail, across to Elizabethtown Point, New Jersey, to take on her engines; five months were required to install and check the machinery, but finally, on March 28, *Savannah*—dubbed by a skeptical New York press the "Steam Coffin"—passed the narrows under Rogers' command, skirted Sandy Hook, and set a course for her home port.[21]

Savannah stayed in Georgia only long enough to load stores and fuel and receive minor adjustments to her machinery. On Saturday morning May 22, 1819, "dark black smoke puffed out of the stack, the paddle-wheels slowly began to move," and *Savannah* made her way downriver toward the Atlantic.[22] Although she had been advertised as "principally for the accommodation of passengers," not a single person booked passage. Nor did anyone offer to ship cargo. *Savannah* sailed with seventy-five tons of coal, twenty-five cords of wood, and a ninety-ton engine.[23] The voyage was all expense and no revenue.

Savannah took twenty-nine wearisome days, a time longer than many sailing vessels, to reach Liverpool. In that month's passage, her engines steamed only three and a half days, but managed to consume nearly all her coal.[24] Hoping to recoup their costs, the owners tried to sell the "steamship" in Europe, but with her dismal record, no buyers stepped forward. Unheralded, *Savannah* "returned to the United States under sail, was sold to pay her debts, and had her engine removed."[25] *Savannah's* sad fate was cautionary; while it might be possible for a steamer (with the assist of sail) to cross the Atlantic, the cost of construction, the need to carry huge amounts of expensive coal (which crowded out space for cargo and passengers), and the public's well-founded skepticism about safety made such a venture impractical and unprofitable. American shipowners appreciated the power of steam, but they also understood its limitations and preferred wisely to put their capital into sail where, due to lower costs, they enjoyed an advantage over their British competitors. More than two decades would pass before another American steamship would cross the Atlantic.[26]

While Americans preferred sail to steam for an ocean passage, geography and history set Great Britain on a different course. An island nation grown rich through her vast overseas empire, she was at the center of the Industrial Revolution. Steam power was her forte, and by the early nineteenth century, stationary steam engines powered machinery in virtually every industry, including mining, textiles, sugar refining, chemical manufacturing, and brewing. Design, construction, and maintenance of these complicated, often unreliable machines demanded new complex technical skills that required levels of knowledge and formal training more sophisticated than that to be had by means of simple apprenticeships. The professions of engineering and machine design were key in this new economy. As steam engrossed land-based industries, inventors saw no reason why the Industrial Revolution should stop at the water's edge. For a nation whose face had long been set to the water, the notion of putting steam to sea resonated deeply. Few localities in the British Isles were better endowed with these advantages than those along the banks of the River Clyde, in western Scotland.

Rising in the south of Lanarkshire, the River Clyde flows ninety-eight miles, passing the city of Glasgow before it merges with the Firth of Clyde, which leads toward the Irish Sea. In its natural state the river was barely navigable to Glasgow, but over the course of the eighteenth and early nineteenth centuries energetic Scots dredged the bottom, constructed embankments and generally improved the river's navigation so that vessels could reach Glasgow.[27] When the Industrial Revolution took hold, with equal energy the Scots connected Glasgow to the interior of the county to exploit rich deposits of coal and iron.[28]

Lanarkshire was the most populous county in Scotland, and its natural resources of coal and iron drew the Industrial Revolution northward. Manufacturing thrived in the region. Shipbuilding, mining, iron founding, and machine works prospered. Engineers and mechanics were in high demand. As the nineteenth century dawned, to bring essential raw materials from the interior to feed these growing industries Glaswegians looked for ways to improve transport on their canals and rivers. Steam power offered possible answers, but only if ways could be found to put cumbersome engines in small boats.

In 1801 William Symington, "the son of the engineer of the Wanlockhead Mines in Lanarkshire," introduced his "New Mode of Constructing Steam Engines and applying their power of providing rotatory and other motions without the interposition of a lever or a beam."[29] Levers and high beams were a normal component of land-based engines. Such height and bulk, however, made them unsuitable for the tight quarters of a vessel and placed enormous weight abovedeck, which compromised stability. By "dispensing with the beam and substituting direct action" through a system of horizontal side levers, Symington was able to construct a more compact, lighter, and less expensive machine suitable for installation on boats.[30]

Built by John Allan at Grangemouth on the Firth of Forth and powered by an engine built to Symington's design at the Carron foundry in nearby Falkirk, *Charlotte Dundas*—named for the daughter of Symington's patron Sir Thomas Dundas—with two barges in tow, steamed up the "Forth and Clyde Canal a distance of nineteen and a half miles, in six hours" in March 1802.[31] *Charlotte Dundas* was a success.[32] While immediately successful, her career as a canal boat was short-lived. *Dundas*'s wheel "made so much Splashing that [canal directors] were afraid of washing down the Canal Banks." They banned her from the canal, and *Charlotte Dundas* was relegated to the less glamorous business of towing barges on the Clyde.[33] Notwithstanding her banishment from canal work, Symington had made an important breakthrough. His "simple type of direct-acting engine" would become "the standard for marine engines."[34]

While *Charlotte Dundas* labored hauling freight, Henry Bell built the first steamboat on the Clyde to carry passengers. Born in Torphichen, Linlithgowshire, a tiny village lying between Glasgow and Edinburgh, Bell came from a family of well-known millwrights. Working with them, Bell learned a great deal about machinery, but he decided to relocate to Glasgow to take up shipbuilding. Later he moved to London to study more formally with the noted, transplanted Scottish engineer John Rennie. With Rennie's encouragement, Bell designed a steamboat, and he presented his plan to the Admiralty in hopes that it might be interested in his work. Later, he recalled their lordships' reaction: "They had no faith in steam navigation."[35]

Bell returned to Scotland and settled in the village of Helensburgh, on the Firth of Clyde, where he and his wife ran a well-known spa and hotel. Since most of the spa's guests came down the Firth from Glasgow by boat or coach, Bell saw an opportunity to attract patrons by offering fast, regular steam service. Resurrecting his earlier steamboat design, he arranged with the Glasgow boatbuilder John Wood to build the hull of a vessel late in 1811, while contracting with two other Glaswegians, John Robertson and David Napier, to manufacture and install the engines and boilers. Christened *Comet*, Bell's steamer took her maiden run on the Clyde on January 18, 1812. After a few more trial runs the Glasgow *Herald* announced on August 5, 1812:[36]

THE STEAMBOAT COMET
BETWEEN GLASGOW, GREENOCK AND HELENSBURGH
FOR PASSENGERS ONLY

Comet gave witness to the possibilities for commercial steamboats, and within a year, their reputations now attached to steam, Wood, Robertson, and Napier had commissions to build and power three new steamboats: *Elizabeth*, *Clyde*, and *Glasgow*.[37] Unlike the United States, where the demand for steamers traveling on protected waters seemed insatiable, steam vessels in Scotland were prohibited from canals, forcing them to operate within a limited network of lochs, rivers, and lakes. Possibilities for expansion, however, did exist for coastwise carriage, as well as short sea connections to Ireland.

By the late eighteenth century 85 percent of Ireland's trade was with Great Britain, virtually all of which crossed the Irish Sea, landing principally at Glasgow and Liverpool. A distance of less than 150 miles, the voyage was well within the performance range of contemporary paddle steamers. Combining their skills in steam engineering and shipbuilding, Glasgow yards turned out an impressive number of steamers; between 1811 and 1820, tonnage registered in Glasgow more than doubled.[38]

Aside from paddle wheels mounted port and starboard and stacks belching smoke, Clyde-built steamers bore little resemblance to their American cousins. Compared to the relatively kind waters of America's rivers, bays, and sounds, vessels crossing open water to Ireland or coasting along the western shore of Scotland and northern England often encountered gale winds and high seas. Vessels built on the American hull form would not survive rough ocean weather, and so Clyde builders relied on the traditional deep draft model for ocean travel. They installed engines in hulls built closely framed with substantial freeboard, adding timbers amidships to support the weight of engines and boilers. In 1815, at the same time as Elihu Bunker inaugurated his steam service from New York to New Haven, *Thames*, built in Port Glasgow, became the first steamship to cross to Dublin. From there she continued her voyage, eventually landing in London, having traveled 758 nautical miles at an impressive average of 6.2 knots. Isaac Weld, a passenger aboard, presented a report to Parliament, writing that the movement of a steam vessel "will always be more rapid than that of an ordinary vessel. In our voyage we did not meet a single vessel that was able to follow us."[39] Within a half-dozen years, regular steam service was offered between Greenock and Belfast, Liverpool and Belfast, Bristol and Cork.[40]

Among the prominent merchants of Glasgow who grasped the future of steam were George and James Burns. Since 1819 the brothers had operated a successful business carrying produce to Liverpool in sailing smacks the locals dubbed "Ranterpykes." The smacks averaged three to four days between Glasgow and Liverpool, a trip steamers could do in one day. Realizing that their smacks were "doomed"—"steam was killing them"—the Burns brothers organized a company to operate steamers to Liverpool. On March 13, 1829, the first steamer of the new Glasgow company passed the light at the mouth of the Firth of Forth heading for Liverpool. She was appropriately named the *City of Glasgow*. The voyage was a success, and the next month *Glasgow* was followed by *Ailsa Craig*, a crack vessel of her day, and the next year by *Liverpool*.[41]

Liverpool was not long in responding to the challenge from Glasgow. Led by David MacIver, a group of investors, with help from James Donaldson (a wealthy Glasgow cotton merchant and rival of the Burns brothers), formed the City of Glasgow Steam Shipping Company. MacIver managed the company from Liverpool, "but he was constantly back and forth, living almost in the engine room of his steamer, urging on extra coals, extra pressure, extra speed, 'to run those Burns' off.'" After a few years of crippling competition, "the scheme of vengeance went a-gley." The two firms merged to create a powerful shipping enterprise resting on Liverpool capital and Clyde-bank shipbuilding— particularly John Wood, builder of the *Comet*, and Robert Napier, cousin to David Napier.[42]

Robert Napier apprenticed under his father, an iron founder in Dumbarton, Scotland. Shortly after completing his training, he worked in Edinburgh for Robert Stevenson, the famed lighthouse builder. In 1814, at age twenty-three, he returned home and settled in Glasgow where, with the aid of a £50 loan from his father, he established his own ironworks. In 1821, when his better-known cousin David decided to construct more expansive works on the west side of the city, Robert arranged to lease the facility that David was vacating.[43] At the time Glasgow had a pressing need for new waterworks, and Robert Napier's first contract was to provide iron pipes for the system. That mundane work was far too ordinary for a man of Napier's ambition; in 1823 he won a contract to supply an engine for the paddle steamer *Leven* being built at Dumbarton for service on Loch Leven. At a time when steam engines were notoriously unreliable and subject to frequent break-downs, *Leven*'s engine proved reliable and durable enough to outlast three hulls. Napier's success with *Leven* put him well on the way to becoming known as the "steam genius."[44]

As his reputation for building fast, reliable vessels grew, Napier came to the attention of the prominent yachtsman Thomas Assheton Smith. A "boorish foxhunting fanatic" who spent most of his time hunting on his grand estate, Smith enjoyed yachting in the waters off Angelsey.[45] Cantankerous and single-minded, a member of the Royal Yacht Club, Smith proposed to his fellow members that they allow steam yachts in an upcoming regatta. Appalled at the thought of their graceful pristine yachts sharing water with steamers belching soot and smoke, soiling their sails and defiling their decks, the members rejected the idea and snubbed Smith. He resigned from the Club. Determined to prove the worth of steam, he turned to Napier and invited him to build a steam yacht. Although not particularly interested in launching yachts (which to the dour Scot must have seemed frivolous), Napier took the contract when Smith offered him the enormous sum of £20,000. At 120 feet in length, sleek and fast, *Menai* was a marvel. Over the next two decades, Napier built at least eight more yachts for Smith at similar prices. In addition to his money, Napier also took from Smith "something much more valuable, the lifelong goodwill and unbounded confidence of this powerful English gentleman."[46]

While laying down yachts filled his coffers, Napier's English competitors in London and Bristol never missed a chance to heap disdain on Scottish shipbuilders. Anxious to prove he was as good as his English brethren, Napier welcomed an 1836 invitation from the East India Company to construct and provide the engines for the paddle steamer *Berenice* for service in the Far East. It was his first opportunity to build engines for an ocean-going steamer, and at the price of £30,000, the largest contract he had ever received. The work went well, and in the spring of 1837 *Berenice* made her maiden voyage to India via the Cape of Good Hope. Upon arriving at Bombay (Mumbai), her captain wrote to Napier, "Your noble ship has behaved well."[47] Reports of the voyage spread his fame and brought Napier to the notice of the East India Company's chief secretary, James Melvill. With his renown riding high, and drawing on the influence of Smith and Melvill, Napier captured the greatest prize of all: an Admiralty contract. The Lords Commissioners asked him to supply engines for two bomb vessels, *Stromboli* and *Vesu-vius*. They went even further, taking the unusual step to assure him that his high reputation made it unnecessary for them "to insist on [his] giving bond for fulfilling your engagement to provide steam-engines you have contracted for."[48] The Commissioners' faith was well placed. Both vessels exceeded expectations. Erasmus Ommanney, captain of *Vesuvius*, described Napier's engine as "incomparable . . . always ready when wanted," and they "never had a screw loose."[49]

As a manufacturer of marine engines with a reputation for reliability, Robert Napier stood far ahead of his peers on both sides of the Atlantic. Demands for his services reached such a level that when his cousin David decided to leave Glasgow to establish a shipyard on the Thames in 1836, Robert stepped forward to lease his cousin's extensive works at Lancefield.[50] As his business grew Napier became increasingly convinced that steam was the future for ocean transport; still, he was enough of a realist to appreciate that many years would pass before steam engines might gain ascendancy over sail on long passages. Steam offered enormous advantages in short sea work, but it presented serious shortcomings on long voyages. In the 1830s, as Napier's esteem grew, shipowners interested in steam came to Glasgow seeking his advice. One such visitor was Patrick Wallace, a London businessman.[51]

In March 1833 Wallace, at the request of "friends" in London, traveled north to Glasgow and Liverpool "prosecuting some inquiries" about building and operating "steam navigation to New York."[52] After spending time with Napier at Glasgow and touring the Lancefield works, Wallace took passage for Liverpool on the coastal steamer *Ailsa Craig*. By coincidence, Napier was aboard as well. As the *Craig* was coming down the Clyde, Wallace pressed Napier on his views about the practicality of transatlantic steamships and whether they could provide regular service across the Atlantic. It was, Napier told Wallace, a question that much interested him; in fact he had made several estimates as to the costs of such an enterprise. Wallace was intrigued. Shortly after he returned to London and spoke with his friends he wrote to Napier about their speculation aboard the *Ailsa Craig*, asking him if he might "minute down an estimate of the expense according to your views per month of a vessel of 800 tons."[53]

Eager at the prospect of being part of a great venture, Napier wasted no time in responding. He began by warning Wallace and his friends that "many things occur that cannot be foreseen." They should stand ready, he wrote, "to meet with strong opposition and other difficulties for a short time."[54] The opposition to which Napier was referring were pronouncements by Doctor Dionysius Lardner, a Professor of Natural Philosophy and one of England's most distinguished academics, who had declared publicly that those who talked of steamships making transatlantic crossings "might as well talk of making a voyage to the moon."[55]

After dismissing Lardner and other naysayers, Napier predicted that transatlantic service from Liverpool to New York not only could be accomplished but would provide "a very great increase of revenue in a short time." He assured Wallace, "I have not the smallest doubt upon my own mind but that in a very short time it will be one of the best and most lucrative businesses in the country." Success, however, was predicated on "having first-class vessels fully suited for the trade in every department," which meant extra expense. At a minimum, to maintain regular twice-monthly service, two vessels had to be built, "cost what they may." In calling for a pair of vessels Napier was, for the purpose of negotiation, being slightly disingenuous. He knew that if Wallace and his friends intended to offer anything comparable to the multiple sailings provided by the American sailing packets, it would require at least four steamships, three to maintain service and one in reserve.[56]

Even for only two steamers, the cost was huge. The vessels must, demanded Napier, be "adapted for great speed . . . and upon no account should the model be sacrificed for the sake of cargo, for the success of the Company depends in having fast sailing steamers as well as good ones." Speed was expensive. Napier wanted ships powered by two engines, "150 horse-power each, or 300 whole," and of not less than 800 tons. Recognizing the incredible strain on such machinery during a long crossing, he insisted that to ensure proper maintenance at sea, a "workshop, with a complete set of tools and duplicates of all parts of the engine that are most likely to go wrong, should be on board." To tend to these machines, according to Napier, the ship required a complement of four engineers, eight firemen, and four coal trimmers. However, since no one was yet willing to risk complete dependence upon steam power, these vessels would also require a full set of sails and a sizeable deck crew to manage them.[57] For a twenty-two-day passage, Liverpool to New York, the ship would carry at least 660 tons of coal which, stowed in compartments (later referred to as bunkers), took up considerable space. Machinery weighing nearly 300 additional tons occupied large parts amidships. With so much belowdeck space given over to the requirements of steam, Napier's ships had room for barely 200 tons of paying cargo. Collins's Dramatic Line packets enjoyed four times the carrying capacity at a fraction of the cost. Napier offered to deliver these vessels at a total price of £34,000 each. At a time when Brown and Bell were launching packets without engines into the East River for Collins at less than $75 per ton, Napier's steamers promised to slip down the ways at over $200 per ton, with nearly half the cost sunk into machinery down below.[58] Comparing operating costs between sailing packets and steamers is difficult; however, Napier estimated the annual pay of the engine crew to be nearly $5,000, a cost completely absent from sailing packets, while the cost of coal would likely run slightly under $2,000 per voyage. Napier left out estimates for the cost of provisions for passengers, piloting, and docking fees.

On the plus side of the ledger, Napier calculated that nearly 90 percent of revenue would come from passenger traffic, all of it cabin (first) class. He proposed charging £30 ($150) and expected a full booking of 100 passengers on each crossing. Like most steamship proponents, he dismissed ferrying low-paying steerage passengers as uneconomical: indeed, by Napier's account it was even more profitable to devote the steamer's limited space to high-value cargo, rather than immigrants.[59] Those unfortunates were better left to be crammed into the holds of packets, whose fares averaged $20. To make their revenue goals, Napier's steamers would have to depart consistently, never missing a voyage, with all cabins occupied and a full hold—all unlikely prospects.

Robert Napier dispatched his "package" to Wallace on April 3. Silence was the response from London. James Napier, in his biography of his father, commented, "No business resulted with Mr. Wallace and his friends, and the project fell through from lack of funds."[60] While Robert Napier was the master of steam engines, clearly his appreciation of steamship operations was limited. From a business point of view, the men in London knew that Napier was proposing to sell them machines they could not afford. Despite the engineer's genius, the limitations of paddle steamers made transatlantic commercial operations a losing proposition. Napier had provided evidence that regular transatlantic steamship service was possible, but not profitable. Until someone was willing to make a large long-term investment while enduring significant financial loss for the sake of speed and regularity, the prospect of steam conquering the Atlantic remained a pipe dream.

CHAPTER SEVEN

The British and North American Royal Mail
Steam Packet Company

NAPIER'S CHASTENING CALCULATIONS, coupled with Lardner's dyspeptic dismissal, gave pause to those who contemplated investing in regular steamship service between England and the United States. It was clear that even if steamships were able to cross the Atlantic, they could not make money doing so.

Following *Savannah*, in 1819 there were several other eccentric crossings. Between 1827 and 1829, the Royal Netherlands Navy's *Curacao* made three voyages from Rotterdam to Dutch Guiana. Built in Dover, England, *Curacao* had two fifty-horsepower engines driving her paddles. Unlike *Savannah* she steamed nearly full-time, but because she was a public vessel she did not need to turn a profit.[1] In 1833 HMS *Rhahdamthus* crossed from Plymouth to St. Domingo. Built in the Royal dockyard at Plymouth, she was named for the son of Zeus and Europa. She was considerably larger and fitted with more powerful engines than either *Savannah* or *Curacao*. In the year following, Cunard's *Royal William* made her voyage from Pictou, Nova Scotia, to Liverpool. That was her only crossing, and at twenty-nine days it was unimpressive. In the same year another Canadian vessel, *Cape Breton*, completed a westbound trip from Plymouth, England, to Sydney, Nova Scotia. Like *Royal William*, it was her only crossing.

Although none of these early vessels was commercially viable, their successful crossings drove interest in steam. In the late 1830s, the British and American Steam Navigation Company of London, the Transatlantic Steamship Company of Liverpool, the City of Dublin Steam Packet Company, and the Great Western Steamship Company of Bristol each built and operated several transatlantic paddle steamers.[2]

Among these early steamers, the Bristol firm's *Great Western* was the most successful, and stayed in service longest even though there were "plenty of difficulties." Her first year's financial results in 1838 were promising, giving her owners hope "that all was bright for the future," but then came the breakdowns of machinery, high price of fuel, and expensive maintenance. According to an American newspaper account, *Great Western*'s "proprietors are so deeply embarrassed by the expense incurred in keeping her employed, that they cannot in reason hazard their funds any further."[3] The lesson was clear. A single vessel could not offer frequent regular service. It would take multiple vessels to run a schedule across the Atlantic to compete with the regularity of the American packets.[4] Plagued by construction expenditures, unreliable machinery, and the need for constant maintenance, private investors could not offer regular steam service and expect a profit.[5] If steam were to conquer the Atlantic, an interest more powerful than profit would have to be found. Such a compelling interest arose in the 1830s as Great Britain and her North American provinces, particularly Nova Scotia, reflected on their place in the Empire while marinating in worry over the uncertain intentions of their ambitious and restless neighbor to the south.

When the peace commissioners representing the United States and Great Britain signed the Treaty of Ghent that ended the War of 1812, they did so on the basis of "Status Quo Ante Bellum," which in the elliptical language of diplomacy meant that the war had changed nothing. All of the issues that had led to war—impressment, neutral rights, status of Native Americans, and boundary claims—were left unsettled. Both sides continued to perceive the other as a potential enemy.[6] Seeing American invasion as a continuing threat—one invasion had taken place during the Revolution and several were attempted during the War of 1812—in 1819 the Duke of Wellington, at the request of the British ministry, presented a detailed report, "The Defense of Canada," in which he called for an elaborate and expensive series of forts manned by an army of ten thousand men to guard against the "enemy."[7]

The Duke's report arrived at a moment when simmering disputes over borders in the Oregon territory and along the line between Maine and New Brunswick, as well as conflicting interests in the matter of the future of Texas—which had recently declared its independence from Mexico—were agitating relations. Although London took some defensive measures, including the building of the impressive "Citadel" in Halifax and opening a secure canal link between Kingston and Bytown (Ottawa), for reasons of economy the home government did little more to bolster the defenses of Canada, which left the Canadians uneasy.[8]

In 1837–38 tensions sparked along the border near the Niagara River. In both Upper (Ontario) and Lower (Quebec) Canada, armed rebellions fueled by long-standing economic grievances, ethnic conflict, and demands for political rights broke out against the ruling oligarchies in these provinces. Romantic recollections of the "Spirit of 1776" aroused sympathies in America. President Martin Van Buren warned citizens of the United States against committing any act that would "compromise the neutrality of this Government."[9] Nonetheless, with the support of sympathetic Americans, guns and volunteers crossed the border to aid the rebels, while the insurgents themselves, when pursued by government forces, often took sanctuary on the American side. In December 1837 Canadian militia crossed the Niagara border into New York to seize *Caroline*, a steamer known to be running guns to the insurgents. After setting her afire the militiamen pushed *Caroline* into the river. She drifted downriver over the falls, and Amos Durfee, an American trapped aboard, was killed. After Durfee's recovered body was exhibited outside a tavern in Buffalo, cries for revenge stirred the border and prompted Sir Francis Bond, lieutenant governor of Upper Canada, to summon the Glengarry militia to stand guard against "an attack from the American frontier by a horde of rapacious brigands."[10]

Farther to the east more border violence erupted when a dispute arose between Maine and New Brunswick over large swaths of valuable timberland in what was dubbed the "Aroostook War." The governor of Maine dispatched a sizeable force of militia to eject trespassing Canadian lumberjacks. With tensions still running high between the United States and Great Britain over the incidents around the New York border, President Van Buren, seeking to defuse the situation, sent General Winfield Scott to oversee a peaceful resolution.[11] Nonetheless, relations were uneasy. The two nations, according to the Canadian historian J. Bartlet Brebner, "bordered on war."[12]

From the rebellions in Upper and Lower Canada and the ongoing strain with the United States, the imperial government took two lessons; first, that the provincial governments in Canada needed to be reformed.[13] Stable, secure provincial governments would be better positioned, not only to address threats of insurrection, but also to shoulder the costs of defending against American encroachments, thus reducing the burden on the motherland. Toward this end London ordered John Lambton, Earl of Durham, to Canada. Durham's 1839 *Report on the Affairs in British North America* was a milestone in Canadian history and would eventually lead to the adoption of "responsible government," a policy granting greater autonomy to the provinces and paving the way for Canadian Confederation in 1867.[14] Recent upheavals had also brought home a second lesson: the need for better transatlantic communication.

Virtually every piece of mail London received—personal letters, diplomatic correspondence, and newspapers—carried the head note "via New York."[15] The failure (particularly in winter), of the royal mail packets to provide fast, direct, and reliable service to Halifax, the only British North American port at which they called, put the carriage of important and sensitive mail, as well as of travelers—businessmen, military officers, and diplomats—under the control of the upstart Americans, who never ceased to brag about the superiority of Yankee packets. Under rising pressure, and having concluded that the Admiralty "knew more about boats than the Post Office," in 1837 the government transferred responsibility for the mail packet service to the navy. Nearly forty vessels suddenly came under Admiralty authority. Of that number, more than half were steam vessels engaged in short sea service primarily serving Ireland and the Continent.[16] With the scratch of a pen, "the strength of the steam navy was doubled overnight." Taken aback, the Admiralty ordered a senior naval officer, Sir William Edward Parry, to London to organize the service.[17]

At the time of his appointment Parry was Great Britain's most famous explorer. In his three epic Arctic voyages in search of the Northwest Passage, he had managed to survive shipwreck, fierce winters, and near-starvation. In 1827 he struck out for the North Pole, and although he never reached that goal, his expedition established a farthest north record (82 degrees 45 minutes) that stood for fifty years. "Oh how I long to be among the ice," he once said.[18]

In a whirlwind of activity, Parry completely reorganized the home packet service. On April 19, 1837, pleased with his work, their Lordships expanded his authority by appointing him Controller of Steam Machinery and Packet Service.[19] Armed with his new responsibilities, Parry pushed to increase the use of steam in the packet service as well as the entire Royal Navy. In the case of the transatlantic mails, however, not even Parry would venture to operate steam packets across the Atlantic, which continued to leave Canada dependent on the slow and unreliable sailing packets.

Frustrated at such neglect, Joseph Howe—the Halifax newspaperman and Nova Scotia's most prominent politician—along with several other Haligonians left for London in the summer of 1838 accompanied by William Crane, who represented New Brunswick, to lobby for steam service to their provinces. Since it was summer, they had the pleasure of departing directly from Halifax aboard the sailing packet *Tyrian*. As if to underscore the importance of their mission, as *Tyrian* ploughed her way east she was overtaken by the steamer *Sirius*, bound home from her pioneering voyage to New York. Since *Tyrian* was "roll[ing] about in a dead calm with flapping sails," making absolutely no progress, her captain sent the mails over to *Sirius*. As he watched from *Tyrian*'s deck, the whisper of smoke disappeared over the horizon, and Howe acknowledged (he later wrote) that he was "not at all pleased with the prospect of being left behind to the tender mercies of wind and canvas, when a few tons of coal would have done the business much better."[20]

After landing at Falmouth the delegation boarded the stage to London, where they met Samuel Cunard, who was in the city on GMA business. At home, Howe and Cunard were political adversaries; in this case, however, they were allies. On August 24 Howe, joined by Crane, wrote to Lord Gleneig, Secretary of State for War and Colonies. Cunard likely helped draft the letter. In dramatic fashion, they pointed out to Gleneig that, despite all the evidence of "the fearful destruction of life and property, the serious interruptions of correspondence [and] the general impression abroad that [they] are neither safe nor suitable sea boats," sailing packets, to their dismay, continued to be employed carrying the mails.[21] This was an issue that transcended the provincial concerns of New Brunswick and Nova Scotia.[22]

If Great Britain is to maintain her footing upon the North American Continent—if she is to hold the command of the extensive sea coast from Maine to Labrador, skirting millions of square miles of fertile lands, intersected by navigable rivers, indented by the best harbors in the world, containing now a million and a half of people and capable of supporting many millions of whose aid in war and consumption in peace she is secure—she must, at any hazard of even increased expenditure for a time, establish such a line of rapid communication by steam, as will ensure the speedy transmission of public dispatches, commercial correspondence and general information, through channels exclusively British, and inferior to none in security and expedition. If this is not done, the British population on both sides of the Atlantic are left to receive, through foreign channels, intelligence of much that occurs in the mother country and the Colonies, with at least ten days, in most cases, for erroneous impressions to circulate before they can be corrected. Much devil has already arisen from the conveyance of intelligence by third parties, not always friendly or impartial; and from the feverish excitement along the frontier, the indefatigable exertions of evil agents, and the irritation not yet allayed in the Canadas, since the suppression of the late rebellions, it is of the highest importance that a line of communication should be established, through which not only official correspondence but sound information can be conveyed. The pride, as well as the interests of the British people, would seem to require means of communications with each other, second to none which are enjoyed by other States.

As the minister responsible for Canadian affairs, Lord Gleneig knew firsthand the problem of communication across the Atlantic. During the rebellion crisis, he had spent many anxious weeks awaiting reliable intelligence from Canada, which often arrived in American packets. To remedy the problem, the cabinet turned to the Admiralty.

Their Lordships were cautious. They had little enthusiasm for taking on the additional complexity and significant costs associated with a transatlantic steam packet service. They were relieved when they turned to Parry for advice and he recommended contracting with private operators, pointing out that he had inherited a number of such contracts when he took over from the Post Office, and that the system worked well. The idea of avoiding direct responsibility appealed to the Admiralty, while contracting out also met the financial needs of a strapped Whig administration that, thanks in part to the expense of putting down the Canadian rebellions, was facing a serious budget deficit.[23] Pushing off costs to private firms was a sensible and obvious answer. On September 24, 1838, "the Treasury authorized the Admiralty to invite tenders for a steam packet service connecting Britain to North America."[24] Parry's office undertook the details, and with unwonted speed, his clerks prepared a public invitation. The advertisement appeared on November 7, 1838.[25]

Steam vessels required for conveying Her Majesty's Mails and Dispatches between ENGLAND and HALIFAX (Nova Scotia), and also between ENGLAND and HALIFAX and NEW YORK.

The deadline for submission was set for December 15. Parry, unwilling to wait for bids to come in over the transom and worried that none might arrive in any case, took the initiative by contacting James Burns's younger brother George, with whom he had done considerable business, inviting him and his partners in Glasgow and Liverpool to bid.[26] Burns was cool to the idea. Fully engaged with his coasting trade, he told Parry that "his hands were full," and he was "determined to let the Atlantic steam business alone."[27]

The reaction from Glasgow dampened enthusiasm for the project. Parry received only two bids. The St. George Steam Packet Company, owners of the *Sirius*, proposed to run a service from Cork to Halifax, with feeder service by small vessels to Liverpool and New York. The Great Western Steamship Company offered direct service from Bristol to Halifax without service to New York.[28] Neither would guarantee anything more than service once a month. Disappointed, Parry found the offers wanting and rejected both.

As usual, winter mail from London took an inordinate amount of time to reach Halifax, and not until January 10, 1839, did details of the Admiralty tender appear in Halifax. Samuel Cunard then moved quickly. Two weeks later the Halifax *Novascotian* noted the departure of "Hon. S. Cunard" aboard the Falmouth packet.[29] For nearly a decade, since his investment in *Royal William*, Cunard had remained keenly interested in the future of steam, but cost remained the issue. However, with the promise of underwriting from the Admiralty Cunard saw new possibilities, and he was willing to endure a risky and uncomfortable winter passage on a coffin brig to make his pitch to the Admiralty.[30]

Raising money was Cunard's chief obstacle; there was little of it available in Halifax, and the experience of *Royal William* still held heavy. Before leaving for England he tried raising capital from friends in Boston but was turned away by Yankee merchants so fully invested in sailing packets that they had nothing left for steam. They did, however, assure him that should he succeed they would see to it that their port would accommodate his ships. Cunard decided to go it alone, carrying a letter of introduction from the province's lieutenant governor, John Campbell, that paid tribute to Cunard as "one of the firmest supporters of the Government."[31]

Using the General Mining Association offices at Ludgate Hill as his headquarters, he forwarded his tender to the Admiralty:

> I hereby offer to furnish steamboats of not less than 300 horse-power to convey the mails from a point in England to Halifax and back twice in each month. Also to provide branch boats of not less than 150 horsepower to convey the mails to Boston and back to Halifax.

He added that he would also provide "boats of not less than 150 horse-power to convey the mails from Pictou to Quebec," and he promised to have the ships in readiness by May 1, 1840, if not sooner. In return he asked for a ten-year contract at £55,000 per year.[32]

The Admiralty was slow to respond. Cunard needed a champion, and in the world of steamships there could be no better supporter than Robert Napier. Cunard, however, was not acquainted with him. To help open the door, he wrote to William Kidston, a commercial agent in Glasgow with whom he had done business, asking him to approach Napier with a proposal to build "one or two steamboats of 300 horse-power and about 800 tons."[33] Given his limited resources, Cunard told Kidston, "I want a plain and comfortable boat, not the least unnecessary expense for show. I prefer plain work in the cabin, and it will save a large amount in the cost."[34] Concerned that the Admiralty, and Napier, might dismiss an overture from a little known colonial, Cunard set off on a bold tack. Using the connections he had formed as East India Tea agent in Halifax, he arranged an appointment with the company's influential chief secretary James Melvill, who Cunard knew was well acquainted with Napier.[35] Melvill offered his support and contacted Napier on Cunard's behalf, who responded quickly. To avoid his previous unhappy experience with Patrick Wallace, Napier advised that Cunard should be prepared for an expensive undertaking. "The cost of these vessels depends on so many different things that it is hardly possible to name a price for them. I have done them as low as £35 per ton . . . but good vessels . . . cannot be done for less than £40 to £42 per ton."[36] If Cunard understood these conditions and remained "in want of vessels," Napier offered to meet him in London. Cunard, eager to get a firsthand view of Napier's extensive facilities, asked instead if he might come to Glasgow.[37]

Within days Cunard was on his way to Scotland. In early March 1839 the two men met at Napier's home, Lancefield House. Cunard had been preparing for this moment. He laid before Napier plans for three vessels, all identical; 800 tons and 300 horsepower. They were, by no coincidence, almost exact copies of the steamer *City of Glasgow*, which Napier had built for the company of the same name in which George and James Burns, James Donaldson, and David MacIver of Liverpool were partners.[38]

Napier was impressed, and perhaps flattered by Cunard's pitch to him, but the Haligonian's real selling point was money. The dangling offer of

a substantial Admiralty mail subsidy meant that while a line of steamships might operate at a loss (almost a certainty), government money
would insure a gain.

Seeing the possibilities, Napier offered to build the vessels at £40 per
ton, a price slightly less than the one he had quoted Patrick Wallace
five years earlier. Cunard thought the price "fair and reasonable," but
observing that "the three vessels [were] all of one size" and could be
built from the existing plans of the *City of Glasgow*, he countered boldly
that a discount of £2,000 per ship was in order. If Napier agreed to that
price, "he would give the order before he left."[39] Napier reluctantly
assented. Remaining, however, was the question of raising the capital to
build the vessels. The Admiralty subsidy was for operation, not construction. Neither Napier nor Cunard had personal resources approaching
what was necessary. Napier, however, had the answer; he invited Cunard
to join him on a short carriage ride to the office of James Donaldson, the
wealthy cotton broker, who expressed interest but told Cunard "that he
never did anything without consulting 'a little friend.'" The friend was
George Burns, and the trio of Napier, Donaldson, and Cunard descended
upon him. Still skeptical about the profitability of transatlantic steam
service but intrigued by the thought of a government subsidy, Burns
asked to speak with Cunard "alone . . . to talk it over." The private
meeting ended "cordially" but with nothing concluded. Burns invited
Cunard to stay for dinner, and joining them would be David MacIver,
who happened to be in the city on business.

Dinner did not go well. MacIver was "dead against the proposal."
Burns, however, despite his previous position, was not so certain. He
saw some "daylight" in the scheme. Napier, who was not at dinner, was
Cunard's last hope. Napier invited Burns and MacIver to breakfast the
next morning. Cunard would later credit him "with the great portion of
the merit of his success," as he managed to sway Burns and MacIver.[40]
However, not even these men commanded enough capital for the project.
To assist them, Burns told Cunard they would have to invite "a few
friends to join us," but first the partners needed a formal agreement.[41]
Burns's lawyer and friend John Park Fleming, a man known to write
"tight" contracts, was up to the task. With "notes which I supplied,"
recounted Burns, Fleming "sat up all night, and wrote out in his own

hand the contract of a co-partnery," thus forming the North American Royal Mail Steam Packet Co., soon to be known simply as the Cunard Line.[42] The "essence" of the contract was to invite other investors to join Cunard, Burns, and MacIver, while leaving the "power to do everything and all things" in their hands.[43] Informally, the three agreed that Cunard would negotiate with Napier on matters of construction, Burns would attend to raising capital, and MacIver would return to Liverpool "to superintend the practical working of the steamers."[44]

With everything in place, on Monday, March 18, Cunard signed a contract with Napier, but only after a last-minute change. Napier, "dread[ing] failure," urged Cunard to build vessels larger and more powerful than the 800 ton, 300 horsepower proposed. The "expense alarmed him" and Cunard balked. Napier offered a compromise—he would enlarge the vessels to 960 tons, 375 horsepower for only an additional £2,000 each, the same figure Cunard had earlier persuaded Napier to deduct. Cunard grabbed the bargain and signed the contract. Napier complained that he had given Cunard "the vessels cheap."[45]

Tuesday, the nineteenth, Cunard left Glasgow and hurried to London. Within a few days of his departure, "entirely through the instrumentality of George Burns" thirty-three investors subscribed £270,000 with Cunard taking the largest portion—£55,000.[46]

In London Cunard wasted no time making his way to the Admiralty and the Treasury, and he found a warm reception. Napier's involvement reassured the Admiralty that the vessels would be well built, while support from Burns and his friends relieved the Treasury of their concerns over finances. Despite some sniping criticism from "English builders" jealous of their Scottish competitors, Cunard reported that when he laid his contract with Napier before Parry and the others, they were "highly pleased."[47] In a deal "made privately with no attempt to have a public letting," their Lordships agreed to terms.[48] That the deal was done privately rankled some members of Parliament, who charged monopoly.

The contract obliged Napier "to build and construct with the best materials . . . three good and sufficient steam ships, each not less than two hundred feet long, . . . not less than thirty-two feet broad between the paddles and not less than twenty-one feet six inches depth of hold." Hoping to gain a sizeable revenue from passengers, their accommodations were of special concern. "Cabins [will be] finished in a neat and comfort-able manner for the accommodation of from sixty to seventy passengers or a greater number." Napier pledged that the cabins would be to the standard of the popular steamer *City of Glasgow*. Although powered by two steam engines, each vessel carried a full suit of sails.

Cunard pressed for a firm and speedy construction schedule. Napier set forth "to have one of the said vessels ready for trial and delivery in the Clyde on or before the twelfth day of March Eighteen Hundred and Forty," followed by a second vessel on the first of April and the third on May 1. He also provided a six-month warranty on the machinery "unless such occurrences may have arisen from neglect or carelessness."

For his part, Cunard pledged payment of £32,000 per vessel, £96,000 total. Sixty thousand pounds was to be paid "during the progress of the work," with balances paid according to a complicated calendar. Cunard and Napier agreed that any disputes that might arise would be submitted for "final and conclusive" arbitration to their mutual friend James Melvill.[49]

On April 23, 1839, the Treasury advised the Secretary of State for the Colonies, Lord Mulgrave, that the new service was being established. The bureaucratic wheels moved with unusual speed and, on May 4, 1839, a formal contract was signed between the Lords of Admiralty and Samuel Cunard representing the British and North American Royal Mail Steam Packets (Cunard Line).[50]

The agreement closely followed Cunard's original proposal, but there were some notable changes. After further discussions with Napier, the number of vessels to be built grew to four and their tonnage to 1,200, and horsepower to 420, and instead of branch service by smaller vessels connecting to New York, Cunard persuaded the Admiralty that west-bound direct service to Boston via Halifax, dropping New York, would be more suitable, with the return also through Halifax. In recognition of the added expense the Admiralty agreed to increase their subsidy to £60,000 for a period of seven years.[51]

Barely a week after the signing, anxious to make arrangements in Halifax and Boston for his line of steamers, Cunard took passage on the steamer *British Queen* bound for New York while Napier and Burns launched the building program. To hasten construction they arranged for the vessels to be built in separate yards. *Britannia*, the first to be laid down, went to Robert Duncan. John Wood built *Acadia*, his brother Charles constructed *Caledonia*, and *Columbia* launched from the yard of Robert Steele.[52]

Cunard was clever and deliberate in his choice of names for the new ships. Two took the name of Roman provinces: *Britannia* and *Caledonia*. In Victorian England classical allusions to empires were always popular, and since these honored Britain and Scotland, they were especially reso- nant. The remaining two names on the sterns, *Acadia* and *Columbia*, looked to the other side of the Atlantic, connecting to the ancient name of Nova Scotia while offering a poetic reference to the United States.

Classical names ending in *ia* became a signature for the line, as did the unusual color of Cunard's funnels. Cunard ordered that the lower four-fifths of the funnel be painted red and the top, as was the custom for steamships, be black to obscure soot deposits. From experience Napier understood that heat rising from below would blister ordinary red paint, and so he "came up with a mixture of buttermilk and fresh ochre that when applied to a funnel, actually took advantage of the heat to literally 'cook' itself onto the metal." What Napier did not foresee, however, was that the heat caused the constituent elements of ochre to combine in a fashion that left a "unique shade of red-orange" that remains to the present the distinctive color of Cunard funnels.[53]

After a long, nineteen-day passage, Cunard arrived in New York City on July 29 to a cool reception. The *Herald* dismissed Cunard's plan "to establish a line of steamboats between England and Halifax" with only a brief mention, and then in a sneering voice, described him as "winding as the serpent that beguiled Eve."[54] He tarried only a few days and then booked a cabin to Boston on the coastal packet *Liverpool*, arriving in the city on August 8. Boston, however, was expecting him.

Bostonians had been following events in London and Glasgow with keen interest. Although Boston still asserted her claim to being Ameri- ca's intellectual and cultural center, her commercial prominence had been overshadowed by New York's, with its growing population five times the size of Boston's and a port that was the greatest in America. In the late 1830s, the fortunes of Boston took a turn for the better, when after years of delay, the Western railroad connecting the city to Albany, and thence to the west and north to Canada, was on the verge of completion. According to local boosters, the railroad would return the city to glory, "not merely as a seat of literature and the arts, not merely as a seaport, where capital, in which they are deficient, had accumulated to a large amount, but as the best market in America for the produce of the West, and the great center and depot of American manufactures."[55]

While iron rails pushed west to Albany, the Eastern Rail Road, with its terminus across the harbor in East Boston, was reaching north to Portland, Maine.[56] The possibility of tying these rail lines to Cunard's steamships at Boston piers intoxicated the city with dreams of Boston becoming the great Atlantic nexus between England and America. "In the course of a few months," bragged the *Boston Evening Transcript*, the completion of these lines "will enable the traveler to reach Boston as soon as New York from Albany, Utica, Rochester, Oswego, Buffalo, Detroit, Louisville, St. Louis, Kingston, Toronto, Montreal and upon his arrival in Boston he will find himself 220 miles nearer to Liverpool than when at New York."[57] A few weeks later a writer in the *Daily Atlas*, reminding his readers about their perpetual rivalry with the city on the Hudson, predicted that with Cunard's steamships, "we shall stand upon a par with New York."[58]

Cunard saw this as well. The success of his enterprise depended upon providing a network of efficient through-connections that would move people, mail, and cargo by land, sea and rail.

"I think," he boasted, that "when the boats are seen, I shall have all the passengers for Boston, and to the east ward of Boston."[59]

Among those ready to welcome Cunard were the proprietors of the East Boston Wharf Company. A group of land speculators who had held extensive real estate on Noddle's Island (East Boston), they were eager to use Cunard to promote their investment.[60] At a crowded public meeting held in Faneuil Hall, with Mayor Samuel Eliot presiding, the proprietors offered Cunard an extraordinary deal. At their own expense (estimated to be $50,000) they promised Cunard a 1,150 foot pier, construction to "commence immediately," with "ample docks for the reception of his steamships, and an extensive depot for coal." The lease was to run "for twenty years without any charge except the customary wharfage on goods shipped and landed." Since the wharf was located across the harbor from the center of the city, the Company agreed "to carry all merchandize to the consignees, and from the shippers, without any charge for ferriage."[61] They owned the ferry. Cunard accepted the offer and appointed one of the principals in the company, Samuel S. Lewis, to be his agent in Boston.

Cunard's plan reverberated far beyond mere matters of commerce. Rapid and regular steamship service to England, according to some, would usher in a new era of Anglo-American relations that had been strained by ongoing diplomatic disputes. "While the governments are arguing about the boundaries he makes a successful incursion with a peace force into the heart of the country." Boston hailed Cunard as the "harbinger of peace."[62]

Halifax was no less exuberant. "We rejoice," proclaimed the *Novascotian*, "that a colonist whose enterprising spirit we have often had occasion to notice, has had the courage to grapple with an undertaking so vast."[63] As soon as Cunard arrived home from Boston, plans to honor him were set in motion. Despite a rainy morning on Friday, August 30, 1839, the elite of Halifax gathered for a grand "Pic Nic" to celebrate Cunard's triumph. Departing from his own wharf at the edge of the harbor, "a little after three the Honorable Samuel Cunard with the 8th Band playing on deck, steamed down the harbor and landed at McNab's Island." The host committee had erected a "spacious marquee" sheltering long tables groaning with food and drink. With the Halifax brewer Alexander Keith presiding, "the day passed agreeably: Toasts, Songs, and Speeches, following each other in rapid succession." As usual, Cunard spoke only briefly, offering thanks to "Her Majesty's Government for their liberal expenditure." Near sunset the festive crowd marched to the wharf, "gratified that a compliment justly due to an enterprising townsman had been properly paid."[64]

CHAPTER EIGHT

Liverpool—Halifax—Boston—New York

ALTHOUGH HALIFAX STOOD as Canada's most important Atlantic port, it was, in the view of the ministry, only a waypoint on the route to the chief population centers of Quebec and Ontario, clustered along the St. Lawrence River. To fulfill his contract and move mail from the Halifax pierhead to the interior, Cunard had pledged to the Admiralty "to provide boats of not less than 150 horse power to convey the mails from Pictou to Quebec and back while the navigation is unobstructed by ice."[1] Located on the northern edge of the province near the Northumberland Strait, Pictou was familiar to Cunard as a key depot from which the GMA shipped coal.

A few days after his return to Halifax, Cunard left for Pictou. Having recently secured the "privilege" of storing coal for his steamers in the Royal dockyard in Halifax, he was keen to check on the arrangements for transporting it from Pictou to Halifax.[2] On Thursday, September 19, he arrived just in time for a grand celebration at which the town was toasting the completion of a railroad from the mines to a loading dock at nearby New Glasgow. Cunard "rejoiced with the knowledge that [his] steamers' bunkers would be filled with GMA coal."[3] Adding to the joy of the moment, in a short speech Cunard told his audience that Pictou would also be the connecting point between stages from Halifax and steamers on the Saint Lawrence. Since this was likely to result in many people passing through, a welcomed prospect, he suggested that the town needed a "good hotel . . . as there will be much travelling, and a good House for the accommodation of strangers will induce many persons to visit this interesting part of the Province."[4]

Cunard appreciated the risks of navigation on the St. Lawrence, a "transportation backwater," and he had been careful in his contract negotiations to include the costs of the river segment in his original estimates.[5] What he had not figured into his calculation were charges for conveying passengers and mail on the overland route connecting Halifax and Pictou. Indeed, had he sought Admiralty support to fill this gap, their Lordships would likely have dismissed the request since they bore no responsibility for anything traveling above the tide line. To close the gap and make "the line of communication to Canada perfect," after having secured the contract to carry the mails across the Atlantic Cunard sought help from the Post Office Department for the inland route. Writing to its secretary, William Maberly, Cunard noted the difficulty of overland passage between Halifax and Pictou.[6] At Maberly's recommendation, the Post Master General instructed Nova Scotia's deputy post master, John Howe, to contract with Cunard for coach service between Halifax and Pictou "three times in each and every week, between the 1st day of May, and the 1st day of November, in each year, and twice in every week, during the remainder of each year" in a time "within 17 hours."[7] Cunard proposed a fare of £2-1-0, less than one-third the rate charged by the slow-moving "waggons," but only on the condition that a subsidy "should be permanently provided for out of the Post-Office revenue of which there is plenty for that purpose."[8] Howe, son of a prominent Loyalist refugee and an old hand in provincial politics, suspected that Cunard, a person with a record of garnering lucrative government contracts, was overcharging. Howe objected to the arrangement, but to no avail.[9] London overruled him. The contract, including a subsidy, was signed on December 14, 1841.[10] With this final piece in place, Samuel Cunard had secured a virtual monopoly on steamship service across the North Atlantic. He stood astride the most important ocean thoroughfare in the world—the link between the United States and Great Britain— while at the same time he extended his reach into the heartland of Canada

via river steamers on the St. Lawrence, railroads from Boston, and overland coaches across Nova Scotia.

In a remarkable display of energy and workmanship, on Wednesday,
February 5, 1840, more than a month ahead of schedule, Wood's yard
crew launched *Britannia*. Dressed "with appropriate embellishments"
and "with easy, regular, undeviating motion," *Britannia* slid into the
Clyde as "Miss Isabella Napier the beautiful daughter of the celebrated
steam engine maker, pronounced her name."[11]

Although now in the water, weeks remained to complete her fitting-
out. Originally scheduled to make her maiden voyage from Liverpool
in mid-March, the best she could now do was to manage a departure
date in early July.[12] Fortunately, Burns and MacIver had a backup plan.
For the Pictou-Quebec river run, they had already purchased *Unicorn*
from the local yard of Robert Steele and Co., "a neatly built and gallant
steamer of about 700 tons."[13] To provide an early and on-time offing for
the new line, they decided to use her "as a sort of pioneer to the undertaking." On May 15, 1840, commanded by Captain Walter Douglas,
Unicorn "hauled out of the Clarence Dock [Liverpool] into the stream.
The passengers came aboard on the 16th, and at noon she rounded the
Rock Light House" bound for Boston via Halifax.[14]

At ten in the morning on Monday, June first, *Unicorn* came alongside
Cunard's Halifax wharf, where a boisterous crowd welcomed her as the
first of "the precursor of a superb line of steam packets" running between
Liverpool, Halifax, and Boston.[15] Her stay at Halifax was brief, just long
enough to leave off mail and twenty-seven passengers. Shortly before
midnight, after taking on coal, fresh stores, and new passengers, she
cast off for Boston, arriving early Wednesday evening. "As soon as
Unicorn was announced by telegraph [i.e., a semaphore signal relayed
from Boston Light] the American and British flags were hoisted at City
Hall, and flown to the breeze from the masts of vessels in the harbor,
and from numerous elevated points along the wharves, and at East
Boston." On the harbor, "the tops of houses were crowded with people,
who cheered the *Unicorn* incessantly as she passed."[16] The United States
Revenue Cutter *Hamilton* gave a "gallant salute," but the "enthusiastic
shouts [of the crowd] were louder than even the roar of the artillery."
On Friday a "collation" was served at "Faneuil Hall, at the expense of

the city, to which the officers and passengers of the *Unicorn* were invited."
Most prominent among the guests was Edward Cunard, "a son of the
proprietor."[17] Even other ports, perennial rivals of Boston, hailed the
moment. The *Baltimore Sun*, lamenting that its city was "stand[ing]
with folded arms," congratulated Boston on "one of the most joyous
occasions in the annals of [the] city."[18] In a swipe at bickering diplomats
and politicians "parading and war-speeching" over the Maine border, a
writer in Keene, New Hampshire's *Sentinel* toasted "The Hon. Samuel
Cunard—The founder of direct Steam Navigation between Great Britain
and the City of Boston—a wise negotiator—while the governments are
arguing about the boundaries, he makes a successful incursion, with a
peaceful force into the heart of the country."[19] Boston had secured the
prize—a line of four ships providing regular service across the Atlantic.

As *Unicorn* prepared to depart, Boston awaited the arrival of *Britannia*.
She had completed her fitting-out and left the Clyde in early June; by
the twelfth *Britannia* was secure in Liverpool's recently completed
Coburg Dock. For several days she was the object of considerable attention, but finally a notice in the *Liverpool Mercury* advised passengers that
on Friday morning, July 3, *Britannia* would leave the dock, and so "all
heavy baggage should be sent on board before that time."[20] At ten A.M.
the gate to Coburg Dock swung open, *Britannia's* master, Captain Henry
Woodruff, gave the command, and the steamer was towed gingerly
through the dock's narrow opening and headed into the river. She moored
off Egremont Slip, where the next day tenders brought out sixty-seven
passengers, including Samuel Cunard and his daughter Anne.[21] Taking
advantage of a favorable tide, *Britannia* passed over the bar at the mouth
of the Mersey River, dropped the pilot, and set a course down the Irish
Sea.[22] By Monday, the sixth, she steamed past Tuskar Light on the
Irish coast, "wind W. blowing fresh," bound to Halifax.

After a stormy crossing, *Britannia* came abreast of Sambro Light
Thursday, July 16, 1840, at about 2:30 in the morning. Instead of
proceeding to the wharf, Woodruff, perhaps for reasons of safety but
more likely to await daylight, when a more public entrance could be
executed, gave the order to anchor. In the morning *Britannia*, described
by Halifax's *Acadian Recorder* as a "felicitous combination of grandeur,

elegance, speed and durability," came up the harbor. She was greeted by "the whole population lining the wharves with repeated huzzahs and shouts." "Every attention" was lavished on Cunard.[23] The stay was brief—seven hours—only enough time to offload passengers and mail, replenish coal bunkers, and take on additional passengers for Boston.

At seven P.M. on Saturday, July 18, the keeper at Boston Light, David Tower, signaled *Britannia*'s approach. The message sent an electric charge through the city. Slowly she made her way past the harbor islands and down the main channel, her bow pointed directly at the steeple of Old North Church. Despite the falling darkness along the shore at the end of the piers, crowds had gathered. Church bells rang and a band on the USS *Columbus* struck up "God Save the Queen." Turning to starboard, *Britannia* hauled into her berth at Cunard's East Boston wharf about ten o'clock, "greeted with a splendid display of fireworks."[24] For the next several days, Boston indulged itself in a "Cunard Festival, culminating in a grand reception at the East Boston Company's Maverick House."[25] "Six stories high," with more than eighty rooms, "its halls, parlors, dining-rooms and chambers were furnished in an elegant manner, equaling any hotel in the United States."[26] From the roof of the hotel a canvas was spread creating a "beautiful and elegantly decorated pavilion," under which two thousand people dined. At the entrance to the pavilion "was a beautiful arch bearing the simple word Cunard, in letters of gold—upon the right the name Fulton, and the American eagle, and upon the left, Watt and the British arms, both elegantly and appropriately painted on canvas." Present was "the highest talent in the land," including Edward Everett, the recently appointed Minister to Great Britain, and Senator Daniel Webster, both ranked among the finest orators in the nation. Seeking to erase any unease lingering from the unhappy experiences of Cunard's Loyalist parents who had fled America, Bostonians hailed him not "as a son of America, but as a grandson." After innumerable toasts and long-winded paeans Cunard rose to return the compliments.[27] He spoke "very briefly," celebrating the ties that bound "Old and New England," but "in a tone so low that his remarks were heard only by a few persons very near the chair."[28] The festival concluded with a "Comic Song," sung like a "dirge," that concluded with the chorus:[29]

How timid and slow, but a few years ago,
The world hobbled on its motion—
Old Europe seemed far as the fix'd northern star.
O'er the boundless expanse of the ocean;
But though it was hard—at the word of Cunard,
Britannia herself is a rover—
Old England awhile, that fast anchored isle,
By steam is now here—half seas over.

Cunard mania consumed Boston. So too did the sweet scent of victory over her nemesis, New York. The British and American Steamship Company, which had been struggling for a year to provide service to New York with its steamer *British Queen*, "a favorite of the New Yorkers," was embarrassed when *Britannia*, on her maiden voyage, beat her across the Atlantic by three days.[30] A month later the company's second steamer, *President*, was also humiliated when she took five days longer to cross than had *Britannia*. British and North American's slumping reputation then crashed when *President* went missing on a winter crossing early in 1841.[31]

In quick succession, and on schedule, *Britannia*'s sisters *Acadia* and *Caledonia* arrived in Boston. *Columbia*, the fourth in the quartet, was the last to enter service, reaching Boston on January 19, 1841, after a "rough voyage."[32]

The city had engineered a remarkable achievement. The *New York Sun* tipped its hat to "the cute Yankees," who by investing in a vast railway network with "iron horses at the rate of 25 miles an hour" and enticing Cunard to their city had "unlocked a vast depot of Western produce" and drawn it into their orbit.[33] Nor were Boston's fortunes limited to her links to the American west, for many believed she was also destined to become "the great thoroughfare betwixt England and the British provinces."[34]

Thanks to Cunard, business in Boston was brisk. Speed and punctuality became the hallmarks of the line. The average voyage from Liverpool was an impressive fourteen days and ten hours—less than half the passage time of a sailing vessel.[35] Equally remarkable was the steamers' punctuality. Twice a month they arrived. "Hackmen" knew "the very hour a steamship is due," and lined up their carriages waiting for fares.[36] From the pier, disembarking passengers were hurried to a railway depot or stagecoach line whose schedules had been coordinated to accommodate the arrival of the Cunarder. For those who intended to remain a day or two in Boston, the nearby Maverick House owned by Cunard's agent Samuel Lewis and his partners in the East Boston Company stood ready to lodge them. Some took the ferry, also owned by the company, across the harbor to stay downtown at the newly finished Tremont House.[37]

Gentlemen hungry for dinner and not apt to be comfortable in unkempt taverns could patronize a "Refreshment House" such as Ford's on Wilson Lane, where "meals are served up at all hours of the day (excepting Sundays) which makes a convenient resort for gentlemen transiently visiting the city."[38] If travelers preferred more elegant surroundings, they headed toward Pearl Street and the former mansion of the China trader Thomas Handasyd Perkins, whose home had been converted into "an inviting house of entertainment." The combination of the opening of the Western Railroad, improved roads, and the arrival of Cunard's steamers generated "a vast increase of business in Boston."[39]

Those Bostonians suspicious of the evils often associated with strangers, and fretful that the arrival of so many foreign "Jack Tars" might be a threat to the moral fabric of the community, were relived to find that the officers and crew of Cunard's ships were pious and religious men. At sea, when weather permitted, Sunday services were held and "all unnecessary work" avoided. When *Caledonia* arrived on her first visit to the city Captain McKellen, "a religious man with a kindred crew," led them off the ship and mustered on the wharf to hear a sermon preached by the renowned Edward "Father" Taylor, minister from the Seamen's Bethel, who "by his wit, pathos and imagination wrought upon the feelings of his hearers in remarkable degree."[40] On the Sunday following, McKellen "marched his crew to church in person."[41]

While public acclaim buoyed his reputation, Cunard's continued success depended upon pleasing the Admiralty and post office and attracting passengers by providing regular and quick passages.[42] Cunard did not disappoint. Not even New England's harsh winters could disrupt the schedule. On February first, 1841, in the face of a "severe easterly snow storm" raging across the harbor, *Acadia* left her East Boston pier at "precisely 2 P.M.," right on time.[43] During the first full year of operation in 1841, Cunard steamers carried 1,454 passengers, all cabin class, to Boston in twenty-one trips, at an average fare of £25 (approx. $135). Total foreign ship arrivals for the same period, including Cunard's, numbered 1,743, landing 8,503 passengers.[44] Representing slightly more than 1 percent of arrivals, Cunard carried 17 percent of passenger traffic.[45] Statistics for mail service were equally impressive. On a single eastbound winter voyage, *Acadia* steamed out of the harbor with thirty thousand letters and "several wagon loads of newspapers."[46] The numbers increased steadily, and by 1845 the Postmaster General estimated that more than six hundred thousand letters left Boston each year, nearly all on Cunard steamers.[47]

The bulk of revenue came from carrying mail and people: cargo was secondary. The North Atlantic routes were oversupplied with sailing tonnage, forcing general freight rates down. Collins's packets, for example, with their lower operating costs and huge cargo capacity, could carry several times the tonnage of *Britannia* and at a much cheaper rate.[48] What cargo Cunarders took aboard was almost always of the type for which shippers were willing to pay a premium—small in bulk, of high value, time sensitive, and frequently perishable. Mail and passengers fit that description and so too did specie, food stuffs, publications, and expensive consumer goods. "The Cunard steamers bring to Boston fresh all the delicious fish known in the English waters" was the claim in one paper.[49] Wealthy Bostonians patronized shops that offered "New and Fashionable Articles" just arrived on "Cunard's Line of Royal Packets." Merchants promised "British Goods of the best manufacture, immediately upon the arrival of each Packet." "Frequent and rapid communication between the old and new country" made it possible for bookstores to stock the latest books, magazines, and newspapers, thus satisfying a growing demand for timely information.[50]

While Boston reveled in her triumph—one local booster bragged that the city "will take the wind out of [New York's] sails"—the Cunard Line almost immediately steamed into troubled waters.[51] Running four vessels across the Atlantic every season, fair weather and foul, had proven far more costly than Cunard and his partners had anticipated. In calculating costs, Cunard, MacIver, and Burns had relied on estimates from Robert Napier, their fellow investor, builder of their engines and the master in steam. Napier likely shared with them the calculations he had produced six years earlier for the ill-fated London venture. In those estimates, for vessels slightly smaller than *Britannia* and her sisters, Napier had calculated a crew of thirty-eight. *Britannia*'s crew numbered eighty-nine. In nearly every category of expense, Napier had undershot the mark, most notably the engineering and the steward departments. Napier called for four engineers, eight firemen, and four coal trimmers. *Britannia* actually shipped six engineers, twelve firemen, and ten coal trimmers.[52] To serve the 100 passengers Napier estimated would book passage (plus the ship's company), a cook and a boy in the galley and two stewards for the salon and the cabins would be sufficient. *Britannia*'s complement of stewards, serving an average seventy (not 100) passengers, numbered twenty-eight, plus a purser, whom Napier had failed to mention. On the revenue side, Napier saw profit at a £30 fare. Cunard charged £25. Income from cargo, estimated at 6 percent of total revenue, was marginal.[53]

In the spring of 1841 Cunard and his partners tallied the books for the first nine months of operation, revealing a grim picture. High operating costs and empty cabins brought mounting losses. Pampered passengers expected a table full of meats, fish, poultry, vegetables, and sweets, which they washed down with full bumpers of wine, beer, and spirits. When done with drinking and eating, satiated passengers thought nothing of leaving glasses half-empty and plates littered with discarded food. Cunard, who adopted the "American Plan" common on packets, whereby food and drink were included in the cost of passage, was furious at the expense and waste and recommended charging extra for wine.[54] MacIver, a businessman far more experienced than Cunard in the world of passenger service, offered advice to his fretful partner:

> About wine or no wine—the more I ponder over this the less like-
> lihood do I see of our getting at a better system than just giving
> wine as we do now—The paying for wine, in practice working,
> may do well enough in a ship with a half a doz passengers, but with
> 80 people it would not work—The purpose of any change that we

might make would be that we should be gainers by the change, but we would not dispense with the carrying all the quantities and qualities of wine as now: in which case, it is palpable, that, with waste of servants, and breakage and the doubtful accts of returns in money; we might soon experience that we had made a change without making a difference. The charging of Hotel prices too for wines would be most impalatable.[55]

MacIver advocated a more subtle approach. Maintain the current system but raise the fare to £40, "which still is too low"; nonetheless, it was the limit to which they could go without losing business. At an average of seventy passengers per trip, the line was already operating under capacity. At a moment when rates in general on the North Atlantic routes were falling, it was difficult to fathom how raising prices would fill cabins, and so fares remained the same and wine continued to be served.[56]

Unable to cut costs at sea or raise prices to a more realistic level, Cunard suggested trimming shoreside expenses. He focused on Boston, where company affairs were in the hands of Samuel Lewis. Acting as the ship's agent, a position better known along the waterfront as the "ship's husband," Lewis had the "authority to make requisite repairs, and attend to the management, equipment, and other concerns of the ship."[57] His job was to anticipate the vessels' requirements before arrival and smooth the way with local suppliers and officials. He engaged harbor pilots to guide the vessel into port. He visited the customs house at the end of State Street to make arrangements for inspectors and appraisers to board as quickly as possible to prevent any delay in clearance and debarkation that might annoy passengers. Likewise, he sought out health officials to avoid the dreaded complications associated with quarantine. Sheaf upon sheaf of government documents crossed his desk in East Boston, all requiring his attention.[58]

Although Cunard's ships took on coal at Halifax, a cautious captain might want to top off his bunkers in Boston with a few more tons to ensure a comfortable passage. For the same reason, he took aboard extra barrels of tallow, an essential lubricant for the engines. Lewis had to ensure that these materials were on the pier, ready to load as soon as the steamer tied up. Once secured to the pier, the first to go aboard the steamer were the customs officers. Lewis trailed close behind, going as quickly as he could to meet with the captain and chief engineer. Aside from the usual requirements, they often had special demands. Ocean voyages, especially winter crossings, took a toll on ships. Engines, pumps, and boilers might need repair requiring special parts and skilled mechanics to install them. Aloft, battered sails, broken spars, and worn rigging called for mending and replacing. On winter crossings the hull was likely to have suffered damage from ice and wanted patching. Interior spaces sought attention as well. Under the watchful eye of the ship's bosun, the crew labored, scraping and painting, preparing for the return voyage.

In a crew of nearly ninety, personnel problems often arose. A few crew members might need medical care; engine rooms and lofty rigging were dangerous places to work on a tossing sea. Lewis had to find doctors and, if necessary, replacements for crewmen unable to sail again. On occasion he found himself with the unpleasant task of helping to extract errant crew out of the hands of local police authorities, or arranging for a minister from a seamen's bethel to come aboard and preach the word of God.

Lewis's most visible and delicate tasks were dealing with passengers and mail. As soon as the passengers heard the call "land" they scurried onto the deck. Having spent days enduring the tedium of the voyage or, in winter, the terror of storms, they crowded the bulwarks to catch the first glimpse of shore—the hills beyond Boston, the loom of the lights along the coast, or the vague outline of a distant church steeple.

As soon as the customs officers cleared the ship, passengers rushed down the gangway. "Busy as the devil in a gale of wind," Lewis was everywhere. Stewards supervised the offloading of luggage—trunks, bags, parcels, all had to be sorted and delivered to waiting carriages and wagons. Passengers in transit were escorted to the nearby ferry to be taken over to Boston to meet local stages or trains that would carry them to distant destinations. No one wanted to wait.

While passengers were going ashore crewmen and local officials unloaded mail and cargo. It was critical for both Cunard and Boston to move as quickly as possible. Cunard's reputation, and subsidy, depended on fast and reliable delivery, while Bostonians reveled in, and profited from, being the first "to know, and having New York wait for the mail to arrive 'via Boston.'"

All of these services were expensive, and shoreside costs at Boston were considerable. In his quest to cut expenses, Cunard aimed his sights on Lewis, whose salary of $4,000 per year exceeded that of a United States senator. Unlike Liverpool and Halifax, where trusted partners and relatives were in charge, affairs in Boston were in the hands of a stranger. Cunard suspected that Lewis and his associates were involved in "a system of expensive cost gaining among Tradesmen's Bills." Lewis, he thought, was taking commissions from his friends or, at the very least, was careless about seeking the best price. Without first consulting MacIver and Burns, Cunard decided to fire Lewis and replace him with his twenty-six-year-old son, Edward.

As usual, MacIver was the voice of caution. He shared Cunard's suspicions about mismanagement, but as soon as he learned of his partner's intentions he warned him that dismissing Lewis at a moment when the finances of the firm were frail was "very impolitic." Lewis was "the only existing link that gives the U.S. folks any connexion with Steamboat matters with this country. We know plenty of the Sympathies and Jealousies of that people . . . but like the other matter [wine] it is incidental to the novelty of a new Trade." To mollify Cunard and his disappointed son, MacIver suggested that "the true way for us to bring this right" was to keep Lewis in place but send Edward "now and again to [visit] Boston [to] keep the system up."[59]

Keeping Lewis in place with Edward looking over his shoulder improved affairs in Boston, but Samuel Cunard's financial problems went beyond steamships. His Canadian investments were also troubled, and his partnership with his brothers Joseph and Henry in Miramichi timber and shipbuilding had turned sour.[60]

Cunard's involvement in this venture had begun two decades before when Joseph and Henry moved to the Miramichi region of northern New Brunswick and, with backing from their elder brother, set up a network of mills and shipyards. As in any natural resource business, it was a speculative enterprise that carried risks. Long periods of time elapsed between setting up camps and sending supplies before timber arrived for sale, which meant tying up capital. In the meantime prices fluctuated widely. An observer writing in the *Novascotian* warned that "the Cunards are making a great dash here [Miramichi] but all I can see of them confirms my opinion of the ultimate smash of the whole concern."[61] The brothers, particularly Joseph, paid little heed to the warnings.

Cunard had also become deeply involved in land speculation on Prince Edward Island. Hoping to capitalize on immigration to Prince Edward Island, Cunard had partnered with George Young, Thomas Brooks, and Andrew Colville to form the Prince Edward Island Land Company in May 1838. Through cash and mortgages they purchased more than 150 thousand acres. Within months, however, the partners fell out when Cunard pushed the appointment of his son-in-law J. H. Peters as the resident agent while Young, practicing his own form of nepotism, insisted upon his younger brother Charles taking the plum job. In the end Cunard bought Young out, but in doing so he caused considerable ill will and inherited a whirlwind of problems. The land scheme would work only if paying tenants could be found. Those who took up the land became quickly antagonistic toward Cunard, who insisted on high rents. When Cunard tried to evict them, they obstinately resisted. Appealing to colonial authorities in London for assistance, he wrote "there is no tenant on the island who cannot pay his rent if he is industrious and sober."[62] Matters later deteriorated to such a point that in 1842 London authorized the deployment of a company of soldiers to help evict those in arrears. Cunard's hard measures won him no friends among the populace of the island or in Nova Scotia. Many of his tenants saw in his tireless pursuit of rents the same upper class callousness toward the poor that had driven them from their oppressive landlords in Ireland and Scotland. One balladeer, known only as Maclean from Raasay, sang[63]

> We left there [Scotland]
> And came out here
> Thinking we would receive consideration
> And that the rent
>   Would not be so exacting.

But Peters is oppressing us, and, if he doesn't die, we must leave
   this place
And Cunard himself a beast.

By early 1842 Cunard's creditors, including the Liverpool bank
Leyland and Bullins, to whom he owed £1,500, were baying at his door.
Christopher Bullins, a man "parsimonious to an extreme degree," was
anxious for his money. He was willing, nonetheless, to wait as long as
Cunard, who was in England on business, remained in the country and
was thus within reach of the law.[64] In early 1842, however, while in
London negotiating with other bankers, Cunard let it be known that
he would soon be leaving for Halifax. Fearful to have him beyond
their legal reach, Leyland and Bullins immediately sought to prevent his
departure. With the hard prospect of debtor's prison, Cunard made a
fast and secret exit to Liverpool, where his friend Duncan Gibb hid him
in a cottage at a very retired spot in Eastham, along the Mersey. The
next day, right on schedule, a Cunard steamer slipped her moorings,
and came down river. As she reduced speed, off Eastham, a small boat
came alongside to deliver a late-arriving passenger, a man from Halifax.[65]
   Cunard's flight home solved his immediate problem, but it left his
partners in a quandary. While Burns and the MacIver brothers, David
and Charles, had taken most of the burden of management at Liverpool,
Cunard was a key part of the company plan. He was the namesake of
the line, its public face, and its chief lobbyist. As dependent upon government support as the firm was, his presence in England was essential. The
embarrassment was too great to ignore. To ensure that Cunard might
return without fear of arrest, the MacIvers struck a deal with Leyland
and Bullins. If they would suspend the legal proceedings, the brothers
would personally guarantee due payment of Cunard's debt. The bankers
agreed.[66]
   Notwithstanding the rescue by his Liverpool partners, Cunard was
still in a financial hole. His obligations to Leyland and Bullins represented only a fraction of the sums he owed and rumors were afoot, as
reported in the *Baltimore Sun*, of the "failure of Mr. Cunard."[67] All told,
between debts he had incurred on the Miramichi, Prince Edward Island,
and money borrowed to invest in his steamships, Cunard owed a

staggering £130,000.[68] As soon as he arrived home he launched a brisk campaign to salvage his sinking fortunes. To raise cash, he sold what he could, including his father's farm in Rawdon, mortgaged his properties in Halifax, and then, exerting every ounce of influence he could muster, he secured a substantial loan from the Bank of Nova Scotia.[69]

In the midst of righting his ship, misfortune hit. On Sunday, July 2, 1843, a thick fog hung over the waters just south of Cape Sable, Nova Scotia. Through the shrouded sea, Captain Neil Shannon, master of the Cunarder *Columbia*, drove his vessel ahead at a brisk 10 ½ knots on a northeasterly heading, bound for Halifax. Just after the watch struck eight bells signaling noon, *Columbia* collided with a ledge, appropriately named Devil's Limb. She hit "gently," and her bow rose up about five feet out of the water.[70] Cunard happened to be in Halifax, and as soon as the news reached him, he immediately organized a rescue effort. Arriving at the scene, he directed rescue of the passengers and crew. Although her hull remained intact, *Columbia* could not be freed from the ledge. The underwriters declared her a total loss, but miraculously not a single life had been lost.

Instead of bemoaning the wreck and asking why the captain had not reduced speed in the fog, published accounts celebrated Cunard's personal conduct. Stories of his rushing to the scene portrayed him as a hero. According to one of the passengers—the wealthy Bostonian Abbott Lawrence—Captain Shannon too behaved with "coolness and courage." According to the line's apologists, it was not a navigational error or excessive speed but the "extraordinary current" that was to blame, and the fact that *Columbia*'s hull survived was "evidence of the superior workmanship and strength of the Cunard steamers." Topping it off, *Columbia* was nearly fully insured.[71]

At the time of the original agreement, neither the government nor Cunard and his partners understood the costs of running regular steamship service across the Atlantic, nor did they appreciate the stress on their vessels. Keeping to schedule year-round with regularity and safety put a heavy strain on the ships and their machinery, and although Napier's engines had proven to be reliable, they were complicated machines that required constant attention. At sea, with limited resources, engineers tended to normal care, mostly lubrication and tightening connections, and minor repairs—but more serious work could only be done in Liverpool where facilities, skilled engineers, and parts were available. Port time, however, was limited. The stay at Halifax was measured in hours. The stopover at Boston was usually ten days to two weeks, while dock time at Liverpool might not be more than three weeks. There was little time for major repairs.[72] To relieve the pressure, Cunard sought an increase in the subsidy to operate an additional ship. Launched in Glasgow, *Hibernia* arrived in Halifax on her maiden voyage May 2, 1843. She was 300 tons larger than the original quartet, and the Napier-built engines produced 50 percent more power.[73] Her entry into service gave a needed respite to the workhorse of the fleet *Britannia*. For nearly three years she had been in constant service, but thanks to *Hibernia* standing in as her relief, she was sent in for a major three-month overhaul.

In the face of *Columbia*'s loss *Hibernia*'s arrival provided only momentary ease on the fleet. To replace *Columbia*, Cunard ordered an additional steamer on the model of *Hibernia*—*Cambria*. By the mid-1840s Cunard had accomplished what few had thought possible. On one voyage alone, April 1845, from Liverpool, *Acadia* delivered to Boston twelve thousand letters and twenty-five thousand newspapers all destined to Montreal.[74] In Liverpool, Halifax, and Boston people could expect the mail within a day or two of the posted schedule, and that mail carried news not more than two weeks old. Passengers could expect to arrive and depart on the same schedule, and cross the Atlantic quickly and safely. Having conquered the run to Halifax and Boston, backed by generous government support and armed with experience and confidence, Cunard and his partners were ready to make a bold move.

From the very beginning Cunard had had his eye on New York. Politics, however, had forced him to Boston. When he was bidding for his first contract, *Great Western* and *British Queen*, both unsubsidized, were in service to New York. Their supporters would have raised a hue and cry against him had he tried to steam into their waters.[75] As the London *Times* observed, "If the Cunard Line of steam packets were to run fortnightly to New York, there would be an end to the Great Western Steam ship Company."[76] Boston was less threatening to their interests and, because it was closer to Halifax, fit more neatly into imperial concerns.

By the mid-forties, however, *British Queen* had been sold and the *Great Western* was facing financial difficulty. Without those ships Great Britain ran the risk of losing all regular steamship service to New York. Cunard and his partners pressed their advantage, and in the summer of 1846 laid a plan before Parliament to offer service to New York.

Debate in Parliament over Cunard's plan revealed a deep undercurrent of opposition. Supporters of the *Great Western* railed that that ship had not received a farthing of support, while Cunard had been given large sums with no public accountability. William Miles of Bristol demanded an investigation. Others rejoined that Mr. Cunard had a fair claim and that his service had been "exceedingly beneficial to the country."[77] In the end the government had little choice but to accept Cunard's proposal, and on July 1, 1846, he obtained a contract opening New York to his vessels and increasing his subsidy. In return Cunard agreed to add four ships, double the number of his fleet, and begin semimonthly service year-round, alternating between Boston and New York and calling at Halifax each way.[78]

CHAPTER NINE

Collins and Congress

THAT CUNARD WAS COMING to its port received a mixed reception in New York City. Periodic attempts to operate steamships to compete with Cunard and Boston had largely failed. The steamer *Massachusetts*, for example, took seventeen and a half days to cross the Atlantic, "a creditable performance, but it was not as fast a crossing as that of the Cunarder *Caledonia*, and it was only a few hours less than was taken by the packet *Yorkshire*."[1] Having garnered considerable profits with square-riggers on schedule, conservative New York shipowners had seen little need to shift their money to steam. Cunard's announcement, however, was a wakeup call.

By the mid-1840s sailing packets were still carrying the bulk of European emigrants and freight—including coal to America for use by the steam packets—but most of the mail, cabin passengers, and more valuable freight arrived in British steamships.[2] Many in New York saw Cunard's impending arrival as stark evidence of Britain's determination to dominate the Atlantic. To stand by while Great Britain seized this trident was a national and economic embarrassment. A writer in the *New London Morning News* pushed the point, demanding that New York City "get her spunk up."[3]

The nation was in a feisty mood. Patriotic emotions were riding high, especially in the popular press. In its inaugural October 1837 issue, New York's hyper-nationalistic *Democratic Review* announced that the goal of the journal was to "rally the mind of the nation from the state of torpor and even of demoralization in which so large a proportion of it is sunk."[4] The editor, John L. O'Sullivan, declared that "the boundless future will be an era of American greatness." America, according to O'Sullivan, was "destined for unparalleled glory." The nation was the keeper of the "promethean fire" of the "natural rights of man." He went on—"With the truths of God in our minds, beneficent objects in our hearts, and with a clear conscience unsullied by the past . . . the gates of hell shall not prevail against us."[5]

A young navy lieutenant, Matthew Fontaine Maury, whose seagoing career had been brought to an abrupt end when his leg was broken in a carriage accident, embraced O'Sullivan's call to national greatness. In a series of essays, "Scraps from the Lucky Bag"—written while he was recuperating from his injury, and published in the widely read *Southern Literary Magazine*—Maury envisioned a glorious future for the republic.[6] His focus was not, however, on O'Sullivan's evangelizing republicanism. Maury saw the nation's destiny through the lenses of commerce, business, and naval power. America, according to Maury, was rightfully "spreading her wings on every sea and sailing before every breeze on the ocean." It was commerce on the sea "which diffuses health and vigor through this happy republic; . . . filling the treasury with revenue; supplying the wants of the government; and ministering to the comforts as well as the necessities of every member of society, from the sea board to the Rocky Mountains—from St. John's and the Lakes to the Gulf of Mexico and the Sabine. It is commerce that furnishes salt for the poor man's bread, and fills the rich man's goblet with wine."[7]

Edward Knight Collins also foresaw a great America. Ever since that spring day in 1838 when he stood on the Battery and fixed his attention on *Sirius* and *Great Western*, Collins was convinced that to achieve the grand future prophesied by writers such as O'Sullivan and Maury, America needed to be strong at sea, and that strength could be had only by embracing steam. Having spent his life in sail, in the winter of 1841

Collins made an astounding proposal. He put forward a plan to build four enormous steamships of 2,500 tons, half again the size of *Great Western* and more than twice the dimensions of *Britannia*, to be powered by engines producing 1,000 horsepower.[8] In a patriotic brag he promised that his steamers would "run off Cunard's packets."[9] Nothing afloat could match these giants in size, speed, or expense. Each ship carried a price tag of $750,000, a sum more than the combined construction costs of the entire Dramatic Line—*Roscius, Siddons, Garrick, Sheridan,* and *Shakespeare*—and five times the cost of *Britannia* and her sisters.[10]

Collins knew such a mammoth project could never gather sufficient private capital. He needed public money. Like "railroads seeking a monopoly or a slice of western lands," or "bankers craving special charters on terms ruinous to their competitors," and "manufacturers asking a tax on incoming goods that would deprive consumers of a choice on prices," Collins turned to Washington.[11] Twice he wrote presenting his plan to President Martin Van Buren, though his timing could hardly have been worse.[12] Not only was Van Buren a Jacksonian Democrat, who as a matter of principle opposed government assistance to private enterprise, but the president was also a lame duck. The previous November the voters had turned against him and elected the Whig William Henry Harrison, who was due to take office on March 4, 1841, barely two weeks away.[13]

Van Buren's political demise could be traced back to Andrew Jackson's war on the Bank of the United States. "Old Hickory's" victory against the bank's president, Nicholas Biddle, had led to rampant financial speculation, and in May 1837, only a few weeks after Van Buren took office, New York City banks shocked the nation by suspending specie payments. The tremors spread quickly, precipitating a nationwide banking collapse during which states repudiated their debts, factories closed, and farm prices and land values fell dramatically. The opposition Whigs heaped blame on the president for the nation's distress, dubbing him "Martin Van Ruin."

As the 1840 election approached, the Whigs, led by Henry Clay and Daniel Webster, played the "Jacksonian card" and nominated William Henry Harrison, a sixty-eight-year-old hero of the War of 1812, for president. To balance the ticket Harrison was joined by John Tyler of

Virginia, a former Democrat. A conglomeration of various factions, strongly supported by business interests and united principally by their hatred of Jackson, the Whigs adopted no platform. The campaign was vicious and personal. Carrying the entire northeast with the exception of New Hampshire, Harrison won by a narrow popular vote, but amassed a wide margin in the Electoral College. Election returns also gave the Whigs fair majorities in both the House and Senate.

Hoping for a better reception, on March 13, 1841, Collins wrote to the new president repeating his proposal that with a three-million-dollar construction loan from the government and an operating subsidy of $15,000 per ship for each round trip he would provide four 2,500-ton steamships beginning monthly service by June 1842—increasing to twice monthly when all four were completed."[14]

Collins's grandiose proposal drew withering criticism from experts. Devastating reports in the American press, which cited the widely respected *British Naval and Military Gazette*, charged that the ships were poorly conceived and that in their passion to race against Cunard, Americans were embracing the "erroneous belief that size gives speed." It was not size that mattered, but "STRENGTH"; especially in steamers "which are to carry passengers . . . as they must be driven through the fiercest gales that rage on the Atlantic." The "scantlings" of Collins's steamers were too lightly built. These vessels were "too large and out of proportionate size, forced through heavy seas [they] will labor and strain even to an alarming degree." British critics pointed out that although Americans were admired for their fast sailing packets, they had yet to learn that a hull designed to be propelled by wind was not necessarily suited for steam, particularly in draft. "In a sailing ship, a good draft of water is necessary, as it enables the ship to hold her course and lay on the wind better, than she would do if she drew a light draft. But a steamer needs not this, as they never use their sails except when the wind is fair, and therefore some of the draft of water could be dispensed with." "Squatting" deep was a severe handicap to paddle wheels since it forced them to dig deeper into the water, inevitably reducing efficiency and increasing fuel consumption. Indeed, it was in the matter of engine efficiency that, according to the *Gazette*, the Americans had committed their most grievous error. According to the writer, "vessels of about

200 feet long and 1000 tons, with 400 horse power, are the best calculated for quick passage across the ocean from point to point, and that
when their dimensions extend beyond this, an increased ratio of power
must be appended, to attain which would be most expensive." Estimates
that it would take only a small increase of seamen and stokers, and only
a few more tons of coal to work a ship of 2,500 tons compared to one of
1,000 tons, was folly. "Machinery and fuel [alone] would occupy nearly
all the space in the vessel."[15] In a final caution, the *Gazette* warned that
"extremes are dangerous, and we advise our New York friends not to
try them."[16]

President Harrison never had a chance to consider these objections and judge Collins's proposal. At his inauguration, March 4, 1841,
a blustery, cold winter day, Harrison spoke outside, not wearing an
overcoat, for nearly two hours—the longest inaugural speech on record.
Pneumonia was the result, and one month later he was dead, his administration the shortest on record.

"His Accidency" John Tyler took the oath on April 6. Since no
president had ever before died in office, Tyler's ascendency was unprec-
edented. Some in Congress, including former president John Quincy
Adams, thought Tyler should be a mere caretaker and should follow the
wishes of the party. Whig leaders Senator Henry Clay of Kentucky and
Secretary of State Daniel Webster agreed; they had intended to manip-
ulate Harrison and now had the same plan for Tyler. The new president,
however, rising to his position, made it clear that he intended to use his
powers. As if that was not offensive enough to the Whig leaders, almost
immediately after his inauguration Tyler, a former Democrat, displayed
alarming recidivist tendencies. Defying the advice of his fellow Whigs,
he refused to support internal improvements and vetoed bills to reestab-
lish a national bank, both measures dear to the party. In retaliation the
Whigs read him out of the party, and in a dramatic public display intended
to humiliate the President, his entire cabinet resigned.[17]

Amidst the political turmoil Collins, the indefatigable promoter,
refused to be deterred. He sent Tyler the proposal he had shared with
Harrison.[18] Though Tyler was not favorably inclined, in Congress Collins
found a sympathetic listener—Congressman Thomas Butler King, chair
of the House Naval Committee. Raised in Massachusetts, King had studied

law with his brother in Pennsylvania, and then moved to St. Simons Island, Georgia, where he practiced law and entered politics.[19] A leading investor in several canals and railroads, and a strong supporter of federal money to support these projects, King had close ties with New York commercial interests. Although a southerner—albeit not a native one— he managed an easy alliance with northern Whigs who shared his political sentiments.

On July 7, 1841, on behalf of the Naval Committee, King brought to the floor H.R.10—"A Bill Making Appropriations for the Pay and Subsistence of the Home Squadron." A routine measure, it called for an appropriation of $789,310 for "two frigates, two sloops, two small vessels and two armed steamers" to protect the nation. It was a pitifully small force, but was in line with Congress's habitually minimal and parsimonious support for the navy.[20] Accompanying the bill, however, was a report from the Whig-controlled committee presented by its chairman.[21] Wrapping his argument in a veil of national security, King crafted a dramatic argument to provide government support for private steamships.

King began by laying out a grim scenario of an America facing threats by sea against which she had no defense.[22] The enemy was Great Britain, which now had a new weapon—steam power. King summoned up fearful images. Because the United States lacked sufficient naval strength, "an enemy employing this new and formidable description of force" could range the coast with impunity. "Our trade," he continued, would be "liable to great interruption, and our merchants to great losses abroad." Land fortification in a condition "too notorious for remark . . . could not defend us against the armed steamers of an enemy." Lest any of his southern colleagues dismiss the threat as one being conjured up for northern interests that stood to benefit from naval shipbuilding contracts, he reminded the House that there were numerous harbors on the Atlantic coast and Gulf of Mexico—but not a fort, from Charleston to Mobile, in a condition to fire a gun. In a comment sure to gain their attention he warned his fellow congressmen, "In the event of a war with France or Great Britain, the fortifications at Pensacola, and perhaps others might be seized and held by the enemy, or any of our unprotected harbors might be entered by fleets of armed steamers, loaded with black troops from the West Indies, to annoy and plunder the country . . . These troops are disciplined and commanded by white officers, and, no doubt, designed to form a most important portion of the force to be employed in any future contest that may arise between Great Britain and the United States." Every part of the nation, according to King, was at risk. "The northern portion of the Atlantic coast . . . would by no means be secure against the rapid movements of such an enemy. The harbor of New York itself might be entered through the inlet at Amboy, and Staten Island Sound, and the fortifications of the Narrows entirely avoided. The city might be sacked or laid under contribution." Indeed, "there is not a harbor on the whole coast, however well defended against sailing ships of an enemy, that these steamers might not enter." Without foundation the report alleged that Great Britain was taking measures "to keep afloat and actively employed on our northern coast . . . a large number of steamers of the largest class, many of them with guns onboard, and the others at all times ready to receive them." The steamers belonged to Cunard.

> These steamers are all in rapid progress of construction; they are to be about 1500 tons burden, and to receive engines of 500-horse power each. Those that have been launched [*Britannia*, *Acadia*, *Caledonia*, *Columbia*] are estimated to be in all respects equal to sixty gun frigates. Thus it is said, the country will be doubly served, and while it pays to the Mail Company £240,000 per annum for the transport of mails, it will defray, by the same payment, the annual charges of the largest and most powerful steam fleet in the world.

Supported by a coal depot at Halifax, once these civilian steamers were converted to warships, they would be able to attack the American coast "before the least preparation can be made to meet them."

The technology of steam had brought astonishing changes, according to the report, "the most formidable vessels the world has ever seen are employed in the transportation of mail, passengers and freight . . . If these vessels can be rendered profitable in time of peace, the security they will afford to persons and property . . . will render them indispensable in time of war." Given such a threat, "it therefore becomes a question of the most urgent and vital importance to the people and Government of the United States, how they can soonest and best provide the means of meeting this new and powerful auxiliary in maritime war."

The report's conclusion was clear. The committee, citing "a gentleman of great respectability and much experience in commercial affairs, and particularly in steam navigation [i.e., Collins]," recommended the establishment of "lines of four steamers from Boston to Havre, of four from New York to Liverpool, of three from Norfolk, via Charleston and Savannah, to Havana, and of three from New Orleans to Havana." It was a plan based on the fanciful notion that with a "guaranty of the Government of less than one million per annum," there was a moral certainty of "receiving back more than half of it from postage on letters and papers, immediately, and the whole in a few years."

H.R.10 passed easily in the House by a vote of 115 to 93; it moved through the Senate with no recorded dissent. When the bill reached the president, he signed it, making no comment on the attached report. Previously, Congress had funded a National Road, but this was the first time they had debated—and shown interest—in using federal government money to subsidize private steamships.

Even though they did not secure support, Collins and King had made a breakthrough and did not give up. For nearly three years the issue remained dormant, but then in the waning days of Tyler's administration they received some unexpected help. In the election of 1844, the Democratic candidate, James K. Polk, ran on a platform of Texas annexation and an American claim, in the face of British opposition, to all of the Oregon country, later to be wrapped into the jingoistic slogan "Manifest Destiny." Polk's campaign rallied the Democrats, stirred the nation, and split the Whigs. When the returns gave him a substantial victory, Tyler interpreted it as an endorsement for Texas annexation. With rumors floating about that the old meddler Great Britain might have designs on Texas, Tyler, a southerner who did not want a potential slave state to slip away, decided it was too risky to delay action until the new administration took office. In his last annual message to Congress, December 3, 1844, the lame duck president took a bold stand: despite the threat of war with Mexico, he would not back down. "It is," he told Congress, "the will of both the people and the States that Texas shall be annexed

to the Union promptly and immediately."[23] Unable to summon the
two-thirds needed to ratify a treaty with Texas, he proposed a joint resolution that required only a majority vote. The resolution passed both
houses, annexing Texas, and Tyler signed it on March 1, 1845, three
days before he left office.[24]

In the same message by which he laid down the gauntlet to Mexico,
Tyler also sent a subtle warning to Great Britain. While the president's
record at home had been lackluster and contentious, Tyler was an advocate of expansionism and free trade and had shown considerable vigor
in foreign affairs. Many of his moves were aimed at checking British
influence. In addition to parrying Great Britain over Texas and supporting
Polk's position on Oregon, he negotiated a treaty with China that challenged British dominance in that region and gave warning that Her
Majesty's government ought not to interfere in Hawaiian affairs where
the United States had special interests. Reporting to Congress before
leaving office, Tyler warned that to defend her interests abroad America
needed both a naval and maritime presence. While "other nations
have added large numbers of steamships" to their fleets, America lagged
behind. To defend herself and expand commerce, Tyler argued, the
nation requires "an extensive steam marine." "I can not too strongly
urge the policy of authorizing the establishment of a line of steamships
regularly to ply between this country and foreign ports." How better to
accomplish this than to follow "the example of the British government."

For once the Whigs agreed with Tyler, and they rushed to get a bill to
his desk. On January 8, 1845, Senator William D. Merrick, a Maryland
Whig and chair of the Committee on the Post Office and Post Roads,
brought in "a Bill to provide for the Transportation of the Mail Between
the United States and Foreign Countries." The bill passed on February
14 and made it through the House on March 3.

The bill gave the authority to the Postmaster General of the United
States, at his discretion, "to contract for the transportation of the United
States' mail between any ports of the United States and a port or ports,
of any foreign power" with the stipulation that the mail had to be carried
"in American vessels by American citizens." Notably, the bill did not
require the Postmaster "to contract," and the timing was left to "whenever, in his opinion, the public interest would be promoted." Bidders

who proposed "to carry the mail in a steam ship or ships" and who agreed in the event of an emergency "to deliver . . . their ships . . . to the United States . . . for the purpose of being converted into a vessel or vessels of war," were to be given preference.[25]

Cave Johnson, a former congressman from Tennessee and President Polk's Postmaster General, entered office charged with administering an act he had voted against.[26] A close friend to the President, Johnson knew little about the functions of his office other than that it offered massive opportunities for patronage.[27] Like most Democrats he had long preached economy in government. With the last-minute measure of March 3, Congress and Tyler had undermined Johnson's plans to reduce expenditures. Not only was the Postmaster invited to award costly contracts, but in the same measure Congress had also reduced postage rates "to the lowest scale in the history of the department."[28] Caught between the Scylla of expense and Charybdis of revenue, Johnson, relying on the freedom of action given him by the bill, steered a political midcourse and did nothing.

While Cave Johnson dug in his heels, members of Congress who favored government assistance for American steamships pressed ahead. Trying to skirt the touchy ideological issue of the propriety of using public money to support private enterprise, they reminded their opponents that while these steamers would be built for civilian purposes, they could be converted easily into ships of war. The argument was timely. By late 1845, war was already looming with Mexico. Not only had the United States annexed Texas, but President Polk insisted that the state's southern boundary was not the Nueces River as historically accepted, but the Rio Grande. When Mexico objected, in January 1846 Polk dispatched General Zachary Taylor with a force of 3,500 soldiers to the Rio Grande. Notwithstanding his concern for economy and a mounting deficit in his department, Johnson—faced with the threat of war—on October 4, 1845, invited proposals to "Carry Mails to Europe, The Gulf of Mexico, and the Pacific" under the authority of the act of March 3, 1845. Seven different routes were noted. At the top of the list was "From New York to Liverpool," semimonthly for eight months, and once a month for the four months of winter (total of twenty round trips). While the proposals should specify the mode of conveyance, whether by steamship or sailing packet, Johnson made it clear Congress had ordered preference to be given to steamships "convertible into ships-of-war." Bids were due by January 31, 1846. Contracts would be awarded by May 1, 1846, with service due to begin May 1, 1848.[29]

Collins moved quickly to prepare his bid on the New York to Liverpool leg. To provide the required semimonthly and monthly service he estimated that four steamships would be required at a total cost of three million dollars. Collins scurried to find investors, including Brown, Shipley Co. of Liverpool, which had long acted on behalf of the Dramatic Line. Their reaction was succinct. Steamships "never will pay."[30] Left to his own devices, Collins announced that he was offering to sell the Dramatic Line to raise funds, but no one stepped forward to buy his packets.[31] Unable to amass sufficient capital, Collins missed the submission date.

By January 31, 1846, Johnson had four bids in hand for the European mails.[32] They included Junius Smith, one of the principal investors in the *British Queen*; A. D. Mann and A. G. Sloo, both New York businessmen with experience in packets; and Edward Mills, a little-known speculator who with several other men had formed the Ocean Steam Navigation Company. Mills and Sloo both bid $400,000 but the latter called for fewer voyages.[33] With the exception of Smith, whose connections were with England, the other three bidders proposed Havre and Bremen as destinations.

After considerable discussion, Johnson selected the bid from Edward Mills. Several of his partners had financial interests in packets. To please them and avoid competition with existing packet lines, Mills ignored Liverpool—New York's most important trading partner—and instead proposed a route to Bremen via Cowes.[34] In the *New York Herald*, Collins's friend James Gordon Bennett questioned why the contract was not given to men with more shipping experience, while the *Washington Union* likened Mills and his associates to "a nest of Wall Street stock-jobbers."[35]

Johnson's controversial acceptance of Mills's bid left him, embarrassingly, without the promise of steamship service on the most important Atlantic route—New York to Liverpool. From his days in Congress, Postmaster Johnson was well aware of Collins's interest in the Liverpool route, and so he arranged a meeting in Washington, which took place on March 6, just as he was delivering his letter to the House announcing Mills's contract.[36] Collins assured Johnson that he was prepared on the Post Office's terms to offer service to Liverpool, semimonthly for eight months and during winter once a month, in ships of 2,000 tons and 1,000 horsepower.[37]

Collins pointed out to the Postmaster that this proposal was almost identical to the one he had shared with Presidents Harrison and Tyler. To fulfill the contract Collins requested an annual subsidy of $385,000, ($19,250 per round trip). He proposed to build five steamers "which vessels shall be built for great speed, and sufficiently strong for naval purposes." The first four would be ready in eighteen months and the fifth as soon as possible. Johnson's principal interest was improving mail service. Hitting hard on that point, Collins reminded Johnson that before the Cunard steamers appeared, the United States had carried the bulk of transatlantic mails. Cunard's steamships, with their speed and regularity, had upended that practice, and to secure that advantage the British Post Office charged higher rates for mail arriving in American ships. Anxious to end the discrimination, Johnson was negotiating with the British; but as long as Cunard, providing regular and speedy transit, dominated mail carriage, Her Majesty's government had little incentive to compromise. "It is a well-known fact," Collins wrote, "that England is now the central point from which our European and Asiatic news is received." Without a competitor to Cunard, Johnson had no leverage. Collins' proposal promised to improve the odds for a postal treaty.[38] Seeing an opportunity to exert pressure on the British, Johnson decided to capitalize on the wide discretion Congress had given him. He ignored the January 31 deadline and forwarded Collins's bid to Congress.

Opposition to subsidies, particularly among southern Democrats, remained strong in Congress, and the annual Post Office appropriations bill brought to the Senate in June 1846 included no funding for the mail contracts. Senator John Niles of Connecticut, former Postmaster General under Van Buren, moved an appropriation of $25,000 each for Collins and Mills. Heated debate followed. Senator William Allen, a Democrat of Ohio, complained bitterly about the government becoming involved with "moneyed connections" and objected to the "injustice of endowing a line from New York."[39] Despite objections the measure passed in the Senate along partisan lines by a narrow vote of 27 to 24. Twenty-one of the 24 Whig members supported the amendment; nearly all the Democrats opposed it.[40] In the Democrat-controlled House, the result was decidedly different. Since Mills had already laid down a vessel, *Washington*—a ship described by one critic as "about as ugly a specimen of steamship building as had ever been seen"—the House agreed to pay him the $25,000.[41] Collins, on the other hand, had yet to begin any construction or sign a contract with the government and received no money.[42]

Shortly after the second session of the 29th Congress convened (December 7, 1846), the chairman of the Senate Naval Committee, Senator John Fairfield, a Democrat from Maine, described by the *New York Tribune* as "not a man of extraordinary talents . . . but with an aptitude for affairs," reported out a bill from his committee authorizing an appropriation of "one million dollars for the building and equipping of four naval steamships."[43] In the midst of a war with Mexico that had been declared May 13, 1846, the bill rode easily through the Senate and went on to the House, where Collins's friend Thomas Butler King was ready to pounce. The bill arrived in the House on February 15, 1847, and was sent immediately to the Naval Committee chaired by King. Two weeks later, March 3, he reported the bill back—supporting the steamship appropriation, but with amendments. Unhappy with Postmaster Johnson's delaying tactics and his granting a contract to Mills and not to Collins, King demonstrated his political clout by adding an amendment that transferred authority over civilian mail steamers from the Post Office to the Secretary of the Navy, who was directed

> to accept, on the part of the government of the United States, the proposals of E.K. Collins and his associates, of the City of New York, submitted to the Postmaster-General, and dated Washington, March 6, eighteen hundred and forty-six, for the transportation of the United States mail between New York and Liverpool.[44]

In Congress, a body increasingly divided by sectional interests, King sought to assure the members that the five steamers awarded to Collins were indeed an important asset to the nation as a whole and not simply a gift to the North. To guarantee his claim he laid down specific requirements. The ships were to be "constructed under the inspection of a naval constructor in the employ of the Navy Department, and shall be so constructed so as to render them convertible, at the least possible cost, into war steamers of the first class." They were "at all times" to be under the authority of the Navy Department. To watch over navy interests, these ships would take "on board four passed midshipmen of the United States Navy, who shall serve as watch officers, and be suitably accommodated without charge to the government."

Debate was fierce, but since it was the last day of the second session of the 29th Congress, members were anxious to leave. When King moved to close debate, the House agreed. Hannibal Hamlin of Maine, a strong supporter, moved the previous question and the bill passed, signed by President Polk the same day, March 3, 1847. The only business left in the late night scramble to finish the session's work was a measure to transfer a strip of land along the Ohio River to the city of Madison, Indiana, and a resolution "for lighting with gas the Capitol and Capitol grounds." Both passed, and Congress adjourned.[45]

King was a hero, and on Wednesday evening, March 23, New York's Astor House was well filled at a dinner to honor the Georgia Whig. Horace Greeley's *New York Tribune* reported that "rarely if ever has so imposing and honorable a tribute been paid by our City to any public benefactor, to any Statesman holding a position short of the highest in the land, as that paid last evening to Hon. Thomas Butler King."[46] Everyone of importance was present: "The Bench, the Bar, the Press, the Halls of Legislation . . . our most distinguished merchants." Known for its elegance and its extensive menu, the Astor House outdid itself. To the "sound of enlivening music . . . the guests were treated to an "elaborate dinner." Collins sat in triumph.

"After the cloth was removed," the toasts began.

In a speech lasting forty-five minutes, "frequently interrupted by irrepressible bursts of applause, with cheers and the ringing of glasses," King "compared the sagacious and wide grasping views of the English Government for the protection and preservation of its Commercial Marine, with the past indolence and inattention of our own." It was essential to act "to prevent a monopoly by England of the Commerce of the World."

When a speaker made reference to the "character and professional conduct of E. K. Collins, Esq. who has contracted with the Government to build the line of steamers," the audience called upon him to speak. "Mr. Collins," according to the writer in the *Tribune*, "wasted no words; he never wastes words or time, but made appropriate answer."

Collins could ill afford to "waste time." His proposal of March 6, 1846, had been far too general to please his new partner, the United States Navy. The two parties would have to agree on design and performance standards, as well as arrangements for payment. Almost eight months would pass, until on November 1, 1847, Collins and the Navy were ready to sign.

As the evening at the Astor House drew to a close, on the other side of the city, along the East River, Mills's steamer *Washington* was completing her fitting-out.[47] Launched in June 1847, and joined in March of the next year by her sister *Hermann*, the ships proved to be poorly built, clumsy, and slow.

Aside from poor construction and inept management, Mills and his partners had fallen into the same error as the British owners of *Great Western* and *British Queen*. Napier had warned, and Cunard had proven, that to maintain regular transatlantic service a line needed not only good ships well-run, but several of them. Two ships were totally inadequate. The *Herald* dismissed the Mills's Ocean Steam Navigation Company as a failure.[48]

On December 28, 1847, a dreary but unusually warm Monday morning, *Hibernia* poked her nose through the Narrows to become the first Cunarder to enter New York Harbor.[49] Her destination, however, was not Manhattan, where the American steamers docked; instead, she held a course steadily northbound to Paulus Hook, New Jersey (Jersey City).

Cunard would have preferred a Manhattan location, but the laws of New York prohibited "aliens" from holding or conveying real estate.[50] New Jersey had no such restrictions, allowing the Associates of the Jersey Company to offer him facilities on their side of the river—two new piers, located on Hudson Street at the foot of Grand Street, and stretching out into the river for 300 feet, built at a cost of $80,000.

Cunard agreed to a ten-year lease. At the head of the piers, the Jersey Company had erected "two large frame buildings designed for storing coal, flanked on each end by a brick storehouse."[51] Close by was the ferry connecting to Manhattan, and behind the piers was a rail line convenient for passengers and mail. For months, workmen had been scurrying to finish the piers while coasting schooners had been delivering tons of coal. The work was barely finished by the time *Hibernia* cast her lines to shore.

New Yorkers did manage one small victory over their New Jersey rivals. At first the Associates had arranged for the Newark customs district to oversee clearances on the Jersey pier. With a plethora of appointed positions (weighers, gaugers, cashiers, clerks, inspectors, etc.), customs houses were a rich mine of patronage. The thought of those spoils slipping though their hands was too much for New York's political establishment, particularly the Collector of Custom and former mayor Cornelius Van Wyck Lawrence. An emergency application was made to Secretary of the Treasury Robert Walker to transfer authority to the New York district. Walker succumbed, and "notwithstanding the opposition" and in defiance of geography, the Jersey City piers came under jurisdiction of the New York Collector.[52]

While noting her arrival, New York's merchants gave *Hibernia* a tepid welcome—nothing compared to what Boston had done for *Britannia*. The city's merchants hosted a dinner for *Hibernia*'s Captain Alexander Ryrie, but newspapers made only brief mention of the event. By the extravagant standards set in Boston for *Unicorn* and *Britannia* it was a lackluster affair—no bands, songs, poems, or over-the-top decorations.[53] Compared even to the attendees who feted Congressman King, the list of guests was quite ordinary. When the host, James DePeyster Ogden, president of the New York Life Insurance Company, rose to speak, he sensed the uneasiness in the room. Rather than celebrating *Hibernia*'s arrival with the usual hyperbolic rhetoric expected at such events, he took a different tone, and assured Ryrie "that the establishment of a Cunard Line to New York would not be looked upon with envious spirit by the American merchants, or regarded with any other than the most kindly feelings."[54] A few days following the dinner, the merchants learned that Edward Cunard, son of the line's founder, would be the company's agent in New York, a sign of the importance Cunard assigned to the new connection. Edward established the firm's office near the tip of Manhattan, at Bowling Green. His personal residence, however, was across the harbor on Staten Island, where he built an elaborate Italianate villa from which "he could watch his ships enter New York Harbor."[55]

Although scheduled to depart on Saturday morning—New Year's Day—*Hibernia* remained at her mooring, held fast by an impenetrable fog. Finally, getting under way on January 2, 1848, she steamed down the harbor carrying "36 passengers and $300,000 in specie" and "diplomatic dispatches from the British embassy." As her paddles splashed and a cannon saluted from the Jersey shore, silence prevailed on Manhattan.[56]

With reluctant admiration, the *New York Herald* was forced to admit that the Cunard Line was making, and "deserved to make, money. They have a glorious harvest before them."[57]

CHAPTER TEN

Competition Begins: Collins versus Cunard

HIBERNIA'S MAIDEN VOYAGE inaugurated Cunard's regular monthly service to New York. Three weeks after her arrival, on the 18th of January, *Cambria* docked, and on the 18th of February *Hibernia* returned, followed in March by *Cambria*. With the advent of spring bringing better weather, Cunard increased the service to twice-a-month departures. Cunard's piers at Jersey City bustled with activity, while across Manhattan on the East River, after considerable delay, work finally got under way on Collins's steamers.

Although the Act of March 3, 1847, had directed the Secretary of the Navy to contract with E. K. Collins for the construction of "four first-class sea-going steamships," Secretary John Y. Mason showed little urgency to move forward. A Virginia Democrat, Mason viewed the order from the Whig-dominated Congress as meddling in his business for the advantage of northern Whig interests.[1] Officers in the service, while fiercely opposed to the secretary's parsimony, were equally resistant to the Collins contract. They doubted that civilian steamships could ever be useful in the navy. In their opinion, no amount of "conversion" could ever make civilian vessels into anything more than what they were intended to be—mail and passenger carriers. To them, the arrangement with Collins was an insincere nod aimed at placating political interests.[2]

From London, where he now spent much of his time, Samuel Cunard followed the debates in Congress with considerable interest. Looking back on his own early experience he shared the opinion of the American naval officers. When asked about the naval viability of his steamers he noted that in his first contract with the Admiralty there was no mention given that his vessels might be "made available for war purposes." In subsequent contracts, he gave in to political pressure and did include such a clause, but, he explained, "I always considered it of no use to the Government," since "the two services cannot be combined." Cunard warned that when the standards of naval construction—heavy framing (often with costly material such as live oak), thick hull planking, reinforced decks, and powerful engines—were applied to civilian vessels, the result would be a "Ship too expensive for Mercantile purposes."[3]

Mason was in no hurry to please Congress. With neither the secretary nor the officer corps in favor of what had been forced upon them, Collins's contract moved through the maddening labyrinth of the Navy Department bureaucracy at a snail's pace. Finally, after nearly eight months of review, Mason summoned Collins to Washington. On November 1, 1847, Collins arrived at the office of the secretary accompanied by his financial backers James and Stewart Brown.

Cousins, the Browns represented the American side of a transatlantic partnership that dominated Anglo-American trade. James's father, Alexander Brown, had been a linen auctioneer in Belfast, Ireland, who for political reasons fled to Baltimore in 1800, and settled in the city with his wife and four sons. Alexander continued in the linen trade and in 1808, with an eye to expanding his operation, he dispatched his eldest son, William, to Liverpool. William did well, and in succeeding years, while his son George remained with him in Baltimore, Alexander spread the firm's influence by positioning John in Philadelphia and James at New York.[4] In the years following the War of 1812, the firm thrived as it drifted away from the linen business to concentrate on the far more promising cotton trade. Alexander established a web of agents in the American South at Charleston, Savannah, Mobile, and New Orleans, who dispatched cotton to Liverpool consigned to William. By the late 1820s William was England's "largest cotton importer." Through his cotton business William became acquainted with a number of American packet lines, including Collins's Dramatic Line, establishing close and often personal relationships with visiting captains from whom he gleaned the latest commercial gossip while entertaining them "at the best hostelry in Liverpool, renowned for its turtle soup."[5]

When Alexander died in 1834, William emerged as the senior partner; but, given the three thousand miles of ocean separating them, the brothers moved with considerable leeway in their particular spheres. Nonetheless, the rise of Liverpool and New York gave William and James special status, and when George and John retired from the firm, the center of authority in America moved to New York with James at the helm.[6] In Liverpool, wanting more time to devote to his political career, William took into partnership Joseph Shipley, an American Quaker from Wilmington, Delaware, who had been associated with the firm for more than a decade. Renaming the firm Brown, Shipley and Company, William left the day-to-day operations in his partner's hands while he pursued a career in politics and philanthropy.

Under Shipley's guidance and with William's support, the Liverpool branch of the firm expanded greatly, moving beyond cotton to become a "large merchant house," which specialized in complicated international currency transactions and letters of credit. Always cautious, and holding its reputation as one of its most precious assets, the firm adopted rigid rules and standards to make certain that "foreign sellers highly valued the reliability of the Browns's guarantees." Avoiding undue risk, they put strict limits on any particular investment and held a diversified portfolio.[7]

As the firm prospered it accumulated considerable capital, much of which they held in reserve for contingencies. Thanks, however, to improved rapid and regular communication provided by steamships, times between transactions shortened and risk fell, reducing the need for hoarding large reserves. William Bowen, Brown's agent in Philadelphia noted, "Now the steamers go so quick there is very little gain in interest."[8] In determining where to invest their excess cash, James in New York and William in Liverpool had very different views.[9]

From the conservative British perspective, it was best to keep "an essentially defensive position; that is, the purchase of low risk securities with appropriately low yields which would serve as secondary reserve in emergencies."[10] It was important, the firm believed, to be as liquid as possible, avoiding long-term investments—"lockups"—that tied up capital. In a letter to James, William made his position clear. "The more I think of it . . . the more I think it is desirable to get every shilling unlocked from fixed property."[11] The English partners were also nervous about any venture that might draw them into direct management of an enterprise, a burden for which they had no appetite or experience. In terms of what was happening on the other side of the Atlantic, while they viewed "the advancement of the United States as certain," they had serious doubts about Americans, who they described as an "extravagant and wasteful people."[12]

James Brown was Liverpool's chief worry. Through their success in creating a highly efficient and profitable enterprise the English partners, Shipley in particular, had built a solid institutional environment that freed the partners of managerial duties while at the same time putting an immense amount of cash into their hands without careful oversight. James was a dabbler who was always on the hunt for "situations that offered the potential of higher returns."[13] He was, in the opinion of his Liverpool partners, overly fond of highly speculative investments in railroads, ironworks, and real estate, and he had a worrisome tendency to mess about in the management of the companies in which he invested. He often made bad choices. Repeatedly, but always politely, William cautioned James against reckless "expansion of outside business interests." He paid little heed. When James informed his brother that he had not only invested heavily in the Collins Line, but also (contrary to the firm's policy) had undertaken managerial responsibilities and drawn his cousin Stewart into the enterprise, his elder brother dropped the veil of conviviality. "I do not know," he wrote to James, "when I was more surprised, astonished and mortified than . . . to find that you had become principals in Collins' Steam Boat Scheme."[14]

At the meeting with the Navy Secretary, Collins and the Browns agreed, repeating the 1846 proposal to carry the United States mail between New York and Liverpool twice each month during eight months of the year, and once a month during the winter months of December, January, February, and March. In return, the government pledged to pay the Line "the sum of three hundred and eighty five thousand dollars per annum, payable quarterly yearly," but not before "Collins and his associates shall have actually commenced the performance of the mail service." If a trip was not made or delayed, the Line would forfeit "pro rata pay." The ships were to be "not less than two thousand tons measurement, and of one thousand horse-power each, to be built for speed, and sufficiently strong for war purposes." Four of the steamers were to be ready for service by May 1, 1849, and a fifth to see service "as early as possibly practicable." Appended to the contract were two "Schedules" which gave full specifications for hull and machinery. Although the 5,000-word contract was written tightly, tucked away in the body of the document was a clause that allowed the builders "the liberty to vary from [the specifications] as in their judgment may seem necessary and proper." The "necessary and proper" clause would prove important.[15]

Although it was generally believed that these three men were signing for the "Collins Line," in fact at the moment no such corporate entity existed. The three were signing as "Associates," and although they now had a signed contract and a generous subsidy they still had to raise sufficient capital, estimated at $2 million, to build the promised steamers. Confident that they would find the money, the three men hurried back to New York. Six weeks after the Washington meeting, on December 13, 1847, the three partners organized a trust and invited William Wetmore and Elisha Riggs to join them as trustees.[16] Both Wetmore and Riggs had extensive experience in international finance, including associations with George Peabody and Co. (Wetmore named his son George Peabody Wetmore), a London-based firm and the Browns's chief competition. Wetmore, from St. Albans, Vermont, had made a fortune in the China trade as a partner in the firm of Wetmore and Cryder, and was one of America's leading merchants and bankers.[17] Born in Maryland, Riggs was a Georgetown dry goods dealer who in 1814 took into partnership George Peabody, then a young man from South Danvers, Massachusetts. Riggs and Peabody moved to Baltimore and eventually opened branches in Philadelphia and New York. In 1829 the firm dissolved in an amicable fashion. Riggs relocated to New York City, retiring to an elegant residence at Number 5 Bowling Green while Peabody moved to London where, with the help of the Browns and Junius Morgan (father of J. P.), he built the most important American trading house in the city.[18] With contract in hand, subsidy assured, and the backing of some of the most powerful men in American finance, Collins was ready to begin construction.

Although he had decades of experience building and operating sailing packets, Edward Knight Collins had never built or managed steamships. Samuel Cunard had had little to fall back upon either, but at least he had Robert Napier, Clyde Bank builders, and the Admiralty to advise him. On the scale that Collins proposed to build and operate steamships no one in America could provide him with a model or a guide. The "sad" performance of the New York–built steamers *Hermann* and *Washington* demonstrated that East River shipbuilders and foundries had much to learn about constructing massive and complicated seagoing machines.[19] Recognizing the local want of experience in design and construction, Collins persuaded the Navy Department to relieve the navy's Senior Chief Engineer John Faron from his regular duties and dispatch him to London, Liverpool, and Glasgow to gather information from experienced shipbuilders, foundries, and shipowners.[20]

Faron left New York in late December 1848. After enduring a winter crossing, he spent several weeks visiting offices, yards, and foundries in London, Liverpool, and Glasgow. By late March, carrying extensive notes and drawings, he booked passage home aboard Cunard's newly launched *Niagara*. Eager to see her machinery at work, Faron managed to pry permission from the ship's commander and chief engineer to go below to observe firsthand the powerful engines propelling the ship across the Atlantic. As he made his way past the trimmers and firemen, he felt the blasting heat of the furnaces, which burned nearly fifty tons of coal per day. He admired the work of the engines, the quiet up and down rhythmic motion of piston rods encased in cylinders more than ten feet high and ninety inches in diameter, connected to shafts two feet wide extending port and starboard, turning immense paddle wheels and driving the ship forward.[21] As he drew close to the machinery from a setting on a safety valve, Faron noticed immediately that contrary to what had been published in the press, *Niagara*'s engines, with ninety-inch diameter cylinders, were operating at a maximum of thirteen pounds of pressure, not the reported ten. Collins's ships, built to compete with

Cunard, were designed to operate at ten pounds. To win the race at sea Faron knew that the American steamers would need more power. He took careful notes, and as soon as he landed in New York he hurried to advise Collins of this new information.[22] Against the advice of many who thought the change unnecessary, and at the risk of increased cost, Collins ordered his cylinders enlarged to a diameter of ninety-five inches with a stroke of nine feet, making them the largest ever cast and powerful enough to beat the Cunarders.[23] Impressed by Faron's report, Collins offered him the post of superintending engineer for the new line.[24]

Unlike his sailing packets (*Sheridan*, *Garrick*, *Shakespeare*, *Roscius*, *Siddons*), whose Anglophile names had been chosen to attract British favor, Collins's steamers were being built to challenge and beat the skilled and experienced Cunard Line. It was a competition that put the honor of the "whole American people" on the line.[25] Their status demanded grand names that reflected the nation's aspirations. Claiming that since Cunard had taken the continents he would take the oceans, Collins announced that his ships would be christened *Atlantic*, *Pacific*, *Arctic*, and *Baltic*.[26] To further twist the lion's tail, Collins made it known that he was painting the stacks of his ships black with a red top, reversing Cunard's color scheme.[27]

Collins awarded the building contracts for *Atlantic* and *Arctic* to the yard of William H. Brown, who was well known for his finely designed packets, as well as for building several steamboats for Hudson River service. Ocean steamships, however, were a new venture for the firm. Contracts for *Pacific* and *Baltic* went to Collins's old friends and partners in the packet business, Brown and Bell. Stillman, Allen Co. (AKA Novelty Iron Works) provided machinery for *Atlantic* and *Arctic*, while the Allaire works supplied machinery for *Pacific* and *Baltic*.

Having grown up in the harsh environment of Cape Cod, fought pirates in the Caribbean, outwitted his rivals on South Street, built one of the country's most famous packet lines, navigated the dangerous political waters of Congress, and allied himself with some of the most powerful financial interests in the Atlantic world, Edward Knight Collins stood ready to conquer the oceans. His triumph, however, had strings attached. Since he was drawing from the public purse, government oversight was required. Well aware of Collins's blunt and independent persona, the Navy Department needed a government monitor who would be a worthy match for him. They found just such an officer in Commodore Matthew Calbraith Perry, appointing him "Superintendent in Chief."[28]

Nicknamed "Old Bruin" for his harsh demeanor and bellowing command voice, Perry was "imperious," "obstinate as a bull," and "as close as an oyster."[29] He was, in short, the perfect officer to supervise Edward Knight Collins, a man much like himself. A strong advocate of steam power, Perry hailed from a distinguished naval family. He had entered the service shortly before the War of 1812, commanded the African squadron, and served as Commodore of the Gulf Squadron in the Mexican War. At the time of his appointment he was Commodore of the Home Squadron, flying his blue pennant from the frigate *Cumberland* moored at the Brooklyn Navy Yard.

Perry's instructions were vague. The Commodore was "to exercise . . . a parental official influence," and "watch the progress of construction . . . suggesting such timely arrangements as will render them [i.e., steamships] more readily available for vessels of war."[30] Although he was described by some as "Meddlesome Matty," in fact he left most of the day-to-day supervision to his assistant, a well-known retired New York packet captain, William Skiddy.[31]

Skiddy and Collins had a less-than-pleasant relationship. Captain Skiddy had once commanded Collins's *Garrick*, and had been dismissed by the owner from his post after a disappointingly long voyage from Liverpool to New York. Skiddy took the dismissal well enough, acknowledging that "Collins had a right to place who he pleased in his Ship," but then added in remembering the incident that Collins in his usual brusque manner had not given him "the courtesy due to my standing and character."[32]

Perry's observations on Collins's ships were generally positive, although he made it clear that had he been present at the beginning he would have done things better, but by the time he arrived *Atlantic* and *Pacific* were well under way and little could be altered. He did note, however, that the steamers were "extravagantly showy."[33]

Construction did not go smoothly. Taking the instructions given him by the directors to "manage the ships as if they were his own,"[34] Collins meddled everywhere, insisting on a number of changes. His experience in the New Orleans trade, for example, convinced him that a flat-bottomed hull, rather than the conventional rounded version, was preferable for speed and carrying capacity and would at the same time provide an interior space better shaped to accommodate the huge forty-ton cast iron bedplate to which the machinery was to be bolted. Fearful about the stress on the hull caused by tough winter passages and vibrations from the machinery, he ordered expensive diagonal iron framing to reinforce the wooden frames.[35]

While keels were being laid Collins and his fellow trustees sought additional investors. In the meantime costs were escalating rapidly. Collins was running out of money and bills were going unpaid. He turned to Congress and the navy for an advance on his subsidy; once again Congressman King carried the day, and despite opposition Congress agreed to advance him $25,000 per month for each ship, the total not to exceed one year's payment, $385,000. Solon Borland, a Democratic Senator from Arkansas, later remarked that "Mr. Collins's tongue seems to have been gifted with the spell of the open sesame to the heart of Congress."[36] The navy ordered payment, but also attached a lien on the ships as security.

Even with the advance Collins was burning through cash at an alarming rate. To raise additional capital, on January 13, 1849, Collins announced that the trustees had applied to the state for a corporate charter allowing them to have a public offering of stock. On April 11, 1849, the New York legislature constituted "a body corporate, by the name of The New York and Liverpool United States Mail Steam Ship Company." Capital stock was set at "two millions of dollars" which included the $385,000 the government had pledged in annual subsidy.[37] The five trustees, referred to as commissioners, were authorized to "receive subscriptions for such capital stock." As soon as a million dollars had been subscribed, at a price of $2,000 per share, the act required them to call a stockholders meeting to elect five directors.[38]

The market took 538 shares. Of that number James Brown purchased 100 shares and his relatives nearly the same amount. Collins bought ninety, Riggs fifty, and Wetmore twenty-five. George Peabody took a token five shares. Between them the Brown family and Collins held 278 shares, more than enough to ensure control of the company.[39] At their first meeting the thirty shareholders elected the "commissioners" to be directors and James Brown, the line's largest investor, as president. On paper the sale of shares brought in $1.076 million; however, since investors were allowed to pay over time, the sale did little to alleviate the immediate cash flow problem.

With spotty records it is difficult to sort out the company's finances. Prior to the stock offering it is likely that the trustees, the Browns in particular, had provided substantial backing—the exact amount is unknown, although the United States Attorney for New York did certify that the five trustees were "sufficient to respond in the sum of five hundred thousand dollars."[40] While the directors struggled, expenses piled up as it became increasingly obvious that the total price of the four ships would far exceed the capital available. Since construction costs were not being paid from public money (the $25,000 monthly advance on the subsidy notwithstanding), Collins and his associates offered no public accounting. Nonetheless, engines for the USS *Powhattan*, under construction at the Norfolk navy yard and comparable in size and power to those aboard the Collins steamers, cost nearly $400,000. Hull construction for the civilian steamers was slightly less than *Powhattan*'s, bringing the entire figure for each of Collins's ships to nearly $800,000.[41] While certain naval features of *Powhattan* might have added expense, Collins's extravagant interior design also increased costs.[42] To meet the enormous bills, in addition to proceeds from sale of stock and subsidy advances, the firm borrowed at least two million dollars from private investors. Even with additional financing, however, the line remained on the brink of insolvency to the point that one of their chief vendors, Novelty Iron Works, warned Collins that they were ready to stop all work on *Atlantic* "unless we receive money."[43] The Collins Line was in debt "before it ever earned a dollar."[44]

Adding to their woes was the slow pace of construction. The port was humming and New York yards were overwhelmed with work. Skilled labor was in high demand and could only be had at premium wages. Between Grand and Twelfth Streets nearly a dozen yards had forty-four vessels on the ways, including Collins's four steamers. In the following year the total number of vessels under construction rose to sixty-three.

More than 2,500 men were working, but even that was not enough—
particularly when cholera arrived. Brought in by passengers aboard an
immigrant ship, the disease ravaged the city. In the shipyards laborers,
fearing contagion, refused to come to work. "It was almost impossible
to get men to work," Collins lamented, "and if they did, they dare not
do half the work they otherwise would have done."[45]

By early 1849, just as the company was going public, *Atlantic* and
Pacific were nearing completion. Determined to make a show of their
launching, Collins announced that he had arranged with the two yards
to launch *Atlantic* and *Pacific* on the same day, February first. As the
hour approached "Notwithstanding the state of the weather," according
to one spectator, thousands of people crowded the yards and shore
between Houston and Twelfth Streets "to witness the interesting spectacle." New Yorkers had never seen such an event firsthand. In the large
open floor space of the mould lofts, carpenters, sailmakers, riggers,
caulkers, and others whose labor and skills had made possible the day
passed along tables groaning with cheese and biscuits and gallons of
rum punch.[46] Excitement and expectation ran high in the yards but so
too did anxiety. Much could go wrong. Tallow used to grease the slip-
ways might freeze, causing the ship to stick; or, once released from her
restraints, if not secure in her cradle she might topple over. Even if all
went well in the yard the chance of danger arising from a nearly 3,000-
ton behemoth careening wildly into the narrow river was ever present.

Atlantic was scheduled to launch first, but she was delayed. During
construction the ways had shifted so that when the workmen attempted
to send her down the incline toward the water she stuck. While crews
worked feverishly lubricating the ways with tallow, the tide was ebbing
and fog was rolling in. The nod was given to *Pacific*. At precisely three
o'clock "the tide served, and the thousands of spectators who had been
watching the vast fabric for some time, raised a tremendous shout as
[*Pacific*] started off."[47] In his "The Building of a Ship," written a year
later, Henry Wadsworth Longfellow captured the emotion and spirit of
such a moment.[48]

[The] master builder
With a gesture of command,

Waved his hand;
And at the word
Loud and sudden there was heard,
All around them and below,
The sound of hammers, blow on blow,
Knocking away the shores and spurs.
And see! She stirs!
She starts, —she moves, —she seems to feel
The thrill of life along her keel,
And, spurning with her foot the ground,
With one exulting, joyous bound,
She leaps into the ocean's arms.

As *Pacific* touched the water, she was saluted by "the booming of guns and the ringing of bells . . . She rode upon the bosom of the waters like a gull." Riding high in the water like a seabird, she sped across the river heading straight for a pier on the Williamsburg side until the crew hurriedly released her anchors, bringing her up within one hundred feet of a disastrous collision. At this point the steam tug *Hercules*, "like a mere pigmy of a boat alongside of this leviathan," came alongside and towed the steamer back to her berth.

While *Hercules* nudged *Pacific* to safety the men at W. H. Brown, "with considerable difficulty," were adjusting the ways to give *Atlantic* a better angle toward the water. Fortunately, a favorable tide kept the water at sufficient height, and at twenty-five minutes past four, she slid into the water.

While crowds onshore stood by to watch this extraordinary dual launching, on the river a small flotilla of steamers and small boats jogged to and fro also waiting for the great moment. Most notable among them was the steamboat *Telegraph*, chartered by Collins, who had "invited a select number of guests to witness the spectacle from onboard her." After watching from the open deck the guests "adjourned to the cabin, where a handsome collation had been prepared," including bumpers of fine champagne.

Although Collins was the central figure of the day, James Brown presided over the festivities. Among the guests aboard *Telegraph* was Captain William Hudson, commanding officer of the USS *Vincennes*, who raised his glass to offer a toast comparing Collins with Archimedes and Benjamin Franklin. The commandant of the Brooklyn Navy Yard, Captain Isaac McKeever, honored "Our Merchant Princes," to which Brown, mindful of the company and the need for their support, added "our Merchants for they are all sovereigns." Also present was Edward Cunard, accompanied by Captain Ganbry Calcroft, Her Majesty's Mail Agent. When Brown turned to offer a toast to the Cunard Line he was told that "Mr. Cunard had gone on shore." Finally, long after dark, *Telegraph* steamed to Fulton Market wharf, where passengers stepped ashore confident of the success of the steamships *Atlantic* and *Pacific*, and looking forward to the launching of vessels which were yet to be built for the New York and Liverpool line of U.S. mail steamers.

However, the ships yet to be built, *Arctic* and *Baltic*, were barely framed up. *Arctic*'s skeletal hull remained on the ways of William Brown's yard next to the spot from which *Atlantic* had been launched, while *Baltic* rested nearby in an equally unready state at Brown and Bell's. In the meantime *Atlantic* and *Pacific* were tied up alongside their piers waiting to "fit out." Despite the toasts, accolades, and waves of self-congratulations, critics harped that these vessels had taken much longer to build than promised by Collins and his associates and, if the rumors were accurate, were far over their original cost estimates. In Washington, southern Democrats, who were never fond of the project, raised questions. Senator Solomon Downs, Democrat of Louisiana, was among the skeptics. On his motion the Senate approved a resolution directing the Committee on Post Office and Post Roads, chaired by Thomas Jefferson Rusk, Democrat of Texas, to "inquire and report to the Senate the facts in relation to the respective contracts for building mail steamships."[49] The investigation consumed four months and produced a 121-page document. Included were reports from Commodore Perry, abstracts of contracts made for the carriage of the Royal Mail, estimates of Cunard revenue, a list of steam vessels in Her Majesty's Navy, and summaries of contracts signed by the Secretary of the Navy for carrying mail, as well as a host of other documents.[50]

The Committee unearthed no wrongdoing, attributing construction delays to the "overpress of work at the steam engine manufactories in the city of New York." Not every member agreed. "Some amongst us," wrote the chair, "are disposed to cavil at the failure of the parties to these contracts to comply with the strict letter of their engagements, and who are willing to punish any delays that may have occurred by a forfeiture of the privileges incident to them."[51] The majority, however, answered that "whatever has been done, has been done with the best intentions." Under the circumstances, the report concluded, Congress ought "to regard these contracts with indulgence, and to retain and establish an enterprise which, without the aid of government must fall short of its mark."[52] With so much already invested, public and private, for the moment at least an indulgence was granted and the contracts honored.

On Wednesday afternoon, April 23, under the command of Captain James West, *Atlantic* cast off from Brown's pier to set out on her sea trials. She "moved slowly out into the stream stern foremost [as] vehement cheers arose from both the dock and those on board."[53] To please the gawking New Yorkers Collins had timed *Atlantic*'s sailing to coincide with the regular departure of *Southerner*, a fast steam packet running between New York and Charleston, also built by William H. Brown. The race was on. Taunting her rival, *Atlantic* went ahead "under easy steam, and waited for [*Southerner*] to come up, when the steam was let out, after which she showed the *Southerner* a clean Pair of heels in the shortest possible space of time."[54] "Delighted" at *Atlantic*'s performance, the next Sunday, Collins, joined by a throng of people, gathered at the pier at the foot of Canal Street to wish her and all aboard a safe voyage to Liverpool.[55]

New York was mad to celebrate Collins's triumph. To memorialize it, local merchants commissioned the city's best-known jeweler and goldsmiths, Ball, Black, and Tompkins, to fashion an extravagant four-piece "service of gold plate." Inscribed on the salver was "To Edward Knight Collins In testimony of the public sense of the great honor and advantage which has been conferred upon this city and the whole country, through his energy and perseverance in the successful establishment of an American line of Transatlantic Steamers."[56]

Nine days out, as she drew near the southwest coast of Ireland, *Atlantic* had to stop her engines and lay becalmed in order for the crew to repair loose and broken paddles damaged during the crossing. When she resumed power the air pump in the port engine failed, forcing her to proceed on one engine and under reduced speed until the pump was repaired. On her inaugural voyage *Atlantic* took an unimpressive thirteen days to cross. Cunard's ships had been averaging twelve and a half days and his *Canada* held the record at eleven days, four hours.[57] Notwithstanding her lack of speed, however, *Atlantic* drew immediate attention in Liverpool. *The Illustrated London News* took the unusual step of dispatching a reporter and an artist to chronicle her historic arrival.[58]

At first glance, what impressed the writer most was *Atlantic's* size. Aside from Isambard Kingdom Brunel's iron-hulled *Great Britain*, lying idle in Liverpool's "Bramley-Moore Dock—a huge mass of iron suffering under premature rust," *Atlantic* was the largest steamship afloat.[59] She boasted accommodations for 150 passengers and a crew that numbered five deck officers, ten engineers, twenty-four firemen, twenty-four coal heavers working in three shifts of eight hours each, thirty-six sailors, a purser, a surgeon, and thirty-eight persons attached to the steward's department. Altogether, *Atlantic* shipped a crew at least twice the size, and expense, of any aboard a Cunard ship.[60]

Size, however, did not necessarily connote beauty, and persistent baiters, accustomed to the clear, sharp profile of packets and clippers, were eager to note that *Atlantic's* lines were awkward and coarse. She was "clumsy." The funnel was "short and stumpy, there is no bowsprit and her sides are painted black, relieved by only one long streak of dark red." Under her bow was a figurehead Neptune carved in colossal dimensions, which one wag asserted was Collins "blowing his own trumpet." In the center of her rounded stern was an "American eagle, clasping the starred and striped shield." Beneath the eagle, scrolled along the curve of the stern in painted letters, the word *Atlantic* appeared and under that the hail "New York."

At seventy-five feet, including paddles, *Atlantic* was so broad that she was too wide to pass into any of the existing Liverpool docks. Anticipating her arrival, as well as that of her equally sizeable sisters, the Liverpool Dock Committee had already begun construction of "a dock at the north end" to accommodate the new steamers.[61] Even the new dock, however, proved tight, and could only be entered at high water.[62] As a result *Atlantic* and other Collins steamers often had to moor in the Mersey River, where they awaited a turn of the tide to bring sufficient water for entering the dock.

Atlantic was a local sensation. Paying six pence apiece for the privilege, more than two thousand people ferried out to board her. In a gesture that was widely approved, Captain West donated the proceeds to the Liverpool Institution for the Blind. A writer for the *Edinburgh Journal* described his visit:[63] "[Like] all the other Atlantic steamers, the run of the deck is almost a straight line. Around the funnel, and between the paddle boxes, is a long wooden house, and another is placed at the stern." The forward house provided quarters for the Captain, officers, a bakery, and—most remarkably—a barber shop "fitted up with all necessary apparatus—with glass-cases containing perfumery, etc.; and in the center is 'the barber's chair.' This is a comfortable, well-stuffed seat, with an inclined back, movable so as to suit people of all sizes; and in this position the passenger lies, and his beard is taken off in a twinkling, let the Atlantic waves roll as they may." The house at the stern served a dual purpose. One part was a smoking room with a direct passage to the cabin below "so that, after dinner, those passengers so disposed, may without the least exposure to the weather, or annoyance to their neighbors, enjoy the weed of old Virginia in perfection." Adjacent to the smoking room was "a small apartment completely sheltered from the weather for the steersman." Unlike sailing vessels, where the helmsman stood at the wheel on an open quarterdeck and took verbal orders from a nearby officer, this sailor steered according to signals relayed to him by bells. From his post on the bridge, an elevated passage between the port and starboard paddle boxes, the officer on watch stood by a wire running aft, linked to the steersman's bell—one pull for port and two for starboard.[64] A similar system connected the bridge to a long box in the engine room, "with five compartments each communicating with a wire fastened like a bell pull to the side of the paddle box. These handles are marked respectively, 'ahead,' 'slow,' 'fast,' 'back,' and 'hook-on;' and whenever one is pulled, a printed card with the corresponding signal appears in the box opposite the engineer, who has to act accordingly."

What truly amazed visitors, however, was the opulence of the appointments below. Two grand saloons, one for social gathering and the other for dining, ran nearly half the length of the ship. Both were finished in the finest woods—"rose, satin, and olive . . . tables [topped] with beautifully-variegated marble." Carpets were "rich, and the coverings of the sofas, chairs, etc., are of superior quality." *Atlantic*'s interior "savored strongly of republicanism." The walls of the saloons displayed "beautifully-finished emblems of each of the states in the Union," while standing in the midst of it all was "a young and beautiful figure, all radiant with health and energy, wearing a cap of liberty, and waving a drawn sword . . . trampling on a feudal prince, from whose head a crown has rolled in the dust."

There were berths for 150 passengers. "The most novel feature about them is the 'wedding berths,' wider and more handsomely furnished than the others, intended for such newly-married couples as wish to spend their first fortnight of their honeymoon on the Atlantic." Each cabin had an "Annunciator," a rope running to the steward's room by which a passenger might summon him. "There is thus no noise of human voices on this ship: the helmsman steers by his bells, the engineer works by the telegraph, and the steward waits by the annunciator."

Having praised nearly everything aboard *Atlantic*, the writer did find one unlovely feature—"spittoons," present "even in the finest saloon . . . places where they would be least expected . . . giving ample facility for indulging in that practice of spitting of which Americans are so fond."

Liverpool was alive with talk of Collins and *Atlantic*. Comparisons were inevitable. With her size and elegance, she made Cunard's ships appear stodgy and common. For the first time since the founding of his line in 1840 Samuel Cunard faced real competition. He had, however, anticipated this moment, and to a degree had been preparing for it.

In May 1847, shortly after learning that Congress had voted Collins his generous subsidy, Cunard wrote to Charles MacIver, who had succeeded to partnership in the firm following the death of his brother David, that unlike other foreign competitors, from whom he did "not apprehend any serious injury . . . The American ships will be different— they will introduce all our improvements, together with their own—we shall have national prejudices to contend with, so that every attention will be required to meet them." Cunard, however, did not "despair of getting our fair share" of a trade that "will yearly increase."[65] MacIver agreed. So too did his Liverpool competitor William Brown, who despite his deep misgivings about Collins, and anger at his own brother James, had become the firm's agent in Liverpool. William shared Cunard's view that Anglo-American trade was growing so rapidly that there was enough for everyone. Staunchly conservative, Brown saw no benefit in competing when collusion would answer. On March 8, 1849, as *Atlantic* was laying alongside her pier in New York preparing for her maiden voyage to Liverpool, Brown wrote MacIver:

> How unpleasant it would be for your vessels and those coming to us to be carrying on a war of mutual injuries . . . I have written to my brother James . . . to see Mr. [Edward] Cunard . . . and if possible to make such arrangements as would prevent injury to either concerns.[66]

It was a complex transatlantic negotiation. Over a year later, on May 29, 1850, MacIver, on behalf of Cunard, and the firm of Brown, Shipley on behalf of Collins, signed a secret agreement in Liverpool. To prevent undercutting, the heart of the agreement established minimum rates for passengers and cargo. Both companies, however, were permitted to charge higher rates, an unlikely prospect. In addition, recognizing that American shippers and passengers would favor Collins's ships on the New York departure, and likewise British interests would favor Cunard's ships leaving Liverpool—a preference that would impact income—the parties agreed to pool revenue and divide it according to a very complex formula.[67] For Cunard and Collins secrecy was essential. Maintaining the appearance of a dramatic and fierce competition between their two lines was vital. If it were revealed, on either side of the ocean, that the two national champions, who received huge public subsidies in exchange for nobly undertaking their patriotic duties, were in fact colluding to maximize their firms' profits, the political and financial fallout would have been catastrophic.

For the press, Parliament, and Congress, unaware of this secret deal, the rivalry between Cunard and Collins was seen as nothing less than an honorable and colorful contest between two great maritime nations.

CHAPTER ELEVEN

Crossing the Atlantic: Life Aboard

NOTWITHSTANDING THEIR REVENUE-SHARING AGREEMENT, in the public eye on both sides of the Atlantic, Cunard and Collins were fierce competitors vying to offer the fastest and safest liners crossing the ocean. By the end of 1850, Collins's quartet— *Atlantic*, *Pacific*, *Arctic*, and *Baltic*—had completed a dozen round trips. In the following year the number of crossings doubled.[1] Praise for the new line was unstinting. According to the *New York Herald*, the engines of the *Atlantic* "were so quiet that conversations could be carried on in the engine room." Passengers enjoyed unwonted luxury and service. "Married gentlemen and ladies amused themselves in spacious drawing rooms, while bachelors repaired to the smoking room or forward saloon, where they whiled away time in the scientific game of brag or poker for six and a quarter cents or more."[2]

Already thrown aback by the impressive performance of the crack American steamers, British pride took another blow in September 1850 when *Pacific* set a new record for an Atlantic crossing—ten days, four and three-quarters hours, a feat giving rise to a popular joke.[3]

A Yankee merchant told an Englishman that Captain Nye [commander of *Pacific*] intended to alter *Pacific*.

Alter her! My word! We thought she had been altered already.
Oh, yes but Capt. Nye intends to make a day boat of her.

In their first full year of operation, Collins's steamers outpaced Cunard's on every crossing, including another astounding performance by *Baltic* in the summer of 1851, when she became the first vessel to cross from New York to Liverpool in less than ten days.[4]

Even more impressively, although they made fewer crossings to New York than Cunard in 1851, the American steamers actually landed more passengers: 4,156 to 4,118.[5] Collins relished his success, and for the moment the line's impressive performance swelled his national prominence and muted the voices that had opposed his subsidy.

For a decade Cunard and his partners had enjoyed the luxury of steaming in the protected waters of subsidy. Relying on their allies in Parliament, the Post Office, and the Admiralty, they had managed to deftly avoid the nuisance of bidding on competitive contracts and instead were able to secure highly favorable snap contracts, whose generous terms allowed the firm to slash rates and "club others out of the business." Having pushed aside all competition, the naturally conservative partners, particularly Charles MacIver who took the lead in management, saw little cause to change and stubbornly refused to consider any alterations in company operations.[6] They considered that the line's chief hallmarks, safety and punctuality, gave them sufficient influence to fend off competitors, hold the subsidy, and thereby preserve their dominance on the North Atlantic. Operating in this protected environment dulled the Cunard Line to the shifting demographics of transatlantic passenger travel. Between 1840 and 1860 the number of overseas voyages made by Americans, in sail and steam (90 percent of which were to England and Europe), increased by an average of 5 percent per year, a figure exceeding population growth or GNP. Fast-sailing packets and Cunard's regular steamers had made ocean travel both increasingly important and popular. The 1850s surge was especially dramatic. In that decade American foreign trade nearly doubled, and the number of overseas trips made by Americans (again mostly to England and Europe) increased nearly threefold over the average for the preceding five years. During this same period, steam, which offered comfortable, quick crossings, took an increasing

Edward Knight Collins (1802–1878), owner of the Dramatic Line and founder of the United States Mail Steamship Company, better known as the Collins Line. LIBRARY OF CONGRESS, PRINTS AND PHOTOGRAPHS DIVISION

Samuel Cunard (1787–1865), Halifax shipping magnate and founder of the British North American Royal Mail Steam Packet Company, better known as the Cunard Line. GETTY IMAGES

1781.   *A View of the Town & Harbour of Halifax: from Dartmouth Shore*

A view of the port and city of Halifax, Nova Scotia, from the Dartmouth shore, 1781. Engraved by Joseph Frederick Wallet.

COLLINS AND CUNARD.

RAISING THE WIND; OR, BOTH SIDES OF THE STORY.

Caricature of Edward Knight Collins (backed by Uncle Sam) and Sir Samuel Cunard (backed by John Bull) trying to blow toy ships across a tub in opposite directions.
Frank Bellew, *The Lantern*, 1852. LIBRARY OF CONGRESS, RARE BOOK AND SPECIAL COLLECTIONS

Robert Napier (1791–1876), Scottish marine engineer who built engines for the Cunard Line. GETTY IMAGES

View of South Street from Maiden Lane, 1828. GETTY IMAGES

View of Boston's North End from the Navy Yard, 1833. Painted by W. J. Bennett.
LIBRARY OF CONGRESS

Uniform button of the Collins Line. Found by
Todd Yerks in a cellar hole in Sharon,
Connecticut, in 2008. PHOTO BY THE AUTHOR

NOVELTY IRON WORKS, FOOT OF 12.th ST.E R. **NEW YORK.**

STILLMAN, ALLEN & Co.

Iron Founders Steam Engine and General Machinery Manufacturers

Lithograph of Endicott & Co. Novelty Iron Works, by John Penniman, at the foot of 12th Street in New York City.

Phineas Taylor "P. T." Barnum (1810–1891), American promoter, showman, and businessman. LIBRARY OF CONGRESS

Bird's-eye view of New York City. Drawn by C. Parsons, published by N. Currier, 1856. LIBRARY
OF CONGRESS

Collins Line steamer *Atlantic*, launched 1849. LIBRARY OF CONGRESS, PRINTS AND PHOTOGRAPHS DIVISION

New-York & Liverpool U. S. Mail Steamer

ARCTIC

-------------------------------------*1853.*

BREAKFAST BILL OF FARE.

Beef Steaks,	Boiled Eggs,
Mutton Chops,	Scrambled Eggs,
Veal Cutlets,	Poached "
Pork Chops,	Omlets,
Chickens,	Potatoes, plain,
Pigeons,	" fried,
Kidneys,	" stewed
Tripe.	Hominy,
Ham,	Mush.
Bacon,	Rice,
Calf's Liver,	Oatmeal Porridge,
Sausages,	Buckwheat Cakes,
Fresh Fish,	Rice Cakes,
Salt Fish,	Hot Rolls,
Fish Balls,	Corn Bread,
Hashed Meats,	Toast dry,
Curry and Rice,	" dip.

COLD MEATS,

J. H. Burnet, Stationer, 61 Wall Street.

Breakfast menu from Collins Line steamship *Arctic*, 1853. THE NEW YORK PUBLIC LIBRARY, RARE BOOK DIVISION

Mary Ann Collins, wife of Edward Knight Collins, lost on *Arctic*, 1854. BY PERMISSION OF
THE COLLINS FAMILY/JESSICA TODD HARPER PHOTOGRAPHY

Cornelius Vanderbilt (1794–1877), investor in steamships and railroads, known as "The Commodore."

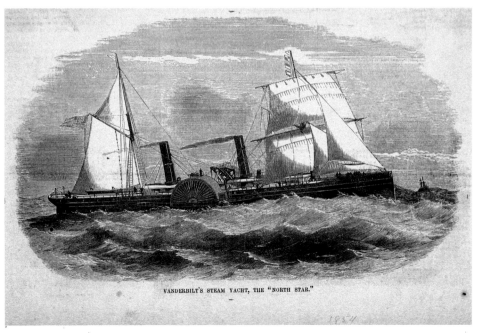

VANDERBILT'S STEAM YACHT, THE "NORTH STAR."

Cornelius Vanderbilt's steam yacht *North Star*.

Collins Line steamer *Adriatic*, fifth and last of the line to be built, launched 1856.
THE MARINERS' MUSEUM, NEWPORT NEWS, VA

This silver goblet was presented by the president and directors of the Collins Line to L. S. Bartholomew, 1st Assistant Engineer, commemorating the maiden voyage of the Atlantic. BY PERMISSION OF CRAIG PRINCE. JESSICA TODD HARPER PHOTOGRAPHY

share of the business from sail. Between 1855 and 1859 the proportion of passengers arriving in New York on steamships jumped from 7 percent to 33 percent.[7] The total number of steam passengers, however, was tiny compared to the more than one-and-a-half million immigrants arriving in America, mostly traveling in steerage aboard sailing vessels.

By their "secret agreement" Cunard and Collins established minimum fares that far exceeded the low fares ($135 versus $20) offered by sailing vessels, and so were able to discourage Liverpool's long lines of emigrant families that would have disrupted their carefully crafted image of elitism. Their passenger lists were composed primarily of well-to-do people (mostly American and British) traveling on personal or government business. Three quarters of the passengers were men. Most travelers, including women, were traveling alone. Families represented only about 20 percent of those onboard.[8] This was a privileged clique who lived comfortably at home and expected the same at sea. When traveling they favored the ambience of fine restaurants, such as New York's Delmonico's on Broadway, and for lodging they preferred the elegance of New York's Astor House, the St. Nicholas, or the Metropolitan. Collins catered to this set. With his flair for the dramatic and an outsized ego, he marketed snobbery; he touted his grand and elegant steamers, designed to shame the stodgy Cunarders, as the only way to cross the Atlantic in fashion. With the largest steward department afloat, the best chefs, finely appointed public rooms, and the promise of a safe voyage faster than Cunard's—all offered under the American flag—Collins appealed to the patriotic sensibilities of the American gloves-and-cane-crowd.

Unlike the plain-style staterooms aboard the Cunarders—six-by-eight-foot cells with bunk beds furnished with a "hard settee, a commode with two wash basins, two water jugs and two chamber pots"—Collins's steamers offered the luxury of "satinwood floors, and French bedsteads and curtains." Jacob Abbott, author of a number of travel books for young readers, described his voyage on *Pacific*:[9] Each cabin, he wrote, was outfitted with a marble wash basin, a dish for soap, and a heavy water pitcher "made broad and flat at the bottom so that it could not be easily upset." A round mirror "was screwed to the wall in such a manner that it could be set in any position required, according to the height of the observer."[10] Passengers were allowed one thousand pounds of baggage, most of which could not fit into small cabins, so the crew stowed it below, but not before passengers scrambled to take out what they would need for the days at sea. Hanging closets were small since the rolling and pitching motion of the ship caused items to swing back and forth in a very unsettling fashion likely to add to the passenger's discomfort. Shelves too were scarce since objects lying on flat surfaces became dangerous projectiles in a heavy sea. Instead, canvas sacks were fixed to the bulkhead. The only natural light that penetrated the cabin entered through an oval-shaped porthole, tightly secured in an iron frame and held shut by a strong clamp and screw that opened inward. Near the door was a rope pull used to summon the steward.

Cabin comfort depended not only upon proper furnishings but also upon keeping it secure and dry. In heavy seas waves crashed over the pitching bow, sweeping aft along open decks, and often cascaded down companionways, flooding into spaces below, including cabins. Cunard's ships were notoriously wet. It was company policy that as soon as the steamer cleared land, stewards hurriedly rolled up the carpets in anticipation of the water that might inundate public rooms, passageways, and cabins. Collins's steamers, on the other hand, with their greater size, high bulwarks, and towering plumb bows, cut the seas sharply, which minimized unwanted water belowdecks.[11]

In good weather, as the steamer ploughed ahead under clear skies and a fair breeze, passengers were able to enjoy a stroll on deck, chatting with family and making new shipboard friends. While men gathered at the leeward rail to smoke and talk, women conversed in a separate sphere on cushioned settees stationed behind sheltered areas about the deck.[12] Access to the quarterdeck or the lookout platforms atop the paddle boxes was prohibited, and conversations with the sailors, aside from officers, was discouraged.

In the evenings, card playing—often for money—parlor games, or singing helped pass the time. One activity in which nearly all on board participated was the daily lottery. Each day passengers placed bets on the distance traveled in the previous twenty-four hours. At precisely noon, the captain appeared on the quarterdeck to take his daily sighting. He then retired to his cabin, and with the aid of a variety of navigation tables, calculated the ship's position and compared it to the previous day's to determine exactly how far the steamer had progressed. It was a complicated procedure and could take an hour or so to complete. In the meantime passengers, most of whom were taking their lunch, eagerly awaited the result, which was posted on a board outside the dining saloon.[13] It might read:

Latitude 44 deg. 26°
Longitude 16 deg. 31°
Distance 270

The passenger whose guess came closest to the actual distance won the pool.

Unwelcomed storms broke the monotony. If the captain permitted, a brave or hardy soul might venture onto the open deck, risking a salt-water soaking or worse. Others preferred dry confinement below. Gathered in the saloon or alone in their quarters they held tight against the pitching and rolling of the ship. Had they failed to secure their cabin porthole, their cabin would likely be swamped with seawater, their belongings soaked and scattered. Green passengers, fearing that the vessel was about to sink beneath them, thought every moment their last. Drowning, however, was not their chief threat; they were far more likely to suffer broken bones, bruises, cuts, burns, and concussions from being thrown down a companionway or tossed out of bed, having a hot bowl of soup spilled in their lap, or being pitched about in a narrow passageway. Six hundred miles from Ireland, bound to Liverpool aboard *Arctic*, John S. C. Abbott (brother to Jacob), a writer for *Harpers Monthly Magazine*, described a storm that made "every timber" creak and groan, with waves coming across the bow that made "the whole fabric shiver." On deck it was "a wild scene. The roar of the gale through our shrouds was almost terrific. It seemed like the voice of an angry God." At breakfast, only five passengers out of nearly 100 aboard sat to eat. Stewards trying desperately to make it across the saloon to their tables were thrown about with the contents of their trays scattered everywhere. It "was a wild scene of uproar and confusion."[14]

Despite the drama and fright of a storm at sea, in all the years of their competition neither Cunard nor Collins lost a ship or a passenger to a violent storm.[15] While they could never master nature, steamships, because of their larger size and powerful engines, could better control their movements against the elements. Smaller sailing vessels could never be anything but subservient to the same forces.

On every voyage, somewhere between the monotony and terror there emerged moments of wonder such as stunning sunrises and sunsets, or dolphins playing in the bow wave. In early September 1851, while commanding *Baltic* on an eastbound voyage, Captain J. J. Comstock recorded in his journal a remarkable sight seen only in northern waters:

> Lat. 52 21
> Long. 23
>
> Between 3 and 4 o'clock this AM there was a most brilliant display of the Aurora Borealis which continued nearly 1 ½ hours. From behind these masses of black there issued immense streams of brilliant yellow light not continuously but at short intensity now fading almost away and now suddenly shooting to the center of the sky producing a most splendid and gorgeous effect.[16]

To Comstock and others aboard *Baltic*, the sight of the Aurora was an experience of supreme beauty. Nearly three years later, in the spring of 1854, Comstock observed another natural work of art, one far more dangerous.

Spring is the time when icebergs calve off Greenland's glaciers and drift slowly southward into well-traveled shipping lanes. On March 10, 1854, *Baltic*, eastbound to Liverpool, was steaming along the great circle route at approximately 52 degrees N. Lat. Although the seas were calm and the wind moderate, the steamer was wrapped in rain and fog. Despite limited visibility Comstock, following company policy, was steaming ahead at full speed. Extra lookouts were posted and told to keep alert. Luckily for *Baltic*, one of them spotted "an immense field of ice looming through the fog thickly filled with large icebergs." Unwilling to risk a late arrival at Liverpool, Comstock, instead of either stopping his engines or altering his course to go round the ice, reduced speed and proceeded into the ice floe, looking for a clear passage. As *Baltic*'s paddle wheels drew her slowly through the ice, passengers curious to see the phenomenon huddled on deck, trying to protect themselves against the cold and rain while fixing their gaze on a beautiful and menacing sight. As they looked out toward the floe, one of the lookouts aloft called a warning to the deck—icebergs! Weeks drifting at sea had softened their sharp features, but they still stood glistening white, high above the water with most of their mass hidden below. Comstock ordered the helmsman to give them a wide berth. As *Baltic*'s bow parted the ice, the passengers heard the crunch and felt a slight tremor; lookouts searched for a passage, but none could be seen. The floe, wrote Comstock in his journal, seemed "a complete labyrinth from which there was no escape."[17] As he moved among "icebergs and large patches of heavy fields [of] ice," Comstock discovered that paddle wheels and ice were a bad match. As the wooden wheels turned and mushed their way through the frozen sea, the ice jammed the mechanisms and tore at the paddles. Up forward, the ship's carpenter warned that the *Baltic*'s stem was showing signs of stress from the press of the ice. With darkness arriving Comstock ordered the engines to be stopped. Through the darkness, *Baltic* drifted, her passengers lying in their cabins kept awake by the sound of ice sliding along the hull. During the night, the wind shifted; in the morning *Baltic*'s lookout spotted a clear channel and the ship resumed her course for Liverpool. Comstock's wise decision to stop *Baltic*'s engines and drift undoubtedly saved his ship.[18]

In addition to parlor games, lotteries, and ocean watching, the principal pastimes on an Atlantic crossing were eating and drinking. Aside from safety, a ship's reputation often hung on the menu. By this measure the Cunard Line fared poorly in comparison to the Collins steamers. According to Charles Dickens, who crossed to Boston aboard Cunard's *Britannia* in 1842, the ship's dining saloon resembled "a gigantic hearse," a suitable venue for the food served.[19]

At one the stewardess comes down with a steaming dish of baked potatoes, and another of roasted apples, and plates of pig's face, cold ham, salt beef; or perhaps a smoking mess of rare collops.

At five, another bell rings, and the stewardess reappears with another dish of potatoes—boiled this time—and a store of hot meat of various kinds; not forgetting the roast pig [followed] by a rather mouldy dessert of apples, grapes, and oranges.

On a later voyage sailing from Boston to Liverpool aboard *Britannia*, a passenger complained that for the first three days out fresh food was available but "thereafter the fish and meat is salted," and often served "cold."[20] Cunard's steamers gave the impression of being prim, proper, and stuffy, an image that Collins was happy to counter with visions of sumptuous elegance, particularly in the galley department where the line sought comparisons with the best establishments ashore.

On a Collins ship a "Steward, two Stewardesses, six Cooks, and a Butcher, with forty Pantry and State Room Servants" stood by to serve passengers. To satisfy the culinary demands of his British and American passengers, Collins ordered aboard ample quantities of beef, pork, and lamb. For an average passage time of ten and a half days, *Baltic* carried in her ice-cooled larder "2000 pounds of Crew Beef, 1500 lbs. Prime do., 250 lbs. Veal, 250 lbs. Pork, 400 lbs. Mutton Lamb, 100 lbs. Sausages, 25 Sweetbreads, 6 Pigs, 12 Kidneys, 50 lbs. Tripe, 6 livers, 12 Ox Tails, 6 Calves Heads, 12 Calves feet." Also stowed below were a wide variety of poultry, turkey, chicken, geese and duck. For cooking and table use, Collins's steamers carried four thousand eggs and six hundred quarts of milk. Relatively small amounts of fish came aboard—"100 lbs. Codfish [and] 50 Haddock." For the more adventuresome diners, *Baltic* stowed 136 wet, live lobsters. Vegetables were in shorter supply: potatoes ranked first—100 bushels along with "2 barrels Turnips, 100 heads Cabbage," and lesser quantities of celery, onions and cauliflower. For after dinner delectation the stewards could tap stores of "70 lbs. Figs, 40 lbs. Prunes, 6 Wiltshire, 4 Stilton, and 2 Cheshire Cheeses." Ample spirits were also provided.[21]

From these stores, typical menu items aboard included the following:

Soups: cream, turtle, potato, Giblet à la Irlandaise
Fish: (stuffed and baked) boiled bass (Hollandaise sauce), turbot (bitter sauce) salmon
Boiled: ham (sugar cured), tongue, beef, turkey (oyster sauce), fowl (parsley), leg of mutton (caper sauce)

Roasted: Beef, veal, mutton, pork (apple sauce), turkey, chicken, goose

Entrees: Macaroni and cheese, filet of pigeon au Cronstadt; fricassees chicken au champignon, coquette du poisson à la Richelieu, chicken in tomato sauce, veal cutlet à la St. Croix or la Zingara, a turtle with baby peas, mutton à la Niverare, oysters, pork and beans

Vegetables: green corn, peas, asparagus, cabbage, new/mashed potatoes, salads: plain or potato

Pastries: puddings (gooseberry, rhubarb, berry, Indian or soufflé), pies (quince, plum, cranberry, apple, red current), calf's feet, jelly, molded rice, apple fritter (hard sauce), almond cup

Desserts: fruits, nuts, olives

Beverages: coffee, frozen lemonade[22]

John S. C. Abbott recounted his dining experience aboard *Arctic* in the year 1852: "We breakfast at eight o'clock, have an abundant lunch at twelve, dine at half past three very sumptuously, take tea at seven, and those who wish it have supper at ten." Beer, wine, and spirits were available all day and into the late night.[23] Aside from evening tea that might be served in one of the saloons, all meals were taken in the main dining saloon.

A single seating was the rule. The dining saloon was "large, airy and beautiful; sixty-two feet long and thirty feet wide." As passengers entered, stewards escorted them to their places at long tables running fore and aft, paralleled by "handsomely cushioned settees with substantial backs to them." Both the tables and settees were secured firmly to the deck. Around the edge of the table was a small lip (fiddle board) to prevent a roll of the ship from sending dishes into a passenger's lap.

At each place was a setting of fine china framed by flatware in the "Tuscan" pattern, designed specifically for the line by the New York silversmith Philo B. Gilbert.[24] Hanging over the table were wooden racks for wineglasses, tumblers, and decanters. On a crossing aboard *Baltic* in 1851, Horace Greeley, editor of the *New York Tribune*, remarked that service aboard the Collins Line "would have done credit to the Astor or the Irving," a reference to New York's two most fashionable eating establishments.[25]

Recognizing that passengers were "brought so closely into contact with each other, and confined to so small a neighborhood that all their sayings and doings" were noticed by everyone, *Miss Leslie's Behaviour Book: A Guide and Manual for Ladies* emphasized the need, for the sake of harmony and conviviality, to skirt any potentially disagreeable situations—particularly discussions of volatile subjects such as politics and religion.[26] In some instances, however, avoidance was impossible, especially when it came to the Atlantic world's most inflammatory topic: American slavery. On one occasion, in a highly publicized incident Samuel Cunard found himself embarrassed by his line's ill treatment of one of America's most famous abolitionists, Frederick Douglass.

Although Great Britain had abolished slavery in 1833, the textile mills of the midlands fed on slave-grown American cotton. Before the Civil War, imports of American cotton doubled in each decade of the nineteenth century until nearly five-sixths of the cotton English mills turned into cloth originated in the southern United States. While British abolitionists condemned slavery and American slave owners in the bitterest terms, British textile mills employed nearly one million workers. According to the *New York Times*, "one quarter of the inhabitants of England [were] directly dependent upon the supply of cotton for their living."[27] Cries of conscience conflicted with economic necessity. The issue of slavery was nearly as contentious in Great Britain as it was in America.

Born into slavery in Talbot County, Maryland, in 1818, at age twelve Frederick Douglass was sold to a family in Baltimore where his mistress, Sophia Auld, took the unusual step of teaching him to read, giving him access to a wider world and the horrors of slavery. In 1838 Douglass fled Baltimore on a train to Philadelphia and eventually arrived in New York, where he married Anne Murray, a free black woman. The couple then settled in New Bedford, Massachusetts. On August 9, 1841, Douglass was in the audience in New Bedford when the famed abolitionist William Lloyd Garrison spoke. Also present was William Coffin, a proprietor of the Nantucket Athenaeum, who was so impressed with Douglass that he invited him to speak at a the Massachusetts Anti-Slavery Society meeting to be held two days later at the Athenaeum. Douglass's speech that day launched his career as a powerful presence, and he soon become one of the nation's foremost leaders in the abolitionist movement.[28] Renowned for his powerful writing and spellbinding oratory, in 1845 Douglass agreed to undertake an extensive speaking tour through England and Ireland to raise funds for the American anti-slavery movement.[29]

Through Samuel Lewis, Cunard's Boston agent, Douglass booked arrangements to travel as a first-class passenger on Cunard's newest vessel, *Cambria*. Once he came on board, however, Douglass discovered that he had been reassigned to quarters in the forecastle, separate from the other passengers, and he was advised to remain secluded there during the crossing. With little choice Douglass moved to the forecastle, and for the first few days of the voyage he stayed in his quarters.

So famous a personage, though, did not long go unnoticed. Several English passengers—with decidedly anti-slavery opinions—took note that Douglass was aboard and asked the ship's master, Charles H. E. Judkins, Cunard's senior commander, to invite him to speak. Judkins agreed, and set about making arrangements. Several American passengers objected vehemently once word of the plan spread. When the moment came for Douglass to address the group, the steward rang the bell and the passengers assembled. Anticipating that some of those aboard disapproved, Judkins, in the gruff manner for which he was well known, announced that when Douglass spoke, anyone who did not wish to hear him could go below. Several of the Americans, angered at the want of respect shown to them, retired. Others, however, stayed topside and grumbled. In a later lecture, "American Prejudice Against Color," delivered to an audience in Cork, Douglass remembered the scene:

> I had not uttered more than a sentence before up started a man from Connecticut, and said "that's a lie." I proceeded without taking notice of him, then shaking his fist he said, again,—"that's a lie." Some said I should not speak, others that I should—I wanted to inform the English, Scotch and Irish on board on Slavery—I told them blacks were not considered human beings in America. Up started a slave-owner from Cuba—"Oh," said he, "I wish I had you in Cuba." Well, said I, ladies and gentlemen, since what I have said has been pronounced lies, I will read not what I have

written but what the southern legislators themselves have written—
I mean the law. I proceeded to read—this realized a general clamour,
for they did not wish the laws exposed. They hated facts, they knew
the people of these countries, who were on the deck would draw
their own inferences for them.

Here a general hurry ensued—"Down with the nigger," said
one—"he shan't speak" said another. I sat with my arms folded,
feeling no way anxious for my fate. I never saw a more boldfaced
attempt to put down freedom of speech than upon this occasion.
Now came the Captain.[30]

Whatever opinions he held on slavery as master of the ship, Judkins
would brook no disturbance. He "ordered the boatswain to call the
watch, and *have three pairs of irons ready at a moment's warning.*" Standing
with the boatswain and the watch, he told the "rioters that he did not
'care a d____n' for them. A few of the passengers called 'throw the
d____d nigger overboard.'" One passenger "put out his fist" at Judkins.
"The captain knocked him down." Once calm was restored, Judkins
told the rioters, "You have behaved derogatory to the character of
gentlemen and Christians," and once again ordered those who did not
want to hear Douglass to go below. For his part, Douglass remained
silent during the uproar. Not wanting to cause more excitement, he
graciously declined Judkins's offer to speak, and for the rest of the voyage
he remained silent, confined to his separate quarters.[31]

After a triumphal tour lasting twenty months, Douglass called on
Cunard's London agent to book return passage home to America in the
spring of 1847. For £40 he purchased a cabin-class ticket aboard *Cambria*
departing Liverpool on April 4, 1847. When he boarded *Cambria* and
inquired about his berth, he was informed to his "surprise and mortifi-
cation that it had been given to another passenger." Accompanied by
Captain Judkins, Douglass returned ashore and presented himself at
Cunard's Liverpool office. Charles MacIver told him bluntly that the
Cunard Line was "not a reformatory society," and that the London
agent "had acted without authority in giving him a cabin." Unless
Douglass agreed "to take [his] meals alone, not to mix with the saloon
company, and give up his berth" for which he had already paid, he

could not travel on *Cambria*.[32] Eager to return home, Douglass accepted these humiliating conditions, but not before he posted a letter to the London *Times*. Reacting to Douglass's account, the *Times* denounced Cunard's actions in a fiercely worded editorial as a "gross injustice," and expressed its "most intense disgust at the conduct of the agents of the *Cambria*, in having succumbed to a miserable and unmeaning assumption of skin-deep superiority by the American portion of their [Cunard's] passengers."[33] With abolitionist sentiment running strong in the popular press, and more importantly within Parliament, Cunard could ill-afford such bad publicity. Nor, however, could he risk antagonizing his American passengers, many of whom were pro-slavery. Finally, after pleading that an "accidental absence from town" had delayed his response, in a letter to the *Times* published on April 13 he defended the line's policy of separate accommodations, while regretting "the unpleasant circumstances respecting Mr. Douglass's passage." He assured readers that "nothing of the kind will again take place in steamships with which I am concerned."[34] Cunard was being disingenuous. As soon as the furor died down the line continued its policy of segregation.[35]

Religion was an equally delicate subject that might disturb the harmony of a crossing. In 1850, Cunard stepped into a controversy—dubbed by the press "Church and Steamboat"—with one of America's most famous preachers, the fiery Henry Ward Beecher. Since proper religious observance was key to keeping up appearances, Cunard, a respected member of the established Anglican Church, issued a standing order to his captains that "one hour every Sabbath morning is to be devoted to the service of the Church of England for the benefit of the crew. Passengers may attend if they desire. The service is to be read by the captain of the ship, and by no other person, except when an English clergyman of the Established Church is present." No other public religious observances "were allowed."[36]

On Saturday, August 31, 1850, Beecher and eight other American clergymen boarded Cunard's *Asia* at Liverpool.[37] As the newest and largest vessel in the fleet, the honor of command was given to Captain Judkins, late of the *Cambria*. Also aboard for the crossing was Samuel Cunard. The next morning, the first Sabbath, as *Asia* was steaming down the Irish Sea "a merchant from Boston, of high standing, called upon the captain, in behalf of a large number of passengers, to inquire if preaching would be allowed." Following company policy, Judkins replied "that it would not." Cunard supported Judkins. With no recourse the ministers retreated to the privacy of their cabins for private prayer. A week later on the following Sabbath, in a move certain to annoy the Americans, Cunard invited a Presbyterian clergyman of the Church of Scotland to preach.

Led by Beecher, the Americans confronted Cunard demanding to know why "a Scotch Presbyterian had been permitted to preach, but an American Methodist clergyman, or Presbyterian, or Congregational had been forbidden?" "Americans," they told him, "were quite unused to such restrictions upon the right of religious worship." In a thinly veiled manner they told him that if this policy of excluding American clergymen was made public, it was likely "to produce ill feeling toward the Cunard Line among Americans" and drive them to turn away from Cunard and book passage on the new Collins Line. "Mr. Cunard quite lost his temper." He would not tolerate such "threats," he sputtered, "that if Americans did not choose to go in his ships, 'd___n them, let them stay away.'" They could, he said, "go to h___l."

Beecher reported all the details of the encounter to his local newspaper, the *Brooklyn Eagle*. Adding a bit of spice to the story and tossing a dart at Cunard, Beecher noted that the saloon where religious services were held on Sundays was the same room that only a few hours earlier had been the scene of late-night "whist and card playing of various kinds [i.e., playing for money], in which Mr. Cunard engaged with relish." When it came to Judkins, Beecher "took off his gloves." While not questioning "his skill in navigation," as a preacher of the word of God the captain came up short. He too was seen in the saloon "playing at cards till late on Saturday evening, preparatory for the Sabbath." It was an "outrage" for "an unordained man and card player to be the sole minister of the Gospel."

Cunard made no response, but in a letter to the *Eagle*, Judkins tried to defend himself. "I do emphatically deny," he wrote, "having played cards." He went on: "If ever I had cards in my hands it was on some occasion of an accidental visit to the saloon when possibly I may have had them in my hands for the amusement of the ladies. I did not play a game of cards on the voyage even for the value of a cent." Judkins's explanation was amusing, but hardly persuasive. Americans, however, were not the only ones critical of Cunard. At home, a number of detractors questioned the very essence of his company—its conservatism.

Later in his career, when the company was undergoing careful scrutiny, Charles MacIver was questioned by a Parliamentary commission as to why he had not made improvements in ships and service to compete with Collins. With the arrogance of a monopolist, he responded defiantly that in those years of operation the line had not "lost a passenger or a letter." The gimlet-eyed manager asserted that he had "deemed both the boats and the management *perfect*, and that was enough."[38] Since *Britannia*'s maiden voyage, he told the commissioners, the line had never seen it necessary to alter "the saloons, the state rooms, the bill of fare, the meal hours, or any of the details." Notwithstanding MacIver's defiant defense, the line's shortcomings were obvious. The ships lacked private baths; did not provide a smoking room for gentlemen, forcing them to take their pleasures on the open deck; nor was there a space for ladies to sit at leisure. It was also charged by the commission that in more than a decade Cunard had not made even a single change to the menu.[39]

British newspapers railed that Collins's success against Cunard was nothing less than a national disaster. When reporting *Pacific*'s record crossing, the *London Daily News* blasted that "the stake is neither more nor less than the ascendancy of the seas." The paper demanded a "searching inquiry." In 1851, London's satirical magazine *Punch* published a cutting ditty:

> A steamer of the Collins Line,
> A Yankee Doodle Notion.
> Has also quickest cut the brine,
> Across the Atlantic Ocean,
> And British agents, no way slow,
> Her merits to discover,
> Have been and bought her—just to tow
> The Cunard packets over.[40]

The partners stood firm and refused to alter course. Their answer to Collins was to continue to do what they had been doing since 1840. In turn, by raising the specter of the Yankee menace they wheedled an increase in their subsidy from Parliament, and with it they added two new steamers to the New York run, *Africa* and *Asia*, wooden side-wheelers both smaller and slower than Collins's ships. In lieu of offering better ships, in the spring of 1851 Cunard announced that the line would provide weekly sailings between New York and Liverpool, but, however, call at Halifax only biweekly. The news did not sit well in Nova Scotia.[41]

Despite these developments, critics were not impressed. They dismissed the new ships as simply "enlarged edition[s] of *Britannia*" with hulls so poorly designed that they "went bowling down the Mersey, causing a sea before enough to swamp a revenue cutter." The London *Times* declared, "The truth must be told—the British steamships have been beaten." The American steamers were of "exquisite model" and they "slip down the Mersey with scarce a ripple at the bow."[42] The line that had launched ten years earlier to wide acclaim seemed to be steaming behind in the American wake.

CHAPTER TWELVE

A Rising Storm in Congress

A S HE BUFFETED against the political winds set against him in Parliament, Cunard did at least have the advantage that few in that body doubted that the nation's far-flung empire depended upon a strong merchant marine, and were willing to see public money used for its support. In the American Congress, however, political winds blew from a different direction. As the debates and votes over subsidies had revealed, American steamship owners, Collins chief among them, did not enjoy strong congressional backing from the government supporting their enterprise.

In arguing against government favoritism Collins's opponents drew strength from the spirit of Andrew Jackson, who in his dramatic 1832 veto of the Bank of the United States bill assailed the "rich and powerful" who "too often bend the acts of government to their selfish purposes." Jackson told Congress, "There are no necessary evils in government, its evils exist only in its abuses. If it would confine itself to equal protection, and, as Heaven does its rains, shower its favors alike on the high and the low, the rich and the poor, it would be an unqualified blessing."[1] Memories of the president's lambasting attack against those who sought to prostitute government through monopoly and special privilege fed Jacksonian suspicion of business interests, particularly those associated with eastern and northern elites. Southern Democrats looked warily upon subsidizing Yankee shipowners. Westerners wondered why transatlantic ships were subsidized but not their river craft. Even owners of sailing packets, Collins's neighbors on South Street, lobbied against granting him subsidies, arguing that "for the carriage of passengers and freight," steamers competed unfairly against them.[2]

While keeping an eye on affairs in Washington, Collins, always the showman, looked for paths beyond politics to enhance his reputation and that of his line. He saw an occasion in January 1850, when P. T. Barnum, dubbed "The Prince of Humbug" and the "Prince of Promoters," announced that he was bringing to America the world's most famous singer, Jenny Lind. Collins saw an opportunity for a public relations coup.

Barnum scheduled Lind to perform in nearly 100 concerts, charging local venues huge fees that sometimes reached the astronomical sum of $10,000 for a single appearance.[3] Unlike Barnum's previous fantastical promotions—the "Fee Jee Mermaid," a bizarre mummified creature of unknown origin, the diminutive "Tom Thumb," or the Native American dancer "fu-Hum-Me"—Lind was real and she was talented. With her beautiful soprano voice, delicate frame, and shy demeanor, she was an international sensation. She had performed in Sweden, Austria, and Germany, and for two years sang in London opera—once in the presence of Queen Victoria. American audiences were ready to embrace her, even more so when she announced that she intended to donate her fees to charity. "Lind Fever" set in.

As soon as the contract was signed, months before the tour was to begin, Barnum launched his publicity campaign. "Perhaps," he announced in the New York newspapers, "I may not make any money by this enterprise; but I assure you that if I knew I should not make a farthing profit, I would ratify the engagement, so anxious am I that the United States should be visited by a lady whose vocal powers have never been approached by any other human being, and whose character is charity, simplicity, and goodness personified."[4] Few people believed Barnum's self-deprecation, but that did not diminish their enthusiasm for the opportunity to pay to see and hear Jenny Lind.

How would Lind come to America? National pride demanded that it be on an American ship. Collins sought out Barnum and persuaded him that to add drama to her crossing and arrival Lind must take passage on the world's largest and fastest steamer, his newly launched *Atlantic*.[5] Barnum could hardly refuse. On July 21, under the command of Captain James West, who carried instructions from Collins to the line's Liverpool agents, Brown, Shipley, to do all in their power to accommodate Lind, *Atlantic* left for Liverpool on her special mission.

After an unimpressive passage of fifteen days, West secured *Atlantic* in Liverpool's Prince's Dock and made his way to the popular Adelphi Hotel, where Lind was staying, to present his compliments.[6] A man of "great worth and striking appearance," the famous captain of *Atlantic* was already the toast of New York City. The poet and socialite Anne Lynch Botta rhapsodized,

> To Captain West of the Steamer *Atlantic*
> The gale of storm, the night may come
> No fear disturbs the breast
> Our ship is strong—our Captain brave
> And we securely rest.
> Long life to him all his Line!
> Health to the gallant West[7]

Lind was preparing to depart for a rehearsal of the *Messiah*, which she was scheduled to perform at the local Philharmonic Room. Clearly struck by the captain, Lind, with a "gracefulness of manner, and that open hearted simplicity of character which forms the distinguishing feature in her attractions," inquired of her visitor "if he had heard her sing?" When he regretted that he had not, she insisted that he accompany her to the rehearsal. With police carving a way through the crowd gathered outside the hotel, the two set off in her carriage. During the ride, West invited Lind to visit his ship. Thus began a close friendship between the "gallant captain" and the "Swedish Nightingale."[8]

Lind's every movement in Liverpool made the front page, with reports reaching America as well. Barnum and Collins were delighted. On Sunday, August 17, Lind attended a service at St. George's Church, where an overflow congregation jammed the pews and ladies, overcome with emotion, were carried out fainting. After the service Lind made her way along streets lined with her admirers toward Prince's Dock to visit *Atlantic*. Queen Victoria could not have received a more reverent reception. Joseph Shipley stood at the gangway to welcome her, as did her friend Captain West. After the captain's private tour, from which "all other visitors were excluded," the "party partook of a superb dejeune."[9]

On Monday Lind performed the *Messiah*, and the next day continued her triumphal visit to Liverpool, driving to Texteth Hospital to be presented with a "tea kettle" in recognition of her charitable efforts on behalf of the institution. Finally, on Wednesday, the day of her departure, thousands gathered near the landing to bid her farewell. The cheering throng pressed so fiercely that Shipley decided, for her safety, to "smuggle" her off from another landing to the waiting *Atlantic*. It was, the *New York Herald* reported, a "sorry disappointment to many, who sought this opportunity to see one whose charms had won all hearts."[10]

On Wednesday morning, August 21, with her cabins fully booked (an unusual circumstance), *Atlantic* cast off and steamed down the Mersey River. On this warm summer day dozens of small boats pranced about, circling dangerously close to the steamer, their occupants straining to catch a last glimpse of "the favorite Jenny." Adding to the moment, the Cunarder *Asia*, also getting under way for New York, steamed abreast *Atlantic* and "fired a salute, a compliment much esteemed by Captain West," who returned the honor with thirteen guns.[11]

Attentive to her audience, amidst all the hubbub the diminutive Lind stood atop *Atlantic*'s starboard paddle box, her appearance "the signal for one thrilling shout, which was echoed along the lines of wharves for fully two miles." Seventy thousand people afflicted with Lind Fever . . . waved hats and handkerchiefs. As *Atlantic* "stood down the river, cheer after cheer greeted [her] until the dim and dingy spires of Liverpool were lost to view."[12]

For the first three days out, heavy weather kept most passengers, including Jenny Lind, confined to their cabins. Few ventured to meals. Stewards responding to the call of cabin bells passed up and down narrow passageways and onto the open deck, trying to keep their footing as they made their way to the leeward rail to dump the foul remains from below. Finally, as the seas calmed and stomachs settled, passengers gathered for meals and conversation. In recognition of the crew's steadfastness Lind offered to give a concert. Toward the end of the voyage, on a foggy evening off the Grand Banks, "for the benefit of the sailors, firemen and servants of the *Atlantic*," Lind sang a full program of ballads, including some from Sweden. To her dismay the fog kept Captain West at his post on the bridge, and so the following evening after the fog had lifted she gave an identical concert for the captain and his officers. Her efforts raised £70 for the crew.[13]

New Yorkers waited anxiously for Lind to arrive. Barnum had orchestrated a gala welcome. To be certain that he would be the first to greet her, he went over to Staten Island so that as soon as *Atlantic* reached the Sandy Hook pilot station he could rush out and board the steamer to stand with Lind and share in receiving the crowd's adulation.[14] When it came to showmanship, however, Barnum had found his match in Edward Knight Collins.

On September 1, Barnum boarded *Atlantic* off Sandy Hook and made his way to Lind's stateroom, where he discovered to his astonishment Collins, sitting with "the peerless Queen of song," the two chatting merrily, surrounded by the dozens of roses Collins had presented to her. Outwitting America's greatest impresario, Collins had taken the pilot boat out to meet his liner. By the time *Atlantic* reached her North River pier, a mass of forty thousand swooning admirers had assembled to hail Lind. "She landed from the steamer, escorted by the captain, on a gang plank covered with tapestry." Behind her followed Barnum and Collins. She passed under "a bower of green trees" to be greeted by Collins's young son John, who presented to her a "magnificent bouquet." From the pier, Lind "entered a carriage [which proceeded] with great difficulty . . . up Canal Street to Broadway. Arriving at the recently opened Irving House, she was prevented from alighting for fifteen minutes by the rush of human beings."[15]

While Lind was launching her triumphal and highly profitable tour of America, another visitor from abroad—with a very different mission— was also attracting enormous crowds: the Irish priest Theobald Mathew, the "Apostle of Temperance." Ordained as a Capuchin monk, Mathew had moved to Cork, where he helped found the Total Abstinence Society, best known for asking people to take "The Pledge," thereby swearing off all liquor for life. Mathew's passionate opposition to drunkenness and his reputation for personal integrity made him one of the most revered figures in Ireland.

Having enjoyed phenomenal success at home, and hoping to reach and redeem the thousands of Irish who had migrated to the United States, Mathew planned to carry his crusade against alcohol across the Atlantic. When the monk, bound by a vow of poverty, looked for passage to New York, Cunard stood silently by while the New York firm of Grinnell and Minturn, eager to curry favor with the large Irish population in their city, quickly offered him a free ticket aboard their packet *Ashburton*. A notoriously slow sailor, *Ashburton* took nearly a month to complete her voyage.[16] When the packet finally tied up at her East River pier on July 2, 1849, the city's notables—including Mayor William Havemeyer, members of the city council, and thousands of New Yorkers, mainly Irish—stood ready to welcome him.[17] For nearly two years, Father Mathew delivered his message of temperance to crowds in hundreds of towns and cities across twenty-five states. Everywhere people gathered to take "The Pledge." Mathew dined with the president of the United States and was received by both houses of Congress, an honor previously granted only to the Marquis de Lafayette. By the fall of 1851 Mathew was physically exhausted and near collapse. He was eager to return to Ireland. Quick to see a chance to tout his ships and embarrass his packet competition, Collins offered Father Mathew free passage home on *Pacific*, a trip the American promised would be shorter and far more comfortable than that he had endured coming out.

The day before his departure, local newspapers published Mathew's long and heartfelt "Farewell Address to the Citizens of the United States." Widely distributed, Mathew's poignant leave-taking made special note of the great generosity of Edward Knight Collins, a "merchant prince," citing him even before the Archbishop of New York. Collins bathed in the publicity as Grinnell, Minturn, and other proprietors grumbled at the unfavorable light cast upon their slow packets.[18]

In the same year that he won acclaim for helping Father Mathew, Collins took another turn on the international stage when the "Great Exhibition of the Works of Industry of All Nations" opened in London.

Better known as the "Crystal Palace Exhibition," after the extraordinary cast-iron-and-glass building erected to house the exhibits, the event was the first World's Fair. Organized by Prince Albert, ostensibly to celebrate all nations, it was in fact a massive propaganda effort designed to highlight Britain's industrial superiority.[19]

When word reached New York that the British organizers had invited the United States to participate, Collins announced immediately "in a most generous and patriotic manner to take all goods marked 'London Exhibition, Hyde Park,' free of charge." On July 2, 1851, Collins stood on his pier at the foot of Canal Street as *Atlantic* cast off, bound for Liverpool. Stowed below were dozens of crates and boxes containing a wide variety of American goods to be displayed at the Crystal Palace.

Upon *Atlantic*'s arrival at Liverpool William Brown arranged an extraordinary banquet aboard the ship in honor of the "Royal Commissioners of the Exhibition, the Executive Committee and a large party of distinguished foreigners." Following the dinner they went ashore to attend a grand reception at the Liverpool Town Hall.[20]

At Liverpool the exhibits were offloaded from *Atlantic* and hurried by train to London. The American display, including a glittering trophy celebrating American wealth and prowess at sea, was applauded. In a clever move to twist Britannia's tail and showcase his line, Collins had carried across the ocean and offered for view the Ball, Black, and Tompkins gold-plated tea service, of "chaste and simple design, plated by unalloyed California gold," which had been presented to him on the occasion of the launching of *Atlantic*. After viewing it a writer for the *London Illustrated News* gushed, "The forms, ornaments and above all, the colour of the gold were really beautiful."[21]

Despite these efforts, good press and public acclaim did not translate into profits for Collins. By late 1851 his line was wallowing in debt and had yet to pay a dividend. Collins's and Brown's emphasis on size, speed, and luxury had proven quite dear. Noting the reckless extravagance of his American rivals, Charles MacIver noted wryly from Liverpool that "the Collins people are pretty much in the situation of finding that breaking our windows with sovereigns, though very fine fun, is too costly to keep up."[22] Cunard's policy of steady ahead, "never in advance of the times, but never far behind them" and "never experimenting" while "avoiding equally extravagance and parsimony," kept his line afloat.[23]

The financial reports were grim. In a report to Congress at the end of 1851, Collins estimated that the average outlay for each round trip was "$65,215; the average receipts for the same were $48,286," which left a deficit of $17,000—a loss of nearly $500,000 for the year.[24]

The Collins Line investors were caught in a terrible bind. Although their secret agreement with Cunard that permitted them to raise passenger fares and cargo rates was still in force (see chapter 9), they would undoubtedly lose customers if they did so. There was no way to increase revenue. Cutting costs was equally problematic. Collins had built his reputation on speed, service, and luxury. Any economies in these areas would undermine passenger satisfaction and endanger his annual subsidy of $385,000 drawn from a consistently skeptical and divided Congress. The avowed purpose of government support was to out-sail the British steamers. Enthusiasm spread inland. In January 1850 a writer for the *Ohio State Journal*, noting *Baltic*'s departure for Liverpool, wrote that a more noble vessel was never launched. According to him, she and her sisters would eclipse Cunard.[25] A correspondent in the *Baltimore Sun* wrote that "it is of some national importance to us not to retire before John Bull."[26]

Hyperbolic speeches in Congress expressed the same nationalistic spirit. When Democratic Senator Robert Hunter of Virginia, a fierce opponent of Collins's, argued on the floor of the Senate that even "if the whole American marine were tomorrow gulfed in the depths of the ocean, commercial British vessels would still bring us the products of foreign countries, and take away the products of our own," George Badger, a Whig senator from Georgia and former Secretary of the Navy, answered that any American who would be willing to accept such a fate must have a "soul dead to the perceptions of national honor and national interest."[27]

Collins had steamed into shoal water. He had launched a preposterously expensive enterprise on a foundation (i.e., subsidy) that had been shaky at best and now showed alarming signs of crumbling. The line could only survive with an increased subsidy, but that subject, like nearly every political question facing Congress, had become inextricably entwined with the controversy over the expansion of slavery in the territories acquired from the Mexican War.

The alarm bell rang on August 12, 1846, shortly after the war began, when David Wilmot—a Jacksonian Democrat from Pennsylvania—moved an amendment to an appropriations bill funding peace negotiations that expressly prohibited the introduction of slavery into any territory acquired from Mexico.[28] The amendment failed, but the issue did not disappear; in 1848, as a result of the war, the United States acquired vast territories from Mexico, and the question of slavery's expansion rose again when the newly acquired territories of California and New Mexico petitioned for admission as Free States. With abolitionist sentiment rising in the north, and the south agitating for a more effective fugitive slave law and the right to carry their slaves into the territories, the issue of admitting two Free States tore Congress and the nation apart along strict sectional lines. Legislatures in the north adopted charged resolutions demanding admission, while in the south equally fiery rhetoric demanded adherence to the doctrine of states' rights. On January 18, 1850, the Whig senator from Kentucky, Henry Clay, sought compromise by offering a series of resolutions aimed at ending the crisis. For seven months the Senate debated Clay's proposals. Bitter exchanges filled the chamber. In a particularly dramatic scene Senator Henry Foote of Mississippi drew a pistol on Thomas Hart Benton of Missouri, who bellowed, "I have no pistols! Let him fire! Stand out of the way and let the assassin fire." To avoid violence, Vice President Millard Fillmore quickly adjourned the body.[29]

By the end of September 1850 moderates in the Senate and House managed to pass several measures through a series of political maneuverings known collectively as the Compromise of 1850. These included the admission of California as a Free State; New Mexico and Utah were established as territories with no limits on slavery; the Texas boundary was established and the state was paid $10 million; slave trading was prohibited in the District of Columbia; and a severe fugitive slave act was put in place.

While the Compromise preserved the Union, it left deep wounds and exposed sharp divisions. Southern members of Congress, principally

Democrats, grew increasingly wary of northern interests who they claimed sought special privileges. Collins provided them a target.

Overall, support for the Collins subsidy was weak in the House and even weaker in the Senate. To bolster his position Collins courted key members to ask for help, including two prominent Whig senators, New York's William Seward and Daniel Webster of Massachusetts. Webster was agreeable and lobbied the House Naval Committee, assuring them that an appropriation for Collins would not "inconvenience" the treasury. For his help Collins offered the senator free passage to Europe.[30]

Relying on their friends in Congress, Collins and Brown put in motion a plan for the greatest lobbying effort Washington had seen since the days when Nicholas Biddle launched his offensive against Andrew Jackson to save the Bank of the United States.

On October 18, 1851, Collins fired the opening gun. Hoping that the Whig administration of President Millard Fillmore, who had succeeded to the office upon the death of President Zachary Taylor in July 1850, would be receptive, Collins wrote to Postmaster General Nathan Kelsy Hall, a New York Whig, asking for an increased subsidy and offering in return to provide biweekly service (twenty-six voyages per year over the current twenty) between New York and Liverpool.[31] Hall supported the request and in mid-November passed it on to the Secretary of the Navy William A. Graham, a former Whig governor of North Carolina, for his approval. Although he had administration support, Collins needed a congressional appropriation. Unwilling to wait for a new session of Congress to introduce a bill, and fearful that any separate bill might draw unwanted attention, Collins and his congressional allies saw an opportunity to slip the request into a routine item of congressional business— a deficiency bill.

It was common for Congress, toward the middle of a fiscal year (at the time ending June 30), to discover that additional appropriations were needed to cover "deficiencies." Such bills were routine and were often used by members to secure special appropriations—in modern parlance, "pork barrel." With the likelihood that such a bill would be introduced for fiscal 1852, Collins set out to lobby Congress in a flamboyant fashion. Since the majority of members of Congress had never seen, let alone been aboard, an ocean steamer, Collins decided to put on a show in Washington with the best stage prop he had—*Baltic*. Joseph Comstock, *Baltic*'s usual commander, was laid up with inflammatory rheumatism; command of the vessel devolved to the first officer, Naval Lieutenant Gustavus Vasa Fox, whom the navy had assigned to the ship so that he might gain "a practical knowledge of steam navigation."[32] While Fox prepared *Baltic* for her Washington debut, Collins, vowing not to "retire before John Bull," left for the capital. Initially, *Baltic* was to arrive soon after Collins, but she was stuck at her pier by ice flows coming down the Hudson. If he could not present his ship Collins decided he would at least summon her commander, and so Collins ordered Fox to join him in Washington. Vital to his campaign, Collins spared no expense for Fox's comfort, putting him up at the fashionable Willard Hotel, the social epicenter of the city. According to Fox's journal he understood that he was "employed lending a hand to the success of further appropriations to aid the Collins Steamers."[33]

On Friday morning, February 27, the *Baltimore Sun* reported that, the ice having cleared, "the noble American steamship *Baltic*" fell away from her North River pier and steered into the Hudson River.[34] Aboard were James Brown and nearly 150 guests, including James Shiles, a Potomac River pilot; Charles King, president of Columbia College; and a gaggle of New York politicians. Most important, given the mission of the voyage, also in company was "the press, there being editors or attaches of almost every paper in the city on board." As she eased from her pier, spectators cheered her departure. "Gaily decked with flags and streamers," *Baltic* moved into the river, while from Cunard's Jersey pier across the river *Canada* fired a salute. As *Baltic* passed the Battery, a "discharge of cannon livened the scene."[35]

After clearing Cape Henry, *Baltic* steamed up Chesapeake Bay and entered the Potomac on Saturday. She passed Mount Vernon in the afternoon, offering the traditional thirteen-gun salute to the first president. To the disappointment of Fox and Collins, who wanted the steamer moored in full view of Washington, Shiles advised against it. The river, he warned, was too shallow to accommodate *Baltic*'s twenty-foot draft. She anchored instead across the river, at Alexandria.

On Sunday morning, as *Baltic*'s crew spent time polishing brass, touching up paint, holystoning decks, and climbing aloft to tie sails into a neat "harbor furl," small boats filled with gawkers came out from both sides of the river and circled the steamer. While Collins, Fox, and the New York passengers stood by to welcome their guests, across the city under the unfinished capitol dome Collins's friend and supporter Senator Seward submitted a motion that "when the Senate adjourns today, it adjourns to meet on Wednesday" so that the members of Congress who had been invited would have time on Tuesday "to visit a steam ship, which is very interesting in its connection with the commerce of the country." Democratic senators Augustus Caesar Dodge of Iowa and Richard Brodhead of Pennsylvania rose to object. *Baltic* was here, Brodhead claimed, for the sole purpose of "giving an entertainment for the purpose of getting money from the Treasury."[36]

With Dodge and Brodhead leading the charge, other senators spoke forcefully against special "interests" and "capitalists"—Collins specifically—who came to Congress seeking special legislation. Democrat Solon Borland of Arkansas took the occasion to lump Collins into that mass of greedy "speculators and large capitalists" who preyed upon the public:

> The honor as well as the interests of this country, and especially the honor of the Senate of the United States, require that we should turn our face from such propositions—turn away with scorn and contempt from all such exhibitions—repudiate the use of such influences for electioneering, lobbying, and log rolling here, for the purpose of controlling and influencing the votes of the members of Congress.[37]

Collins's boorish behavior, Borland concluded, was a "direct insult" to "any one having the honorable impulses of a man and a patriot in his bosom."

If Borland truly believed what he was saying, he was living in a mythical world distant from Washington. In the history of the U.S. Congress, the 1850s stand as one of the high points of exactly the "electioneering, lobbying and log rolling" he objected to. It was, according to one historian, a "plundering generation."[38] Collins was much in the game. To reach members of Congress he hired one of the best known and most successful purveyors of political influence, the former clerk of the House of Representatives, Benjamin B. French. One of a swarm of lobbyists known as "borers," he worked the Hill incessantly.[39]

The assault took Seward aback. What he thought was a benign motion to take a congressional holiday had instead unleashed turmoil. It was clear the strains of division that had marred the debate over the future of newly acquired territories and had resulted in the unsettling compromise acts of 1850 had taken a toll on congressional comity and cleaved the body along party and sectional lines. After two hours of "spicy debate," the vote was 21 in favor of adjournment to visit the *Baltic* with 19 opposed. The vast majority of southern Democrats (excepting those representing maritime interests) voted in opposition. All of the Whigs but one, Jackson Morton of Florida, cast their votes in favor. Collins took note.[40] Like so much else in Washington, the matter he brought before Congress had to overcome the polarization of north and south.

Tuesday, March 2, was a "beautiful spring day," rhapsodized a writer for the *Baltimore Sun*, an ideal setting for "that perfect Novelty, *Baltic*, the most beautiful, fastest, and strongest steamer now afloat," to welcome aboard "the whole world and the rest of mankind."[41] Among them were Millard Fillmore, "the President of the United States, Cabinet Ministers, Senators [not all], members of the House of Representatives, distinguished visitors from Baltimore and Annapolis," and hundreds of others, including those invited and many not invited, who came anyway.[42] According to Fox, as the wine and liquor flowed freely, "confusion and disorder" took hold. In the midst of the press of visitors Collins received a telegram delivering disturbing news. *Atlantic*, which had just arrived at New York, had suffered an "accident" on her westbound crossing and was unable to make its next voyage. *Baltic* would have to leave immediately for New York to take her place. As the guests stumbled ashore, Fox, happy to see the disorderly guests depart, gave the order to bring up steam.[43]

Baltic's excursion up the Potomac made an impression—not entirely favorable. For some the ship's "extravagant finish and furniture," coupled with "the expensive entertainment," evinced "bad management" and had a "blighting effect" upon Collins and his line.[44] Rumors circulated that the *Baltic* was "supplied with a tea set—cups, saucers, etc. made of gold which cost five thousand dollars." Her supporters described such accusations as "blarney and humbug."[45] To them *Baltic* was the greatest ship "in all the waters of the globe."[46] Critics, however, held steadfast to their accurate view that the sole purpose of *Baltic*'s visit to Washington was to pry money out of the treasury.

As *Baltic* made her way back to New York the House was wrapping up H.R.207, a bill "to supply deficiencies in the appropriations for the service of the fiscal year ending the thirtieth of June, one thousand eight hundred and fifty-two." On March 27, the bill passed by a vote of 95 to 76. Despite heavy lobbying, however, the bill made no mention of a steamship subsidy.[47] Having lost the first round, Collins turned his attention to the Senate.

When H.R.207 arrived in the Senate the bill was dispatched to the Finance Committee, chaired by Senator Robert Hunter, a Virginia Democrat. For two weeks the committee reviewed the bill until finally it appeared on the calendar for Wednesday, April 21.

Not surprisingly, with a southern Democrat as chair, the bill that emerged from committee made no mention of Collins. Knowing such would be the case, Collins's friends in Congress were primed to offer amendments. On Wednesday morning the Senate convened, and, in its usual manner, turned first to routine matters before undertaking what promised to be a long and serious debate on H.R.207. However, in a deft parliamentary move, Collins's nemesis Senator Brodhead of Pennsylvania subverted the routine, and by clever use of parliamentary procedure, struck the first blow. Taking advantage of the fact that the calendar for each day always began with a reading of petitions, Brodhead asked permission of the Senate president, William R. King of Alabama, to present a resolution from the Board of Commissioners of the incorporated district of the County of Philadelphia. By Senate rules, since the resolution was not directed at that body, the proper response was to deny the request. King, however, a Democrat and an ally of Brodhead's in the battle against Collins, disregarded normal procedure, and even while admitting that the resolution was "not a paper which properly comes before the Senate," he allowed it to be read and entered. The wording was harsh, direct, and self-serving. It submitted that the "sums of money payed to endow the Collins steamers of New York, and similar projects to pamper the overgrowth of that city, with her dictation to the rest of the country . . . be better spent to build the Sudbury and Erie railroad, connecting the Lakes with the Atlantic."[48] The commissioner's petition shredded the veil of principle and revealed a truth. Some in the body may well have opposed the Collins subsidy out of principle; however, others just wanted the largesse served up to them. For Collins it was a distinction without a difference.

Following Brodhead's devilry, which previewed the acrimony to come, the morning business continued until the Finance Committee reported out the Deficiency Bill.[49] Numerous amendments came to the floor, most of which were handled quickly and with little discussion. Then Senator William Gwin of California, Chairman of the Naval Committee and one of the few Democrats to support Collins, stood and offered an amendment providing for "additional compensation for increasing the transportation of the United States mail between New York and Liverpool in the Collins Line of steamers to twenty—six trips per annum . . . at the rate of $33,000 per trip."[50] Although the measure called for only six additional trips per year, the total request of $858,000 was more than double the original subsidy. Democratic Senator Thomas Jefferson Rusk of Texas, one of the few southerners to support Collins, proposed an amendment aimed at placating the opposition. In Collins's current contract the government could terminate the agreement only by purchasing the four steamers at fair value. Likely to be very costly to the government and a boon to Collins, Rusk proposed "that it shall be in the power of Congress, at any time after the 31st day of December 1854, to terminate the arrangement for the additional allowance on giving six months' notice."[51] Rusk's amendment would hang Collins on the tenterhooks of Congress.

Rusk's amendment was added to Gwin's, but even that failed to appease the opposition. Led by Senator Borland, dissenters tried first to delay debate to give themselves time to organize. Borland argued that since Gwin's amendment was "likely to give rise to considerable discussion," its consideration should be withheld until other less controversial amendments were settled. The motion failed, discussion began, and for more than a month, off and on, the bill appeared on the Senate calendar and was debated on the floor more than a dozen times.[52]

As debate wore on, each side dug in its heels. Numbers were tossed about, with senators disputing each other's calculations. In its May 8, 1852, edition the *New York Evening Post* compiled a useful summary comparing the expense of running a Collins ship versus a Cunard vessel.[53]

	Collins	Cunard
Payroll for two months	$9,000	$5,400
Consumption coal, one round Trip @$5 per ton	10,000	7,000
Insurance, depreciation For two months	23,333	16,068

While each side conjured up its own numbers, on one point there was no disagreement. Collins's ships were more costly to operate than Cunard's. The question was whether the United States government ought to pay such exorbitant sums.

Senator Borland answered with a resounding no, and on May 12 he took the floor to launch an attack "against the Collins Line of Steamers and against special legislation—the doctrine of Protection—and all Monopolies." Borland, known for his colorful prose, compared the Collins Line to a "huge and hungry Boa Constrictor, fast winding its tortuous and fearful folds about the body and limbs of this Congress." After speaking for more than two hours, the former doctor from Arkansas turned to William King, president pro tem—"My strength has failed me, and I am unable to stand on my feet any longer." He asked that he be allowed to continue another day. Despite bitter divides within the chamber, on this occasion courtesy prevailed. The senator would be permitted to resume his remarks the following Monday. When obviously refreshed, Borland rose again and "spoke until a late hour," repeating his opposition to special legislation, monopolies, and Collins.[54]

Other senators, taking less time than Borland but no less vigorous in their language, spoke in opposition. In the end Collins's Senate supporters—including Gwin, Rusk, and others—managed to hold the line. On May 31 the chamber approved the amended bill by a vote,

27 to 19. Eighteen of the 19 votes against the measure came from the South and West.[55]

Although the bill had survived in the Senate, the House—to which the amended measure would have to return—was in doubt. Knowing his line could not survive without the added money, Collins turned to James Brown for help. Brown enlisted the aid of the company representative in Philadelphia, William Bowen, an English Quaker who had been with the Browns for more than twenty years, as their agent first in Manchester and then in Philadelphia. Having spent upward of $10,000 to bring *Baltic* to Washington, Collins and James Brown decided to double down and supplied Bowen with ample cash (rumors reported upward of $20,000), dispatching him to Washington. Knowing that the amended bill would have to return to the House for approval, Bowen made his first visits to members of the House Committee on Ways and Means, to whom the bill was assigned. He paid particular attention to an influential Philadelphia congressman, John Robbins, to whom he reported he brought "influence from various quarters to vote in favor, if not to keep out of the way."[56] Bowen also launched a charm offensive, calling to the city Jenny Lind's friend, the gallant Captain James West. Suave, debonair, and handsome, West was quite unlike Collins's other gruff sea dog commanders, as much at ease in the salon as he was barking orders from the quarterdeck. He was the captain, trumpeted the *Baltimore Sun*, who had "crossed the wide Atlantic two hundred and eight times!" and who "Jenny Lind remembers in her prayers."[57]

Rumors also circulated that Cunard had sent agents to Washington to lobby against Collins, a charge he fiercely denied.[58] In any case, Bowen left nothing to chance, and with the aid of Brown's deep purse he dispensed lavish gifts. To certain parties "important to our cause" he sent "wild cherry brandy, sparkling Moselle, Brandies and scotch whiskey." Some, less interested in liquors, received direct cash to help in their reelections. Reason, buttressed by Bowen's gifts, prevailed. The committee voted to support the Collins subsidy. On the floor both sides paraded the usual shibboleths. On one side—the ships were too big and expensive. It was all a monopoly and a plot by the Whigs to raid the treasury. The other countered that national pride demanded that the

United States not cower before John Bull. For Collins and his backers, the vote was alarmingly close. With Rusk's amendment providing for a six-month termination attached and the subsidy intact, the bill passed 89 to 87 with the South and West standing in opposition.[59] When Bowen informed James Brown of the result, "Quite satisfactory" was the characteristically understated response.[60]

Brown and Collins had survived the battle, but the war was hardly over. Bowen warned Brown, "I hope Collins will keep quiet and not crow too loudly, 1854 will soon come around when we will want all our friends."[61]

It had been a costly victory. The line's image had been tarnished badly by revelations of excessive cost and bad management, as well as the verbal assaults leveled in Congress. Collins could take little comfort from his narrow victories in the 32nd Congress. He had managed to survive this political gale, but worse storms were gathering on the horizon.

CHAPTER THIRTEEN

Vesta

NEWS OF COLLINS'S VICTORY in Washington came as an unwelcome surprise in Liverpool and London. Most British observers
had expected, and hoped, that the subsidy would go down to defeat, a
victim of America's growing sectional crisis, leaving Cunard in
command of steam on the North Atlantic.[1] The notion that Britannia
might not continue to rule the waves set the British popular press,
accustomed to celebrating the nation's mastery of the seas, into a frenzy
of foreboding. Adopting a rueful tone, the London *Times* noted that
although it had taken "very strenuous exertions" in both houses of
Congress to carry the day for Collins and that "the majority was small,"
nonetheless "the appropriation was large." The empire's most influential newspaper went on to add that England "must prepare herself for a
still more vigorous contest or she must abandon dominion of the seas."
The widely read *Illustrated London News* sounded the tocsin as well,
warning that "with the exception of the United States of America no
other country" could challenge Great Britain on the Atlantic.[2]

The timing of Collins's victory, and the alarms it set off in England,
worked to Cunard's advantage. Since his line's earliest days accusations
of political manipulation and monopoly had been pitched against it.
Thanks to performance at sea and friends at home, for the most part

Cunard had managed to fend off the charges, but under increased pressure by the early 1850s, Parliament felt compelled to appoint a select committee "to investigate the mail packet contracts." While the committee held hearings to scrutinize the company's activities and audit its finances, a group of London and Liverpool investors, sensing a chance to advance themselves at Cunard's expense, petitioned the Board of Trade "for a charter of limited liability in order to start a line to compete with Cunard." Already stretching to fend off Collins, Cunard predicted ruin if he had to fight on the domestic front as well. Rallying as much political support as he could muster, and relying on his longtime allies in the Post Office and Admiralty for aid, Cunard argued that he and his partners, all men experienced in shipping and steam, had risked their own personal fortunes to establish regular steamship service across the Atlantic. It would be blatantly unfair, he wrote, to permit a group of investors with no experience, hiding behind the legal protection of limited liability and enjoying potentially greater capital resources, to compete with them. The committee supported Cunard, pointing out in its report that the line "has of late years had to contend against serious foreign competition" against "vessels . . . much more powerful [i.e., Collins]" and therefore was deserving of support.[3] The Board of Trade agreed and denied the petition.[4]

To those who charged that the subsidy was extravagant and unfairly won, Cunard countered by noting that his steamers provided what no other line offered—weekly service to America even in winter. His line provided twice as many trips from New York as did Collins's. Answering critics who accused him of ignoring innovation, Cunard promised that the company's newest steamer, *Alps*, would be screw-driven and iron-hulled.[5] Those with an eye to technical design countered that the fault was not, however, in propulsion or in hull material, but in design. Napier's engines were the most powerful in the world, but still the Cunarders lagged behind Collins's steamers. *Arabia*, for example, one of the line's best ships, was described as a "fair weather boat, [that] with favorable gales . . . can skim the seas with a wonderful rapidity; but let an adverse wind cross her path, and she is nowhere."[6] The solution, according to one puckish—and anonymous—Cunard captain, was to put "Glasgow engines" in Yankee hulls.[7]

While critics on both sides of the Atlantic pricked at Cunard and Collins, their ships, like the steam pistons that drove them, passed back and forth across the Atlantic with a rapidity and regularity that astounded the world. In New York, Saturday was often the day for departure. One Saturday morning a writer for the *New York Herald* stood with a crowd near the Collins pier at the end of Canal Street and watched "quite a fleet of ocean steamships" depart: *Arctic* for Liverpool, *Union* for Aspinwall, *Star of the West* for San Juan, *Alabama* for Savannah, *Marion* for Charleston, and *Roanoke* for Richmond. In a single year Collins and Cunard alone accounted for seventy trips from New York to Liverpool.[8]

These were "years of buoyant foreign trade." Having repealed the restrictive Corn Laws in 1846, Britain was moving toward free trade, and was eager to import American raw materials and foodstuffs to supply its mills and feed its workers. In return she sent manufactured goods, money to invest, and thousands of immigrants, mainly Irish fleeing the famine, to the United States and Canada.[9] Where once people, goods, and information traveled only at the speed of a ship sailing before the wind or the pace of a trotting horse, now steam power carried them over land and sea at speeds never before imagined. Travel time between continents by ships had reduced to weeks, distances between cities by railroads to hours, and thanks to the telegraph, messages moved overland in minutes.[10] For some the seemingly unstoppable rise in the tempo of commercial and everyday life caused stress and anxiety. Reflecting on these dramatic changes the *New Hampshire Gazette* repeated a common refrain: "What would our fathers have said?"[11]

Even in their leisure pursuits, Americans were addicted to speed. Sailing for recreation had become a passion among affluent Americans. In 1851, the members of the New York Yacht Club dispatched the schooner yacht *America* to compete in the Royal Regatta at Cowes. She bested the British in a brilliant race and captured a large silver trophy, since known as the America's Cup. In October 1851, during a public dinner honoring the victory, toasts were offered to the superiority of American ships. The gathering offered a special salute to Collins for having "knocked aback" the British.[12] Winning races, particularly against the British, was very popular.

America's passion for speed on the water extended inland to lakes and rivers. Newspapers reported dramatic scenes on the Mississippi River, where shallow-draft steamboats, with pressure in their boilers rising to extreme and dangerous limits, raced against one another. Owners, ignoring the risks, and driven by the belief that no one would "take passage upon a boat that has been beaten in a fair race," pushed their lightly built craft to the edge of tolerance and sometimes beyond, with deadly consequences.[13]

Speed on the water was not the sole province of steam machines. Sail still had its place.[14] While never matching Collins or Cunard on the race across the Atlantic, New York's sailing packets continued to log respectable times. Their fame, however, was blanketed by the astonishing times being set by the greatest commercial sailing vessels ever launched— clipper ships whose record was one of unsurpassed performance, setting passage times for sailing ships that have never been broken.

Designed to carry high-paying cargo, their sleek hulls and acres of sail aloft allowed clippers to make fast voyages over long distances. In 1848, the discovery of gold in California opened a new route for American clippers carrying "Forty-Niners" around Cape Horn to San Francisco. News that one of the sailing greyhounds had entered port drew thousands of spectators to the waterfronts of Boston, New York, and San Francisco. How many days out were they from Canton, Calcutta, or California, spectators wondered; what new record had been set? The New York lithographer Nathaniel Currier memorialized them for the masses in his cheap and dramatic popular images.[15]

With packets crisscrossing the Atlantic, steamships setting new records, and clippers bounding home from exotic places, Americans were justly proud of their maritime prowess. It was the nation's golden age at sea. At its heart was a madness for speed.

Speed, however, carried risk and cost. Commenting on the nation's addiction to going ever faster on land and sea, the editor of *Harper's Magazine* asked, where in all this mania was the line between "healthy enterprise and heedless audacity?"[16] When margins of victory were reduced to minutes, what was the point of the contest? When a new record was claimed, vigorous questions were posed about the accuracy of the timekeeper, the geographic points from which voyages were measured, and the impact of weather and breakdowns. In reporting a voyage of three thousand miles, a writer in New Orleans' *Times-Picayune* asked, was it not "fanciful if not farcical," with the margin of victory so narrow, "to decide upon the merits of two splendid and splendidly handled vessels on a difference of minutes?"[17]

"Farcical" or not, to be the fastest boat across, even when measured only by minutes, brought fame to the captain and his ship. In July 1854 when *Baltic* beat *Arabia* from Liverpool to New York by a mere four minutes, American newspapers from New York to New Orleans proclaimed that "winner's colors" now belonged to Collins.[18] Aside from titles, records attracted premium-paying passengers, mail, and freight.[19] Captains, who often received a share of the passenger fare in addition to salary, had ample incentive to pour on speed. Of Collins's first four captains, three—James Luce (*Arctic*), James West (*Atlantic*), and Ezra Nye (*Pacific*)—were hard-driving masters who had spent their early years commanding fast packets and clippers.

Luce, a native of Rochester, Massachusetts, captained his first vessel before he was twenty-one. Later he sailed as master on the Red Star Line packets *John R. Skiddy* and *Constellation*. Ezra Nye, who also hailed from Massachusetts, commanded the Swallow Tail Line packets *Independence* and *Henry Clay*. James West sailed in command of *Shenandoah* for the Philadelphia and Liverpool Line.[20] Joseph Jesse "J. J." Comstock (*Baltic*), was unique among Collins's captains, as he was the only one who had previously been master of a steamship. Both Comstock and his father had been involved in building and running fast passenger steamers down Long Island Sound from Providence and Stonington, Connecticut, to New York City.[21] J. J. Comstock had commanded the fast steam packet *Massachusetts*. However, regardless of where they hailed from, sail or steam, coastal or oceanic, all four captains had a reputation for speed.

Sea voyages are inherently perilous. Ships crossing the North Atlantic in any century, sail or power, face nature's dangers—including fog, storms, and drifting icebergs—as well as human-caused hazards: fire, collision, foundering, or (due to faulty navigation) running ashore. Speed enhanced every danger. Nonetheless, in the face of stiff competition, owners pressed and rewarded those captains who kept to schedule, forcing them to balance speed against safety.

Poor visibility compounded nearly every peril. At night and any time in fog, the range of vision from the deck or a lookout post aloft can be reduced dramatically. Few places in the world are as cursed by heavy fog as the well-traveled waters of the northwest Atlantic, where the cold Labrador Current and the warm Gulf Stream merge. With no means of determining the presence of other vessels, or signaling its own position except by sounding the ship's bell or stationing a crewman at the bow blowing a tin horn, a steamer plowing ahead at full speed in fog or darkness ran the risk of collision with another ship, striking an iceberg, or running up on an unforgiving shore.[22]

In dangerous waters a careful captain might reduce speed and post extra lookouts, but those precautions cost time and imperiled the schedule; besides, there were no laws or regulations that required him to take any special measures. The chance of collision was dismissed. Caught up in the enthusiasm for setting records, one observer boldly claimed that for "steamships like the *Arctic*, it is safest to run at the highest speed, even if there should be a collision, as their great movement must be in their favor." Rudyard Kipling later made famous this "ram-you-damn-you liner" approach to navigation in his tale of Grand Banks fishermen, *Captains Courageous*, wherein small boats either get out of the way of the big boats or go to the bottom. But, as one callous promoter of speed confidently declared, there was actually very little chance of an accident since "the ocean highway is so broad that the chances of collisions at sea are no more than one to a thousand against such a possibility."[23]

In his journal in which he documented more than two dozen crossings, J. J. Comstock, master of *Baltic*, recorded fog on more than half his voyages, but on only one of those occasions did he reduce speed. In the spring of 1854, a "friend" of Collins's gushed that in nearly five years of service and dozens of crossings, "not a life has been lost by neglect, carelessness or accidently."[24]

Although the Cunard Line spouted "speed and safety" and boasted, like Collins, that it too had never lost a life at sea, it put its captains under pressure to "win back fully the honors snatched from them by the boats of the Collins Line." The line's senior captain C. H. Judkins defied company instructions to reduce speed in fog, arguing "that the best way to handle an encounter with a patch of fog is to tear through it at full speed."[25]

On the morning of April 20, 1853, Judkins gave a swaggering demonstration that a fast passage trumped safety. *Arabia*, under his command, had arrived off Sandy Hook. Her crossing time put her in a fair way to beat Comstock's record on *Baltic*'s clocked two years before at nine days, nineteen hours, and twenty-six minutes. The captain was jubilant. The weather at the Hook, however, was foul: dense fog and a pelting storm. The harbor entrance was tricky. At low water the depth across the bar was less than twenty-four feet. *Arabia* drew nearly twenty-eight feet. Company rules stipulated that steamers "shall not come up to the city, unless there is a clear sky, or the atmosphere is such as will assure the captain that he can bring the vessel in without sustaining any damage." Having come so close, Judkins, who had entered the port many times, and who had no intention of missing a chance to beat the Yankees, ignored the advice of the pilot and the company rule. "Capt. Judkins paid no attention to the state of the weather as he was set on a 'crack trip,' and, therefore, ran his vessel into port in the midst of a storm and fog, that in hundreds of other instances the captains of the Cunard steamers have never ventured to do."[26] Fortunately, *Arabia* arrived safely at her Jersey City pier. Judkins's dramatic entrance into the harbor proved, however, disappointing. *Arabia*'s time failed to beat *Baltic*'s.

While Comstock held the record westbound, his fellow New Englander James Luce, master of *Arctic*, held the eastbound record (set February 1852)—nine days, seventeen hours, and fifteen minutes. On Saturday morning, September 2, 1854, *Arctic*, with Luce in command, fell away from her Hudson River pier to begin a regular crossing to Liverpool with a full load of passengers—"nearly 400 souls."[27] The deck crew, engineering, and stewards department numbered 135. One hundred and eighty-five passengers booked passage in first class and seventy-five sailed up forward in second class cabins.[28] Included in the roster were forty-three women, twenty-three children, and two infants.[29]

First officer Robert Gourley had charge of the deck department. Under him served two mates, four quartermasters, two boatswains, twenty seamen, and two boys. As second in command he was expected to possess all the skills of the captain, particularly navigation, should

Luce become incapacitated. It was often the case, especially on large vessels, that neither the master nor the first officer supervised the crew directly; that task was left to the second and third mates. In the case of *Arctic*, second mate William Baahlam and third mate Francis Dorian had charge of the deck crew, which was divided into two watches.[30]

The engine department was the domain of Chief Engineer J. W. Rogers, the son of Moses Rogers, who was master of the *Savannah* during her pioneering voyage. J. W. had begun his service with Collins serving aboard *Atlantic*. As "chief" he was responsible for the largest department—six assistant engineers, twenty-four firemen, and twenty-four coal passers (trimmers). The latter two, working in the heat, grime, and dust of the ship's coal bunkers, were known as the "black gang." Under way, *Arctic* burned two to three tons of coal per hour. In the bunkers, coal passers filled their wheelbarrows, always being careful to take coal evenly, port and starboard, so as not to impact the ship's stability, and brought it to the firemen to heave it into the furnaces. Rogers also had care of the maintenance and operation of all the machinery aboard, including boilers, engines, paddle wheels, and pumps.

Purser John Geib, the ship's business manager, directed the stewards department, including the galley, and saw to the overall comfort of the passengers. Geib's staff included the chief cook, five assistants, a baker, a pastry cook, vegetable cook, butcher, and storekeeper. Also under Geib's direction were thirty-eight to forty stewards and stewardesses who tended to the daily needs of the passengers, serving in the saloon and tidying up cabins. The chief stewardess, Anna Downer, was a young African American woman from New York.[31]

Arctic's engine crew, deck department, and stewards lived and worked in three carefully divided worlds. The deck crew prided themselves as being part of a centuries-old maritime fraternity of seafaring. While on watch, fair weather and foul, they worked topside, standing at the wheel, scurrying aloft to set and reef sails, repairing rigging, pumping the bilges, swabbing the deck, chipping paint, and performing numerous other duties. Off watch they took refuge in the dark, confined world of the forecastle, where they ate together, slept, smoked, and swapped salty yarns. Like generations before them, when they were at work, *Arctic*'s sailors could look up and see the sky, feel the breeze, and wipe the salt spray from their faces. Proud of their place aboard ship, they often scorned the rest of the ship's company. They dismissed the burly men covered with coal dust who were sweating below as little more than factory workers, and considered prancing stewards simply servants and waiters. These "workers," however, who composed nearly four-fifths of the crew, presented a new reality for the maritime world. They had none of the skills of seamen manning the ship. They could not, in the tradition of the sea, "hand, reef, or steer." They heaved coal, oiled machinery, and served meals, which in the eyes of "sailors" condemned them to be nothing more than cogs in an industrial machine at sea.[32]

Although *Arctic* and her sisters shipped large crews, the cost of people was not their largest expense. For packets and clippers the wind was free. For steamships, machinery and coal were expensive. Collins might have cut costs by reducing speed, but that was never an option, and so he sought other means.[33] One economical measure was to ensure that captains and chief engineers took aboard only enough coal (estimate of 1,000+ tons) for a single crossing. Extra coal took up valuable space that might be filled with paying cargo, while its weight put the hull deeper in the water, which increased resistance and reduced speed, and so to please their owners, captains filled their bunkers on a tight margin. Some erred in their fuel estimations. A tough voyage, particularly pushing west against strong winds, might require more coal than estimated. On at least two occasions New York–bound Collins ships diverted to Halifax to resupply, and in one instance, December 1850, after a "boisterous passage" that took several more days than planned, and with her bunkers nearly empty, *Baltic*, the fastest in the Collins quartet, was forced to make an embarrassing and unscheduled call at Provincetown on the tip of Cape Cod to take on coal.[34] Such mistakes, widely reported, cost time and reputation.

Coal and engine maintenance were the largest operational costs for both Cunard and Collins.[35] On a normal crossing, *Arctic* burned an average of nearly eighty tons per day. When in New York Collins's ships took on Cumberland coal, which was mined in Maryland and shipped from Baltimore by coastal schooner to the piers at the foot of Canal Street.[36] In Liverpool, Brown, Shipley purchased locally mined coal. In both ports it took the crew, working in a swirling cloud of choking coal dust, two or three days to complete bunkering, and then another miserable day was spent wiping down the coal dust that had drifted onto every surface and into every crevice in the ship.

At prices ranging between five and six dollars a ton, plus shipping, a full load of coal might cost eight to ten thousand dollars per round trip.[37] At the end of every voyage clerks and owners scrutinized the engineer's log, checking that he had done everything possible (except reduce speed) to cut consumption. Collins, whose tattered balance sheet gave him reason to check reports carefully, was particularly observant. Unlike Cunard, who seems to have left most of the detailed management of his line to MacIver and Burns, Collins scoured every line item.

Collins's interest in steam and economy drew him to the work of Brooklyn engineer and inventor James Frost. Like many of his contemporaries, Frost abhorred what he considered to be the colossal waste of steam power. In 1841 he secured a patent for a "repeating expansive engine" that sought to use steam more efficiently.[38] Continuing to advance his theories, Frost was promoting a new kind of steam by the late 1840s for which he coined the word "stame"—dry, superheated steam—that he claimed produced three to four times more energy than regular steam.[39] To test out stame, in 1852 the East River shipyard of Lawrence and Foulkes launched the tug *Joseph Johnson*, equipped with one of Frost's devices consisting of a pair of large pipes that conveyed "common steam" through the boiler, by which it was superheated. Benjamin Isherwood, the United States Navy's chief engineer, witnessed the experiment and declared it a success.[40]

Confident of these results, in the summer of 1854 Collins ordered that *Arctic* be fitted up to carry Frost's invention into "practical use."[41] Soon, however, a defect was discovered. Superheated dry steam "burned out" *Arctic's* pipes. To reduce the potential for damage, Chief Engineer Isherwood suggested using stame and "common steam" in combination, which "produced a better effect than using the former alone." Rogers and Collins agreed and pushed to complete the installation along these new lines, hoping to make a trial run to Boston in early September. Their plans were upended, though, when *Pacific*'s engines failed. When she was taken out of service for repairs, *Arctic* was called up to replace her. Although some of the stame equipment had been installed, the work would have to wait to be completed until *Arctic* returned, when all would be made "perfect."[42] On September 2, with some modest modifications having been made to her engines, *Arctic*—with Luce in command—departed for Liverpool.[43] With her paddle wheels churning, and assisted by a northwest breeze, *Arctic* made it to Liverpool in ten days, a decent but not record-breaking time.

After discharging passengers and mail to the landing, *Arctic* stood by in the river awaiting permission to enter a dock. Dock space in Liverpool was limited and expensive, particularly for vessels as large as *Arctic*.[44] Even more irksome, Liverpool's port charges, including towing, customs fees, and lighthouse duties, were nearly five times the rates charged in New York.[45] American owners complained bitterly about delays and costs. They also alleged that local officials discriminated against them, giving preferential treatment to vessels of their own port. Since the authorities could not be persuaded to reduce rates, the best way to cut expenses was to move quickly and minimize time in the dock. For the Collins Line this was the job of Brown, Shipley agents, who pressed hard for the quickest turnaround possible. "Fastness . . . in all things" was the line's reputation.[46] Stevedores hurried aboard to open hatches, unloading freight onto the dock apron to be carted away by teamsters to nearby spacious brick warehouses, awaiting delivery to customers in Liverpool and beyond.

In those same warehouses, other men were busy pushing iron-wheeled dollies laden with boxes and barrels that were packed with cloth and machinery from Manchester, cutlery from Sheffield, hardware from Wolverhampton, and earthenware from Staffordshire, all marked "New York via *Arctic*."[47] At the loading dock, clerks checked bills of lading while warehousemen slid heavy freight onto wagons drawn up in line waiting to ferry the cargo to the steamer. In addition to lumbering commercial freight wagons, smaller wagons from local hotels arrived with mounds of passenger luggage, bulky items including "steamer trunks" too large to stow in small cabins.

By early Wednesday morning, September 21, with cargo secured and full bunkers, *Arctic* had steam up and was ready to leave the dock. With a favoring tide the gates opened as a tug stood ready to escort her to a mooring opposite George's landing.[48]

On the landing there was considerable bustle. The steam tug *Samson* was tied up alongside, ready to ferry passengers out to the steamer. All through the morning Hackney carriages had been delivering passengers from hotels and boarding houses. As was usual a considerable crowd, including many who had come to say goodbye, had gathered about the landing.

Typical for the fall westbound crossing, the ship was fully booked, mostly with Americans heading home.[49] In each decade since 1830 the number of Americans traveling abroad had doubled.[50] Leaving home in the spring and early summer, the rich and well-to-do traveled across to Great Britain and the continent to visit their relatives and take in Europe's great cities, historic sites, and spas. It was a seasonal migration, and by early fall, with trunks full of "souvenirs" and lots of memories, travelers made their way to Liverpool, anxious to book passage before the fall winds turned the Atlantic mean.

Among the first-class passengers waiting to board was a small group connected by family and business. Mary Ann Collins, Edward Knight Collins's wife, and their children Mary Ann, age eighteen, and Henry, fifteen, were on their way home to New York after a summer abroad. With her and the children was her young brother James Ennis Woodruff, who was returning to his post in St. Louis as agent of the Collins Line, and his wife. The family of the line's president and chief investor, James Brown, was also preparing to board. The Brown entourage included James's eldest son, William, and his wife, Clara, with their two-year-old daughter, Grace Alice Jane, and her nurse. Joining them were James's two sisters, Grace and Maria. Grace was accompanied by her husband, George Allen, and their infant son, Herbert.[51]

Other distinguished passengers also stood about the landing, including Antoine Alfred Agenor, tenth Duc de Gramont; Prince de Bidache, a French diplomat en route to Washington; and William Comstock, brother of *Baltic*'s captain. Nearly lost in the crowd of passengers and the horde of well-wishers was a small, frail-looking eleven-year-old boy, Willie Luce, son of the captain who was preparing for *Arctic*'s departure. Always in poor health, Willie had accompanied his father on the eastbound passage and was returning with him to New York.[52]

Slowly passengers made their way onboard *Samson*. The short trip out to *Arctic* was unpleasant. Liverpool tugs, work boats with little in the way of passenger amenities, were notorious for being dirty and cramped. By eleven A.M. *Samson* had finished her ferrying duties and all were aboard. *Arctic* dropped her mooring lines and, as the last bags of mail were being hurled over the bulwark, steamed down the river, firing a salute to the city as passengers crowded the rail cheering and waving. Taking advantage of the tide, Luce, with the advice of the pilot standing by him, guided the steamer over the bar at the river's mouth. After dropping the pilot Luce ordered a westerly course across the Irish Sea. By midafternoon, clear of land, *Arctic* steered more southerly, heading down the Irish Sea toward St. George's Channel and thence into the Celtic Sea and the Atlantic. From the bridge, Luce signaled full speed. Down below, firemen went to work, and with rhythmic motions fed the furnaces. Gradually pressure in the boilers reached fourteen to fifteen pounds—enough to drive the *Arctic*'s thirty-five-foot diameter paddle wheels at nearly sixteen revolutions per minute, propelling her at a steady thirteen to fourteen knots. Rogers kept a careful eye on the engines. Frost's devices had worked well on the way over, and he and the captain looked for a record on the return voyage.

Not long after losing sight of land, at 3:30 in the afternoon, the sound of the gong invited passengers to dinner—a sumptuous meal, followed by tea at seven, and for those still hungry, supper at ten. After dinner, as the passengers settled into their cabins, they prayed that this first day at sea would be followed by others that could be summed up by a simple diary entry: "Nothing of special note occurred."[53]

As *Arctic* approached the southern tip of Ireland she changed course again. Off to the starboard side was Cape Clear Island (Fastnet Rock), the departure point on a long arc that stretched across the North Atlantic to Cape Race at the southern tip of Newfoundland. This line on Luce's charts, the great circle route, marked the shortest distance on the earth's surface between these two points. After several days of steaming against swells pushed toward them by brisk westerly winds, *Arctic* reached the midpoint on her route. Luce ordered a gradual change of course toward the southwest in the direction of Cape Race. The new course brought

Arctic across the shallows of the Grand Bank, where the chilly Labrador Current spilled into the warm waters of the Gulf Stream, creating a rich feeding ground for fish below and the constant threat of fog above. After nearly a week, by the twenty-sixth as she approached Newfoundland's Cape Race, heavy fog swaddled *Arctic*. Luce posted two lookouts forward, but eyeing a chance for a record westbound crossing, and perhaps wanting to give his partially altered engines a full test, he refused to reduce speed. While *Arctic* steamed steadily ahead to the west, on the small French island of St Pierre the French bark *Vesta* was preparing to get under way.[54]

Located in the Gulf of St. Lawrence, barely fourteen miles from the southern coast of Newfoundland's Burin peninsula, the rocky island outcrops of St. Pierre and Miquelon were the last vestiges of France's empire in North America.[55] Close by the rich fishing grounds off Newfoundland and Nova Scotia, the islands were critical bases for the French cod-fishing fleets. Each spring hundreds of "graviers"—mostly young men from the ports of Saint-Malo and Granville in Normandy, as well as Basques from Saint-Jean de Luz—arrived on the islands. Through the spring, summer, and early fall they worked spreading and drying codfish, preparing it for shipment to markets. At the end of the season, usually around the feast of Saint Michael (Michaelmas), as the weather turned cool, they gathered their few belongings and boarded vessels for home.

Owned by the Société Terreneuvienne of Granville, one of the largest companies involved in French cod fishing, *Vesta* was a relatively new vessel. Designed for the North Atlantic trade, she had an iron hull to protect her against ice, while below she was divided into three watertight compartments. Bark-rigged, with auxiliary steam and a screw propeller, *Vesta*, at 250 tons, was a well-built, sturdy vessel. When she departed St. Pierre on the twenty-sixth, her captain Alphonse Duchesne had a full cargo of fish and oil, a crew of fifty, and 147 fishermen bound happily home.[56]

Like Luce, Duchesne was well acquainted with fog, and he treated it with equal unconcern. As soon as *Vesta* cleared the harbor, Duchesne set a southeasterly course, taking him into the Atlantic past Cape Race sixty miles to the north. Moving briskly under both engine and sail, *Vesta* plowed ahead at ten knots.[57]

On Wednesday the twenty-seventh, at the sound of the eight bells marking noon, it being too foggy to take a sighting, Luce walked to the chart house to calculate *Arctic*'s position by the less precise method of dead reckoning. At this point in the voyage, seven days out from Liverpool, Luce was particularly concerned to get an accurate plot. On his last westbound crossing he had, through a "navigational error," grounded *Arctic* near Tuscar Rocks, County Wexford.[58] Although she had suffered no damage, *Arctic*'s misfortune had left a mark on his reputation. His calculations put the ship approximately sixty miles southeast of Cape Race crossing the Grand Banks east of Virgin Rocks.[59] From there to Sandy Hook, careful to keep sufficient sea room between his ship and the dangerous shores of Nova Scotia and Cape Cod, Luce plotted a clear path to New York. Indeed, given his position and speed—an impressive thirteen knots—Luce calculated that if he could maintain speed, he might beat Joe Comstock's westbound record of nine days, sixteen hours, and fifty-two minutes set by *Baltic* only two months before.[60]

As he put his charts aside and headed for the saloon to join the passengers, Luce ordered the ship's location entered into the log. The passengers, having heard the steward's summons, had already begun to take their seats at the long dining tables.[61] Elsewhere aboard, deck and engine crews moved about as the watch changed. For the lookout on the bow the change of watch could not have come too soon. Of all the duties aboard none was more important or tedious than standing lookout in fog. For hours the lookout had faced into a chill damp wind, unable to see more than a few hundred feet ahead. Aside from the slight rushing sound made by the bow cutting through the water, and the steady thump of the paddle wheels, he stood his post in eerie silence. In fog some captains sounded signals—bells or whistles—but that was not the order of business on a Collins ship.

Barely fifteen minutes into the new watch, out of the fog, two points to starboard, suddenly appeared the menacing shape of a vessel heading straight for *Arctic*, a vessel with all sails set and a stack belching smoke. Having no means of communication other than his panicked voice, the lookout ran aft toward the bridge calling "Stop her, stop her—steamer ahead."[62] Passengers in the saloon heard the cry, which raised considerable "excitement among the ladies." One of the passengers, James Smith of Mississippi, tried to calm the room; as he spoke, they felt "a slight jar to [the] ship, accompanied by a crashing noise against the starboard bow." Smith reported that "it was a moment of awe and suspense" but nothing to be concerned about. "We all seemed to satisfy ourselves that the shock was slight, and that, as we were on [a vessel] so large and strong, no serious damage had happened or could happen to such a ship, in an occurrence of such a nature." Just to satisfy himself, however, Smith followed the captain onto the deck to survey the situation.[63]

CHAPTER FOURTEEN

The *Arctic* Disaster

GRABBING THE BULWARK, Smith stood motionless. What he saw horrified him. *Vesta* had struck *Arctic* on the starboard side forward. The bark's iron prow had sliced through *Arctic's* wooden hull at the waterline, splintering the thick pine planks and shattering several of her diagonal cast iron frames. The French vessel too had been damaged. The force of the impact had torn open *Vesta's* bow, part of it breaking off and impaling itself in *Arctic's* hull. Inside moments, with an eerie, violent, death-like shudder, *Vesta* broke clear of the steamer—but not before the iron fluke on her starboard anchor had ripped another hole in *Arctic's* side. On deck, *Arctic's* crew and passengers rushed to the starboard side to look down on the bark as *Vesta* passed alongside, barely clearing the paddle box. Screams of panic could be heard from *Vesta* as her foremast, whipped by the force of the collision, toppled over the side, leaving a mass of broken timber and tangled rigging. With the wind spilling from her sails and a gaping hole in her bow, *Vesta*, cloaked in fog, sheered away.[1]

In an attempt to lift the gash above the waterline, Captain Duchesne ordered crew to go forward and lighten "the vessel by the head." Crewmen heaved boxes of salt cod, luggage, and anything else they could find over the side. Others, frantic for their own lives and believing that they were doomed, ignored the captain's order and hastily launched two small boats hoping to reach the safety of *Arctic*. The first capsized as soon as it hit the water, drowning all, while the second managed to pull away—but in the men's blind haste to get to the steamer through the fog they failed to notice *Arctic* turning toward them. Luce, trying as best he could to call the ship's company to emergency stations while also calming passengers, never saw *Vesta*'s boat, and within minutes *Arctic*'s giant thirty-five-foot starboard side paddle wheel shredded the small craft, spewing the frantic Frenchmen into the sea. From *Arctic* a deckhand threw a line toward the struggling men, but only one sailor, Jassonet Francois, was able to take hold and make it to the steamer. The others perished.

Despite first appearances, *Vesta* was not sinking. Thanks to Duchesne's quick thinking and the crew's swift action, *Vesta*'s bow came up high enough that the rush of water pouring in ebbed sufficiently to give the men time to stuff the gaping hole with "one hundred and fifty mattresses, paillasses and other effects of the crew and passengers." Once the hole was plugged, the men rushed to reinforce the forward bulkhead with "boards and planks." With the bulkhead holding and her pumps working at full capacity for the moment, *Vesta* was safe. *Arctic* was nowhere in sight. Believing that he had been abandoned by the steamer, Duchesne set a course for the closest port—St. John's, Newfoundland.[2]

Luce had not abandoned *Vesta*. "Seeing," he reported, that "the bows of the strange vessel seemed to be literally cut or crushed off for about ten feet, and seeing that she must instantly sink in a few minutes, and taking a hasty glance of our own ship, and believing we were comparatively uninjured, my first impulse was to endeavor to save the lives of those onboard this sinking vessel." With "a total want of anticipation" that his own situation required every man remain onboard, Luce made a fateful, and fatal, decision. He ordered two boats lowered to hasten to *Vesta*'s aid.[3]

Since *Arctic* carried only six lifeboats, Luce's actions left him with only four small rescue craft, each capable of taking aboard no more than fifty people. In retrospect, a mere six boats for 400 people, passengers and crew, was irresponsible, but *Arctic* was in full compliance with the law.[4] In accordance with an 1852 act of Congress providing "for the better Security of the lives of Passengers on board of vessels propelled in whole or part by Steam," *Arctic* and other steam vessels her size (more than 1,500 tons) were obligated to carry only six lifeboats, a number calculated not on the number of people aboard, but rather on an archaic measure of tonnage. That not every person was guaranteed a "seat" seems callous (and illegal) by modern standards, but just as no airline passenger expects a parachute, so nineteenth-century passengers accepted the lack of lifeboats for everyone, placing implicit faith in the Almighty and competent officers.[5]

Ironically, while the lifeboat seats were woefully inadequate, the same 1852 act required that "every vessel propelled by steam, and carrying passengers, carry aboard a sufficient number of good life-preserver[s], made of suitable material," available "in convenient and accessible places . . . for each and every passenger."[6] Luce's decision to send a third of his boats away risked the lives of people for whom he was accountable. As the first boat pulled in the direction of *Vesta*, with chief officer Gourley in command and six sailors at the oars, Luce received bad news. After surveying the damage below, the ship's carpenter, George Bailey, reported that *Arctic* was "leaking fearfully." Immediately, Luce stopped the launch of the second boat and tried to recall the first, but Gourley was too distant to hear the command. The captain's decision had cost him not only a boat but his first officer and a half dozen experienced seamen, nearly one-quarter of the entire deck crew. Gourley and his men never found *Vesta*, nor were they ever heard from again.

An hour after Gourley disappeared, Luce decided to begin abandoning his ship. He ordered a boat lowered. As he began to load it with women and children a rush of male passengers and crew pushed them aside. Luce ordered the boat to stand by the ship, but to his "dismay," the people in the boat panicked and cut the painter connecting them to the steamer, drifting into the fog and never to be seen again.[7]

While panic took over on deck, the engineers, firemen, and trimmers down below, even as water floated up around their ankles, worked feverishly to do all they could to keep the boilers fired. Pumps were started, and in a desperate attempt to combat the incoming rush of water, Chief Engineer Rogers reversed the bilge injectors so that instead of drawing water from outside for the boilers they sucked it up from the flooding bilges. Nonetheless, despite these efforts water continued to wash its way steadily aft, filling the long uncompartmentalized hull.

On deck, passenger James Smith looked on as the desperate and macabre scene of chaos spread. From his station atop the paddle box Luce was barking orders but few were listening. "[M]ost of the officers and men [were] running here and there on the deck, getting into an evident state of alarm." As the vessel took on a starboard list, aft on the quarterdeck "women and children were collected . . . seemingly resigned to their fate."[8]

To compensate for the growing list to starboard, Luce ordered all passengers to the port quarter while crew scrambled forward to release the heavy starboard anchor. For the moment, Smith noted, it worked and "our ship seemed to right herself somewhat . . . but it was too evident that Captain Luce himself as well as all hands, was becoming increasingly aware of our danger." Grasping at his only hope, abandoning any thought of providing assistance to *Vesta* or recovering Gourley and his crew, Luce turned his mortally wounded ship west and made for the coast of Newfoundland fifty miles distant.

It was a forlorn hope. The decision to steam for land probably hastened *Arctic*'s fate, for the forward motion of the ship forced more water into the hull. No longer the "Greyhound of the Sea," *Arctic*, her bow down and the list to starboard increasing, steamed toward her tragic fate. On deck the passengers and crew watched the water lapping up toward them as they cornered themselves on the port quarter, struggling to keep their footing on a wet deck sloping down toward the steadily rising sea. Smith recalled seeing the "deep seated thoughtful look of despair on their faces" as they stood in stupefied silence watching their universe collapse. "Wife and husband, father and daughter, brother and sister, would weep in each other's embrace."[9] The Brown and Collins families stood near one another "and talked little but composedly."[10]

In an attempt to give his pumps a chance to gain on the flooding, Luce ordered the ship's carpenter to try fothering; that is, stretching a sail over the hole in the damaged hull. The force of the water, he hoped, would push the canvas into the opening, thus stemming the flow. Bailey tried twice to no avail. The hole was too large, and jagged pieces of iron left behind by *Vesta* tore the sails apart.

Luce was losing control. Men were going "about the decks in a sort of bewilderment as to what was best to be done." Some went to the pumps, others broke open the liquor cabinet in the saloon, and many simply stood by, stunned. While the crew knew their duties in ordinary circumstances, they had never been drilled for emergencies. Nor had passengers ever been advised about what to do in an unexpected situation. The logic and order of the ship was torn to pieces.

With Gourley gone—an officer who if still onboard "would have kept the sailors to their duty"—Luce could not control the crew. *Arctic*'s remaining boats were insufficient for those left aboard. Luce's attempts to restore order were futile, and they collapsed completely when, driven up from the rising waters below, the engine room crew burst onto the deck. These men knew firsthand that the ship was going down. There was a mad scramble on deck and a rush to lower boats. Stewards who had been pleased to serve passengers now became mortal enemies. Burly firemen pushed aside women and children as they made for the boats. Luce, in a vain effort to save "ladies and children," ordered second mate William Baalham to launch a boat and follow aft to await his commands. As soon as the crew saw the boat swung out, they rushed Baalham, and "no sooner did she touch the water than men from the ship threw themselves into her and around her in all directions. Those who first gained a place in the boat picked up those who were nearest to them . . . The seamen naturally were the strongest and came first." Within minutes the boat was filled with twenty-five "desperate men" who, in defiance of the captain's orders, cut the line and rowed away from *Arctic*; no women or children were among them.

Panicked men offered no mercy to the weaker. They continued to rush the boats. One boat slipped from her lines and plunged into the water, drowning more than two dozen people. The survivors managed to right her. She pulled away with eighteen crew and one male passenger. A fourth boat managed to get into the water successfully. She carried away two dozen people, including some women, but then drifted away and was lost. Smith recorded the melancholy scene. "Some few gentlemen exert all their powers to prevail on others to work at the pumps, but all to no purpose, the ship kept on gaining in quantity as steadily as time progressed." It was, he knew, "only a question of how many hours or minutes we would be above water."[11]

Convinced "that the ship must go down in a very short time" Luce, with the help of passengers and third mate Francis Dorian, broke out axes and saws and began to hack away at every floatable item they could find, putting over the side spars, sails, "and such other materials as we could collect . . . to form a raft." Luce ordered Dorian to lower one of the last boats and bring her around to stand by as they attempted to launch the raft. "They had made considerable progress in securing the spars together when an alarm was given that the ship was sinking." To avoid being sucked down by the rapidly sinking steamer Dorian shoved off with four male passengers, twenty-six crew, and several empty seats.

In *Arctic*'s dreary and disheartening final moments, even more craven acts played out. Under the pretense of going over the side to help plug the hole, chief engineer Rogers and a dozen of his men took a small boat carried on the deckhouse forward and lowered it into the water. Smith, hoping to join them, leaped over the side, but once in the water he was unable to reach Rogers. Luckily he found a tiny raft of three planks lashed together, and on it he floated away. Meanwhile the boat full of engineers pulled from the ship. They too would be lost.

In this bleak demonstration of human depravity, two heroes emerged. Stewart Holland, the son of Isaac Holland, assistant master of arms of the United States Senate, had signed aboard *Arctic* as an apprentice in the engineering department. When the rest of the engine room crew fled, Holland remained behind. To draw attention in the hope that a passing vessel might hear it, Luce gave the young man the task of firing off the ship's signal cannon. Holland remained by his gun until swept from the deck.[12] Checking for crew or passengers on a last sweep below, Luce discovered chief stewardess Anna Downer doing her duty, working a manual pump "with all the power she could command." Luce ordered her on deck. He told her "that it was as useless for her to attempt to pump out the ship, as it would be to attempt to pump out the ocean." She defied his command, answering that she would "pump as long as I can work my arms."[13] In light of all else that took place aboard the *Arctic*, the bravery of Holland and Downer shone as bright lights in an otherwise dark story.

By 4:30 in the afternoon, little more than four hours after the collision, with her decks nearly covered by the sea and waves lapping over the bulwarks, *Arctic* was in her final throes. Passenger George Burns, one of the lucky few in Dorian's boat, described what he saw when at the last moment Luce ordered the raft put over the side. Almost immediately "a rush was made . . . headlong over the bulwarks on to the raft."[14] By then "the sea was now flush with the dead lights. In less than three minutes the stern sunk—the foam went boiling over the tumbling heap of human beings—many were dashed forward against the pipe. I heard one wild yell (still ringing in my ears) and saw the *Arctic* and the struggling mass rapidly engulfed."[15]

Three lifeboats remained in sight but, fearing that if they approached the sinking ship they might be overwhelmed by people clamoring to get in their boat, they stood off. "We were," remembered Burns, "forced to abandon them to fate."[16] They abandoned nearly 300 people, most either floating on the surface buoyed by their life jackets, or clinging to the half-submerged raft. Although the best available, *Arctic*'s life jackets were crude devices constructed either of a collection of sealed tin cans or India rubber bladders sewn together. The India rubber preservers "leaked out air about as fast as you could blow in," while the "tin ones did good service." If they were still alive after the initial shock of going into the water, "good service" meant keeping people afloat only long enough, in the forty-five degree water, to succumb to hypothermia, which might have happened in as little as thirty minutes.[17] According to steward Peter McCabe, who was clinging to an uncompleted "imperfectly constructed raft," it was a grisly scene. "Those who had life preservers did not sink, but floated with their ghastly faces upwards reminding those who still remained alive of the fate that awaited them."[18]

One survivor, the captain, suffered a fate that was both tragic and miraculous. As the ship went down, Luce recounted, "I found myself on the surface after a brief struggle with my own helpless child [Willie] in my arms when I again found myself impelled downwards to a great depth and before I reached the surface a second time I nearly perished and had lost my hold on my child." As he gasped for air, searching frantically for Willie, an "awful and heart rending scene presented itself to my view; women and children struggling together . . . calling on each other for help and imploring God to assist them."[19] The ship was gone, but then, in a fashion, she reappeared. As *Arctic* plunged 600 feet to the bottom, her descent accelerated by the weight of her heavy iron machinery, the power of the water tore her apart. Then as she hit bottom, the impact sent buoyant pieces of the hull, deadly projectiles, to the surface.[20] The largest was a paddle box. Detached from the hull, it broke the surface in a violent eruption and, according to Luce, "just graz[ed] my head." He was spared, but Willie was not, for as the box came crashing back down, it fell with its full force "on the head of my darling child [and] I beheld him a lifeless corpse on the surface of the waves."

By dusk the scene was silent. Of the six lifeboats, three had disappeared. Three remained in the area, two in command of second mate Baalham and a third under the command of third mate Dorian. A dozen men, including Luce, found strange refuge on the deadly paddle box still afloat. Among them was Grace Brown Allen's husband, George, who had watched as his wife and child were swept away along with Mary Ann Collins and her two children.[21] Collins's brother-in-law James Woodruff was also huddling in the box, but at some point during the long night, he slipped into the cold Atlantic. Passenger James Smith was floating nearby amongst the wreckage, holding himself up on a flimsy piece of debris. Francois, the fisherman who had been rescued from *Vesta*, and a mess boy occupied a small raft, while other bits of debris that had been lashed together drifted nearby, five firemen clinging onto it for dear life. The largest number, however, took refuge with McCabe on the raft.

As the temperature dropped, rolling swells driven by light winds from the west and southwest rocked the boats, the rafts, and the paddle box. None of the boats carried any emergency gear; no food, water, or compass. Second mate Baalham, unwilling to float aimlessly, took his cue from the direction of the wind and waves and decided to strike for Newfoundland. Baalham was a good seaman, and after a day and a half of rowing, he brought his two boats (twenty passengers, twenty-five crew) to shore early on the morning of the twenty-ninth on a rocky beach at Broad Cove (Renews) on Newfoundland's Avalon Peninsula, sixty miles south of St. John's. Leaving Purser John Geib in charge with instructions to get everyone to St. John's, Baalham rushed to the nearest fishing village and chartered a small schooner to return to the scene of the fated steamer.

As Baalham's boat was pulling for Newfoundland, McCabe and seventy-five others remained near the site of the wreck, clinging to their makeshift raft. That night, McCabe remembered, was "cold and foggy."[22] Through the darkness he watched as the waves "washed away [the] living freight . . . Every minute one or more of our unfortunate fellow passengers [dropped] into their watery grave."[23] The women were "the first to go; they were unable to stand the exposure more than three or four hours."[24] At dawn McCabe, who had secured himself to the raft by running his left leg under a taut line, looked about the raft. He was alone.

Lacking Baalham's skill at boat-handling and navigation, Dorian kept his boat hove to near the site of the sinking, hoping that other vessels might be in the area. His lifeboat overcrowded, low in the water, with barely six inches of freeboard, Dorian had to use "despotic means" to keep command. To prevent being swamped, he ordered a sea anchor out to hold the boat into the wind. Through the night the men bailed furiously with all the sapping strength they could summon. They managed to endure the night. The following afternoon deliverance arrived. The lookout standing watch on the bark *Huron*, bound from New Brunswick to Quebec, spotted Dorian and the raft. *Huron*'s commander, Captain A. Wall, altered course for the lifeboat. As soon as its occupants were safely aboard, Wall sent a boat to the raft to rescue McCabe. After hearing how many people had been aboard *Arctic*, Wall crisscrossed the area for the rest of the day and through the night in search of additional survivors. He displayed "extra lights, fired rockets and kept a horn blowing [but] his endeavors were fruitless."[25] In the morning (September 29), *Huron* resumed course for Quebec. Late that afternoon, Wall spoke with the ship *Lebanon*, bound for New York. Offered passage directly home, eighteen of the rescued, including Dorian, transferred to *Lebanon*. The others remained aboard *Huron* and continued on to Quebec.[26]

Despite his best efforts at searching, as Wall bore away he unknowingly left behind several others in the water who had managed to survive the sinking by floating on pieces of wreckage. Fortunately another vessel, *Cambria* (not the Cunarder), was passing through the area, bound from Greenock to Quebec. In his report, *Cambria*'s captain John Russell told an extraordinary story.

> On the 29th of September, the weather being very thick and hazy, and having been so for several days, about 8 A.M. it suddenly cleared away, when a sailing ship [*Huron?*] was seen in the distance steering in the same direction. At 9 A.M. the mate called me, saying there was some singular looking thing ahead. I immediately took the glass and went aloft. I distinctly saw one human being standing on some boards waving his hands.[27]

The man frantically gesturing was the French fisherman Jassonet Francois. He had managed to stay alive, although the mess boy had slipped away and drowned. Russell went on to describe the scene. "We soon reached him, and running up with the ship close by him, we threw out ropes and put some hands overboard, who caught him as he laid hold of the ropes, and he was thus brought on board. He was very much exhausted." Although in immediate need of attention, Francois refused to go below. Instead he pointed to the sea—"More man, Englishman." Russell understood. "I immediately went abaft with my glass in my hand, and distinctly saw five pieces of wreck, at separate distances from each other, about two miles on our weather beam, and on three pieces human beings were distinctly visible." It took a while to tack to windward, but about two P.M. Russell was able to send a boat to the largest piece of wreckage, the remnants of the paddle box. They returned with Luce, George Allen, and a young German passenger, Ferdinand Keyn. The rest had drowned.

As Luce and the others were "put to bed," Russell approached "another raft on which were two persons [firemen], who being taken into the boat, it proceeded in the direction of two other rafts, from which were taken three persons [firemen] and one person on the other [James Smith]." As they came aboard, Russell asked about other survivors. For the entire day *Cambria*'s lookouts stood at the masthead searching, but no other survivors were found. It was hopeless, and as darkness fell the seas turned rough and the fog rolled in. All about the site flotsam— bedding, trunks, boxes, barrels, and life preservers in great quantity— was floating about, but no living being was seen. "I then proceeded on my voyage," Russell remembered, "a heavy gale, which no raft could have lived through with people on it having sprung up." As crew tended to the survivors *Cambria* resumed her course to Quebec. It would take several days to arrive. Luce spent much of his time composing a report to Edward Collins.

While *Arctic*'s tragedy was playing out, Captain Duchesne and his crew, in a remarkable display of seamanship, were able to shore up *Vesta*'s crushed bow well enough to make the two-and-a-half day trip to St. John's. On Saturday morning, September 30, *Vesta* limped through the harbor's narrow entrance into St. John's just ahead of a severe gale that, had she still been at sea, might well have doomed her. Her unexpected arrival quickly drew attention. As she approached the wharf, onlookers gaped at the sheared-off bow and shattered rigging and marveled that she had survived. Duchesne reported that *Vesta* struck *Arctic* in a heavy fog. The steamer, according to him, had suffered minor damage, and then Duchesne told the stunned community that *Arctic* had steamed away, abandoning *Vesta* to damage that at the time appeared fatal. For nearly two days a community steeped in seafaring tradition buzzed with the remarkable story of the *Vesta* and her captain, while damning the cowardly desertion of the American steamer. Embarrassed by what appeared to be the despicable behavior of his countrymen, the American consul, W. H. Newman, was greatly relieved late Sunday when the *Arctic*'s survivors who had gone ashore at Broad Cove arrived to share their own story of woe.[28]

Although several days had passed since *Arctic*'s sinking, making the odds of finding anyone still alive highly unlikely, Newman launched a search. Locals, who from their own experience were familiar with disasters at sea, rushed to help. Newfoundland's Anglican bishop, Edward Field, offered his yacht. The Warren brothers, St. John's fish merchants, offered their brig *Ann Eliza*. To the profound dismay of many in St. John's, however, the royal governor declined to send out a public vessel. In any case, nothing but wreckage was ever discovered. Newman was anxious to report the tragedy, but since Newfoundland had no telegraphic connection to the mainland, dispatches had to be sent by mailboat to Halifax and thence over a series of unreliable connections via New Brunswick and Boston to New York.[29] It took ten days for the news from Newfoundland to reach the city.

Totally unaware of what had happened in the North Atlantic, New York's newspapers declared *Arctic* "overdue" on October 4th. No one was particularly alarmed. Despite the firm schedules that were promised, steamship arrivals often varied by days. Collins explained that *Arctic*'s delay was most likely caused by "some disarrangement in her machinery," a reoccurring excuse in the early days of the line, and in this instance perhaps related to the experiment with stame.[30] Uneasiness grew, however, when on October 6th the Cunard steamer *Canada* docked from Liverpool. Having left England on the twenty-third, her crew confirmed that *Arctic* had indeed sailed on schedule.[31] The next day George Templeton Strong, a prominent New York lawyer and compulsive diarist, recoded in his journal that "people who've friends on board [*Arctic*] begin to talk nervously about her." At a Trinity Church vestry meeting that night, he observed, when the evening gun sounded from the Navy Yard several men announced, "There's the *Arctic* at last." It was, he noted, a mistake.[32]

On Tuesday, October 10, *Lebanon* arrived off Sandy Hook with the baleful news. The pilot boat *Christian Berg* brought seventeen of the survivors up to the city. Hoping to avoid attention, Dorian remained aboard *Lebanon* and did not step ashore until the eleventh. By that time the story had swept the city, also fueled by the receipt of a telegram from Halifax. The Collins office at 56 Wall Street was jammed with people demanding information about friends and loved ones. As rumors circulated, the unreliable telegraph connection went dead, compounding the confusion and uncertainty. Learning that he had lost his wife, brother-in-law, daughter, and young son, Collins left the city. Unable to answer the unceasing questions and overwhelmed with grief, he retreated to Larchmont, where he remained in seclusion. When told that he had lost his son, two daughters, a daughter-in-law, and two grandchildren, James Brown, president of the line, reportedly fell to his knees, crying

"My children, my children!"[33] The wreck of the *Arctic*, reported the *Herald*, "completely absorbed the public mind."[34]

Luce's report, however, published by a sensationalized press avid for lurid details, finally gave the public what it wanted: the truth about what had happened aboard *Arctic*. He described how firemen and others rushed for the boats, pushing aside women and children. When he ordered a boat over the side to take on passengers the crew "cut the ropes, and disappear[ed] astern in the fog." Another boat was torn from her davits by panicked crew and fell into the sea. When one boat was successfully launched, "men leaped from the top of the rail, twenty feet, crushing and maiming those who were in the boat." The chief engineer and fifteen of his men had abandoned the ship in the last available lifeboat. Less than two hours after the collision, Luce found "that not a seaman was left aboard." Others recounted even more hideous sights. Down below in the saloon, where only a day before gentlemen and ladies had been associating in polite company as stewards scurried about answering the call for service, "passengers had broken up the bar; the liquors were flowing down the scuppers. . . . strong, stout-looking men [were] on their knees, in the attitude of prayer; others, when asked to do anything, were immovable, perfectly stupefied."[35] The stewards were not present. They had rushed on deck and joined the rest of the crew in a mad dash for the boats. The final count told the story. Of the approximately 400 people aboard only sixty-one crew and twenty-four passengers had survived; not a single woman or child was among them.

Arctic's tragedy exploded into a national drama. Strong, the diarist, noted that the news "stopped all the workings on Wall Street . . . and kept brokers and lawyers and businessmen of all sorts around the news-paper offices and telegraphs."[36] The initial shock of the loss soon gave way to recrimination and despair. Taking his lesson from Psalm 77:19— "Thy way is in the Sea, and thy paths in the great waters,"—the well-known Presbyterian minister Cortlandt Van Rensselaer voiced a Promethean view of the sinking. In a much-reprinted sermon he asked if Americans, in their headlong rush to "annihilate time and space," had gone too far and suffered the consequences of greed and hubris.[37] Others read an even more damning message into the tragedy. In their sober view *Arctic*'s plunge to the bottom of the North Atlantic had taken down not only innocent women and children, but had dragged American character into the depths as well. To prove their point, they cited the example of HMS *Birkenhead*.

Barely a year and a half earlier, February 26, 1852—a moment still fresh in the public's memory—the British troopship HMS *Birkenhead* had been steaming east from Simon's Bay bound to Algoa Bay, both in South Africa. Aboard were soldiers of the 74th Regiment and the Queen's Royal Regiment, many of them accompanied by their families. At two o'clock in the morning "with no warning whatsoever, a deafening crash shattered the silence of the night and the *Birkenhead* came shuddering violently to a stop,. . . impaled helplessly on the apex of an uncharted rock."[38] It was a fatal blow. Through a wide gash in the hull water poured in and the ship began to go down. Lieutenant Colonel A. Seton, the soldiers' commanding officer, ordered his men to the pumps, instructing them "to preserve order and silence."[39] As the men pumped vigorously, ship captain Robert Salmond sent the women and children into the first cutter, telling the cutter's coxswain "to pull away immediately."[40] Other boats followed with additional women and children. As they moved off, *Birkenhead* slipped suddenly off the rock and plunged into deep water. As she went down Salmond gave his final command: "Save yourselves. All those who can swim, jump overboard and make for the boats. That is your only hope of salvation."[41] Lieutenant Colonel Seton, fearing "that any rush for the boats would mean certain death for the helpless women and children" [raised] his hands above his head, and with his voice torn with deep emotion, ordered the regiments "to stand fast." Seton's order "was heard by every man . . . and this, to their eternal honour, they did to the very last man."[42] Nearly all of the soldiers perished, but their bravery saved the lives of others, including seven women and thirteen children. Salmond's call for "women and children first," and the steadfastness of the soldiers, embodied the Victorian ideal of manly selflessness and signified the special place that women were accorded in Anglo-American society.[43]

In his sermon Van Rensselaer remembered the *Birkenhead* and proclaimed the conduct of its soldiers "Britain's highest military achievement." Their behavior was tragic, but nonetheless glorious and self-sacrificial. What then to think of the American men, passengers, and crew aboard *Arctic*, who "treacherously desert[ed] feeble and delicate women and shut their ears to cries from little children" as they either drank themselves into numbness or rushed to the boats to save themselves? In stark contrast to the despicable actions of the men aboard his ship, Luce, in his report to Collins—circulated widely in both American and British newspapers—wrote that the women, including Mrs. Collins, gave proof to their virtue and nobility by standing aside from the hysteria sweeping across the steamer, and who, "after the first fright was over, were as calm as could be imagined and seemed perfectly resigned to whatever might be their fate."[44] Third mate Francis Dorian, who left in the last boat (men only aboard), remembered that as he looked back he saw that "the ladies exhibited the most admirable coolness, and stared death in the face with a heroism which should have put to the blush the men who deserted and left them to their fate."[45] Of all the condemnations, the most powerful came from the redoubtable Henry Ward Beecher, pastor of the Plymouth Church in Brooklyn and Captain Judkins's nemesis on *Asia*. It was an attack on hubris, wealth, and human behavior. "In the morning the waiters served the titled and rich [but] in the evening the lusty strength of the engineer was a greater title than money or coronets."[46]

In this sordid scene of cowardice and desertion, one figure stood apart—Captain Luce. American newspapers, desperate to find someone to praise, held him up as the tragic hero. He certainly had suffered tragedy, specifically the loss of his son, but he had also made the mistake of ordering his first officer and six seamen off *Arctic* at precisely the moment when experienced hands were most needed aboard the ship. During the four agonizing hours of *Arctic*'s demise, authority collapsed, the ship was in chaos, and her captain was little more than an observer. Extant accounts mention no attempt on his part to take control of the situation, nor does he seem to have done much to organize the building of the raft or to have taken any other measures that a commander ought to have done. Instead Luce is most often presented in a tender tableau standing on the paddle box, embracing his son as the ship goes down. Indeed, in the iconic image of the sinking ship's last moments, marine artist James Buttersworth painted Luce standing boldly on the paddle box. The enterprising New York City lithographer Nathaniel Currier, knowing his audience's ravenous appetite for disaster scenes, produced a popular print from the painting.

Luce's behavior had been highly questionable, but few criticized him. One exception was a writer in the Middleton, Connecticut, *Constitution*, who in response to the laudatory reports in the New York City newspapers asked why an "incompetent commander" who had brought "destruction upon a crowd of helpless beings committed to his care" ought not to be punished. Where is the justice, he asked, if "an officer of the army or navy on slight appearances of misconduct is court martialed . . . but if the commander of a ship, on board of which are five hundred souls, shows such a want of seamanship and care that his vessel is lost and half his passengers are sent into eternity, the public 'regrets' the 'accident,' and with a few stereotyped expressions of horror, forgets the subject altogether."[47] Privately, Strong, a man who in his diary entries was more given to description than judgment, concluded that Luce "was not equal to the emergency, [and] a commander more energetic and thoughtful than Luce could have saved crew and passengers."[48] Strong kept his criticisms to himself, as did many others in New York society. What was remembered and repeated was the sight of Luce standing at his post while the vessel was sinking, embracing his son Willy. In an era when captains of packets and steamers were idolized, it was easier to blame the tragedy on common, cowardly sailors, and the soot-covered black gang rising from the ship's bowels below, than to call into question the competence of the commander on the quarterdeck.

In a nation in which seafarers were held in high regard, British commentators offered some excuse for Luce. "At least," commented the *Times*, "he had the merit of remaining by his ship to the last."[49] They granted no such grace to Collins and his partners. Luce, they noted, "in carrying on at all hazards, without any regard to signals or precautions, without previous preparation in the escape of boats for all the contingencies of an Atlantic run," was simply following orders. "Had the *Arctic* been provided with a sufficient number of boats, there would not have been any undue precipitancy on the part of the crew to break discipline. When 400 people are struggling for possession of a boat which will contain but 20 or 30—and life is the prize of success, death the penalty of failure—it is not difficult to see that not every man will remain a martyr to duty." The fault rested clearly with Collins. "More than 300 valuable lives have been lost through the neglect of the owners, the evil customs of the line, and the cowardly desertion by the crew of the *Arctic*."[50]

Some responses were theatrical and self-serving. On Friday, October 13th, Edward Cunard, his father's agent in New York, announced that company orders had been given "to furnish two additional life boats for each steamer." At the time British law actually required fewer lifeboats than did American regulations.[51] The following Monday, "a life boat was conspicuously paraded through the streets, having painted on it 'Life boat of Cunard Steamship *Canada*.'" One observer asked, "Could it have been a taunt, a boast, an advertisement to secure passengers?"[52] Cunard had also ordered shipped aboard his vessels "large bells which will be rung in the fog and [directed] that hereafter the steam whistle will be freely used."[53]

Collins too announced new safety measures including the addition of five lifeboats, "nested on deck with crew assigned," and the installation of watertight compartments in his ships. In reaction to criticism of Captain Luce's apparent inability to maintain discipline among the crew, the company advertised that henceforth it was providing each of its officers "with two cases of Colt's revolvers, with instructions that if ever another of *Arctic*'s calamities with its heartless desertion occurred, to use them."[54]

Captain James Luce never went to sea again. He "swallowed the anchor," moved to New York City, and became a founder of and surveyor for the Great Western Marine Insurance Company. On July 9, 1879, he died in the comfort of his home at New Rochelle.

In the midst of national furor Collins was silent. He remained at Larchmont, grieving his personal loss while also contemplating the future of his line. *Arctic*'s sinking shook the very foundation upon which his line had been built—public subsidy. Despite the persistent carping in Congress Collins had managed to survive by presenting his ships as mighty symbols of American enterprise, power, and character. The grand image that he and his associates had so carefully erected was dissolving. If Collins had any doubt about the extent to which his line's reputation had been tarnished, it was removed when he read President

Franklin Pierce's annual message to the second session of the 33rd Congress, December 4, 1854. Although he hailed from New Hampshire, Pierce, a "Doughface Democrat"—a political trimmer with southern sympathies—had never been a friend to New York's maritime interests. According to the president, contrary to the grand and exalted vision of the American merchant marine that shipowners on South Street and elsewhere had conjured up to secure public acclaim and congressional largesse, it was an enterprise in need of "serious reflection." It was time, Pierce said, "to revise the existing laws." In an obvious reference to *Arctic*, he reminded Congress that[55]

> In most of the States severe penalties are provided to punish conductors of trains, engineers, and others employed in the transportation of persons by railway or by steamboats on rivers. Why should not the same principle be applied to acts of insubordination, cowardice, or other misconduct on the part of masters and mariners producing injury or death to passengers on the high seas, beyond the jurisdiction of any of the States, and where such delinquencies can be reached only by the power of Congress?

Pierce's message was unwelcome news. So too was the announcement that another New Yorker, Cornelius Vanderbilt, "The Commodore," was preparing to launch his own Atlantic steamship line. Known for his fierce, predatory behavior, Vanderbilt's entry into the contest sent a shudder along the keel of the Collins Line.

CHAPTER FIFTEEN

Commodore Vanderbilt

SAMUEL CUNARD WAS IN LONDON when he learned of the *Arctic* disaster. In order to be closer to the center of his business he had left Halifax and taken up residence at Bush Hill, a seventeenth-century mansion just outside of the city.[1] In a letter published in the *Times* he blamed the misbehavior of *Arctic's* crew and passengers for the loss of life and praised Captain Luce "as a firm and resolute man." To allay any fears about the safety of his own ships, he noted that the lifeboats aboard his steamers "are quite sufficient to carry every person in the ship" and could be "launched, equipped and manned in three minutes." He reminded his readers that his line "have been so fortunate as to carry about 100,000 passengers across the Atlantic without injury to one of them."[2]

While Cunard was reassuring the public about the safety of his ships, he was also contending with another challenge. The Admiralty had taken up several of his steamers for service in the Crimean War.

The Crimean War broke out between Czarist Russia and the Ottoman Empire in 1853. Unwilling to allow Russian advances in the Black Sea that threatened their interests, Great Britain and France entered the war on the side of the Ottomans in March 1854. Without the means to move their massive armies overland, including horses and mountains of supplies, the Western powers had to rely on the long sea passage through the Mediterranean and into the Black Sea. Pressed to provide transport, the Admiralty faced a daunting logistical challenge. Only steam-powered vessels had the capacity and speed to move allied forces to the theatre of war. Unfortunately, the Admiralty had neither sufficient experience with steam nor ships to fulfill that mission. Samuel Cunard, however, could assist on both fronts. According to his contract he was obligated to relinquish his ships for wartime service, but rather than waiting to be summoned, Great Britain's best-known shipowner preempted any official call and, in a clever political move that gained him national acclaim, offered his ships for service with "no haggle of price, no driving good bargain."[3] Eventually, the Admiralty took up for service fourteen Cunard steamers, including several on the American route. With so many ships dedicated to the war effort, the company was unable to maintain its regular Atlantic schedule, forcing it to curtail calls at Boston and reduce its New York arrivals. The line's scaling back, however, did little financial harm to Cunard. A grateful government agreed to pay him twice the normal charter rate. Cunard's service in the Crimean War was later recognized when the Queen conferred a baronetcy on him.

Under the uncertain circumstances brought onto them by war and disaster, it was in the best interests of Cunard and Collins to continue to abide by their agreement to fix prices and share revenue. At a moment when both lines, in their weakened condition, might be vulnerable to competition, stability was critical. In late 1854 that stability was threatened when Cornelius Vanderbilt, one of New York's most rapacious businessmen, announced his entry into the transatlantic steamship competition.

Cornelius Vanderbilt, according to a contemporary observer, "evinced more energy and 'go-aheadativeness' in building and driving steamboats" than any American alive.[4] He was descended from four generations of immigrants (Van der Bilt) who had settled on Staten Island during the period of Dutch rule, a family that during its first century in the New World avoided any notable success. The early generations were "plodding, unimaginative tillers of the soil" whose "saving characteristic seems to have been a steadfastness of purpose which drove them to make their living in relatively unfavorable surroundings and rear large broods of children." Cornelius, described as "a big-bodied, husky, black-eyed lad," grew up on the island pitching hay and hoeing potatoes and sailing small boats over to Manhattan.[5] In 1810, at age sixteen, he borrowed $100 from his provident mother, the only person in his extraordinary career who could "dominate" him.[6] With that money he left the farm, bought a periauger (a small two-masted boat), and launched a ferry business between Manhattan and Staten Island. Decades later, on his way to becoming the richest person in America, he shifted to owning steamboats and railroads. Generally an unsentimental man, Vanderbilt was noticeably nostalgic when he recalled the day when he first set sail across the harbor. "I didn't feel as much real satisfaction when I made two million . . . as I did on that bright May morning sixty years before when I stepped into my own periauger, hoisted my own sail, and put my hand on my own tiller."[7]

"Cornele, the boatman," did well. During the War of 1812 while the British Navy prowled outside New York Harbor, Vanderbilt secured several lucrative government contracts for carrying supplies to the various American military posts defending the port. After the war he expanded into the coasting business, sailing north to Providence and Boston and venturing south as far as Charleston.

In 1817, only a decade after Robert Fulton's *Clermont* had made its inaugural voyage up the Hudson, Vanderbilt, tired of tacking and jibing across the harbor, abandoned sail and shifted to steam, taking command of the steamer *Mouse*, owned by Thomas Gibbons, crossing between New York City and New Brunswick, New Jersey. After a dozen years with Gibbons, Vanderbilt launched his own steamboat business in 1829, running up the Hudson River to Albany. Success on that route brought him enough profit and experience to expand his growing steam empire to Long Island Sound, where in 1840 he began providing service to Stonington, Connecticut, and Providence, Rhode Island. Within a few years "The Commodore," a title laid on him by the *Journal of Commerce*, "owned and operated more steamboats than any other man in the country."[8]

Not even the Sound, however, could contain the Commodore's ambitions. In 1853, recognizing an opportunity to take advantage of the horde of crazed Americans raring to get to California's goldfields, Vanderbilt, along with several partners, focused on building a route across the

Central American nation of Nicaragua that, by a series of roads, rivers, lakes, and a canal, would connect the Atlantic and Pacific Oceans. It was a grandiose scheme marked by political infighting, diplomatic intrigue, a failed filibustering expedition, and blackmail. In the midst of this wild and unruly free-for-all, Vanderbilt wrote a note in his own barely decipherable hand informing Charles Morgan and Cornelius Garrison, two of his partners with whom he had the falling out, "I won't sue you for the law is too slow. I'll ruin you. Sincerely yours."9 His threat was real. Revenge was Vanderbilt's favorite policy, so to keep him at bay his former partners paid him off. In two years he took payments from them of more than $1.2 million—an agreement later described in a court decision as "immoral."10 Immoral or not, it became one of Vanderbilt's favorite, and highly lucrative, tactics—threaten to compete, then take the payoff instead. In the Nicaragua adventure Vanderbilt emerged as the only person who profited.11

By the early 1850s Vanderbilt—by his own account worth more than $11 million, returning him 25 percent a year—was swimming in cash and looking for new opportunities. Remaining focused on steamships, a business he knew well, the Commodore cast his predatory eye toward the North Atlantic.

Vanderbilt's interest in transoceanic steam peaked when he and his family, accompanied by several friends, took a vacation cruise during the spring and summer of 1853 aboard his yacht *North Star*. At 270 feet and nearly two thousand tons, *North Star* was larger, and possibly more luxurious, than the Royal Yacht *Victoria and Albert*.12 Vanderbilt offered command of his yacht to one of New York's most famous masters, the former skipper of the Collins Line packet *Roscius*, Asa Eldridge. It was a voyage, Vanderbilt told his friend New York senator Hamilton Fish, by which he intended as an American to "give credit to the enterprise of our country."13 In four months *North Star* steamed more than fifteen thousand miles. Although he was snubbed on occasion by English and European elites who viewed him as a crude, ill-educated parvenu, Vanderbilt made an impression nonetheless. After his yacht docked in Southampton, Vanderbilt and his party took the train to London, where his arrival attracted great attention.14 He attended dinners given in his honor by the American minister to Great Britain, Joseph Ingersoll; by

Thomas Sidney, Lord Mayor of London; and by George Peabody, the most prominent member of the expatriate American community.

The cruise over, Vanderbilt returned to New York. Although the tangled affairs in Nicaragua continued to engage him, his European travel had set him to thinking about steam travel on the Atlantic. He had not been oblivious to the profits to be had, but he had seen small advantage in trying to compete with Collins and Cunard, both of whom, through political connections, enjoyed generous public subsidies. Vanderbilt had little regard for Collins. He was, in the Commodore's estimation, a weak character and a poor businessman. His ships were needlessly extravagant; his line's costs were out of control; his business had yet to turn a profit; his entire enterprise floated along by the grace of the Browns and the federal government, to whom he had servilely prostrated himself. The Commodore also knew from his own experience that after nearly five years of hard service, Collins's ships would be wearing out. Soon he would face repair and refitting costs that could exceed his original outlay for construction.[15] With Collins facing increasing financial woes, and Cunard partially sidelined by the war, Vanderbilt decided to pounce.

North Star had proven to be an extraordinarily useful vessel. Built by Vanderbilt's nephew Jeremiah Simonson, she was smaller than any of Collins's vessels and not as fast, but she was highly economical. Her crew costs were lower, she burned only about one-third the amount of coal as Collins's behemoths, and—most important—Vanderbilt owned her outright. He had no partners to satisfy and no debt to service. Vanderbilt commissioned Simonson to build a sister vessel, *Ariel*, and advertised that with the two vessels he would carry the mails for a payment of $15,000 per voyage, less than one-half the subsidy paid to Collins.[16]

In his *New York Herald* James Gordon Bennett, Collins's longtime supporter, welcomed the announcement, proclaiming "competition is the life of business." Without criticizing Collins, he noted that as a result of *Arctic*'s loss and Cunard's withdrawal, "steamship lines between Europe and this continent have been materially reduced. There is room for more Atlantic steamships and just in the nick of time we have a man to fill in the deficiency."[17] Collins thought otherwise. Vanderbilt's plan unnerved him. While his line had yet to make a profit, his gentlemanly "arrangement" with Cunard was working nicely, providing stability and predictability. His remaining ships *Pacific*, *Baltic*, and *Atlantic* were providing regular service. With the continued backing of the federal government he might even hope to become profitable. Much depended, however, upon his line maintaining an unblemished character as America's standard-bearer on the Atlantic, a status that had been sorely diminished by the *Arctic* disaster. When Vanderbilt asked for a private meeting, Collins, eager to avoid a fight with the wealthiest man in America, agreed.

On an early January day in 1855 Vanderbilt arrived at Collins's South Street office. The pleasantries were brief. Collins offered a deal. He would support Vanderbilt's proposal to Congress if the Commodore agreed to ask for the same mail subsidy that he received, $33,000 per voyage. "You cannot possibly do it for less," he told the Commodore. "[It's] why [even with the subsidy] I am not making any money by my steamers as all the world knows." "No," Vanderbilt retorted, he would not up his request. He then cleverly turned the tables on Collins, who had long survived by waving the flag. "I am patriotic in the matter. If an Englishman can do it for $16,000 I'm sure I can. I won't admit that a Britisher can beat us in anything." Collins, whose ships were steaming in a sea of red ink, was incredulous. When he reminded Vanderbilt of the heavy losses he was suffering, the Commodore shot back, "You've got into a business that you don't understand. Let me have an opportunity and I'll make it pay." In the past he had been able to extort tribute from businesses by threatening to enter into competition with them. Wisely, they generally preferred to pay the Commodore to stay away rather than challenge him. More interested in a quick profit than a long war, Vanderbilt tried a variation of his blackmail strategy on Collins. He offered to sell *Ariel*, still on the stocks, at $250,000, stating that if Collins would take her at the price he named, and arrange to send his ships to the Allaire Works for repair, a firm the Commodore virtually owned, he would agree not to compete with him before Congress. Collins shot back that *Ariel* was not worth more than $100,000. She was too small and slow "to sustain the reputation of [his] line." Vanderbilt's price was "extravagant." The additional $150,000 was nothing less than "hush money." Indignant, Collins refused, and the meeting ended on a cold note. Rebuffed by a man for whom he had no regard, Vanderbilt was stunned at Collins's "stupidity." While Simonson went ahead preparing *Ariel* for sea, the annual congressional subsidy drama in Washington was under way. Vanderbilt the hunter, "accustomed to bringing down his game," pointed his gun at Collins.[18]

On December 4, 1854, the second session of the 33rd Congress had convened. Democrats controlled both chambers as well as the presidency. At the tail end of the first session the Senate had taken up action on a bill that aimed at abolishing Collins's subsidy. Still reeling from the bitter bruising debates over the infamous Kansas Nebraska Act, which effectively repealed the controversial Missouri Compromise and opened new territory for slavery, the Senate was in an ugly, disputatious mood. Collins's stalwart ally, the Whig senator from New York William Henry Seward, moved to block the bill against attempts by the Democrats, led by the senator from Tennessee George Washington Jones, to enact it. With the clock ticking toward adjournment, Seward held the floor and taunted the Democrats. He refused to yield. "I intend," he said, "to speak out the time of the Senate." Furious at being outmaneuvered, Jones responded angrily: "I will fight the Collins steamers from this day out." The debate was heated and often personal. Unable to come to a resolution, the Senate adjourned without taking action, postponing the bill to an indefinite period.[19] Supporters of the Collins Line celebrated the postponement, claiming it a signal triumph and a defeat of the petty and un-American-like attempts to kill off the line.[20]

But the battle had been only deferred, not concluded. Since no action had been taken in the first session, when Congress reconvened, Ohio congressman Edson Olds, chairman of the Post Office and Roads Committee, presented a new Ocean Mail Steamer Appropriation Bill (H.R.595) that preserved Collins' generous annual subsidy of $858,000.[21] Having narrowly avoided death in a carriage accident in early January, in which his horse "took fright and dashed ahead for several blocks at full speed," Collins rushed to Washington to lobby for the bill.[22]

On February 15 Olds presented the bill and spoke at length in support of it. One year before his committee had reported out a bill "abolishing the Present Ocean Mail Steam Service." During that debate Olds had vigorously attacked Collins, indeed arguing the very notion of subsidies to be "un-American."[23] Having completely reversed himself, and now in conflict with his own party and the administration, Olds had much to explain. He began by recounting "the process by which my own prejudices have been removed, and my preconceived opinions so radically changed." He told his colleagues he had given "the ocean mail steamer service a patient and thorough investigation" that, "notwithstanding all my preconceived prejudice, has so far changed my views upon the subject, as to induce me, not only as an act of national policy, but also in justice to [support] Mr. Collins, and his associates."[24]

The "patient and thorough" investigation to which Olds referred had been conducted by a nine-member committee chaired by Daniel Mace, Democrat of Indiana, that had been charged with inquiring "into everything connected with appropriations for the mail steamship service." Mace, no friend to Collins, did his best to conduct a "thorough" investigation, but Collins's wily congressional allies did all they could to thwart the committee's proceedings by restricting the scope of its charge and denying it clerical support, allowing it a clerk for only twenty days over a seven-month period. After months of frustration during which the committee tried to conduct an investigation into the complex world of steamships without adequate support, in July 1854 they presented a whitewashed report with "no conclusions." Not surprisingly, they had not found any corruption in Congress, nor could they prove that Collins had not fulfilled his contract.[25] Olds, claiming that Collins had been vindicated, apparently saw more in the report than its authors.

In his rambling speech, Olds went on to summon testimony from a wide number of experts; however, most of the information he cited had already been made public. Among the carefully selected quotations he inserted into the *Congressional Globe* were ones from both the American and British Postmaster Generals, James Campbell and Viscount John Charles Canning (son of the former illustrious prime minister). Olds scoured the navy ranks as well and presented testimony from Captain Charles Stewart, the revered commander of "Old Ironsides" in the War of 1812, as well as from Commodore Matthew Calbraith Perry. Introducing Perry was a clever move and struck a resonant chord. He had just returned from his epic voyage "opening Japan." Leaving Hong Kong on September 11, 1854, Perry left his squadron in China and took the long way home via Europe, pausing at various ports to bask in the accolades and honors showered upon him. The last leg of his triumphal tour, Liverpool to New York, was aboard the Collins liner *Baltic*. Perry arrived home to national acclaim, and Olds took advantage.

Reaching into the grab bag of the past to buttress his position posed risks. When charged that he had allied himself with "the old fogies of the navy bureau," Olds rehearsed testimony from leading contemporary American ship designers and scientists including Francis Grice, the designer of Perry's flagship *Powhattan*, and the Irish-born Oliver Byrne, a highly regarded mathematician, engineer, and prolific author who lived in Philadelphia.[26] In an appeal to nationalism and the spirit of "Young America," Olds proclaimed to his colleagues, "We have the fastest horses, the prettiest women, and the best shooting guns in the world, and we must, also, have the fastest steamers. Nothing short of this will answer the expectations of the American people. The Collins line steamers must beat the British steamers."[27] If those who listened were waiting for some new revelation that explained Olds's change of heart, they were disappointed. In his attempt to explain why he had "radically changed," Olds offered nothing but warmed over arguments heard many times before.

Taken aback by Olds's epiphany, William Smith of Virginia, a fellow Democrat, rose to share his "inexpressible surprise to the speech of the gentleman, who was the last member from whom he expected to hear such a remarkable summersault." It filled him with amazement. To the amusement of the House, Smith's sharp political barbs likened Olds's conversion to that of St. Paul's on the road to Damascus. "The conversion of the apostle—the great persecutor of the Christians of that day— was scarcely less marvelous than the sudden and unexpected conversion of the Chairman of the Post-Office Committee." Olds, tongue in cheek, expressed the hope that his conversion was "as pure as that of St. Paul's." That was too much for Smith, who saw nothing in it but "corruption." The congressman from Virginia ought to have been more careful. Before his election to Congress Smith, enjoying the benefit of lucrative post office contracts, had run a line of passenger and mail coaches in Virginia. Through a series of clever maneuvers he had arranged to extend his service on a variety of spur routes from which he collected extra fees and earned the nickname "Extra Billy."[28]

The jousting continued. Olds asked Smith, "If the gentleman was so opposed to extras," how had he got the name of "Extra Billy"? Smith's hypocrisy being all too evident, Olds's question produced laughter in the chamber. As it died away, Olds gave one last prick to "Extra Billy." When it came to finding ways to exploit government contracts, Olds claimed, Smith "ought to understand it better than anybody else."

While Olds waged war in the well of the House, Collins unleashed a lobbying barrage on Congress. When he learned that senator James Pearce from Maryland might speak against the bill, he went immediately to visit him and secured his vote.[29] Some members in opposition clung to Jacksonian principles and stood firm against all subsidies, but for most members of Congress the issue was simply one of how much and to whom? Only one speaker, William Barry of Mississippi, raised the "frightful misfortune" of the *Arctic*. "If [Collins] had spent in lifeboats for that vessel the money which they spent in ginger-bread ornaments and decorations, there might have been hundreds of valuable lives saved."[30]

Notwithstanding the opposition, the bill passed the House on February 17 by a vote of 99 to 82. It reached the Senate floor ten days later, provoking a day-long debate during which Collins's critics offered a variety of poison-pill amendments aimed at weakening the bill. But through the day each was defeated until finally on a final vote of 26 to 22 the bill passed and was sent to the president.[31]

Olds's astonishing defection, the base debate in the House, and the foul odor of corruption sparked a fierce public reaction to Collins's victory. It began in Horace Greely's *New York Daily Tribune*, the nation's largest newspaper and ordinarily an advocate to "enterprise." After recounting the unhappy history of the Collins Line, dubbing it "a harvest of glory, but no money," Greeley struck hard:

> Now if Congress had thrown away this vast sum in a freak of generosity or folly, we might have regretted the waste of money, but we would not have been called to deplore a still graver calamity. The evil in this case is that Congress was not deluded—it was

corrupted. Where the money came from we do not legally know—
we can only give a Yankee guess—but that money passed this
bill—money not merely expended on borers and wheedlers and
the usual oyster cellar appliances of lobby legislation—but money
counted down unto the palms of members of Congress—this is as
clear as the noon day sun.

Greeley lambasted members of Congress "who but a few months
ago were breathing out threatenings and slaughter against the Collins
job," but now following the abrupt conversion of Congressman Olds,
they had reversed their position. Greeley selected Olds for particular
attention. "What," the editorialist asked, "can have wrought the miraculous transformation of the savagely virtuous Chairman of the House's
Post Office Committee? Brief is the interval since he was loudest in his
denunciations of the Collins job, and now 'Behold he prayeth.' Of course
he hath pondered well the Divine assurance 'Ask, and ye shall receive.' "
Greeley's piercing attack concluded with a lamentation—"Woe to the
American people . . . when members of Congress are bought and sold
like horses."[32]

Despite his threat to challenge Collins for a congressional subsidy,
publicly Vanderbilt remained on the sidelines. In retrospect, given his
wealth and character, this seems surprising. Reviewing these events
some decades later, and citing them as examples of corruption, Gustave
Myers, a fierce socialist critic of American business, suggested "that for
years a secret understanding had been in force between Collins and
Vanderbilt by which they divided the mail subsidy funds." To fool the
public and Congress, however, into thinking that they were fierce
competitors and "to give no sign of collusion," these "steam beggars"
went through the public appearance of warring upon each other.[33] Myers
was a biased judge; yet with his secret—and successful—agreement
with Cunard still in force, and his desire to avoid confrontation with a
rival as rapacious as Vanderbilt, Collins was anxious for a deal. It is
likely that the two men, preferring collusion over competition, came to
an understanding.

In its final form the bill gave Collins nearly everything he wanted,
including repeal of the potentially troublesome proviso tucked away in

the 1852 deficiency bill that allowed Congress to terminate his contract with only six months' notice.[34] The repeal, however, was contingent upon Collins fulfilling a promise he had made nearly ten years earlier to build five ships. When challenged in the past as to why he had not built the fifth ship Collins answered that, given the size and speed of his four steamers, an additional vessel was not needed.[35] *Arctic*'s demise, however, now forced him to accept new construction.

On the same day that Greeley's scathing article appeared in the *Tribune*—Saturday, March 3—the House and Senate gathered for the last session of the 33rd Congress. The day turned into a carnival of nearly two dozen last-minute appropriations, including money to build public buildings in Kansas and Nebraska, support for the army, roads in the west, fortifications in numerous places, a host of funds set aside for rivers and harbors, and a variety of other measures, including a number of private relief acts. During debate over the private acts, the morning's agenda was interrupted by a message from the president: he had vetoed the Ocean Steamer Act.

Although the bill authorized payments to several lines, Franklin Pierce sidestepped that fact and took direct aim at Collins, pointing specifically to the repeal of the six months' notice. "In this repeal, the objections are, in my mind insuperable." Pierce chastised Congress. By approving the Collins subsidy and abandoning any element of control over the line, they were giving up "all future discretion as to the increased service and compensation, whatever changes may occur in the art of navigation, its expenses, or the policy and political condition of the country." It was irresponsible to give Collins "a donation of such magnitude" that would "deprive commercial enterprise of the benefits of free competition and establish a monopoly in violation of the soundest principles of public policy and of doubtful compatibility with the Constitution."[36]

In a body under great pressure to finish its business so that members might head for home, Pierce's veto hit like a sudden gale. Congressman Robert Hunt, a Democrat from Virginia, denounced the "abominable veto" as evidence "of the rapid march of tyranny over the liberties of the people." Another member exclaimed "a Revolution has commenced," and cried for impeachment. The clerk of the House noted in the *Congressional Globe*, "Shouts of 'Order! Order!' and tumultuous confusion."

When order was restored, a vote to override was taken—79 in favor and 98 opposed. Pierce's veto stood.[37]

Pierce's signature on the veto, Collins's supporters suspected, had been guided by the evil hand of Cornelius Vanderbilt. In an age when so much was for sale, even the president was not immune. "Vanderbilt is rich and bids high to carry his points, especially his enmities; and President Pierce has sold himself, and his friends, too so often, that his influence has become a marketable commodity. Fifty thousand dollars is supposed to be about the present price of a veto involving a million dollars."[38]

As the furor over the veto subsided, the House returned to its flurry of appropriations, where the "corruption involved [was] too great for analysis."[39] Activity stretched into the evening. Pages scurried along the corridor between chambers bringing to each side bills that had been gaveled through in the last minutes of the session. Shortly after Pierce's veto had been read, a message arrived from the Senate—a request for the House to approve the Naval Appropriations bill, "with sundry amendments," twenty-nine in all.[40] The bill authorized more than eleven million dollars: pay for sailors and officers, repairs to navy yards, munitions, ships, and numerous other budget lines. When pressed by members to read the provisions of the bill Congressman John Phelps of Missouri, chairman of the House Conference Committee, replied that in the few minutes available to him he could not read the full texts, but he would nonetheless "endeavor to make the action of the committee as intelligible as I can." Phelps gave a brief summary of most of the provisions, including one tucked away toward the end of the bill.

Collins's friends in the Senate, most likely led by Seward, had done well. They maneuvered to insert in this last-minute bill, festooned with something for everyone, an enormous plum for Collins. Following section 7, which set the salary of the assistant astronomer at the Naval Observatory, section 8 provided "For the transportation of the mails from New York to Liverpool and back, Eight hundred and nineteen thousand five hundred dollars."[41] No conditions were attached to the provision. However much Pierce may have grumbled, vetoing the entire bill to punish Collins was politically impossible. Congress had outfoxed him.

Although Collins had won, he would pay a high price. Critics swooped in. According to the *Boston Daily Atlas*, Congress had acted "in the most blind and reckless fashion." The *New Hampshire Patriot* called his machinations "The Collins Steamer Swindle," while a writer in *The Texas State Gazette* wrote that "there is a corruption in Congress which is more widespread than we are aware of." The *New York Post* denounced the Collins line as an "avaricious monopoly."[42]

Vanderbilt launched his own attack, going public in the *New York Daily Tribune* with a withering 3,000-word denunciation of Collins. The Commodore took the high road, wrapping himself in the garb of a true Jacksonian celebrating the virtue of free enterprise in a world of laissez-faire economics wherein the government stood aside, allowing "unfettered trade and unrestrained competition." He began his letter by telling readers that he rarely had "taken any notice of newspaper calumnies" against him, but the charge of bribery that had been lodged against him in the press was one "that I am not at liberty to overlook." After dismissing that charge and "other animadversions," Vanderbilt launched his attack on Collins.

> Now, I have made no attack upon the Collins line, though I have never regarded, and do not now regard any particular line of steamers as one of the institutions of the country, to foster which is the duty of the citizens, and to venture to compete with which is treason. I am not inimical to that line, nor have I entertained thoughts of ill will toward the gentleman who founded it. I would not detract anything from the credit to which they are entitled. I congratulate them on the prosperity which has hitherto attended their enterprise and perhaps, ought to applaud them for that ingenuity in its management. Commencing with a capital of about $1,000,000 they have been enabled, by means of large loans from the Government to aid them in the construction of their ships, and the still larger contributions from the public Treasury for carrying the mails.[43]

Notwithstanding the favors Collins had extracted from Congress, Vanderbilt was still in the fight. He announced defiantly "that the Atlantic Ocean was wide enough for two lines of steamers." For the moment, the Commodore had managed to substitute his ugly public image of the rapacious tycoon out to ruin his competition with that of a patriot willing to do the work demanded by the government without the huge bonus guaranteed to Collins. Lest anyone doubt his commitment, early in April, shortly after *Ariel* launched, he announced in the press that he was "determined to start a new line of steamers between New York and Havre," to be conducted by the converted yacht *North Star* and the newly built *Ariel*.[44] Vanderbilt understood that going head to head on the New York–Liverpool run against the heavily subsidized lines of Cunard and Collins was bound to be a money loser, so instead he chose the New York–Havre route.[45]

Secure from the threat of Vanderbilt, Collins steamed ahead. In spite of all his woes, the irrepressible grandstanding entrepreneur announced that for his fifth promised steamer he was going to build a vessel "larger, faster, grander than anything afloat, regardless of cost."[46] It would be the "most forcible illustration that could be given of human ingenuity" and the largest steamship in the world.[47] To design and build her he engaged George Steers, the man who had created the schooner yacht *America*, which in 1851 had won the Royal Regatta race at Cowes. In the tradition of the Collins Line she would be named *Adriatic*. Once she was in service Collins would again have four first-class steamers at his disposal—*Pacific*, *Baltic*, *Atlantic*, and *Adriatic*.

The enormous size of the vessel, and Collins's insistence on experimenting "with new kinds of valves and other features intended to reduce fuel consumption" made his investors, particularly those in Liverpool, increasingly nervous.[48] Having been virtually dragged into Collins's enterprise, which seemed always to teeter on the brink of political and financial disaster and which had never turned a profit, Brown, Shipley were hostile to the proposal. In a world that demanded flexibility and ready access to capital, they were anxious to make and keep everything as available as possible, and were deeply distressed that a good deal of their money was locked up with Collins. When Collins informed them that he was building *Adriatic*, they bluntly refused to help subsidize the project. They later demanded to know how Collins intended to pay the one million dollars the new vessel was estimated to cost, likely making her the most expensive vessel ever built in the United States, and when the monies owed to them (£82,000) would be remitted.[49]

Early in 1856, while Collins struggled to complete *Adriatic* and fend off his political foes, and the Crimean War dragged to a close, the Admiralty released Cunard's ships back to regular service.[50] To dramatize his return Cunard announced that the line's newest steamer, *Persia*, would make her maiden voyage to New York, departing on January 26. Built by Robert Napier and Sons at Glasgow, this was Cunard's first iron-hulled vessel. At 3,300 tons and 3,600 horsepower, *Persia*, with *Adriatic* still under construction, was the biggest and most powerful steamer on the Atlantic.

Determined to uphold the prestige of his line and not be left in *Persia*'s wake, Collins decided to use *Pacific* to challenge Cunard and embarrass *Persia* on her maiden voyage. To beat the Cunarder he needed a bold captain ready to push for speed, and so he sought out his old friend and fellow Cape Codder Asa Eldridge, who had commanded Collins's *Roscius* and *Garrick* in the days of the Dramatic Line, always delivering fast passages.[51] When Collins sold the line, Eldridge left packets to command clippers, including the famed *Red Jacket*, which he drove to a record crossing by sail—New York to Liverpool in thirteen days and one hour. The voyage was equally remembered for Eldridge's arrival when in a "beautiful piece of seamanship" he brought *Red Jacket* up the Mersey "under her own sail with every stitch drawing." While hundreds watched from the shore, "at exactly the right moment he gave the order: her upper sails crumpled, the wind was spilled from her courses, and the Captain shot his great ship into the wind and backed her alongside the dock" in a maneuver "that not one shipmaster in a hundred would have dared to try."[52] Eldridge had also commanded Vanderbilt's *North Star* on her European tour. Offered command of *Pacific*, Eldridge vowed to Collins that he would beat *Persia*.

On Friday, January 18, 1856, after an eastbound passage during which she encountered "severe gales," *Pacific* arrived in Liverpool.[53] *Persia*, only a few days down from the Clyde under the command of Cunard's senior captain C. H. E. Judkins, was also in port preparing to sail for New York on the twenty-sixth.

Eldridge rushed to get his ship to sea before *Persia*. Stevedores worked over the weekend to load coal and stores. In an unusually rapid turnaround, by Tuesday the twenty-third *Pacific* was ready for sea. Eldridge gave the command, and *Pacific* steamed down the Mersey bound for New York. Three days later *Persia* got under way, but not before a grand dinner was held the evening before in the ship's saloon, with numerous toasts offered to the ship and her captain, who promised to best *Pacific*. It was a race, and the betting was heavy that *Persia* would make the crossing in a record eight days.[54]

From Sandy Hook the pilots kept a careful watch for the steamers. Concerns arose when, after ten days, there were "no signs of either *Pacific* or *Persia*."[55] On February 9 *Persia* finally arrived. Judkins reported that the long crossing had been particularly difficult. When his ship reached "the eastern edge of the [Grand] Banks she encountered a vast field of ice, in working through which, nearly all the floats of her wheels were broken."[56] Three days later, holding out hope that *Pacific* too might have suffered damage to her wheels and was making slow progress toward New York, Collins chartered the steamer *Alabama* to seek her out and the navy dispatched the brig *Arctic*. Hope faded, however, as days passed with no news. On March 1 the *Liverpool Mercury* noted that the ship *Edinburgh*, recently arrived at Glasgow from New York, had spotted "a large quantity of broken ice, and on it saw a quantity of broken cabin furniture, fine ornamental doors with white or glass handles, a ladies workbox, and some other articles such as would be in use in the cabin of a first class ship or steamer."[57] For weeks Collins remained hopeful, telling his New York associates that he believed it impossible for her to be crushed in the ice.[58] In its April 5, 1856, issue, *Frank Leslie's Illustrated Newspaper* concluded that *Pacific* had met an awful fate.[59]

Lost at sea, *Pacific* was never heard from again.[60] One hundred eighty-six people were aboard. She most likely struck an iceberg or was crushed in "a vast field of ice." To avoid future disasters of sort Collins ordered his steamers not to cross north of forty-five degrees "until after the 1st of August."[61]

Collins was again an object of both pity and scorn. "We admire," noted the *Georgia Telegraph*, "Mr. Collins's heroic incredulity, and sympathize in his misfortune," but at the same time "the shock of these catastrophes" had undermined "public confidence," particularly in light of "the fact that the Cunard Line has sailed twice as long with twice the number of steamers—but without an accident."[62]

For the credibility of his line, Collins had done all he could to mask his reliance on British investors and keep secret his arrangement with Cunard. It was vital, particularly at moments of disaster (*Arctic*, *Pacific*) that the public believe that the line was a patriotic enterprise. If his image as a loyal American crumbled, so too would his support in Congress, without which he could not survive. Unfortunately, a public scuffle between former Collins and *Pacific* captain Ezra Nye and Brown, Shipley went public, and exposed the considerable involvement of Collins's Liverpool partners.

Another Cape Codder, Nye hailed from Sandwich. Reputed to be a tough and short-tempered master, he made his reputation running fast passages on *Independence*, a packet on the Swallowtail Line, which he commanded for ten years.[63] In 1845, when the Swallowtail Line launched the *Henry Clay*—at the time the largest packet on the Atlantic—Nye took command. In 1850 Collins lured him away from packets and offered him command of the newly launched *Pacific*. For five years Nye captained the steamer on her runs between Liverpool and New York.

By late 1854, having commanded at sea for more than twenty-five years, Nye had thoughts of retirement. As a condition of employment, however, Collins had required that his captains take stock in the company, which they could sell when they left his employ. Nye held a considerable number of shares valued at twenty thousand dollars. Since the company's dire financial situation made it unlikely that a public sale would yield that amount, and Nye assumed that any new captain, according to company policy, would have to purchase stock at its original value, he began a personal recruiting effort to find someone to take his place and purchase his stock.

In the fall of 1854, Captain Oliver Eldridge was a passenger aboard *Pacific* on a crossing from Liverpool to New York. Taking action on his plan, Nye asked if Eldridge might be interested in commanding *Pacific* and buying his stock. Eldridge indicated interest and, as Nye recounted in a letter widely republished in the press, "On arriving at New York, by my advice, he applied to Mr. Collins for the *Pacific* when I should resign." Collins gave his approval. With this understanding in place, Nye agreed to remain in command for one more year. He would make his last crossing in October 1855, and when he came ashore in New York he fully expected to be greeted by the *Pacific*'s new captain and a check for twenty thousand dollars. Instead he was met with the startling news that his brother Asa, not Oliver, would take command of *Pacific*. Brown, Shipley had, "without his approval and contrary to his wishes," overridden Collins while at the same time "waiving the condition originally imposed on the commanders of these ships, of taking a certain amount of the stock." Out a job and in danger of losing twenty thousand dollars, Nye was furious. "Foreign agents," he alleged, had done this to him. In more letters published widely in the press Nye let loose at the Browns. According to him Brown, Shipley had boasted "that these were their own ships, and they would do what they pleased with them."[64] Nye's accusations of "foreign owners" hit home. So too did his disturbing suggestion that Asa Eldridge's unexpected appointment had caused several of *Pacific*'s officers to depart the ship in protest, leaving her in the hands of an inexperienced crew. The *Chicago Times* reported, "The whisper which has been about for years that the Collins Line was really owned by British capitalists received confirmation from the lately published letters of Capt. Nye."[65] Having done his best to wreak revenge, Nye, albeit twenty thousand dollars poorer, retired to his home in Newark, New Jersey, never to return to sea.

Critics railed against Collins and were quick to point out that with *Pacific* lost, and only two ships left—*Baltic* and *Atlantic*—it would be impossible for him to satisfy his contract. To plug the void, Collins chartered two steamers, *Nashville* and *Quaker City*, but neither had the capacity or speed to allow Collins to fulfill his obligations. A third steamer, *Ericsson*, lasted longer in his service, but was equally disappointing. As a consequence Collins failed to meet the requirements of his government contract, which permitted the Secretary of the Navy to fine him thirty-six thousand dollars.[66]

By the spring of 1856, with two ships gone, hundreds of lives lost, a giant vessel under construction plagued by machine failures and escalating costs, mounting financial losses, a public increasingly skeptical of the whole enterprise, partners at odds with one another, and dark clouds gathering in Congress, the Collins line was headed for disaster. In a somber mood the hitherto steadfast Collins wrote to his friend Thurlow Weed—the powerful New York politician and a leader in the newly formed Republican Party— that he no longer could count votes and he no longer cared. He was helpless to fight the trend, and would accept his fate. "If this Congress sees fit," he wrote, "to surrender the honor of the nation, which has cost us so dearly, so be it, Amen!"[67] In January 1856, anticipating that Collins's friends in Congress would launch an effort to renew his subsidy at the extra rate, the Postmaster General made a preemptive strike, damning such an appropriation as a "mere gratuity."[68] As usual, Collins's fate rested in Congress.

CHAPTER SIXTEEN

End of the Line

COLLINS'S SUPPORTERS BIDED their time until May 8, 1856, when Whig congressman Lewis D. Campbell, of Ohio, chair of the House Ways and Means Committee, presented H.R.316, a bill "making appropriation for the transportation of United States Mail by Ocean steamer."[1] Section 7 of the bill authorized $819,500 for Collins, which included the extra compensation, roughly the sum he had been receiving since 1852.[2] Illinois congressman Jesse Norton proposed that Vanderbilt too be given a subsidy, but the chair first refused to recognize him, then did so, allowed Norton to read his amendment, and promptly declared it out of order.[3]

For more than three months the House took no further action, until August 15, when the bill returned to the floor. It was near the end of the session, and as usual the House had accumulated a backlog of bills, which allowed little time for debate. Campbell asked that the House permit five minutes for debate on the bill. With the reins firmly in their hands Collins's foes moved quickly. Five minutes proved enough time for them to add an amendment that directed "the Secretary of the Navy . . . to give notice . . . to terminate" the additional allowance, nearly a half-million dollars, that Collins had enjoyed since 1852, and return to the original (1847) sum of $385 thousand. In a forlorn effort to avoid defeat Collins's supporters managed to delay final action until the next day. Their efforts proved futile. On Saturday, August 16, the amendment was approved 144 to 25. Only a single southern congressman voted in Collins's favor. With sentiment so clear there was no need, and no time, for a roll call, and the bill as amended passed by voice vote. It went immediately over to the Senate, where Seward worked to remove the reduction. In a floor vote he lost, 26 to 9. On the bill's final vote the margin was even worse, 34 to 2; the only senator joining Seward was the Michigan Democrat Charles Stuart. Not a single senator from the south stood in support of Collins.[4] In high dudgeon the *New York Herald* laid the defeat "entirely to the jealous and niggardly spirit of the South and southwest which forgetful of the advantage that they owe to us take every opportunity of manifesting their hostility to our interests." They were "ungrateful and stupid."[5]

On August 18 President Franklin Pierce, harboring no love for Seward, who had cleverly outmaneuvered him the previous year, signed the bill that cut the subsidy to the original level of $385,000.[6] Labeling Congress's act as a fatal stab, the *Herald* lamented, "Congress has closed its labors by dealing the worst blow it could at one of the noblest triumphs of American skill and enterprise."[7] Still harboring deep resentment toward Collins, Captain Ezra Nye challenged the *Herald*'s statement of "American skill and enterprise," pointing out that the "notorious control exercised over [the line] by Mr. Brown of Liverpool" undermined any claim that Collins might make for public support.[8] In his judgment, Congress had acted in a patriotic fashion by refusing to support a foreign enterprise.

Collins was stunned. He still bragged that his remaining ships, *Baltic* and *Atlantic*, were still the largest and finest American steamers afloat, but secretly he understood that even they were sailing in troubled waters. After years of hard service both were in dire need of major repairs that some predicted might equal the original cost of the ships.[9] Whatever hope was left for the line's survival rested in the promise of the thus-far unlucky *Adriatic*.

At eleven o'clock Monday morning, April 7, 1856, George Steers gave the signal, and as everyone "listened with great anxiety to the measured strokes of the hammers and sledges below," *Adriatic*—"in gallant style" and to the sound of a band—slid slowly down the shipyard ways at the foot of Seventh Street and into the East River. In front of a cheering crowd of fifty thousand people she "ploughed her way across the river, bringing up against the docks on the Williamsburg side." As soon as she was secure, Collins and a horde of invitees adjourned from the ship yard and made their way to the Pacific Hotel on Broadway for a grand banquet.[10] In front of hundreds of enthusiastic diners the mayor of New York, Fernando Wood, introduced the "eminently patriotic" Edward Knight Collins.[11] Playing on his favorite theme of patriotism, Collins launched a rebuttal to Nye's charges that "English capitalists" had invested in his ships. He told his cheering throng of guests "that not a dollar of the capital invested" in his ships "is owned by English merchants. Mr. James Brown is a naturalized citizen, and has been for more than fifty years, and there is not a Brown interested in them who is not a citizen of this country." Collins was skirting the truth. The interests of the Browns—Liverpool and New York—were so entwined that it would have been impossible to separate one from the other. Brown, Shipley did have a management role and financial interest in the Collins Line. To admit that, however, would have destroyed Collins's carefully wrought public image of a patriot and further weakened whatever political influence he had left in Congress. Harkening back to one of the original arguments for building his steamers, he told his audience, "You might think that a merchant had no other interest than that of a mere pecuniary character; but from a very early period of my life I have taken the deepest interest in our navy, and I have watched its growth and progress with as much solitude as any other man; and when I wanted to build these ships I pointed out their advantage as war vessels, if they should ever be required as such." Collins went on, noting that "the company have already expended three millions of dollars upon [*Arctic* (lost), *Baltic*, *Atlantic*, *Pacific* (lost), and *Adriatic*] and where, I ask, will the government find another company that would be willing to do the same?" He heaped scorn on his domestic critics. "Every nation has acknowledged what we have done, and I am sorry to say that the only opposition we have met has been from home . . . Now it is with individuals as it is with nations—imbecility provokes insult; and but for the Collins steamers England would have laughed at the steam power of America."[12]

A few days after her launch *Adriatic* was towed to a nearby pier adjacent to the Novelty Iron Works where painters, machinists, joiners, upholsters, and a host of other artisans went to work upon her interior, while many thousands of admiring spectators came to view "this noble triumph of American skill and industry" in which no expense had been spared.[13] As was his wont, Steers had sculptured a sleek, graceful hull reminiscent of the fastest American clipper ship.[14] Her plumb stem and elegantly rounded stern assured onlookers that *Adriatic* was destined to be a record-setter, and although four feet shorter than Cunard's *Persia*, her gross tonnage was slightly greater, allowing Collins to claim her as the largest steamer on the Atlantic. Unfortunately, in September 1856, as *Adriatic* was still fitting out, Steers, only thirty-five years old, "awaiting the completion of his work with anxiety yet with confidence," suffered a tragic accident. While riding on Long Island his horse took fright and ran away, throwing him to the ground and causing fatal injuries.[15] Steers's untimely death denied Collins a wise voice precisely at a time when he needed it most.

However well Steers crafted her hull, *Adriatic* could only speed through the water as fast as her powerful machines could turn the paddle wheels. To build these engines Collins returned to his friends George and Horatio Allen, proprietors of the Novelty Iron Works—the largest marine engine company in the United States and the firm that had produced engines for *Atlantic* and *Arctic*. George was the only one of his family to survive *Arctic*'s sinking, losing both his wife and infant son. His brother and partner Horatio, a renowned engineer, was a designer of railroad locomotives who had joined the firm to build marine engines.[16] As with locomotives, designers of ships' engines sought to achieve maximum power with the lowest fuel consumption, to be delivered by engines of the lightest weight. Horatio Allen's design promised to deliver such engines for *Adriatic*. Instead of the conventional and well-proved side lever engines that powered the fleets of both Cunard and Collins, Allen proposed a new design—an oscillating engine. Devoid of levers, beams, or linkages, Allen's engine connected directly to the crank turning the paddle wheels. The elimination of the complicated connecting apparatus common to the side lever engine reduced weight, space, and cost. However, to work properly Allen's huge 100-inch diameter cylinders "had to be mounted on a pair of trunnions, large projections supported by bearings, so that they could rock back and forth as the shaft revolved." While in many ways advantageous, this arrangement also presented a number of risks, mostly concerning steam leaking out and air coming in.[17] Nonetheless, with the promised efficiency of these engines, the chance of producing high speed while burning less coal promised cost savings too inviting to resist. Collins agreed to Allen's plan, causing the *New York Tribune* to trumpet that *Adriatic* would "prove the fastest steamer afloat."[18]

American commentators showered superlatives on *Adriatic*, lavishing praise on her interior designed by William Gibson, whose work was done in the most luxurious manner and excited surprise and admiration.[19] She was also described as the "safest." The lessons from *Arctic* were clear: *Adriatic*'s hull was divided into eight watertight compartments, was abundantly supplied with lifeboats, and had numerous fire pumps. However, the safety feature that drew the most attention was a "calcium light which she carried at her foremast head" that provided "not only a security against a collision with another vessel but, by enabling the lookout to discover objects at a distance of three or four miles in the dark, will greatly lessen the chances of accidents at night."[20] The maritime reputation of the nation rested on this "noble" ship. "Her triumph will be our triumph, her defeat will be our defeat," exclaimed the *New York Tribune*.[21] *Adriatic* would "beat the Cunarders or sink!" observed the London *Times*.[22] The steamer would be ready to sail in September under the command of the line's senior captain, James West.

However, Steers's sudden death left the project without a firm hand in charge. Allen's innovations failed nearly every test; valves leaked, rubber packing deteriorated, and condensers failed. "In disgust" Collins dismissed Allen and sought help from F. E. Sickels, a well-known engineer who had apprenticed at the Allaire Works, where in 1841 he invented a steam valve—known as the "Sickels cut-off"—that vastly improved the efficiency of steam engines.[23] Collins engaged Sickels to "place [his] apparatus in the *Adriatic*." Novelty Iron Works, despite its failure, was kept on to "supply the necessary materials" and continue to install the remainder of the ship's machinery. Furious and embarrassed, Allen did all he could to interfere and continually interrupt Sickels. In the midst of this pier-side spat Collins, in a rush to get to sea, and over the objections of Sickels who warned that the engines were not yet ready, ordered a sea trial. *Adriatic* left her pier on October 3. Within minutes of casting off word came up from below that the engines were "not properly keyed together," meaning that the port and starboard paddles could not be synchronized. *Adriatic* limped back to the pier. According to *Scientific American* the engines were "badly botched."[24] Ignoring the fact that he had been warned by Sickels, Collins fired him and returned the work to Allen, making this the third try at building engines that might work. Not easily dismissed, Sickels, claiming that he had "undertaken to do this great feat gratuitously, for the honor of American mechanism," sued Novelty for patent infringement as well as damaging his "fame and reputation." The case dragged on for ten years until the court found in his favor.[25]

Finally in early November 1857, fourteen months late, *Adriatic* was brought around to the Collins pier on the Hudson River at the foot of Canal Street. On November 23, with only thirty-seven passengers aboard for a winter crossing, she was ready to depart on her maiden voyage to Liverpool. "Several thousand persons had gathered at every available place in her neighborhood" to watch the historic event. At noon Captain West ordered the lines cast off. First, *Adriatic* had trouble clearing *Baltic*, which was tied up aft of her, but then matters grew worse. As she moved out into the stream, a strong flood tide took hold. Tugs *M.D. Petell*, *Sarah Brown*, and *James Smith*, and the port's largest and most powerful tug, *W. H. Webb*, hurried alongside to render assistance.[26] As she moved further into the river *Adriatic* struck the end of the pier, causing the crowd in a panic "to jump and run in every direction." No sooner had that "excitement subsided than the two metallic lifeboats forward of the wheel-house came in contact with the end of the pier and were instantly broken to pieces. The steamer's bow was by this time carried clear around against the *Baltic*." As she slid along her sister's port side, two additional lifeboats "were driven up against the stern of the *Baltic*, and both of them were completely destroyed." To the amazement of onlookers *Adriatic*, by now seeming to be completely out of control, continued her disorderly dance into the stream with the strong tide carrying her upstream. Like Gulliver, *Adriatic* dragged behind her four tugs still tethered and trying desperately, but unsuccessfully, to bring the behemoth under control. Gradually, *Adriatic* began to make headway speed as her huge paddles gripped the water. "As soon as the crowd perceived her moving out they commenced to cheer and kept up a continuous voice of hurrahs for over ten minutes." From across the river at their Jersey pier, from where they had been watching the spectacle, the crew of the Cunarder *Arabia* offered a nine-gun salute. "As the engines of the *Adriatic* worked up . . . to their full power," she passed the Narrows, and after dropping the pilot Captain West laid a course for Liverpool, never stopping to replace the four lost lifeboats.[27]

In seaman's terms, *Adriatic* might well have had a Jonah aboard.[28] After enduring such an ignominious start, the steamer's luck continued to fade. In the mid-Atlantic the chief engineer reported to West alarming news that the "journals," a part of the shaft connecting the engines and paddles, were overheating. West ordered the engines shut down, and for twenty-seven hours, *Adriatic* slugged her way ahead under sail until the journals cooled.[29]

"Finally on Thursday the 3rd instant [December]," reported the *Illustrated London News*, "after a run of ten days four hours from New York," *Adriatic*, 'the long expected and noble ship,' " entered the Mersey River. There to greet her was her challenger *Persia*, with whom she exchanged salutes. Built "to beat the *Persia* if not all creation," on her first crossing *Adriatic* had taken more than a day longer than the Cunarder's time in crossing.[30] Perhaps, commented the *Illustrated London News* with a slight whiff of superiority, "when her machinery is in good working order she will improve her rate of speed."[31]

While *Adriatic* may not have set a speed record, she was still the largest steamer afloat and certainly the most "magnificent." Anxious to show off American prowess, for two days Captain West opened his vessel to visitors who ferried out from Rocky Slip on the Birkenhead side of the river.[32] On Wednesday the 9th *Adriatic*, with only twenty-four passengers aboard, left for her return to New York, arriving on the twenty-first, a disappointing twelve-day crossing, during which her engines were plagued again by overheated journals. She steamed up the

Hudson, tying up on the south side of the Collins pier, and sat there idle in need of expensive repairs, none of which the company could afford. Collins ordered her out of service.

Adriatic's elder sisters *Baltic* and *Atlantic* were in even worse condition. Hard driving had ravaged them, and in every department they were in dire need of extensive refitting.[33] When *Atlantic* returned to New York on January 6, 1858, Collins ordered her laid up on the north side of the pier opposite *Adriatic*. *Baltic* was alone at sea.[34] Passengers intending to sail with Collins scrambled to make alternative bookings while the post office loaded mail on other steamers, including Cunard's.

Collins was sinking. In 1850 the line had carried an average of eighty-four passengers on each crossing—a number that peaked at 136 in 1855, the year Cunard's ships were away in the Crimea. But the bottom fell out in 1856, as Collins only averaged sixty-six passengers per crossing and only forty-two in 1857.[35] The financial headwinds bore down on Collins with gale force, while the losses of *Arctic* and *Pacific* remained haunting tragedies.

While Collins struggled to remain afloat, Cunard, always cautious and keeping a steady eye toward economy and safety, steamed ahead. By mid-1857 Cunard had more than twenty ships at sea, all built in Scotland, and despite Samuel Cunard's conservatism, more than half were iron-hulled and screw-driven, making the fleet the largest and most modern in the world.[36]

With this impressive fleet Cunard was able to keep his ships full and on a demanding schedule. Cunard steamers carried 5,378 passengers in 1856; slightly more, 5,430, in 1857. In stark contrast, the numbers for Collins in those years were 1,739 and 1,635 respectively. Just as investors were fleeing from Collins it was rumored that Cunard's stock was selling at a 200 percent premium, but since it was valued so highly, "very little is ever sold."[37]

Cunard's organization was simple and highly successful. After the founder left Halifax for London in the mid-1850s, his eldest son, Edward, "took control of the Halifax, Boston and New York end of the business."[38] In Boston the company's agent Edward Bates, who had succeeded Samuel Lewis, managed affairs for the port. Completing the management team on the American side was Edward's younger brother William, who oversaw Halifax operations.[39] Although Samuel Cunard remained the face of the firm, direct management was left to Charles MacIver in Liverpool, who had succeeded his brother David and who directed ship operations. At Glasgow the Burns brothers (George and James) oversaw ship construction, and when necessary, traveled to London to lobby the government and parliament on behalf of the company.[40]

Charles MacIver's obsession with detail and his extraordinary work ethic often earned him something more opprobrious than the title of martinet. When he learned that sailors aboard *Cambria* expected a half-day off on Saturdays, he wrote to the ship's master, John Leitch, "My own time of working is nine hours a day without a break for meals or anything else and . . . Saturday is one of the busiest days."[41] MacIver was punctilious in all matters related to his ships, but no more so than in his concern for safety.

Between *Britannia*'s first voyage in 1840 and the eve of the American Civil War (1859), thirteen steam vessels went down on the Atlantic, an average of one every eighteen months.[42] Hundreds of lives were lost, more than 500 combined on *Arctic* and *Pacific* alone, but not a single one was aboard a Cunard ship.[43] T. T. Vernon Smith, Provincial Engineer for New Brunswick and a highly regarded expert on steamships, offered a damning comparison between the ships of Collins and Cunard. He noted that *Pacific*, which "in all probability" struck ice, "was stove and went down." *Persia*, he went on to observe, "when five days out struck also. The collision broke a large hole through the plates of her iron bow." Unlike *Pacific*, however, doomed by her fragile wooden hull, *Persia*'s iron hull, divided into watertight compartments, endured the blow, "and she was enabled to reach New York in safety."[44]

Even when negligence was at work, the Cunard Line emerged with its reputation intact. When two Cunarders, *Europa* and *Arabia*, as a result of confusion on the part of their masters, collided in the open ocean off Newfoundland, critics found reason to praise the British ships and their crews while taking a swipe at Americans. In a letter published in a number of American newspapers from "a [English] gentleman who was a passenger on the steamship *Arabia*," the writer noted that while "the collision was certainly one of the most alarming ever luckily it was between two Cunard steamers, instead of an American and a Cunarder."[45]

Even though the American ships were larger, fancier, and often faster, "the American public had the impression that the Cunard vessels were better handled and could get out of difficulty if they ever got into it . . . The officers [knew] that they could rely upon their men in case of emergency."[46] Mark Twain, a great fan of the Line, later remarked that Cunard "wouldn't hire Noah without ten or more years of training."[47]

By the end of 1857 the Collins Line was in a desperate situation. Rumors swirled about the future of the line. Collins, according to one report, was going to run his ships at reduced speed, thereby saving four thousand dollars per voyage. Another suggested that Cunard might buy them, that the Czar was eying the steamers, that France was making an offer.[48] Collins's investors were silent. Their mounting losses in steamships were only part of a larger crisis facing the entire nation.

Having gone on a national spree of speculation in land and railroads, America was in the midst of a financial panic precipitated by the sudden collapse, in August 1857, of the Ohio Life Insurance and Trust Company. As financial tremors spread outward, shaky investments collapsed. Interest rates ratcheted up, loans were called, mortgage holders defaulted, and commodity prices declined.[49] Because of the complicated web of business interests, a fabric that packets and steamships had helped weave across the Atlantic, the financial crisis spread to England and the continent. While Collins's woes preceded the Panic, his prospects for recovery turned even bleaker as his investors, seeking to preserve their own interests, refused to risk additional capital. Having "used up all [his] available means," Collins turned to his most important backer, James Brown. Embarrassed that he had ignored the advice of his Liverpool partners to avoid risky investments in railroads and steamships, Brown was neither willing nor able to lend more money.[50] His answer to Collins was succinct. "Messrs. Brown Brothers Co. declined to make further advances without additional security."[51]

On February 3, 1858, when *Baltic* returned from her regular Liverpool run, instead of the loud cheering crowds who often gathered along the waterfront to welcome her home, there to greet her was the somber-faced James C. Willet, Sheriff of New York County, holding a writ of attachment for $636,890 on behalf of Brown Brothers. Collins had sixty days to raise the money or see his ships seized and put up for auction.[52]

With the Collins Line now officially and publicly "insolvent," other creditors petitioned the court to secure their debts. Acting on behalf of the government, the United States Attorney Theodore Sedgwick Jr. submitted a motion for an injunction before the United States Circuit Court to prevent the sale of the steamers until the government was repaid $115,000 in past due fines owed to them by Collins for "failures of time under the contract."[53] The city of New York claimed $39,000 in back taxes.[54] The court, however, refused to order an injunction and Sheriff Willet advertised the auction for 12:30 P.M. on April first at the Collins pier. Shortly after noon Stephen Bogart, one of the city's best-known auctioneers, arrived.[55] At first Bogart suggested holding the auction on the deck of the *Adriatic*, but then decided to sell the ships at the end of the pier, "from which point a portion, at least, of all three [ships] could be seen." Accompanied by Deputy Sheriff George Bonsel and Clarkson Porter, "attending on behalf of the creditors," Bogart ascended to the top of a gallery running around the end of the pier, a platform from which in the halcyon days of the Collins Line thousands of people had stood to bid adieu to each of his gallant vessels, the symbols of American prowess at sea as they departed for Liverpool. By contrast, at the auction barely a "hundred persons [were] present, and [they were] not much interested . . . in the event for which they were assembled."

As Bogart began "reading the notice of sale under execution" a clerk from Sedgwick's office interrupted him insisting that potential bidders be notified that the government held a lien of $115,000 against the Collins steamers and that any buyer would incur this claim. Anxious to move on and avoid delays, Bogart retorted that the "company insists that this is paid off." Just as Bogart finished that reply, which few in the audience believed, "an agent from the Board of Supervisors of New York spoke up to say that the Board had a lien on the *Atlantic* for taxes amounting to $39,000." Those debts however, were minor compared to the announcement by Clarkson Potter, representing himself and Brown Brothers, who "desired to notify bidders" of the substantial "lien on all the steamers held by them." Bogart then called above the noise of the crowd that a further claim for $3,000 had been filed by the crew of *Atlantic* for back wages. Bogart finished the preliminaries warning that the successful bidder will "buy the property with whatever valid claims put in actually bind the property in law," which altogether reached the staggering sum of nearly $800,000.

Bogart began and the crowd fell silent. He "announced the terms of the sale as 20 percent cash down, and the balance the next day." A reporter for the *Herald* provided a detailed account. "Now gentlemen . . . how do you like them put up; separately or all together? No choice? Then I will put the three up together, and I will thank you for a bid. What do you say? What bid will I get? Give me something. (An imposing silence.) Well, I'll give you time to make up your calculations." For five minutes the crowd shuffled about. Bogart resumed. "What am I going to have? Gentlemen, bid something; let us start them." Soon beginning to sound a bit desperate, Bogart pleaded, " 'Gentlemen, give me a bid, if you please; anything at all.' " At this point Potter, leaning over the rail, gave a prearranged signal to a figure down below, acting as his straw, who raised his hand and called out "$50,000." Bogart took the bid. "Fifty now, let me hear seventy-five." Nothing. "Give me sixty. Can't I get sixty? You'll never get such steamships again at such a price. No one will build you ships to sell you at that price. Who will give me fifty-five?" Seeing no hands in the air, Bogart called again for a five-minute break. Resuming, he asked, "No advance on $50,000? Going for $50,000. Once—twice—the third and last time—no other bid? Sold for $50,000." The reporter called to Bogart, "Who are they sold to?" Potter identified Dudley R. Fuller. Perplexed, the reporter asked "a sailorish looking individual (who proved to be one of the hands of the Collins line) which was Mr. Fuller, and he answered—'I wish to h—l you would show him to me, for I want to see my new boss.' " Fuller, an iron merchant, was in fact an agent for James Brown. "The whole affair," even with the two five-minute breaks, "did not occupy more than twenty-five minutes."

As the crowd on the pier slowly dispersed and made their way up Canal Street, across the river at the Jersey piers of Cunard dozens of men were bustling about. *Arabia* had left the day before and ware-housemen were still busily sorting out her cargo of boxes and bales waiting to be carted off to consignees. On the same day that *Arabia* sailed, *Persia*, the queen of the fleet, came alongside.[56] The pier was alive with activity.

Although they now owned the line, Potter and Brown had no intention of resuming service; they were finished with steamships. They advertised the ships for sale.[57] In Washington, Collins's political friends scurried for cover. President James Buchanan refused to "sanction" payments that Collins claimed were owed to him.[58] The Senate launched an investigation "to ascertain the amount of stock which is or has been, held by foreigners in ocean mail steamers."[59] On the other side of the capital the House, in a similar punitive mood, voted to withhold more than $50,000 from Collins for failing to transport "the mails from New York to Liverpool, and back."[60] Nor was the public sympathetic to an enterprise that had bought the influence of "dissolute politicians."[61]

More than a year passed before that "melancholy spectacle—the rotting Collins steamers" found a buyer.[62] The North Atlantic Steamship Company, a firm formed by the combination of the Panama Railroad and the Pacific Mail, bought the three ships. In a complete reversal of Collins's business plan, the new company, more interested in quantity than quality, stripped the steamers of their luxury appointments, gutted the elegant staterooms, and crammed 900 army-style bunks into every nook and cranny they could find. *Atlantic* and *Baltic* took the New York to Panama run, while *Adriatic* went into service on the Pacific side, ferrying passengers between Panama and San Francisco. On her first voyage, in October 1859, *Baltic* carried 900 passengers.[63]

Through the whole tempest of the line's dissolution one voice was silent—that of Edward Knight Collins. According to the *Herald*, his connection to the line had "ceased." His friends had abandoned him. Since he was not a mortgage holder, Collins gained nothing from the sale of the ships and was, by his own account, out several hundreds of thousands of dollars. He made a claim against the Post Office alleging that they had failed to pay him moneys owed. Seward promised to help him, but Congress was so deeply divided by party and section that they could not even find enough common ground to pass an ordinary Post Office deficiency bill, let alone agree to fund Collins's controversial request. Furious that "love of country" had cost him his fortune, Collins surrendered any hope of compensation and turned to other interests.[64]

Ever the risk-taker and speculator, early in 1856 when affairs were turning sour on his shipping business, Collins had invested in an Ohio mining venture located near the river town of Wellsville. According to newspaper reports and promotional material, the area was a veritable Eden. "This land is covered with oak, timber, and has valuable quarries of stone, of potter's and fire clay," and most importantly, "the best coal available for the market."[65] Traveling anonymously, referred to only as a "gentleman from New York," and "accompanied by an unidentified "fine old English gentlemen," Collins "scoured the hills and dales of southeastern Ohio." He was impressed by the abundance and quality of the deposits of iron ore, coal, limestone, and fireclay.[66] Revealing his identity, he purchased a large tract of land in Wellsville from Henry Iddings for $35,000. In May Collins's agent Samuel Wilkes began construction of two blast furnaces, and in July 1856 Collins, accompanied by his sister Sexta, and his next-door neighbors from Larchmont, Ira and Sarah Todd, arrived to survey his property. At the moment, however, when he was trying desperately to resuscitate his failing steamship business, Collins could ill afford to remain in Ohio as affairs were collapsing in New York, and so he returned east, leaving his operations in the hands of Wilkes. Wilkes was a poor choice, however, always starting construction but never seeming to finish, and in 1858 Collins fired him and decided to take management into his own hands.[67]

In the midst of all this, a widower for four years since the tragic loss of his wife, son, and daughter, Collins fell in love with his neighbor Sarah Todd. Sometime after the trip to Ohio with Collins the Todds divorced, and early in 1858 Sarah, thirty-five years old, and Collins married. To please his new wife Collins built a substantial house in Wellsville, directly across the road from the newly completed Cleveland and Pittsburgh railway station and, appropriately, named it "Collinwood."[68] The Ohio residence, while smaller, with its two-story front porch, resembled Larchmont. Apparently using Collinwood only as a seasonal residence, Collins engaged Iddings as his caretaker.[69]

By 1860, as a result of the debacle of his steamship line and disappointing returns on his Ohio properties, Collins needed to raise cash. Larchmont was his largest remaining asset. For nearly two decades he had enjoyed the peaceful surroundings of his 300-acre residence overlooking Long Island Sound; the centerpiece was a "fine styled old mansion, in a lawn of fourteen acres of lofty shade trees, native and imported, innumerable and of great variety." In addition there was a "garden tastefully designed and stocked with fruits." Also dotting the estate were several outbuildings, including a farmhouse, yachtsman cottage fronting on a fine harbor, and a bowling alley.[70] "No estate within one hundred miles of New York" was of "equal size" and offered "the diversified advantages and real elegance" of Larchmont.[71]

Between 1850 and 1860 the population of New York City nearly doubled.[72] Such a dramatic increase intensified the problems of urban life and for reasons similar to those that had driven Collins to leave the city twenty years earlier—crowded streets, poor housing, pollution— prosperous city residents continued to look for ways to escape the miasma surrounding them. They looked to the healthier, relaxing environment of the country. Taking advantage of these migratory impulses, and desirous to sell his property to its highest value, Collins conceived a plan to carve up and sell Larchmont piecemeal.

In July 1860 he hired landscape architects Frederick Law Olmsted and Calvert Vaux, partners who were at the time involved in designing Central Park, to prepare a topographical survey of his estate.[73] At Collins's direction the firm divided the entire property, with the exception of the manor house and about fifty adjoining acres that he retained for himself, into "three distinct parcels each having a water front and most splendid sites."[74] Within each of these parcels Olmsted and Vaux laid out more than fifty individual building sites.[75] Collins the country gentleman had become a suburban land developer. Olmsted and Vaux delivered the completed plan in 1862. On January 3, 1863, Collins took out a large advertisement in the *New York Herald*. The headline read, "Opportunity for Capitalists or Persons desiring Country Residences." Employing the hyperbole of the real estate agent he extolled the property as a place where "every building site commands a fine view of the Sound and surrounding country. Two-thirds of the sites have water front. The place is perfectly healthy, water excellent and air invigorating." Aiming at men working in the city, but desirous of living in the country, Collins pointed out that Larchmont was only "18 miles by New Haven rail- road." Businessmen "can reach the city from this place in less time than from Harlem by the avenue cars." Although the nearest local station was two miles away from Larchmont, that was about to improve, for as soon as "Chatsworth is made a station, now in contemplation (depot already built) the distance will be only half a mile."[76]

The *Herald* ran Collins's advertisement through the month of January. Collins's timing was bad. Winter and the Civil War dampened interest. Sales were slow. In February, expecting that a public auction might draw more attention, Collins turned to the New York auctioneer James Miller to conduct a sale. Miller offered the property on February 28th.[77] Sales continued to be disappointing. Collins waited two more years before going to market again. On June 20, 1865, two months after the war had ended, Miller brought the remaining property up. To spur interest he advertised a "peremptory sale . . . without reserve."[78]

Sales improved and with their newfound cash Collins and his wife, after making arrangements in early 1867 to rent the Larchmont mansion to Mrs. William Tucker to run as a "first class boarding house," the couple moved to the Tremont section of New York City (the Bronx). There they made plans for a summer visit to Collinwood.[79] In late 1869, however, he canceled his arrangement with Mrs. Tucker and moved his family—including his son Thomas, his wife, two half-sisters, a niece, two domestic servants, and an Irish laborer—back into his Larchmont mansion.[80]

Moving back to Larchmont did nothing to solve Collins's rising financial woes, and in 1871 he was forced to sell his remaining interests in the property.[81] The new owners converted the mansion into a hotel, a summer rendezvous for rusticating New Yorkers. On the grounds they abandoned Olmsted's garden plan, offering instead "contemporary and inexpensive cottages" on "building plots of various dimensions." To entice city residents out the new owners announced that thanks to improved service the commuting time was only "45 minutes from Forty-Second Street by the New Haven railroad."[82]

For the last time Collins packed off from Larchmont and moved back to the Bronx, where he retired into obscurity. So completely did Collins cut himself off from society that in 1873 the *New York Herald*, his onetime champion, referred to him as the "late Edward Knight Collins." His family rushed to correct the error and reported that Collins was in Wellsville "actively engaged in developing and bringing into market his coal and iron property."[83] Mining, however, proved no improvement over steamships. His Ohio investments were described as being of "some value or no value." By 1877 he was back in New York City, leaving behind in Wellsville unpaid debts mounting to at least $36,000.[84]

In the Bronx Collins and Sarah led a difficult life. Collins had virtually nothing left. Sarah was estranged from Collins's three sons, and the couple lived in "straightened circumstances."[85] In late 1877 a group of friends, taking pity on him, made an appeal for money for his support. It was a gracious effort, but it was too late. On Tuesday morning, January 22, 1878, having not shown any signs of illness, Edward Knight Collins, "Commodore [of] the now almost forgotten Collins Line," rose from his bed and died, age seventy-six. The following Monday the Reverend George Dixon conducted services from the home. "Representatives from all the Steamship Lines in the vicinity attended, as did many persons who have business associations with him." Collins was buried in Woodlawn Cemetery. His obituary appeared in the *New York Times* and later circulated in several newspapers across the country. The public, however, was less interested in his death and more intrigued by the behavior of Collins's family.

In a will he made in 1867 Collins left all his "household furniture of every kind, and all my silver and plate" as well as carriages and horses to Sarah. He also left her his holdings in Ohio. Whatever else was left was to be sold and Sarah, who was also named executrix, was to receive one-third of the proceeds. The remaining, by 1878 a piddling amount, was to be divided in equal shares amongst his surviving three sons— Edward, John, and Thomas—and his three half sisters.[86] As soon as Sarah offered the will for probate, Edward claimed that a second will, executed in 1872, existed that benefitted them. The first, he charged, was written at a time when their father was under the pernicious influence of his wife, who in a certain ante-nuptial agreement had transferred "to her a large part of his estate."[87] In true Dickensian fashion the suit dragged on for more than decade until the judge found that "the plaintiff (Edward) has not proved his case."[88] As Sarah and the sons tussled over the financial remains of their late husband and father, Edward Knight Collins rested in an unmarked grave in Woodlawn Cemetery.[89] Neither his widow nor children would pay for a monument. There is none there today.

EPILOGUE

SAMUEL CUNARD RETIRED from active management of his company in 1863, leaving his son Edward as the senior partner. In declining health, two years later, April 28, 1865, with Edward and William by his side, he died. Unlike Collins, in death Sir Samuel was remembered, revered, and celebrated. He was buried with great dignity at Brompton cemetery, Kensington, in a grave marked, in contrast to Collins, by a dignified monument. His hometown of Halifax, hailing Cunard as an illustrious son, erected a statue to him on the waterfront. Members of Parliament eulogized him, while the *Times* wrote, "His name will hereafter be written in the Roll of England's 'Merchant Princes' who have built up her power no less vigorously than her statesmen and commanders by the arts of war."

Unlike Cunard, the name Collins has disappeared from the sea. For a brief period, less than a decade, Edward Knight Collins sought boldly to challenge the British on the North Atlantic. He could claim some victories—record-setting passages, a reputation for elegance—but the loss of *Arctic* and *Pacific*, the stigma of corruption, sectional division, and partisan politics defeated him. No steamship line could provide regular service across the Atlantic without a substantial regular subsidy.[1] Cunard had one. Collins lost his. "By 1870 there was not a single

American-flag passenger liner on the North Atlantic, nor were there any under construction, nor were there any being planned."[2]

If Collins's failure was not sufficient evidence to warn away potential investors, during the Civil War the Republican-controlled Congress enacted a series of measures that made a near wreck of America's merchant marine. To finance the war, Congress levied a 2 percent tax on hulls and a 3 percent levy on marine engines. To avoid these taxes, as well as the risk of capture or destruction by roving high seas Confederate raiders, northern shipowners sold their vessels to foreign buyers. Between the losses inflicted by raiders and foreign sales, more than one million tons of America's prewar merchant fleet was lost.[3]

Unfortunately, the post–Civil War period proved to be an even worse time for the American merchant marine. In the years after Appomattox the nation faced a series of complex issues that pressed on the national consciousness and drew interest away from the sea.

Among the issues confronting the nation Reconstruction stood foremost. A nation torn apart needed to be reunited, and a prostrate South rebuilt and reformed so that it might return to the Union. Lincoln's mild and forgiving policy "to bind up the nation's wounds" died with him, leaving a defeated South to the mercy of Radical Republicans. For more than a decade, until the South was "redeemed," issues swirling around Reconstruction dominated national discourse.

Secondly was the West. Even as the United States struggled to reunite, it continued to expand. The conclusion of the Civil War brought stability and with it the opportunity for Americans to follow the advice of Horace Greeley, who famously wrote, "Go west, young man, go west and grow up with the country."[4] To entice families to move west, in 1862 Congress passed the Homestead Act, which offered free land to those who would settle and farm. Access to the west was greatly improved by the construction of thousands of miles of railroad, including the completion of the transcontinental line (1869), all built with generous government support. A flood of settlers, many of them immigrants who had arrived in foreign ships, headed west.[5]

While Reconstruction and the settlement of the West occupied public attention, a third development—the dominant influence of business and industrial interests—put political power into the hands of friendly

Republican congresses eager to do all that they could to support domestic industries by imposing high tariffs on foreign goods. After the war, shipowners petitioned to be permitted to return ships they had sold foreign back to American registry. Congress, under pressure from ship-building interests, refused, arguing that the American merchant marine ought to be rebuilt by new construction in domestic yards. Unfortunately, American shipyards had fallen behind in adopting new technologies and were ill-prepared to meet modern standards. A logical answer was to import materials from abroad—a solution roundly denounced by American iron and steel interests, who persuaded Republican congresses to impose high tariffs to protect their "infant industries." Orthogonal in their thinking, Congress, believing it was helping the shipbuilding industry, managed instead to drive up the cost of constructing ships in America to a point that by 1889 the price of a ship in the United States was 40 to 75 percent higher than that being charged in English or German yards.[6] The difference in cost would have meant less if American owners had been permitted to buy foreign ships and register them in the United States. Congress refused. Only American-built vessels could register. Preventing competition with lower-cost foreign carriers, the law precip-itated a downward spiral in the number of American vessels in foreign trade. From 1870 to 1900, while American foreign trade more than doubled, the number of American flag vessels in that trade decreased by nearly 50 percent and carried less than 10 percent of those imports and exports.[7]

While Collins's miscalculations played their part, Congress's inability to develop a consistent national policy toward the merchant marine is the main cause for America's decline at sea. Today, although most of American commerce moves by sea, only 1 percent is carried in Amer-ican ships, nor is there a single American-flag passenger vessel or cruise vessel registered in international service.[8] In total numbers of vessels registered (2015), the United States ranks twenty-second among the world's fleets. The United Kingdom stands at fifteenth.[9]

Unlike the United States, Great Britain did continue to support her merchant marine, and Cunard remained the nation's iconic firm. In the twentieth century, however, two wars and the loss of her empire drained

Great Britain of the resources needed to support her merchant fleet. The Cunard Line fell victim to austerity, and with reduced government support, it was unable to overcome the twentieth century's greatest challenge: technological advancement. Just as travelers in the days of Edward Knight Collins and Samuel Cunard sought fast passage across the Atlantic, so did travelers in the post–World War II period. And so they boarded jets instead of booking passage on an ocean liner, which carried them far above the Atlantic as they journeyed between continents. The Cunard Company struggled until 1998, when Carnival Cruise Lines, an American Corporation operating more than one hundred cruise ships—none of them flying the American flag—made a historic announcement: Carnival had purchased Cunard. For reasons of prestige, history, and tradition (that is, marketing), Carnival has retained the treasured name, and today in the elegant lobbies of *Queen Mary 2*, *Queen Victoria*, and *Queen Elizabeth*, portraits of Samuel Cunard gaze down at thousands of passengers who are going to sea for "fun." Carnival proudly embraces the legendary traditions of Samuel Cunard—safety, service, and elegance—but in a final irony the Queens of the line fly the flag of Bermuda.

Liverpool too suffered from changes in technology and traveling habits. As ships grew larger, her port facilities were found lacking. A bar at the mouth of the Mersey hampered access to deep draft Atlantic liners, and the docks, while adequate, were a challenge to pilots who struggled to maneuver the liners between stonewalls. Liverpool's access to the industrial midlands continued to work in her favor for cargo, but not for passengers. Most travelers were bound for either London or the Continent. In that case, Southampton was a better choice. That city was closer to London and the Continent as well.

What remains standing from the epic maritime struggle between the United States (Collins) and Great Britain (Cunard) is New York City. The demands the steamships of Cunard and Collins exerted on her resources obliged her to develop skills and institutions to support large-scale trade. Her financial houses, Brown Brothers being the most important at this time, dwarfed those of her U.S. competitors. Like a vigilant and voracious spider, New York sat at the center of an intricate web of commerce. Gobbling up the competition, she grew and grew, until in the modern era she achieved global dominance in the fields of finance, business services, and corporate management. In this, too, Edward Knight Collins and Samuel Cunard played their part.

ACKNOWLEDGMENTS

This book began at sea. I made my first voyage offshore more than three decades ago when the Sea Education Association invited me to sail with their students aboard the schooner *Westward* from Lunenburg, Nova Scotia, to Woods Hole, Massachusetts. I was aboard to teach maritime history. Although I had been teaching a course, "America and the Sea," at Northeastern University, as well as a summer graduate program at Mystic Seaport, I had very little actual experience on the ocean. Following my journey on *Westward* I was invited to teach aboard a number of other vessels sailing along the coast of New England, the Great Lakes, and the Caribbean. Those experiences have led to many years of continuing travel at sea across the North Atlantic.

In 2007 Cunard invited me to join *Queen Mary 2* as a guest lecturer on an Atlantic crossing. Since that day my wife and I have crossed eighteen times on this magnificent ship. While *Queen Mary 2* is modern in every way, she is also wrapped in the past. From the color of her stack to the historic photos along her passageways, guests are reminded of the long history of the Cunard line. That Cunard (the name, at least) has survived for more than 175 years is remarkable. In his early years, however, Samuel Cunard had stiff competition from the American Edward Knight Collins.

I must first acknowledge the pioneering work of the late Edward "Ted" Sloan, my colleague at Mystic who introduced me to Collins. Ted's work on the "secret agreement" between Collins and Cunard was extremely useful, as was his article on *Baltic*'s visit to Washington. I am indebted also to the work of John F. Langley, Cunard's biographer and chairman of the Cunard Society. Professor Andrew Popp at the University of Liverpool introduced me to Lucy Kilfoyle, a Liverpudlian scholar whose knowledge of that city was of inestimable assistance. Also in the UK is Michael Gallagher, manager of public relations and historian for Cunard Lines, whose support I very much appreciate.

As is her wont, Linda Smith Rhoads, editor emerita of *The New England Quarterly*, answered my call and applied her keen editorial eye. My editor George Gibson also stood by and rendered assistance, prodding me when necessary, while offering kind direction through his careful editing. To his colleagues at Bloomsbury, Jacqueline Johnson and Jenna Dutton, and copyeditor Kirby Gann, I offer my thanks as well. And to my agent, Jill Kneerim, gratitude for steering me away from "rocks and shoals." Captain Albert E. Therberge, Jr., NOAA Corps (ret.), informed me in matters of ocean currents and water temperature. My colleague at Northeastern University, Carey Rapport, Distinguished Professor of Electrical and Computer Engineering, assisted me in calculating the size and weight of iron cylinders. I owe a special debt of gratitude to Lorraine Harper, a Collins descendant, who provided me with guidance and information concerning the family, and to Lynne Crowley at the Larchmont Historical Society, who also read and commented on the manuscript.

On both sides of the Atlantic a number of institutions offered exceptional help. In the UK both Archives and Special Collections at the Universities of Glasgow and Liverpool have provided important advice and materials. In the United States the staffs at Mariners Museum and Mystic Seaport Museum were exceptional in their service. I could neither have found nor navigated my course through the considerable amount of genealogical information available had it not been for the New England Historic Genealogical Society. The Public Archives of Nova Scotia was most welcoming, particularly Garry D. Shutlak, who helped me track down sources. As usual, the shelves of the Boston Athenaeum yielded up valuable material while providing a quiet and congenial place for research. The digital resources of the Boston Public Library and the Library of Congress allowed me to search far and wide without leaving my computer. Other institutions in this list include the following: the

Rhode Island Historical Society; the New York Historical Society; University of Rochester's department of Rare Books and Special Collections; Yale University; the United States National Archives; the United States Postal Museum; and Truro Historical Society and the Truro Public Library. Donna Selvaggio, chief librarian at the United States Merchant Marine Academy, King's Point, assisted me with finding data about the current status of the U.S. Merchant Marine. Robert Beresford shared the history of Wellsville with me, while William Iddings provided valuable insight into the history of "Collinwood" in the same town. Ms. Maryann Byrnes of Woodlawn Cemetery provided information concerning Collins's burial site. As has been the case in everything that I have written, I owe a debt of thanks to the Snell Library Northeastern University where Jamie Dendy, Head Librarian for Research, has more than earned his title.

Finally, to my wife, Marilyn, who has joined me in this voyage, I say again—Thank You!

BIBLIOGRAPHY

Primary Sources

University of Glasgow, Archives
  Napier Collection

University of Liverpool Library,
  Special Collections and Archives,
  Cunard Archives

Mariners Museum Library
  Erastus Smith Steamship
  Papers Collection

Mystic Seaport Museum Blunt
  White Library
  William Skiddy Papers

New England Historic Genealogical
  Society
  Genealogical material accessed via
  AmericanAncestors.org
  Files are available at New England
  Historic Genealogical Society,
  Boston, MA:
    Case File M103013A, February
    6, 2014
    Case File M103012A-2, April
    14, 2014
    Case File M103013A
    Addendum, July 9, 2014

New York Historical Society
  Records of Brown Brothers
  Harriman

Public Archives of Nova Scotia
  Papers of Phyllis Ruth Blakeley

Rhode Island Historical Society
  Journal of the U.S. Steamer *Baltic*,
  1850–1855, Comstock Family
  Papers

University of Rochester, Rush Rhees
  Library, Department of Rare Books
  and Special Collections
    Correspondence of William Henry
    Seward

United States National Archives
  RG 41 Bureau of Marine Inspection
  and Navigation
  Custom House Documentation for
  the Port of New York

Yale University
  Matthew Calbraith Perry
  Letterbook, microfilm

Newspapers/Magazines

Acadian Recorder (Halifax)
Baltimore Sun
Boston Columbian Sentinel
Charleston City Gazette
Connecticut Current (Hartford)
Democratic Review (New York City)
Farmers' Cabinet (Amherst, N.H.)
Hartford Courant
Harpers New Monthly Magazine
Illustrated London News
Liberator
Liverpool Mercury
Madisonian (Richmond, KY)
National Advocate (New York City)
New Bedford Mercury
New London Morning News
Times-Picayune (New Orleans)

Newport Mercury
New York Gazette
New York Journal of Commerce
New York Mercantile Advertiser
New York Spectator
New York Times
New York Tribune
North American Review
Novascotian (Halifax)
Nova Scotia Royal Gazette (Halifax)
Nova Scotia Weekly Chronicle (Halifax)
Otsego Herald (New York)
Pittsfield Sun
Rochester Telegraph (New York)
Times (London)
Waldo Patriot (ME)

Books/Articles

Abbott, Jacob. "The Novelty Works." *Harper's New Monthly Magazine* (May 1851): 721–34.
———. *Rise of New York Port*. New York: Charles Scribner's Sons, 1939.
———. *Square Riggers on Schedule: The New York Sailing Packets to England, France and Cotton Ports*. Princeton: Princeton University Press, 1938.
——— and Jennie Barnes Pope. *Sea Lanes in Wartime: The American Experience 1775–1945*. New York: Archon Books, 1968.
Armstrong, John, and David Williams. "The Perceptions and Understanding of New Technology: A Failed Attempt to Establish a Transatlantic Steamship Liner Service, 1824–1828." *Northern Mariner* 17, no. 4 (2007): 41–56.
Arnell, J. C. *Atlantic Mails: A History of the Mail Service between Great Britain and Canada to 1889*. Ottawa: National Postal Museum, 1980.
———. "Samuel Cunard and the Nova Scotia Government Vessels *Earl of Bathurst* and *Chebucto*," *Mariner's Mirror* 54, no. 4 (1965): 337–47.
Atkins, T. B. *History of Halifax City*. Belleville, ON: Mika, 1973.
Babcock, Laurence. *Spanning the Atlantic*. New York: Alfred A. Knopf, 1931.
Baines, Thomas. *History of the Commerce and Town of Liverpool*. London: Longman, Brown, Green and Longmans, 1852.
Bartlett, Walter. *The Old Merchants of New York City*. New York: Carleton Publishers, 1862.
Bauer, K. Jack. *A Maritime History of the United States: The Role of America's Seas and Waterways*. Columbia: University of South Carolina Press, 1988.
Bemis, Samuel Flagg. *Pinckney's Treaty: America's Advantage from Europe's Distress*. New Haven: Yale University Press, 1960.

Berton, Pierre. *The Arctic Grail: The Quest for the Northwest Passage and the North Pole, 1818–1909*. Toronto: Archer, 2001.

Bigelow, Henry B. and William Schoeder. *Fishes of the Gulf of Maine*. Washington: Government Printing Office, 1953.

Bittermann, Rusty. *Rural Protest on Prince Edward Island: From British Colonization to the Escheat Movement*. Toronto: University of Toronto Press, 2006.

Black, Henry Campbell. *Black's Law Dictionary*. St. Paul: West Publishing Co., 1968.

Blunt, Edmund March. *The American Coast Pilot*. New York: Blunt, 1815.

Bourne, William Oland. *Gems from Fable Land: A Collection of Fables Illustrated by Facts*. New York: Charles Scribner's Sons, 1853.

Bowley, Arthur L. *Wages in the United Kingdom in the Nineteenth Century*. Cambridge: University Press, 1900.

Bradley, Francis B. C. *The First Steamer to Cross the Atlantic*. Salem: Essex Institute, 1925.

Brebner, J. Bartlett. *Canada: A Modern History*. Ann Arbor: University of Michigan Press, 1960.

Broadberry, Stephen and Bishnupriya Gupta. "Cotton Textiles and the Great Divergence: Lancashire, India and the Shifting Competitive Advantage, 1600–1850."CEPR Discussion paper No. 5183, August 2005.

Brooke, Richard. *Liverpool as It Was During the Last Quarter of the Eighteenth Century, 1775–1800*. Liverpool: J. Mawdsley and Sons, 1853.

Brown, Alexander Crosby. *Women and Children Last*. New York: G.P. Putnam's Sons, 1961.

———. "A Footnote to the Loss of the *Arctic*." *The American Neptune Magazine* 19 (April 1959): 128–32.

———. "The Steamer *Vesta*: Neglected Partner in a Fatal Collision," *The American Neptune Magazine* 20 (April 1960): 177–84.

Brown, John Crosby. *A Hundred Years of Merchant Banking*. New York: Privately printed, 1909.

Buchnea, Emily. "Transatlantic Transformations: Visualizing Changes over Time in the Liverpool-New York Trade Network, 1763–1833." *Enterprise and Society* 15, no. 4 (December 2014): 687–721.

Bullard, Thomas R. *Sails, Steam and Subsidies: The Career of Edward Knight Collins*. Oak Park: Privately printed, 1990.

Burrows, Edwin G. and Mike Wallace. *Gotham: A History of New York*. New York: Oxford University Press, 1999.

Busch, Laurence. *Steam Coffin: Captain Moses Rogers and the Steamship Savannah Break the Barrier*. n.p: Hodos Historia, 2010.

Butler, Daniel Allen. *The Age of Cunard*. Annapolis: Lighthouse Press, 2004.

Chadwick, French Ensor. *Ocean Steamships: A Peculiar Account of their Construction, Development, Management and Appliances*. New York: Charles Scribner's Sons, 1891.

Chernow, Ron. *Alexander Hamilton*. New York: Penguin Books, 2004.

Choules, John O. *The Cruise of the Steam Yacht* North Star. Boston: Gould and Lincoln, 1854.

Codinach, Guadalupe Jimenez. "An Atlantic Silver Entrepot: Vera Cruz and the House of Gordon and Murphy." In *Atlantic Port Cities: Economy, Culture and Society in the*

Atlantic World, edited by Franklin W. Knight and Peggy K. Liss, 135– 60. Knoxville: University of Tennessee Press, 1991.

Cohen, Ira. "The Auction System in the Port of New York, 1817–1837." *Business History Review* 45, no. 4 (Winter 1971): 488–510.

Cohn, Raymond C. *Mass Migration under Sail*. Cambridge: Cambridge University Press, 2009.

Colledge, J. J. *Ships the Royal Navy*. 2 vols. New York: Augustus M. Kelley, 1969.

Conrad, Margaret, Alan Finkel, and Cornelius Jaenen. *History of the Canadian Peoples*. 2 vols. Toronto: Longmans Co., 1993.

Corlett, E. C. B., "The Screw Propeller and Merchant Shipping." In *The Advent of Steam*, edited by Robert Gardiner, 83–105. London: Conway, 1993.

Crammond, William, ed. *The Annals of Banff*. Aberdeen: New Spaulding Club, 1891–92.

Cutler, Carl. *Greyhounds of the Sea*. New York: G.P. Putnam's Sons, 1930.

———. *Five Hundred Sailing Records of American Built Ships*. Mystic: Marine Historical Association, 1952.

Dalzell, Robert F. *American Participation in the Great Exhibition of 1851*. Amherst: Amherst College Press, 1960.

Dawson, Robert. *Isaac Hicks: A New York Merchant and Quaker, 1767–1820*. Cambridge: Harvard University Press, 1964.

Deas, James. *The River Clyde*. Glasgow: James Maclehouse, 1876.

DeConde, Alexander. *The Quasi-War: The Politics and Diplomacy of the Undeclared War with France, 1797–1801*. New York: Charles Scribner's Sons, 1966.

DeFoe, Daniel. *A Tour through the Whole Island of Great Britain*. Edited by P. N. Forbend, V. R. Owens, and A. J. Coulsen. New Haven: Yale University Press, 1991.

Dictionary of American Fighting Ships. 8 vols. Washington: Government Printing Office, 1959–1981.

Dept. of Commerce. *Historical Statistics of the United States*. 2 vols. Washington: Department of Commerce, 1975.

Dodd, George. *An Historical and Explanatory Dissertation on Steam Engines and Steam Packets*. London: Printed for the author, 1818.

Douglass, Frederick. *Frederick Douglass Papers*, Series Three; *Correspondence*. Edited by John R. McKitigan. New Haven: Yale University Press, 2009.

Douglas, James. "The Steamship *Unicorn* on the St. Lawrence Branch of the Cunard Company in 1849." In *Transactions of the Literary and Historical Society of Quebec, Sessions of 1908–09*, no. 28. Quebec: Chronicle, 1910.

Downing, Andrew Jackson. *The Architecture of Country Houses*. New York: D. Appleton and Co., 1850.

Drago, Harry Sinclair. *The Steamboaters*. New York: Bramhall House, 1967.

Duncannon, John Victor. *Rawdon and Douglas: Two Loyalist Townships in Nova Scotia*. Belleville, Ontario: Mika Publishing Co., 1989.

Dupont, Brandon, Drew Keeling, and Thomas Weiss. "Passenger Fares for Overseas Travel in the 19th and 20th Centuries." Paper presented for the Annual Meeting of the Economic History Association, Vancouver, BC. August 15, 2012. 1–47. http://eh.net/eha/wp-content/uploads/2013/11/Weissetal.pdf.

Dupont, Brandon and Thomas Weiss. "Overseas Travel by Americans, 1820–1860." *Cliometrica* (2013): 319–39.

Eaton, Arthur Wentworth Hamilton. *History of King's County, Nova Scotia.* Salem: Salem Press, 1910.

Ewen, William H. *Days of Steamboats.* Mystic, CT: Mystic Seaport Museum, 1988.

Fahmer, Alvin A. "William 'Extra Billy' Smith, Governor of Virginia, 1864–1865: A Pillar of the Confederacy." *Virginia Magazine of History and Biography* 74, no. 1 (1966): 68–87.

Feys, Torsten. *The Battle for the Migrants.* St. John's, Newfoundland: International Maritime Economic History Association, 2013.

Fingard, Judith. "The 1820s: Peace, Privilege, and the Promise of Progress." In *The Atlantic Region to Confederation: A History,* edited by Phillip A. Buckner and John A. Reid. Toronto: University of Toronto Press, 1994.

Fishbaugh, Charles Preston. *From Paddle Wheels to Propellers.* Indianapolis: Indiana Historical Society, 1970.

Flayhart, William Henry III. *The American Line, 1871–1902.* New York: W.W. Norton and Co., 2000.

———. *Disaster at Sea: Shipwrecks, Storms, and Collisions on the Atlantic.* New York: W.W. Norton, 2003.

———. *Perils of the Atlantic: Steamship Disasters, 1850 to the Present.* New York: W.W. Norton and Co., 2003.

Fleming, James Brown. *John Park Fleming.* Glasgow: James Maclehose and Sons, 1885.

Flexner, Thomas. *Steamboats Come True.* New York: Viking Press, 1954.

Flounders, Eric and Michael Gallagher. *The Story of Cunard's 175 Years.* Ramsay, Isle of Man: Ferry Publications, 2014.

Fogg, Nicholas. *The Voyages of the Great Britain.* London: Chatham Publishing, 2002.

Fontenoy, Paul E. "Ginseng, Otter Skins, and Sandalwood: The Conundrum of the China Trade." *The Northern Mariner/Le Marin du Nord* VII, no. 1 (January 1997): 1–16.

Foreman, Amanda. "The British View the War of 1812 Quite Differently than Americans Do." *Smithsonian Magazine* (July 2014): 17–21.

Fowler Jr., William M. *American Crisis: George Washington and the Dangerous Two Years After Yorktown, 1781–1783.* New York: Walker Books, 2011.

———. *Jack Tars and Commodore: The American Navy 1783–1815.* Boston: Houghton Mifflin Co., 1984.

Franklin, Benjamin. "The Internal State of America: Being a True Description of the Interest and Policy of that Vast Continent." Vol. 10 of *The Works of Benjamin Franklin.* Edited by John Bigelow, 63–70. New York: G.P. Putnam's Sons, 1904.

Frittelli, John. *Cargo Preference for U.S. Flag Shipping.* Washington: Congressional Research Science, 2015.

Fry, Henry. *The History of North Atlantic Steam Navigation*. London: Sampson, Low, Marston and Co., 1896.

Gerriets, Marilyn. "The Impact of the General Mining Association in the Nova Scotia Coal Industry, 1826–1850." *Acadiensis* 21, no. 1 (Autumn 1991): 54–84.

———. "The Rise and Fall of a Free Standing Company in Nova Scotia: The General Mining Association." *Business History Review* 34, issue 3 (1992): 16–48.

Goodrich, A. T. *The Picture of New York and the Stranger's Guide*. New York: A.T. Goodrich, 1828.

Graham, Gerald S. "The Ascendancy of the Sailing Ship, 1850–1885." *Economic History Review* 9, issue 1 (August 1956): 74–88.

Grant, C. L., "Cave Johnson: Postmaster General." *Tennessee Historical Quarterly* 20, no. 4 (December 1961): 323–49.

Grattan, T. C. *Civilized America*. 2 vols. London: Bradbury and Evans, 1859.

Green, Constance McLaughlin. *Eli Whitney and the Birth of American Technology*. Boston: Little, Brown, 1956.

Greenhill, Basil. "Steam before the Screw." In *The Advent of Steam: The Merchant Ship Before 1900*, edited by Robert Gardiner, 11–27. Annapolis: Naval Institute Press, 1993.

Hargest, George E. *History of Letter Post Communication between the United States and Europe, 1845–1875*. Washington: Smithsonian Institution Press, 1971.

Harley, C. Knick. "Ocean Freight Rates and Productivity 1740–1913: The Primacy of Mechanical Invention Reaffirmed." *Journal of Economic History* 48, no. 4 (December 1988): 851–876.

Harper, Lawrence C. *The English Navigation Laws*. New York: Columbia University Press, 1969.

Harris, R. Cole, ed. *Historical Atlas of Canada*. 3 vols. Toronto: University of Toronto Press, 1987–93.

Harrison, Henry. *Lancashire Place Names*. London: Eaton Press, 1911.

Hart, Douglas. "Sociability and 'Separate Spheres' on the North Atlantic: The Interior Architecture of British Atlantic Liners, 1840–1930." *Journal of Social History* 44 (Fall 2010): 189–212.

———."The Grand Saloon and Victorian Propriety." *Powerships* no. 298 (Summer 2016): 24–29.

Haven, Gilbert and Thomas Russell. *Incidents and Anecdotes of Rev. Edward T. Taylor*. Boston: The Boston Port and Seamen's Society, 1871.

Hawthorne, Nathaniel. *American Notebooks*. Edited by Randall Stewart. New York: Russell and Russell, 1962.

Hayler, William B., ed., *Merchant Marine Officer's Handbook*. Centreville, MD: Cornell Maritime Press, 1990.

Hearn, Chester. *Tracks in the Sea: Matthew Fontaine Maury and the Mapping of the Oceans*. Camden: International Marine, 2002.

Hickey, Donald R. "American Trade Restrictions during the War of 1812." *Journal of American History* 68, no. 3 (December 1981): 517–38.

Hill, Hamilton Andrew. *Memoir of Abbott Lawrence*. Boston: Privately printed, 1883.

Hodder, Edwin. *Sir George Burns, His Times and Friends*. London: Hodder and Stoughton, 1890.

Homans, J. Smith, and J. Smith Homans, Jr. *Cyclopedia of Commerce and Commercial Navigation*. 2 vols. New York: Harper and Brothers, 1858.

Hoogenboom, Ari. *Gustavus Vasa Fox*. Baltimore: Johns Hopkins Press, 2008.

Howe, Henry. "Destruction of the Ocean Steamer *Arctic* by Collision with the *Vesta*, a French Propeller, on the Banks of Newfoundland." In *Outrageous Seas: Shipwreck and Survival in the Waters Off Newfoundland, 1583–1893*, edited by Rainer K. Baehre, 281–308. Montreal: McGill–Queens University Press, 1999.

Howe, Joseph. *The Speeches and Public Letters of Joseph Howe*. Edited by William Annard. 2 vols. Halifax: The Chronicle Publishing Co., 1909.

Howley, Frank. *Slavers, Traders and Privateers: Liverpool and the African Trade and Revolution*. Birkenhead: Countryvise, 2008.

Hubbard, Walter and Richard F. Winter. *North Atlantic Mail Sailings, 1840–1875*. Canton, Ohio: U.S. Philatelic Society Classics, 1988.

Hughes, T. E. "The Cunard Story." *Sea Breezes*, July 1965. 503–19, 584–600, 663–681, 742–763.

Hunter, Lewis C. *Steamboats on the Western Rivers*. Cambridge: Harvard University Press, 1949.

Hyde, Francis E. *Liverpool and the Mersey: An Economic History of a Port*. Liverpool: David Charles, 1971.

Hyde, Francis E., Bradbury B. Parkinson, and Sheila Marriner. "The Nature and Profitability of the Liverpool Slave Trade." *The Economic History Review* 5 (1953): 368–77.

Jarvis, Adrian. *Liverpool Central Docks: 1799–1905: An Illustrated History*. Liverpool: National Museums and Galleries, 1991.

———. *The Liverpool Dock Engineers*. Stroud: Alan Sutton, 1996.

Jasanoff, Maya. *Liberty's Exiles: American Loyalists in the Revolutionary World*. New York: Knopf, 2011.

Johnson, Emery. *History of Domestic and Foreign Commerce of the United States*. 2 vols. New York: Burt Franklin, 1964.

Jones, Thomas. *History of New York During the Revolutionary War*. 2 vols. New York: New York Historical Society, 1879.

Kellett, John A. *Glasgow: A Concise History*. London: Blond, 1967.

Kemp, Peter, ed. *The Oxford Companion to Ships and the Sea*. New York: Oxford University Press, 1976.

Killick, J. R. "Sir William Brown." *Oxford Dictionary of National Biography*. Oxford University Press, 2004.

Kirkland, Edward Chase. *Men, Cities and Transportation in New England History, 1820–1900*. 2 vols. Cambridge: Harvard University Press, 1948.

Kittredge, Henry C. *Shipmasters of Cape Cod*. Boston: Houghton Mifflin, 1935.

Knoblock, Glenn. *The American Clipper Ship, 1845–1920*. Jefferson: McFarland and Company, 2013.

Kouwenhoven, John A. *Partners in Banking: An Historical Portrait of a Great Private Bank, Brown Brothers Harriman and Co., 1818–1868.* Garden City: Doubleday, 1968.

Kowski, Francis R. *Country, Park and City: The Architecture and Life of Calvert Vaux.* New York: Oxford University Press, 1998.

Krichtal, Alexey. "Liverpool and the Raw Cotton: A Study of the Port and Its Merchant Community, 1770–1815." MA Thesis, Victoria University of Wellington, 2013. http://researcharchive.vuw.ac.nz/xmlui/bitstream/handle/10063/2952/thesis .pdf?sequence=1.

Labaree, Benjamin, William M. Fowler, Jr., John B. Hattendorf, Jeffrey Safford, Edward W. Sloan, and Andrew W. German. *America and the Sea: A Maritime History.* Mystic, CT: Mystic Seaport, 1998.

Lane, Wheaton. *Commodore Vanderbilt: An Epic of the Steam Age.* New York: Alfred A. Knopf, 1942.

Langley, Harold D. "William Ballard Preston." In *American Secretaries of the Navy,* edited by Paolo Coletta, 1:243–55. 2 vols. Annapolis: United States Institute Press, 1980.

Leslie, Eliza. *Miss Leslie's Behaviour Book: A Guide and Manual for Ladies.* Philadelphia: T. B. Peterson, 1859.

Lindsay, W. S. *History of Merchant Shipping and Ancient Commerce.* 4 vols. New York: AMS, repr. 1965.

Longworth's American Almanac New York Register. New York: D. Longworth, 1801.

Longworth's American Almanac New York City Business Directory. New York: Thomas Longworth, 1841.

Lord, Lindsay. *Nautical Etiquette and Customs.* Centerville: Cornell Maritime Press, 1987.

Lovett, Robert W. "Rundell, Bridge and Rundell: An Early Company History." *Bulletin of the Business History Society* 23, no. 3 (September 1949): 152–62.

MacArthur, William Forrest. *History of Port Glasgow.* Glasgow: Jackson, Wylie and Co., 1932.

MacDonell, J. A. *Sketches Illustrating the Early Development and History of Glengarry in Canada.* Montreal: Wm. Foster Brown, 1893.

MacGregor, George. *The History of Glasgow.* Glasgow: Thomas Morrison, 1881.

MacKinnon, Neil. *This Unfriendly Soil.* Kingston: McGill–Queens University Press, 1986.

MacNutt, W. S. *The Atlantic Provinces: The Emergence of Colonial Society.* (Toronto: McClelland and Stewart, 1965.

McDonald, James S. "Memoir of Governor John Parr." *Collections of the Nova Scotia Historical Society.* Vol. 14:41–79. 1910.

McFarland, Raymond. *A History of New England Fisheries.* Philadelphia: University of Pennsylvania Press, 1911.

McKay, Richard. *South Street.* Riverside City: 7-C's Press, 1969.

Maginnis, Arthur J. *The Atlantic Ferry.* London: Whittaker and Co., 1893.

Maguire, John F. *Father Mathew: A Biography.* London: Longman, Green, Longman, Roberts and Green, 1863.

Maier, Pauline. *Ratification: The People Debate the Constitution, 1787–1788.* New York: Simon and Schuster, 2010.

Maischak, Lars. *German Merchants in the Nineteenth Century.* Cambridge: Cambridge University Press, 2013.

Maury, Matthew Fontaine. *Lanes for Steamers Crossing the Atlantic.* New York: The Underwriters, 1855.

Meeker, Ralph. "Part 1: History of British Shipping Subsidies." *American Economic Association Publications,* third series, vol. 6, no. 3 (August 1905): 1–229.

Melville, Herman. *White Jacket.* New York: Viking Press Library of America, 1982.

———. *Moby Dick.* New York: Viking Press Library of America, 1983.

———. *Redburn: His First Voyage.* New York: Viking Press Library of America, 1983.

Miles, Vincent. *The Lost Hero of Cape Cod.* Yarmouth Port: Historical Society of Old Yarmouth, 2015.

Milne, Graeme. *Trade and Traders in Mid-Victorian Liverpool.* Liverpool: Liverpool University Press, 2000.

Miskolcze, Robin. *Women and Children First: Nineteenth Century Sea Narratives and American Identity.* Lincoln: University of Nebraska Press, 2007.

Morison, Samuel Eliot. *"Old Bruin": Commodore Matthew Calbraith Perry.* Boston: Little, Brown Co., 1967.

Morris, Edward. *Life of Henry Bell.* Glasgow: Printed for author, 1854.

Morris, Richard B. *The Peacemakers.* New York: Harper and Row, 1965.

Morrison, John H. *History of New York Ship Yards.* New York: Wm. E. Sametz, 1909.

Morse, Jedediah. *The American Gazetter.* Boston: Thomas and Andrews, 1804.

Murray, E. M. *A Brief History of Dalhousie University.* Halifax: Dalhousie Million Committee, 1919.

Myers, Gustavus. *History of Great American Fortunes.* 3 vols. Chicago: C. H. Kerr Co., 1909–1910.

Napier, James. *Life of Robert Napier.* London: William Blackwood and Sons, 1904.

North, Douglass C. "Ocean Freight Rates and Economic Development, 1750–1913." *Journal of Economic History* 18, no. 4 (December 1958): 537–55.

———. "Early National Income Estimates of the U.S." *Economic Development and Cultural Change* IX, No. 3 (April 1961): 387–96.

Nye, David E. *American Technology Sublime.* Cambridge: MIT Press, 1994.

N.A. "Ocean Steam Navigation." *North American Review* 99, issue 205 (October 1864): 483–523.

Olivera, Ruth R. and Lilane Crete, *Life in Mexico under Santa Anna, 1822–1855.* Norman: University of Oklahoma, 1979.

Olmsted, Frederick Law. *The Papers of Frederick Law Olmsted.* 9 vols. Edited by Charles C. McLaughlin. Baltimore: Johns Hopkins Press, 1977–2015.

Ommer, Rosemary E. "The 1830s: Adapting Their Institutions to Their Desires." In *The Atlantic Region to Confederation,* edited by Phillip Buckner and John Reid, 284–306. (Toronto: University of Toronto Press, 1995.)

Orrok, George A. "Development of the Steam Condenser" *Power and the Engineer.* June 1, 1909.

Parker, Captain H. and Frank C. Bowen. *Mail and Passenger Steamers of the Nineteenth Century.* London: Sampson, Low, Marston and Co., 1928.

Parry, Ann. *Parry of the Arctic.* London: Chatto and Windus, 1963.

Parry, Edward. *Memoirs of Sir W. Edward Parry.* London: Longman, Brown, Green, Longmans and Roberts, 1857.

Pasley, Jeffrey L. "Democracy, Gentility, and Lobbying in the Early U.S. Congress." In *The American Congress: The Building of Democracy,* edited by E. Zeilzer, 38–62. Boston: Houghton Mifflin, 2004.

Penn, William. *The Papers of William Penn.* 5 vols. Edited by Richard and Mary Maples Dunn. Philadelphia: University of Pennsylvania Press, 1981–1987.

Pennypacker, Samuel W. *The Settlement of Germantown, Pennsylvania.* Philadelphia: William J. Campbell, 1889.

Perkins, Edward. *Financing Anglo-American Trade: The House of Brown, 1800–1880.* Cambridge: Harvard University Press, 1975.

Philip, Cynthia Owen. *Robert Fulton.* New York: Franklin Watts, 1985.

Picton, J. A. *Memorials of Liverpool.* 2 vols. London: Longmans, Green, 1875.

———. Extracted and Annotated, *City of Liverpool Municipal Archives and Records from AD 1700 to the Passing of the Municipal Reform Act, 1835.* 2 vols. G. Wormsley, 1886.

Poor's Manual of Railroads in the United States. New York: Publications, 1903.

Pratt, Julius W. *A History of United States Foreign Policy.* New York: Prentice Hall, 1965.

Preble, George Henry. *A Chronological History of the Origin and Development of Steam Navigation.* Philadelphia: L.R. Hamersly and Co., 1895.

Report of Commissioners Relative to Encroachment and Preservation of the Harbor of New York. Albany: C. Van Beathuysen, 1856.

Rankin, John. *A History of Our Company.* Liverpool: University of Liverpool, 1908.

Rich, Shebnah. *Truro Cape Cod Land Marks and Sea Marks.* Boston: D. Lothrop and Company, 1883.

Ridgely-Nevitt, Cedric. *American Steamships on the Atlantic.* Newark: University of Delaware Press, 1981.

Rogers, John. *Origin of Sea Terms.* Mystic, CT: Mystic Seaport Museum, 1985.

Rowland, Kate. "The Mount Vernon Convention." *Pennsylvania Magazine of History and Biography* 11, no. 4 (January 1888): 410–25.

Rozwadouski, Helen. "'Introduction' Reconsidering Matthew Fontaine Maury." *International Journal of Maritime History* 28, no. 8 (May–June 2016): 388–93.

Sabine, Lorenzo. *American Loyalists: Biographical Sketches of Adherents to the British Crown in the War of the Revolution.* 2 vols. Boston: Little, Brown, 1847.

Salley, A. S. *Marriage Notices in the South Carolina Gazette and Its Successors, 1732–1801.* Albany: Joel Munsell's Sons, 1902.

Samson, Daniel. "Industrial Colonization: The Colonial Context of the General Mining Association, Nova Scotia, 1825–1842." *Acadiensis* 29, no. 1 (Autumn 1999): 3–28.

Savage, Carleton. *Policy of the United States toward Maritime Commerce in War*. 2 vols. Washington: Government Printing Office, 1934.

Schroeder, John H. *Matthew Calbraith Perry: Antebellum Sailor and Diplomat*. Annapolis: United States Naval Institute Press, 2001.

Schwartz, Joel. "Housing." In *The Encyclopedia of New York*, edited by Kenneth Jackson. New Haven: Yale University Press, 1995.

Sellers, Charles. *The Market Revolution: Jacksonian America, 1815–1846*. New York: Oxford University Press, 1991.

Shaw, David W. *The Sea Shall Embrace Them: The Tragic Story of the Steamship Arctic*. New York: The Free Press, 2002.

Sheldon, George W. "Old Shipbuilders of New York." *Harpers New Monthly Magazine* 65, issue 386 (July 1882): 223–42.

———. "Shipping Merchants of New York." *Harpers New Monthly Magazine* 84 (December–May 1892): 457–71.

"Ships and Shipmasters of Old Providence." Providence: Providence Institution for Savings, 1919.

Siebert, Wilbur H. *The Loyalists of Pennsylvania*. Columbus: The University, 1920.

Silliman, Benjamin and C.R. Goodrich. *The World of Art and Industry*. New York: G.P. Putnam's Sons, 1854.

Skempton, A. W. *A Biographical Directory of Civil Engineers in Great Britain and Ireland*. London: Marshall, 1987.

Sloan, Edward P. "Collins versus Cunard: The Realities of a North Atlantic Steamship Rivalry, 1850–1858." *International Journal of Maritime History* 4, no. 1 (June 1992): 83–100.

———. "The *Baltic* Goes to Washington: Lobbying for a Congressional Steamship Subsidy 1852." *Northern Mariner*, no.1 (January 1995): 19–32.

Shattuck, Lemuel. *Report to the City of Boston for the Year 1845. Embracing Collateral and Statistical Researches Illustrating the History and Condition of the Population and Their Means of Progress and Prosperity*. Boston: John H. Eastburn, City Printer, 1846.

Smith, Edgar C. *A Short History of Naval and Marine Engineering*. Cambridge: Cambridge University Press, 1937.

Smith, Myron J. and Robert C. Weller, eds. *Sea Fiction Guide*. Metuchen: Scarecrow Press, 1976.

Smith, Philip Chadwick Foster. *The Empress of China*. Philadelphia: Philadelphia Maritime Museum, 1984.

Spear, John R. *Nathaniel Brown Palmer*. New York: MacMillan and Company, 1922.

Spikes, Judith Doolin. *Larchmont, NY: People and Places*. Larchmont: Fountain Square Books, 1991.

———. *Larchmont (Images of America)*. Charleston: Arcadia, 2003.

Stauffer, John, ed. *The Works of James McCune Smith*. New York: Oxford University Press, 2006.

Starkey, David. *British Privateering Enterprise in the Eighteenth Century*. Exeter: University of Exeter, 1990.

Steel, Edward M. *T. Butler King of Georgia*. Athens: University of Georgia Press, 1964.

Stein, Douglas. *American Maritime Documents, 1776–1860*. Mystic, CT: Mystic Seaport Museum, 1992.

Stiles, T. J. *The First Tycoon: The Epic Life of Cornelius Vanderbilt*. New York: Alfred A. Knopf, 2009.

Stilgoe, John. *Lifeboat*. Charlottesville: University of Virginia Press, 2003.

Still, William and Gordon Watts. "Steam Navigation and the United States." In *The Advent of Steam*, edited by Robert Gardner and Basil Greenhill, 44–82. London: Conway Maritime Press, 1993.

Stuart, Charles B. *The Naval and Mail Steamers of the United States*. New York: Charles B. Norton, Irving House, 1853.

Summers, Mark W. *The Plundering Generation: Corruption and the Crisis of the Union, 1849–1851*. New York: Oxford University Press, 1987.

Sumner, William H. *History of East Boston with Biographical Sketches of the Early Proprietors and an Appendix*. Boston: J.E.T. Horn, 1858.

Sutherland, D. A. "1810–1820: War and Peace." In *The Atlantic Region to Confederation: A History*, edited by Phillip Buckner and John Reid , 234–60. Toronto: University of Toronto Press, 1995.

Tann, Jennifer, ed., *The Selected Papers of Boulton and Watt, Vol. 2: The Engine Partnership, 1775–1825*. Boston: MIT Press, 1981.

Thoreau, Henry David. *Cape Cod*. New York: Penguin Books, 1987.

Trollope, Francis. *Domestic Manners of the Americans*. London: Whittaker Treacher, 1832.

Troxler, Carole. "A Loyalist Life: John Bond of South Carolina and Nova Scotia." *Acadiensis* 19, no. 2 (Spring 1990): 72–91.

Tucker, Spencer and Frank T. Reuter. *Injured Honor: The Chesapeake-Leopard Affair*. Annapolis: Naval Institute Press, 1996.

Tuckerman, Bayard, ed. *Diary of Philip Hone, 1828–1851*. 2 vols. New York: Dodd, Mead and Co., 1889.

Tunzelman, G. N. *Steam Power and British Industrialization to 1860*. Oxford: Clarendon Press, 1978.

Tyler, David Budlong. *Steam Conquers the Atlantic*. New York: D. Appleton Century Company, 1939.

United Nations Conference on Trade and Development. *Review of Marine Transport 2015*. New York: United Nations, 2016.

United States Patent Office. *Inventions and Designs Issued by the United States from 1790 to 1847*. Washington: J. and G. S. Gideon, 1847.

Van Rensselaer, Cortlandt. *God's Way in the Deep*. Philadelphia: C. Sherman, 1854.

Voorsanger, Catherine Hooper and John K. Howett. *Art and the Empire City, 1825–1861*. New York: Metropolitan Museum of Art, 2000.

Ward and Locke's Guide to Liverpool. London: Warwick House, 1881.

Warwick, Sam and Mike Roussel. *Shipwrecks of the Cunard Line*. The Mill: History Press, 2012.

Watson, P. H. "The Two Hundredth Anniversary of the Halifax Dockyard." Halifax: Occasional Papers No. 5, Maritime Museum of Canada.

Webber, Mabel Louise, ed. "Register of the Independent Congregational Church of Charleston, S.C., 1784–1815." *The South Carolina Historical and Genealogical Magazine* 33, no. 1 (January 1934): 29–54.

Webster, Daniel. *The Papers of Daniel Webster.* 14 vols. Edited by Charles Wiltse and Michael T. Birker. Dartmouth: Dartmouth University Press, 1974–1989.

Weigold, Marilyn. *Long Island Sound: A History of Its People, Places and Environment.* New York: New York University Press, 2004.

Weld, Isaac. "Passage from Dublin to London." In *An Historical and Explanatory Dissertation on Steam Engines and Steam Packets,* edited by George Dodd. London: Printed for the author, 1818.

Wellsville [Ohio] Historical Society. *Before the Memory Fades.* Wellsville: Wellsville Historical Society, 1950.

Wertkin, Gerard C. *Encyclopedia of American Folk Art.* New York: Routledge, 2004.

Wetmore, James C. *The Wetmore Family of America.* Albany: Munsell and Rowland, 1861.

Williams, David M. "Abolition and the Redeployment of the Slave Fleet, 1807–1811." *Journal of Transport History,* 11/2 (1973): 103–15.

Williams, Frances. "The Heritage and Preparation of a Statesman, John Y. Mason." *Virginia Magazine of History and Biography* 75, no. 3 (July 1967): 305–30.

Williams, Gomer. *History of the Liverpool Privateers and Letters of Marque with an Account of the Liverpool Slave Trade.* Liverpool: Edward Howell, 1897.

Williamson, James. *The Clyde Passenger Steamer.* Glasgow: James Maclehose and Sons, 1904.

Woodruff, Ceylon Newton, and Maurice R. Herod, comps. *Woodruff Chronicles.* 2 vols. Glendale: Arthur H. Clark Company, 1971.

Works of the Writers Program of the Works Projects Administration for the City of New York. *A Maritime History of New York.* Brooklyn: Going Coastal, 2004.

Wyld, Henry C. K. *The Place Names of Lancashire.* London: Constable, 1911.

Year Book City of Charleston, 1883, The Centennial Year of Incorporation. Charleston: The News and Courier Book Press, 1883.

Young, Henry. "Treason and Its Punishments in Revolutionary Pennsylvania." *Pennsylvania Magazine of History and Biography* 90 (1966): 287–313.

Zahe, Nuala. "Economy." In *The British Atlantic World 1500–1800,* edited by David Armitage and Michael Braddick, 51–68. Houndmills, Basingstoke, Hampshire and London: Palgrave Macmillan, 2002.

Online Sources

Government
Great Britain

Colonial Land and Emigration Commissioners July 1849 Colonization Circular Number 9, "Abstract of Orders in Council for Promoting Order and Health in British Passenger

Ships in North America," p. 23. https://www.nla.gov.au/ferguson/14614278/1849
    0731/00000009/17-24.pdf
Parliament, *The Budget* (Hansard, May 18, 1838), http://hansard.millbanksystems.com
    /commons/1838/may/18/the-budget

United States

Biographical Directory of the United States Congress, 1774–Present, http://bioguide
    .congress.gov/biosearch/biosearch.asp
Library of Congress, A Century of Lawmaking for a New Nation, https://memory.loc.gov
    /ammem/amlaw/lawhome.html
  House Journal
  Senate Journal
  Senate Executive Journal
  Journals of the Continental Congress
  Annals of Congress
  Congressional Globe
  United States Statutes at Large
  U.S. Serial Set
United States Geological Survey, Geographical Names Information Systems, Pamet
    River, https://geonames.usgs.gov/apex/f?p=gnispq:3:0::NO::P3_FID:616807
United States National Park Service, Pamet Area Trail System, https://www.nps.gov
    /caco/planyourvisit/pamet-area-trails.htm
United States Senate, "Bitter Feelings in the Senate Chamber," http://www.senate.gov
    /artandhistory/history/minute/Bitter_Feelings_in_the_Senate_Chamber.htm

Massachusetts

Massachusetts General Laws 1833 Chap. 0186. An Act to Incorporate the East Boston
    Wharf Company. http://www.archives.lib.state.ma.us/handle/2452/112186

Libraries/Museums

New York Public Library, "Maury and the Menu: A Brief History of the Cunard Steamship
    Company," http://www.nypl.org/blog/2011/06/30/maury-menu-brief-history
    -cunard-steamship-company
International Slavery Museum, "Liverpool and the Transatlantic Slave Trade," http://
    www.liverpoolmuseums.org.uk/ism/srd/liverpool.aspx
Victoria and Albert Museum, "Trade Beads," http://www.vam.ac.uk/content/articles/t
    /trade-beads/
The Preservation Society of Newport County, http://www.newportmansions.org/explore
    /chateau-sur-mer
Guide to Allen Family Papers, Hagley Museum and Library, http://findingaids.hagley
    .org/xtf/view?docId=ead/1978.xml

American Presidency Project

Van Buren, Proclamation January 5, 1838, American Presidency Project, http://www
.presidency.ucsb.edu/ws/?pid=67317

Avalon Project

The Federalist Papers, http://avalon.law.yale.edu/subject_menus/fed.asp

Proceedings of Commissioners to Remedy Defects of the Federal Constitution, Annapolis in the State of Maryland September 11, 1786, http://avalon.law.yale.edu/18th
_century/annapoli.asp

Constitution of the United States, http://avalon.law.yale.edu/18th_century/usconst.asp

Frame of Government of Pennsylvania, May 5, 1682, http://avalon.law.yale.edu/17th
_century/pa04.asp

Treaty of Amity and Commerce between the United States and France 1778, http://
avalon.law.yale.edu/18th_century/fr1788-1.asp

Treaty of Peace and Amity signed at Tripoli June 4, 1805, http://avalon.law.yale.edu
/19th_century/bar1805t.asp

Treaty of Ghent, 1814, http://avalon.law.yale.edu/19th_century/ghent.asp

"Annual Messages of the Presidents," http://avalon.law.yale.edu/subject_menus/sou.asp

Treaty of Paris, 1783, http://avalon.law.yale.edu/18th_century/paris.asp

Miller Center

James Madison War Message, June 1, 1812, http://millercenter.org/president/madison
/speeches/speech-3614

Madison, James Proclamation of State of War with Great Britain June 19, 1812, http://
millercenter.org/president/madison/speeches/speech-3615

Other

Catskill Archives, "Progress of Steamboat Movements," http://www.catskillarchive
.com/rrextra/abrw05.html

Cunard, High Speed Coach Line, https://ns1758.ca/cunard/cunard01.html

Cunard Steamship Society, Cunard Heritage, http://cunardsteamshipsociety.com/2010
/01/08/cunard-heritage/

Hamilton, Alexander, *The Papers of Alexander Hamilton*, Digital Edition, ed. Harold C.
Syrett, http://rotunda.upress.virginia.edu/founders/ARHN.html

"Histoire des Iles St. Pierre et Miquelon," http://grandcolombier.com/category/english/

Institute for Ocean Technology, Ice Database, https://web.archive.org/web/20110827
064151/http://www.icedata.ca/index.php

Lambton, John, Lord Durham's Report on the Affairs of British North America. Edited with
an introduction by Sir C. P. Lucas et al. 3 vols. (Oxford: Clarendon Press, 1912).
http://www.archive.org/stream/lorddurhamsrepor01durhiala/lorddurhamsrepor0
1durhiala_djvu.txt

"Loss of the Steamer Arctic," http://steamerarctic.blogspot.com/

"Measuring Worth," https://www.measuringworth.com/datasets/exchangepound/result
.php

Population History of Boston, http://www.iboston.org/mcp.php?pid=popFig

Population History of Philadelphia, http://physics.bu.edu/~redner/projects/population
/cities/philadelphia.html

Population History of New York City, http://physics.bu.edu/~redner/projects/popu
lation/cities/newyork.html

Population History of Baltimore, http://physics.bu.edu/~redner/projects/population
/cities/baltimore.html

"Shipwrecks of the Cunard Line," http://www.cunardshipwrecks.com/fleet.html

Great Circle Route, http://mathworld.wolfram.com/GreatCircle.html

"Liverpool Pilotage Services, Our History," http://www.liverpoolpilots.com/ABOUT-US

Lu, Alicia, "Are Trains Safer than Planes," http://www.bustle.com/articles/83287-are
-trains-safer-than-planes-statistics-are-clear-about-which-mode-of-transporta
tion-is-safest

"Ship's Husband," *Free Dictionary*, http://legal-dictionary.thefreedictionary.com/Ship's
+husband

"The Geography of Transport Systems," https://people.hofstra.edu/geotrans/eng/ch8en
/conc8en/fuel_consumption_containerships.html

"4 Phases of Cold Water Immersion," http://beyondcoldwaterbootcamp.com/4-phases
-of-cold-water-immersion

"Hypothermia," http://www.seagrant.umn.edu/coastal_communities/hypothermia#time

Shipbuilding History, "Jeremiah Simonson," http://www.shipbuildinghistory.com/ship
yards/19thcentury/simonson.htm

Find A Grave, http://findagrave.com/

"Mark Twain on the Cunard Line," *Mount Ida Chronicle* 4, issue 219, May 9, 1873, http://
paperspast.natlib.govt.nz/newspapers/mount.-ida-chronicle/1873/5/9/6

"Go West, Young Man, Go West," *Dictionary of American History* (Farmington: Gale
Group, 2003), http://www.encyclopedia.com/doc/1G2-3401801733.html

Maury Klein, "Financing the Transcontinental Railroad," *History Now Journal of the
Gilder Lehrman Institute*, https://www.gilderlehrman.org/history-by-era/develop
ment-3west/essays/financing-transcontinental-railroad

Lipsey, Robert, "U.S. Foreign Trade and the Balance of Payments, 1800–1913," NBER
Working Paper No. 4710, April 1994, http://www.nber.org/papers/w4710

Philosophical Transactions, "Extracts of Two Letters Written by the Mr. Adam Martindale," Philosophical Transactions, vol. 5, January 1, 1670 http://rstl.royalsociety
publishing.org/content/5/57-68/2015.full.pdf+html

"Memoirs and Portraits of One Hundred Glasgow Men," http://gdl.cdlr.strath.ac.uk
/mlemen/index.html

Introduction

1 Rear Admiral Joseph A. Smith quoted in Edward W. Sloan, "'Vulcan Now Rides in Neptune's Barge': Steam Propulsion and Seafaring Enterprise in Post-Civil War America," paper delivered at the Third Conference on American Economic Enterprise, Tarrytown, New York, October 10–11, 1980. (np)

Chapter One: The New Nation

1 Benjamin Franklin, "The Internal State of America: Being a True Description of the Interest and Policy of that Vast Continent" in *The Works of Benjamin Franklin*, edited by John Bigelow (New York: G.P. Putnam's Sons, 1904) 10:395.

2 Kate Rowland, "The Mount Vernon Convention," *Pennsylvania Magazine of History and Biography* 11, No. 4 (Jan. 1888): 424.

3 *Proceedings of Commissioners to Remedy Defects of the Federal Constitution, Annapolis in the State of Maryland September 11, 1786*, Avalon Project at Yale Law School, http://avalon.law.yale.edu/18th_century/annapoli.asp.

4 *JCC* 31: 677–80; 32:74.

5 Ron Chernow, *Alexander Hamilton* (New York: Penguin Books, 2004), 241.

6 Constitution of the United States, Avalon Project at Yale Law School, http://avalon.law.yale.edu/18th_century/usconst.asp.

7 Avalon Project at Yale Law School, Federalist Eleven, The Utility of the Union in Respect top Commercial Relations and a Navy, http://avalon.law.yale.edu/18th_century/fed11.asp; Federalist Twelve, The Utility of then Union in Respect to Revenue, http://avalon.law.yale.edu/18th_century/fed12.asp; Federalist Thirteen, Advantage of the Union in Respect to Economy in the Union, http://avalon.law.yale.edu/18th_century/fed13.asp.

8 Federalist Eleven, Avalon Project.

9 For a complete analysis of ratification see Pauline Maier, *Ratification: The People Debate the Constitution, 1787–1788* (New York: Simon and Schuster, 2010).

10 U.S. *Senate Journal* 1st Cong., 1st Sess., 8 (April 6, 1789).

11 Avalon Project at Yale Law School, Frame of Government of Pennsylvania, May 5, 1682. http://avalon.law.yale.edu/17th_century/pa04.asp.

12 Vessels engaged in coastwise or fishing were "enrolled" while vessels operating in foreign commerce were "registered." *Black's Law Dictionary* (St. Paul, MN: West Publishing Co., 1968); Douglas Stein, *American Maritime Documents, 1776–1860* (Mystic, CT: Mystic Seaport Museum, 1992), 74, 135.

13 *United States Statutes at Large: Duties on Merchandise imported into the United States.* Act of July 4, 1789, ch. 2, *Stat.* 1, 24–27.

    Duties on Tonnage. Act of July 20, 1789, ch. 3, *Stat.* 1, 27–28.

    Regulation of the Collection of Duties on Tonnage and on Merchandise. Act of July 31, 1789, ch. 5, *Stat.* 1, 29–49.

    Light-houses, Beacons, Buoys, etc. Act of August 1, 1789 ch. 9, *Stat.* 1, 53–54.

    Registering and clearing of Vessels in the Coasting Trade, and regulating the Coasting Trade, etc. Act of September 1, 1789 ch. 11, *Stat.* 1 55–64.

    Establishment of the Treasury Department. Act of September 2, 1789, ch. 12, *Stat.* 1, pp. 65–67.

    Act for the Collection of Duties on Tonnage suspended in part, etc. Act of September 16, 1789, ch. 15, *Stat.* 1, 69–70.

    Act for the Registering and Clearing Vessels, and Regulating the Coastal Trade, explained and amended. Act of September 29, 1789, ch. 22. *Stat.* 1, 94–95.

14 Approved unanimously same day. *Annals of Congress*, 1st Cong. 1st Sess., 8 (April 8, 1789).

15 Robert Lipsey, "U.S. Foreign Trade and the Balance of Payments, 1800–1913," 686; Gordon C. Bjork, "The Weaning of the American Economy: Independence, Market Changes, and Economic Development," *The Journal of Economic History* 24, issue 4 (December 1964): 557.

16 Conversation with George Beckwith, October 1789, *The Papers of Alexander Hamilton* Digital Edition, ed. Harold C. Syrett (Charlottesville: University of Virginia Press, Rotunda, 2011).

17 Labaree et al., *America and Sea A Maritime History* (Mystic, CT.: Mystic Seaport, 1998), 169, 171.

18 Philip Chadwick Foster Smith, *The Empress of China* (Philadelphia: Philadelphia Maritime Museum, 1984), 23–24; Paul E. Fontenoy, "Ginseng, Otter Skins, and Sandalwood: The Conundrum of the China Trade." *The Northern Mariner/Le Marin du Nord* VII, no. 1 (January 1997): 5.

19 Fortenoy, p. 4; *Historical Statistics of the United States.* (Washington: U.S. Department of Commerce, 1975), 2: 905.

20 K. Jack Bauer, *A Maritime History of the United States: The Role of America's Seas and Waterways* (Columbia: University of South Carolina Press, 1988), 53.

21 Table from Robert E. Lipsey, "U.S. Foreign Trade and the Balance of payments, 1800–1913," NBER Working Paper No. 4710 Issued in April 1994 NBER Program(s): DAE ITI, p. 10. http://www.nber.org/papers/w4710.pdf.

22 Population History of Boston, http://www.iboston.org/mcp.php?pid=popFig; Population History of Philadelphia, http://physics.bu.edu/~redner/projects/population /cities/philadelphia.html; Population History of New York City, http://physics.bu.edu /~redner/projects/population/cities/newyork.html; Population History of Baltimore, http://physics.bu.edu/~redner/projects/population/cities/baltimore.html

23 *Historical Statistics* 2: 886; Workers of the Writers Program of the Work Projects Administration for the City of New York, *A Maritime History of New York* (Brooklyn: Going Coastal Inc., 2004), 82.

24 Jefferson opposed a proclamation of neutrality, while Hamilton argued in favor. Washington sailed between the two and issued his proclamation never using the word "neutrality."

25 Aside from the usual provisions of peace, friendship, and commercial relations, the treaty provided special rights for both parties, including the obligation to provide a "safe harbor" in time of crisis while denying such privilege to the nation with which either country was in conflict. Avalon Project, *Treaty of Amity and Commerce between the United States and France 1778*, http://avalon.law.yale.edu/18th_century /fr1788-1.asp.

26 Quoted in Alexander DeConde, *The Quasi-War: The Politics and Diplomacy of the Undeclared War with France, 1797–1801* (New York: Charles Scribner's Sons 1966), 381n.

27 William M. Fowler, Jr., *Jack Tars and Commodores: The American Navy 1783–1815* (Boston: Houghton Mifflin, 1984), 34–59.

28 Early in 1793 Great Britain and France went to war. Aside from a short interval (1802–1803, Peace of Amiens), and a brief respite following Napoleon's abdication (1814), the struggle continued until Napoleon's final defeat at Waterloo (1815) and exile to St. Helena.

29 "Blockade. A marine investment or beleaguering of a town or harbor. A sort of circumvallation round a place by which all foreign connection and correspondence is, as far as human power can effect it, to be cut off." Black, *Black's Law Dictionary*. The United Sates recognized Britain's right of blockade; controversy, however, existed over the definition of contraband.

30 President Jefferson to the Appointed Minister to France (R. Livingston), September 9, 1801, in Carleton Savage, ed., *Policy of the United States Toward Maritime Commerce in War* (Washington: Government Printing Office, 1934), 1:234.

31 Savage, 27.

32 Labaree, *America and the Sea*, 194.

33 *Historical Statistics*, 2: 886.

34 Douglass C. North, "Early National Income Estimates of the U.S.," *Economic Development and Cultural Change* IX, 3 (April 1961), 390.

35 Lipsey, "U.S. Foreign Trade," 1.

36 The Tripolitans announced their declaration of war by chopping down the American Consul's flagstaff. Circular issued by James Cathcart, U.S. Consul, Tripoli, 15 May, 1801, in *Naval Documents Related to the United States Wars with the Barbary Powers*, (Washington: Government Printing Office, 1939), 1:454.

37 *Treaty of Peace and Amity*, Signed at Tripoli June 4, 1805. http://avalon.law.yale .edu/19th_century/bar1805t.asp

38 Lord Sheffield (John Barker Holroyd), *Strictures on the Necessity of Inviolably Maintaining the Navigation and Colonial System of Great Britain* (London, 1806) in *The Naval War of 1812: A Documentary History*, ed. William S. Dudley (Washington: Department of the Navy, 1985), 1:21.

39 Sentence of the Vice-Admiralty Court of Nassau, New Providence in the Case of the Brig *Essex*, Joseph Orne Master in *Naval War of 1812*, 1:20.

40 Thomas Jefferson, *Fifth Annual Message*, December 3, 1805, http://www.presidency .ucsb.edu/ws/?pid=29447.

41 *The Naval War of 1812*, 1:62.

42 Act of April 18, 1806, ch. 29, *Stat.* 1, 379; Act of December 19, 1806, ch.1, *Stat.* 2, 410.

43 *The Naval War of 1812*, 1:26–27. For a view of the consequences of the engagement, see Spencer C. Tucker and Frank T. Reuter, *Injured Honor: The Chesapeake-Leopard Affair* (Annapolis: Naval Institute Press, 1996).

44 Act of December 22, 1807, ch. 5, *Stat.* 1, 451.

45 Labaree, *America and Sea*, 199; George Cabot to Timothy Pickering, November 11, 1808, Henry Cabot Lodge, ed., *Life and Letters of George Cabot* (Boston: Little, Brown, 1878), 398.

46 Bauer, *A Maritime History*, 65.

47 *The Naval War of 1812*, 1:69.

48 *Historical Statistics*, 2:761.

49 *Historical Statistics*, 2:1106.

50 Act of March 1, 1809, ch. 24, *Stat.* 2, 528–33.

51 Act of June 28, 1809, ch. 9, *Stat.* 2, 550–51.

52 Act of April 4, 1812, ch. 49, *Stat.*1, 700.

53 Quoted in Robert Greenhalgh Albion and Jennie Barnes Pope, *Sea Lanes in Wartime* (New York: Archon Books, 1968), 111.

54 James Madison War Message, June 1, 1812, http://millercenter.org/president/madi son/speeches/speech-3614

55 Proclamation of a State of War With Great Britain, June 19, 1812, http://millercenter .org/president/madison/speeches/speech-3615.

56 For a description of the early naval battles see Fowler, *Jack Tars and Commodores*, 162–84.

57 Donald R. Hickey, "American Trade Restrictions during the War of 1812," *Journal of American History* 68, no. 3 (December 1981), 517–538.

58 *A Proclamation*, November 13, 1813; *Naval War of 1812*, 2:328.

59 Amanda Foreman, "The British View the War of 1812 Quite Differently than Americans Do," *Smithsonian Magazine*, July 2014, http://www.smithsonianmag.com/history/british-view-war-1812-quite-differently-americans-do-180951852/?page=2.

60 Treaty of Ghent, 1814, http://avalon.law.yale.edu/19th_century/ghent.asp.

61 *Times*, December 27, 1814.

Chapter Two: From Cape Cod to New York City

1 Edwin G. Burrows and Mike Wallace, *Gotham: A History of New York* (New York: Oxford University Press, 1999), 428.

2 This part of Cape Cod may also be referred to as the "Outer Cape."

3 Thoreau made two trips to the Cape. Henry David Thoreau, *Cape Cod* (New York: Penguin Books, 1987).

4 Thoreau, *Cape Cod*, 189.

5 In its western portion the Pamet is an estuary. On the eastern side it is a freshwater habitat. United States Geological Survey, http://geonames.usgs.gov/apex/f?p=gnis pq:3:0::NO::P3_FID:616807; Pamet Area Trail System, https://www.nps.gov/caco/planyourvisit/upload/FinalPametrackcards.pdf.

6 Sheenah Rich, *Truro Cape Cod or Land Marks and Sea Marks* (Boston: D. Lothrop and Company), 85.

7 John T. Cumbler, *Cape Cod: An Environmental History of a Fragile Ecosystem* (Amherst: University of Massachusetts Press, 2014), 39–79.

8 Thoreau, *Cape Cod*, 158.

9 Rich, *Truro Cape Cod*, 275–86.

10 Richard B. Morris, *The Peacemakers* (New York: Harper and Row, 1965) is the best source for negotiations leading to peace and independence. Definitive Treaty of Paris 1783, http://avalon.law.yale.edu/18th_century/paris.asp.

11 Raymond McFarland, *A History of New England Fisheries* (Philadelphia: University of Pennsylvania, 1911), 134.

12 Henry C. Kittredge, *Shipmasters of Cape Cod* (Boston: Houghton Mifflin, 1935), 14–15.

13 Marriage notice of Captain Israel G. Collins and Mary Ann Allan, *Marriage Notices in the South Carolina Gazette and Its Successors, 1732–1801* (Albany: Joel Mansell's Sons, 1902), 124. This information is in direct contradiction to Rich, *History of Truro Cape Cod*, 391, and other secondary sources claiming the marriage was either in Liverpool or New York. The naming of her son "Knight" does suggest that there may have been a family connection with Admiral Sir Edward Knight, but no proof has been discovered. Another author asserts that she was the daughter of a Mersey River pilot, William Knight. Thomas R. Bullard, *Sails, Steam and Subsidies: The Career of Edward K. Collins* (Oak Park, Illinois: Privately Printed, 1990), 9.

14 Rich, *Truro Cape Cod*, 391.

15 *New York Gazette*, October 24, 1801; George W. Sheldon, "Merchants of Old New York," *Harper's Magazine* (Dec. 1891–May 1892): 468; Extensive genealogical information is contained in Case No. M103013A and M103013A-2 at the New England

Historic Genealogical Society, Boston. Israel's movements can be followed in contemporary newspapers, e.g., *Charleston City Gazette*, April 9, 1801, and March 15, 1805.

16 Mabel Louise Webber, ed., *The South Carolina Historical and Genealogical Magazine, Published Quarterly by the South Carolina Historical Society* 33, No. 1 (January 1834). "Register of the Independent Congregational Church of Charleston, SC, 1784–1815," 53.

17 The shortest distance between two points on a sphere is a segment of a great circle. Wolfram Mapworld, http://mathworld.wolfram.com/GreatCircle.html.

18 Edmund March Blunt, *The American Coast Pilot* (New York: Blunt, 1815), 162.

19 *Liverpool Mercury*, March 31, 1815; *Otsego Herald* [New York], June 1, 1815.

20 Boston *Columbian Sentinel*, August 10, 1815; *New York Courier*, June 29, 1815.

21 "Auction," *Cyclopedia of Commerce and Commercial Navigation*, edited by J. Smith Humans and J. Smith Humans Jr. (New York: Harper and Brothers, 1858).

22 Abraham G. Thompson, "Auction System in New York," *The Merchant's Magazine and Commercial Review* 10 (Jan–June 1844): 154–57; Ira Cohen, "The Auction System in the Port New York, 1817–1837," *Business History Review* 45, no. 4 (Winter 1971): 494.

23 Thompson, "Auction System," 157.

24 Charles Sellers, *The Market Revolution: Jacksonian America, 1815–1846* (New York: Oxford University Press, 1991), 41.

25 Thompson, "Auction System," 156.

26 Robert A. Davison, *Isaac Hicks: New York Merchant and Quaker, 1767–1820* (Cambridge: Harvard University Press, 1964), 91. Emily Buchnea, "Transatlantic Transformations: Visualizing Changes Over Time in the Liverpool-New York Trade Network, 1763–1833," *Enterprise and Society* 15, no. 4 (December 2014): 64.

27 Robert G. Albion, *Rise of New York Port* (New York: Charles Scribner's Sons, 1939), 95–121; Constance McL. Green, *Eli Whitney and the Birth of American Technology* (Boston: Little Brown, 1956), 40–96. Before 1794 cotton exports were too small to bother to calculate. In 1794 2 million pounds were sent out. In 1815 the number jumped to 83 million pounds, and by 1820 it had reached 128 million pounds. *Historical Statistics of the United States Colonial Times to 1970* (Washington: Department of Commerce, 1975) 2:899. See also Sven Beckert, *Empire of Cotton: A Global History* (New York: Vintage Books, 2014).

28 Francis Trollope, *Domestic Manners of the Americans* (London: Whittaker Treacher, 1832), 28.

29 Trollope, *Domestic Manners*, 28.

30 "New Orleans," in Jedediah Morse, *The American Gazetteer* (Boston: Thomas and Andrews, 1804), n.p.

31 Trollope, *Domestic Manners*, 28.

32 Albion, *Rise of New York Port*, 95–121.

33 Albion, *Rise of New York Port*, 96.

34 Timothy Pitkin, *A Statistical View of the Commerce of the United States of America* (New Haven: Durrie and Peck, 1835), 58.

35 John Harvey Treat, *Deaths in Truro, Cape Cod* (Salem: Salem Press, 1891), 21; Charles Burr Todd, *A General History of the Burr Family* (New York: The Knickerbocker Press, 1891), 470.

36 *New York Gazette*, March 20, 1820, and various other issues.

37 Sheldon, "Merchants of Old New York," 468.

38 A. T. Goodrich, *The Picture of New York and the Stranger's Guide* (New York: A. T. Goodrich, 1828), 460–461; Burrows and Wallace, *A History of New York City*, 251.

39 [New York] *Commercial Advertiser*, October 17, 1817; *Liverpool Mercury*, December 1, 1817.

40 Robert G. Albion, *Square-Riggers on Schedule* (Princeton: Princeton University Press, 1938) remains the standard work on the history of the New York packets.

41 For declining freight rates see Douglass North, "Ocean Freight Rates and Economic Development 1750–1913," *Journal of Economic History* 18, no. 4 (Dec. 1958): 537–555; Edward Chase Kirkland, *Men, Cities and Transportation: A Study in New England History, 1820–1900* (Cambridge: Harvard University Press, 1948) 1:82–86; Sellers, *The Market Revolution*, 43; Albion, *Rise of New York Port*, 390.

42 Judith Doolin Spikes, *Larchmont, New York; People and Places* (Larchmont: Fountain Square Books, 1991), 58.

43 *Rochester Telegraph*, January 31, 1825; Albion, *Rise of New York Port*, 114.

44 Rich, *History of Truro*, 270; Sheldon, "Merchants of New York," 469–70.

45 Rich, *History of Truro*, 391.

46 Spikes, *Larchmont*, 58; Portrait of Mary Ann Woodruff in family possession; Entry in Woodruff Family Bible; Ceylon Newton Woodruff and Maurine R. Herod, comps., *Woodruff Chronicles* (Glendale: Arthur H. Clark Co., 1971), 2:22; *Longworth's American Almanac New York Register* (New York: D. Longworth, 1801), 316; Edward K. Collins and Mary Ann Woodruff Matrimonial Notice *National Advocate*, January 6, 1826. A note: the family Bible gives the year as 1825.

47 *The Insurance Times* (1880) 13:776.

48 Oliver L. Barbour, "Frazer v. Western," in *Reports of Cases in Chancery Argued and Determined in the Court of Chancery of the State of New York* (New York: Banks, Gould and Co., 1847), 221–41.

49 *Historical Statistics of the United States* (Washington: Department of Commerce, 1975) part 2:886.

50 Ruth R. Olivera and Lilane Crete, *Life in Mexico under Santa Anna, 1822–1855* (Norman: University of Oklahoma Press, 1979), 91.

51 "Vera Cruz," *The American Gazetteer*, n.p.

52 Olivera, *Life in Mexico*, 17.

53 Guadalupe Jimenez Codinach, "An Atlantic Silver Entrepot: Vera Cruz and the House of Gordon and Murphy," in *Atlantic Port Cities: Economy, Culture and Society in the Atlantic World*, ed. Franklin W. Knight and Peggy K. Liss (Knoxville: University of Tennessee Press, 1991), 150.

54 *New Bedford Mercury*, January 5, 1826.

55 Edward K. Collins Household, 1840 U.S. Federal Census, New York City Ward 15, New York County, New York; 73. The census lists several people in the home. Other than family members these are most likely servants and perhaps employees of the firm. Thomas does not appear in the Federal censuses for 1840, 1850, or 1860 but he does appear in 1870; *The New York City Business Directory for 1840 and 1841* (New York Publication Office, 1840), 181; Joyce Gold, "SoHo" in *The Encyclopedia of New York City*, ed. Kenneth Jackson (New Haven: Yale University Press, 1995), 1088.

56 Thomas R. Bullard, *Sails, Steam and Subsidies*, 10.

Chapter Three: Liverpool

1 *New York Mercury*, October 5, 1831.

2 *Shakespeare* Certificate of Registry, January 27, 1835, RG 41 Bureau of Marine Inspection and Navigation, United States National Archives.

3 Myron J. Smith and Robert C. Weller, *Sea Fiction Guide* (Metuchen, NJ: Scarecrow Press, 1976), ix–xxix.

4 Robert G. Albion, *Square-Riggers on Schedule* (Princeton: Princeton University Press, 1938), 153; Herman Melville, *White Jacket* (New York: Viking Press Library of America, 1982), 743.

5 Albion, *Square-Riggers*, 153.

6 John R. Spear, *Nathaniel Brown Palmer* (New York: Macmillan Co., 1922), 43.

7 Spear, *Nathaniel Brown Palmer*, 73–75.

8 *New London Gazette*, April 24, 1822. While Palmer was among the first to sight Antarctica, it would be some time before its identity as a continent would be established.

9 Carl C. Cutler, *Greyhounds of the Sea* (New York: G.P. Putnam's Sons, 1930), 96.

10 Cutler, *Greyhounds*, 95–96.

11 The advantages of the flat-floor design were described by Captain Charles H. Marshall of the Black Ball Line:

> During my being in the line from 1823 to 1832, I do not think the models of the ships were much changed; but they were increased in size. The general impression then among merchants, and even among nautical men, was that to produce fast sailing it was necessary to build the ships with sharp bottoms, by giving them much dead rise and consequently abridging their carrying qualities. It has been found, however, that our predecessors were altogether mistaken in their notion of gaining speed by *dead rise*; it has such a tendency to increase the draft of water, as to produce no speed! The effect of [flat floor] is to give buoyancy, and with fine ends so as to secure good steering, the ship will evidently go faster through the water. Quoted in Albion, *Square-Riggers*, 90–91.

12 Henry C. Kittredge, *Shipmasters of Cape Cod* (Boston: Houghton Mifflin, 1935), 128. Spear, *Captain Nathaniel Brown Palmer*, 154.

13 Richard McKay, *South Street* (Riverside, CT: 7 C's Press, 1969 rev. ed.), 199.

14 *Shakespeare*, Certificate of Registry.

15 Albion, *Square-Riggers*, 334; Kittredge, *Shipmasters*, 129; Bullard, *Sails, Steam and Subsidies*, 54.

16 *Connecticut Current*, July 18, 1836.

17 *Historical Statistics of the United States* (Washington: Dept. of Commerce, 1975) 2:898.

18 Bayard Tuckerman, ed., *Diary of Philip Hone, 1828–1851* (New York: Dodd, Mead and Co., 1889), 1:90.

19 Quoted in Albion, *Square-Riggers on Schedule*, 96–97.

20 *New York Journal of Commerce*, July 15, 1836.

21 Calculation taken from Robert G. Albion, *The Rise of New York Port* (New York: Charles Scribner's Sons, 1939), 394.

22 Benjamin Blower, *The Mersey, Ancient and Modern* (Liverpool: Edward Howell, 1878), 26; *Ward and Locke's Illustrated Guide to Liverpool* (London: Warwick House, 1881), 3. Over the years the topography of Liverpool has changed dramatically. I am grateful to Lucy Kilfoyle, who has pointed out to me that today the "waterfront vista suggests a decidedly flat hinterland."

23 Thomas Baines, *History of the Commerce and Town of Liverpool* (London: Longman, Brown, Green and Longmans, 1852), 425.

24 J. A. Picton, *Memorials of Liverpool* (London: Longmans, Green, 1875) 1:6.

25 Baines, *History and Commerce*, 61.

26 City of Liverpool, *Selections from the Municipal Archives and Records*, Extracted and Annotated by Sir James A. Picton (Liverpool: G. Walmsley, 1883), 1–3.

27 The source of the name "Liverpool" is a matter of some conjecture. See for example Henry C. K. Wyld, *The Place Names of Lancashire* (London: Constable, 1911); Henry Harrison, *Lancashire Place Names* (London: Eaton Press, 1911), and Baines, *History and Commerce*, 52–74; "Liverpool Pilotages," http://www.liverpoolpilots.com/about-us.

28 Francis E. Hyde, *Liverpool and the Mersey: An Economic History of a Port* (Liverpool: Newton Abbott, David and Charles, 1971), 2, 27; L. Gittens, "Salt, Salt Making, and the Rise of Cheshire," in *Transactions of the Newcomen Society* (2005) 75:139–59.

29 T.C. Barker, in "Lancashire Coal, Cheshire Salt and the Rise of Liverpool," *Transactions*, vol. 103 (1951), 83.

30 Barker, "Lancashire Coal," 83.

31 "Extracts of Two Letters, written by the ingenious Mr. Adam Martindale to the Publisher from Rotherton in Cheshire, November 12 and November 26, 1670, concerning the Discovery of a Rock of Natural Salt in that Country," *Philosophical Transactions* (December 12, 1670): 5:2015.

32 Barker, "Lancashire Coal," 98.

33 Blower, *The Mersey*, 26.

34 For a detailed account of the Navigation Laws see Lawrence A. Harper, *The English Navigation Laws: A Seventeenth Century Experiment in Social Engineering* (New York: Columbia University Press, 1969); George L. Beer, *The Old Colonial System* (New York: Macmillan Company, 1912); a modern overview may be found in Nuala

Zahedieh, "Economy," *The British Atlantic World, 1500–1800*, ed. by David Armitage and Richard Braddick, (Houndmills: Palgrave Macmillan, 2002), 51–63.

35 Daniel Defoe, *A Tour Through the Whole Island of Great Britain*, ed. P. N. Furband, V. R. Owens, and A. J. Coulsen (New Haven: Yale University Press, 1991), 288.

36 Richard Brooke, *Liverpool as it was During the Last Quarter of the Eighteenth Century, 1775–1800* (Liverpool: J. Mawdsley and Sons, 1853), 233.

37 International Slavery Museum, "Liverpool and the Transatlantic Slave Trade," http://www.liverpoolmuseums.org.uk/ism/srd/liverpool.aspx.

38 Francis E. Hyde, Bradbury B. Parkinson and Sheila Marriner, "The Nature and Profitability of the Liverpool Slave Trade," *The Economic History Review*, New Series 5, no. 3 (1953): 374.

39 "Liverpool and the Transatlantic Slave Trade."

40 "Liverpool and the Transatlantic Slave Trade."

41 Quoted in Frank Howley, *Slavers, Traders and Privateers: Liverpool, the African Trade and Revolution 1773–1808* (Birkenhead: Countyvise, 2008), 1; on December 9, 1999, the Liverpool City Council passed a formal resolution apologizing for the city's part in the slave trade, "Liverpool and the Transatlantic Slave Trade."

42 "Trade Beads," Victoria and Albert Museum, http://www.vam.ac.uk/content/articles/t/trade-beads/.

43 Sven Beckert, *Empire of Cotton: A Global History* (New York: Vintage, 2004), xv–xvi.

44 Since Liverpool slave traders rarely brought their cargoes home, the *Somerset* decision had little direct impact upon their business.

45 Beckert, *Empire of Cotton*, 37. One of the chief threats to the Liverpool slave trade was when attacks by the French and Spanish navies, as well as privateers, interrupted the normal flow of slave traffic. Liverpool, however, was quick to answer, shifting from slaving to wartime privateering, an enterprise equally risky but employing the same derring-do characteristic of slaving. David J. Starkey, *British Privateering Enterprise in the Eighteenth Century* (Exeter: University of Exeter Press, 1990), 134–35; See also Gomer Williams, *History of the Liverpool Privateers and Letters of Marque with an Account of the Liverpool Slave Trade* (Liverpool: Edward Howell,1897).

46 Hyde, *Liverpool and the Mersey*, 35; David M. Williams, "Abolition and the Redeployment of the Slave Fleet, 1807–1811," *Journal of Transport History* 11, issue 2 (1973): 103–15.

47 Beckert, *Empire of Cotton*, 39.

48 Beckert, *Empire of Cotton*, 64.

49 Beckert, *Empire of Cotton*, 66.

50 Stephen Broadberry and Bishnupriya Gupta, "Cotton Textiles and the Great Divergence: Lancashire, India and the Shifting Competitive Advantage, 1600–1850," August 2005, CEPR Discussion Paper No. 5183. http://ssrn.com/abstract=790866.

51 *Ward and Locke Guide to Liverpool*, 1; Alexey Krichtal "Liverpool and Raw Cotton: A Study of the Port and its Merchant Community, 1770–1815" (MA Thesis, Victoria University of Wellington, 2013), 22–24. http://researcharchive.vuw.ac.nz/xmlui/bitstream/handle/10063/2952/thesis.pdf?sequence=1.

52 *Ward and Locke Guide to Liverpool*, 89.

53 Hyde, *Liverpool and the Mersey*, 9.

54 Adrian Jarvis, *Liverpool Central Docks, 1799–1905: An Illustrated History* (Liverpool: National Museums and Galleries on Merseyside, 1991), 8.

55 Quoted in *City of Liverpool Municipal Archives and Records from A.D. 1700 to the Passing of the Municipal Reform Act, 1835*, extracted and Annotated by Sir James A. Picton (Liverpool: Gilbert G. Wormsley, 1886) 2:47.

56 Baines, *History and Commerce*, 344–45.

57 Baines, *History and Commerce*, 344–45; Hyde, *Liverpool and the Mersey*, 13.

58 Baines, *History and Commerce*, 346.

59 Quoted in S. Austin, J. Howard, and G. and C. Pyne, *Lancashire Illustrated* (London: Fisher and Sons and Jackson, 1831), 32.

60 A. W. Skempton, *A Biographical Directory of Civil Engineers in Great Britain and Ireland* (London: Marshall, 1987), 652.

61 Hyde, *Liverpool and the Mersey*, 14.

62 Hyde, *Liverpool and the Mersey*, 247; Liverpool Old Dock: Down to Bedrock," https://gerryco23.wordpress.com/2010/09/14/liverpool-old-dock-down-to-the -bedrock/. For a description of the engineering challenges facing dock construction at Liverpool, see Adrian Jarvis, *The Liverpool Dock Engineers* (Stroud, Gloucester- shire: Alan Sutton Pub. Ltd, 1996).

63 Hyde, *Liverpool and the Mersey*, 14.

64 Quotes are taken from Melville, *Redburn: His First Voyage* (New York: Viking Press, Library of America, 1983), 176, 179.

65 Melville, *Redburn*, 180.

Chapter Four: Dramatic Line

1 Albion, *Square-Riggers*, 280–81.

2 *Newport Mercury*, September 24, 1836.

3 Cutler, *Greyhounds*, 95.

4 Albion, *Square-Riggers*, 44, notes that in 1823 a Boston packet line did adopt uniform names *Amethyst, Emerald, Sapphire,* and *Topaz*.

5 *Times-Picayune*, February 9, 1837.

6 For a detailed description of the vessels see *Certificates of Registry—Garrick* October 1836; *Sheridan* January 28, 1837; *Siddons* December 29, 1837; *Roscius* November 25, 1838, RG 41, National Archives; *Baltimore Sun*, August 16, 1838.

7 *Liverpool Mercury*, February 2, 1838.

8 Albion, *Square-Riggers*, 235–36. Not until the mid-1840s did packets begin to board a significant number of steerage passengers. Albion, *Square-Riggers*, 247–48.

9 Edwin Burrows and Mike Wallace, *Gotham: A History of New York City to 1898* (New York: Oxford University Press, 1999), 650.

10 United States Census 1850 Mamaroneck, Westchester County, New York. The fourth child, Henry, was born in 1839.

11 Burrows and Wallace, *Gotham*, 649–50.

12 Certificate of Registry, December 29, 1837.

13 *New York Spectator*, December 28, 1837.

14 *New York Spectator*, December 28, 1837; Gerard C. Wertkin, *Encyclopedia of American Folk Art* (New York: Routledge, 2004), 161.

15 *New York Spectator*, November 29, 1838.

16 Bullard, *Sails, Steam and Subsidies*, 13.

17 *Liverpool Mercury*, February 2, 1838.

18 *The Farmer's Cabinet*, October 26, 1838; *Waldo Patriot*, December 12, 1838; Albion, *Square Riggers*, 235.

19 *Newport Mercury*, November 30, 1839.

20 *New York Weekly Herald*, March 19, 1842. Collins sold *Shakespeare* in 1838, Albion, *Square-Riggers*, 292; actual safety records are difficult to assess. Albion, *Square-Riggers*, 202, estimates one death for every 500,000 miles. In 2015 the fatality rate for commercial air was 0.07 per billion miles. "Are Trains Safer than Planes," http://www.bustle.com/articles/83287-are-trains-safer-than-planes-statistics-are-clear-about-which-mode-of-transportation-is-safest.

21 Albion, *Square-Riggers*, 230–31.

22 Brandon DuPont, Drew Keeling, and Thomas Weiss, "Passenger Fares for Overseas Travel in the 19th and 20th Centuries." Paper presented for the Annual Meeting of the Economic History Association, August 15, 2012, p. 11n, http://eh.net/eha/wp-content/uploads/2013/11/Weissetal.pdf.

23 *Liverpool Mercury*, February 2, 1838.

24 *The Complete Works of Ralph Waldo Emerson, Centenary Edition*, http://www.rwe.org/chapter-ii-voyage-to-england/.

25 Emerson, http://www.rwe.org/chapter-ii-voyage-to-england/.

26 Harriet Martineau, *Retrospect of Western Travel* (New York: Haskell House, 1969) 1:21, 26.

27 DuPont, Keeling, and Weiss, "Passenger Fares," 3, http://eh.net/eha/wp-content/uploads/2013/11/Weissetal.pdf.

28 Albion, *Square-Riggers*, 240; DuPont, Keeling, and Weiss, "Passengers Fares," 12, 15.

29 Herman Melville, *Moby Dick* (New York: Viking Press Library of America), 795.

30 A form of "forced" recruitment. Peter Kemp, ed., *The Oxford Companion to Ships and the Sea* (Oxford: Oxford University Press, 1976); John G. Rogers, *Origins of Sea Terms* (Mystic, CT: Mystic Seaport Museum, 1985).

31 In 1840 American tonnage in foreign trade totaled 763,000 tons. Using as an average 500 tons, the number of registered ships is in excess of 1,400. Albion, *Square-Riggers*, 321–44, lists 345 men as packet captains in the forty-year period 1818 to 1858. See also p. 274 for number of packets; *Historical Statistics of the United States*, part 2 (Washington: Department of Commerce, 1975), 750.

32 A seaman's day (twenty-four hours) was divided into periods of duty of four hours. So that men would not be always serving the same watch, the evening watch (1600–2000) was divided into two two-hour watches. Kemp, *Oxford Companion to Ships and the Sea*, 926.

33 Albion, *Square-Riggers*, 202.

34 Joanna C. Colcord, *Roll and Go Songs of the American Seamen* (Indianapolis: Bobbs-Merrill Company, 1924), 10.

35 Albion, *Square-Riggers*, 157.

36 Rich, *Truro Cape Cod*, 390; Kittredge, *Shipmasters*, 129.

37 J. M. Rigg, "Madden, Richard Robert, 1798–1886," *Dictionary of National Biography*. (Oxford: Oxford University Press, 2004).

38 Robert Jamieson, *The New Excitement; or a Book to Induce Young People to Read*. (Edinburgh: W. Innes, 1841), 110–14; *New York Herald*, February 4, 1840.

39 *Liverpool Mercury*, December 17, 1841; *Times-Picayune*, October 24, 1842.

40 Burrows and Wallace, *Gotham*, 712.

41 Burrows and Wallace, *Gotham*, 712.

42 Joel Schwartz, "Housing," in *The Encyclopedia of New York*, ed. Kenneth T. Jackson (New Haven: Yale University Press, 1995), 565–69.

43 Burrows and Wallace, *Gotham*, 718.

44 Burrows and Wallace, *Gotham*, 798; A. J. Downing, *The Architecture of Country Houses* (New York: D. Appleton Co., 1850), 23.

45 1840 U.S. Census New York City Ward 15, New York County, New York; Edward K. and Mary Ann Collins, grantors/John Niblo, grantee, 18 April 1846, New York County, New York, Liber 479, Page 8, New York Land Records, 1630–1975; Stephen Camberleng, Master of Chancery, grantor/Edward K. Collins. Grantee, August 15, 1845, Mamaroneck, Westchester County, New York, Book 112, Page 1, New York Land Records, q1630–1775, New England Historic Genealogical Society: Case nos. M103013A, M103013A-2 (addendum). Judith Doolin Spikes, *Larchmont, NY: People and Places* (Larchmont: Square Books, 1991), 56–65.

46 Henry C. Collins was born in 1839. 1850 U.S. Census Township of Mamaroneck, County of Westchester, State of New York, July 23, 1850.

47 In 1845 Ann was twenty-three, Sexta eighteen, and Mary Ann twenty-one. 1850 U.S. Census.

48 Henry B. Bigelow and William C. Schroeder, *Fishes of the Gulf of Maine* (Washington: USGPO, 1953), 478–84.

49 Spikes, *Larchmont*, 80.

50 George Henry Preble, *A Chronological History of the Origin and Development of Steam Navigation* (Philadelphia: L.R. Hamersly and Co., 1895), 179.

Chapter Five: Samuel Cunard

1 William Penn to The Free Society of Traders, August 16, 1683, *The Papers of William Penn*, eds. Richard S. Dunn and Mary Maples Dunn (Philadelphia: University of Pennsylvania Press, 1982) 2:443.

2 Samuel W. Pennypacker, *The Settlement of Germantown, Pennsylvania* (Philadelphia: William J. Campbell, 1899), 14.

3 *The Papers of William Penn*, 2:490n; Pennypacker, *The Settlement of Germantown*, 6. The Mennonites were an Anabaptist sect.

4 Pennypacker, *The Settlement of Germantown*, 6.

5 Pennypacker, *The Settlement of Germantown*, 18.

6 Other variations on the name include Cunreds and Conrad.

7 Wilbur H. Siebert, *The Loyalists of Pennsylvania* (Columbus: The University Press, 1920), 84; Henry Young, "Treason and Its Punishment in Revolutionary Pennsylvania," *Pennsylvania Magazine of History and Biography*, 90 (1966), 287–313.

8 William Heath to John Hancock, August 14, 1782, quoted in William Fowler, *American Crisis* (New York: Walker Books, 2011), 84.

9 G. P. Browne, "Guy Carleton," *Dictionary of Canadian Biography*.

10 Shelburne to Carleton, February 18, 22, 1782, Papers of Sir Guy Carleton, Canadian National Library and Archives (microfilm).

11 Thomas Jones, *History of New York during the Revolutionary War* (New York: New York Historical Society, 1879) 2:262.

12 Maya Jasanoff, *Liberty's Exiles: American Loyalists in the Revolutionary World* (New York: Knopf, 2011), 147–75.

13 Sir Guy Carleton to Governor Andrew Snape Hamond, August 25, 1782. *Report on American Manuscripts in the Royal Institution of Great Britain* (London: His Majesty's Stationery Office, 1904–1909) 2:90–91.

14 James S. MacDonald, *Memoir John Parr*, Collections of the Nova Scotia Historical Society, (1910) 14:45, https://archive.org/details/14a15collectionsof14novauoft; Neil MacKinnon, *This Unfriendly Soil* (Kingston: McGill–Queens University Press, 1986), 12.

15 Beamish Murdock, *A History of Nova Scotia* (Halifax: James Barnes, 1865) 1:247.

16 T. B. Akins, *History of Halifax City* (Belleville, Ontario: Mika, 1973, repr.), 85.

17 MacDonald, *Memoir John Parr*, 7.

18 MacKinnon, *This Unfriendly Soil*, 17.

19 Phyllis R. Blakeley, "Samuel Cunard," *Dictionary of Canadian Biography*.

20 Lorenzo Sabine, *The American Loyalists: Biographical Sketches of Adherents to the British Crown in the War of the Revolution* (Boston: Little, Brown, 1847) 1:345.

21 There is confusion over Murphy's first name. John G. Langley, *Steam Lion: A Biography of Samuel Cunard* (New York: Brick Tower Press, 2006), 137, acknowledges that Thomas was also known as John. Documents contained in the Loyalist Claims as well as genealogical and local history sources indicate that Murphy's name was John. John Murphy, Rawson, Nova Scotia: Memorial, Account of Losses, and Evidence, Canada, Loyalist Claims, 1776–1835; John Victor Duncanson, *Rawdon and Douglas: Two Loyalist Townships in Nova Scotia* (Belleville, Ontario: Mika Publishing Co., 1989), vii.

22 Many of the white slave owners relocated in the West Indies. *Year Book City of Charleston, 1883, The Centennial Year of Incorporation* (Charleston: The News and Courier Book Press, 1883), 416.

23 MacDonald, *Memoir John Parr*, 16.

24 Quoted in Carole Troxler, "A Loyalist Life: John Bond of South Carolina and Nova Scotia," *Acadiensis* 19, no. 2 (Spring 1990): 78.

25 Although precise documentary evidence is lacking, this seems the likely sequence of events.

26 Signed March 1802, the Peace of Amiens lasted until May 1803.

27 Murdock, *History of Nova Scotia*, 3:124.

28 Murdock, *History of Nova Scotia*, 3:124–25.

29 The Halifax Grammar School was established in 1780. Atkins, *History of Halifax City*, 169.

30 Judith Fingard,"The 1820s: Peace, Privilege, and the Promise of Progress," in *The Atlantic Region to Confederation: A History*, eds. Phillip A. Buckner and John G. Reid (Toronto: University of Toronto Press, 1994), 265; D. A. Sutherland, "1810–1820: War and Peace," in Buckner and Reid, 258; Judith Fingard,"Charles Inglis," *Dictionary of Canadian Biography*; Susan Buggey and Gwendolyn Davies, "Thomas McCulloch," *Dictionary of Canadian Biography*; Langley, *Steam Lion*, 24–25; Thomas McCulloch, *Stepsure Letters* (Toronto: McClelland and Stewart, 1960), depicted the model Nova Scotian as standing with a hoe in one hand and a Bible in the other.

31 Samuel Cunard to Thomas McCulloch quoted in Langley, *Steam Lion*, 25.

32 Atkins, *History of Halifax City*, 157.

33 Advertisement, *Nova Scotia Weekly Chronicle*, December 10, 1813.

34 After the war nearly £10,000 of customs receipts collected in Maine were used to help found Dalhousie University in Halifax. E. M. Murray, *A Brief History of Dalhousie University* (Halifax: Dalhousie Million Committee, 1919), 2; Atkins, *History of Halifax City*, 163–64.

35 Blakeley, "Cunard," *Dictionary of Canadian Biography*.

36 Arthur Wentworth Hamilton Eaton, *History of King's County, Nova Scotia* (Salem: Salem Press, 1910), 755–56. The Duffus family is mentioned frequently in the history of Banff. William Crammond, ed., *The Annals of Banff* (Aberdeen: New Spalding Club, 1891–92), passim.

37 Blakeley, "Cunard," *Dictionary of Canadian Biography*; Atkins, *History of Halifax City*, 166.

38 Atkins, *History of Halifax City*, 187.

39 Atkins, *History of Halifax City*, 173.

40 F. Lawrence Babcock states that at about this time Cunard went to Boston and "served in a ship-broker's office." Babcock offers no documentation for this statement. It seems unlikely. F. Lawrence Babcock, *Spanning the Atlantic* (New York: Alfred A. Knopf, 1931), 10.

41 C. Arbuthnot to H. Goulburn, August 2, 1816, quoted in J. C. Arnell, "Samuel Cunard and the Nova Scotia Government Vessels *Earl Bathurst* and *Chebucto*," *Mariners' Mirror* 54 (4): 337–38. "Chebucto" comes from the Micmac word meaning "Chief Harbor." It was the place name given to the peninsula that includes Halifax. Thomas J. Brown, *Place Names in the Province of Nova Scotia* (Halifax: Royal Printers and Lithographers, 1922).

42 Cunard to Sir James Kempt, May 28, 1822, quoted in Arnell, "Samuel Cunard," 340.

43 In a ten-year period seven packets were lost. J. C. Arnell, *Atlantic Mails: A History of the Mail Service between Great Britain and Canada to 1889* (Ottawa: National Postal System, 1980), 89.

44 Peter Burroughs, "James Kempt," *Dictionary of Canadian Biography.*

45 G.M. to Lord Bathurst, January 5, 1822, quoted in Arnell, "Samuel Cunard," 342.

46 Arnell, "Samuel Cunard," 342.

47 Jeffrey to Rt. Hon. E. G. Stanley, March 14, 1833, quoted in Arnell, "Samuel Cunard," 347; J. C. Arnell, *Steam and the North Atlantic Mails* (Toronto: The Unitrade Press, 1986), 23.

48 Rosemary E. Ommer, "The 1830s: Adapting Their Institutions to Their Desires," in Buckner and Reid, *The Atlantic Region*, 284.

49 Arnell, *Atlantic Mails*, 64.

50 Arnell, *Atlantic Mails*, 69.

51 Arnell, *Atlantic Mails*, 73.

52 The children of Abraham and Margaret:
>   Mary (b. 1784 d. 1811)
>   Samuel (b. 1787 d. 1865)
>   William (b. 1789 d. 1824)
>   Susan (b. 1792 d. 1815)
>   Edward (b. 1798 d. 1880)
>   Joseph (b. 1799 d. 1865)
>   Thomas (b. 1799? d. 1828)
>   John (b. 1800 d. 1844)
>   Henry (b.1804 d. 1885)
>
> Langley, *Steam Lion*, 137–40.

53 Daniel Samson, "Industrial Colonization: The Colonial Context of the General Mining Association, Nova Scotia, 1825–1842," *Acadiensis* 29, no. 1 (Autumn 1999): 12.

54 John Boileau, *Samuel Cunard: Nova Scotia's Master of the North Atlantic* (Halifax: Formac Publishing Company, 2006), 31–33.

55 Lewis Bliss to Henry Bliss, February 5, 1831, Public Archives of Nova Scotia, vol. 3010 F 31.

56 Cunard was hardly alone. Given the nature of Nova Scotia's economy, virtually all businesses were tied to government support both provincial and empire.

57 For a history of the company see Robert W. Lovett, "Rundell, Bridge and Rundell— An Early Company History," *Bulletin of the Business Historical Society* 23, no. 3 (Sept. 1949): 152–62.

58 The success of the GMA was relatively short-lived. Improvements in techniques for burning American anthracite and improved transportation brought the price of American coal lower. Marilyn Gerriets, "The Rise and Fall of a Free-Standing Company in Nova Scotia: The General Mining Association," *Business History Review* 34, issue 3 (1992): 17–20.

59 Samson, "Industrial Colonization," 18.

60 Gerriets, "The Impact of the General Mining Association in the Nova Scotia Coal Industry, 1826–1850,"*Acadiensis* 21, no. 1 (Autumn 1991): 61.

61 Quoted in W. S. MacNutt, *The Atlantic Provinces: The Emergence of Colonial Society* (Toronto: McClelland and Stewart, 1965): 185.

62 Langley, *Steam Lion*, 38–41.

63 Blakeley, "Cunard," *Dictionary of Canadian Biography*.

64 Langley, *Steam Lion*, 103–4. The complicated role played by the GMA, in their "dream of dominion" (28), and Cunard's participation is described in Samson, "Industrial Colonization."

65 MacNutt, *The Atlantic Provinces*, 200. "Responsible Government" embodied the belief that ministers of government ought to be responsible to the majority in an elected assembly.

66 Aside from his May 3 speech, Cunard is mentioned as speaking publicly on only one other occasion—the arrival of *Britannia* in Boston. Blakeley Papers, Public Affairs Nova Scotia, vol. 3011 F 17. This description of politicking refers to the conduct of the popular politician Joseph Howe in the campaign of 1836. J. Bartlett Brebner, *Canada: A Modern History* (Ann Arbor: University of Michigan Press, 1960), 177.

67 Blakeley, "Cunard," *Dictionary of Canadian Biography*.

68 Blakeley, "Cunard," *Dictionary of Canadian Biography*.

69 This point is well made by Samson, "Industrial Colonization," 22.

70 Langley, *Steam Lion*, 48.

71 *Acadian Recorder*, May 14, 1831; Langley, *Steam Lion*, 50–51.

Chapter Six: Steam

1 Jennifer Tann, ed., *The Selected Papers of Boulton and Watt* (London: Diploma, 1981), 17.

2 George Henry Preble, *A Chronological History of the Origin and Development of Steam Navigation* (Philadelphia: L.R. Hamersly and Co., 1895), 24–25.

3 Fulton registered the name as *North River Steamboat*. *Clermont* was the name of Robert Livingston's country estate. Cynthia Owen Philip, *Robert Fulton* (New York: Franklin Watts, 1985), 204.

4 Preble, *A Chronological History*, 53–57.

5 Shreve's design was the prototype for the traditional Mississippi River steamboat. Placing the paddle wheel at the stern also offered protection against floating debris common in the rivers. James Thomas Flexner, *Steamboats Come True* (New York: Viking Press, 1954), 344–45; Harry Sinclair Drago, *The Steamboaters* (New York: Bramhall House, 1967), passim.

6 Quoted in Marilyn E. Weigold, *Long Island Sound: A History of Its People, Places and Environment* (New York: NYU Press, 2004), 38; William H. Ewen, *Days of the Steamboats* (Mystic: Mystic Seaport Museum, 1988), 41–42; *Baltimore Patriot*, March 27, 1815.

7 Weigold, *Long Island Sound*, 38.

8 Travel by train was not an option. The first successful scheduled railroad in the United States did not begin operation until 1830.

9 Charles Preston Fishbaugh, *From Paddle Wheels to Propellers* (Indianapolis: Indiana Historical Society, 1970), 231; "Progress of Steamboat Movements," http://www .catskillarchive.com/rrextra/abrwo5.html. Individual vessels can be found in *Merchant Steam Vessels of the United States 1790–1868*: "The Lytle-Holdcamper List" (Staten Island: Steamship Historical Society of America, 1975).

10 Quoted in David E. Nye, *American Technological Sublime* (Cambridge: MIT Press, 1994), 57. These exaggerated claims failed to recognize the work of a considerable number of French, English, and Scottish engineers.

11 William Still, Gordon Watts, and Bradley Rogers, "Steam Navigation and the United States," in *The Advent of Steam*, eds. Robert Gardiner and Basil Greenhill (London: Conway Maritime Press, 1993), 64.

12 Edgar C. Smith, *A Short History of Naval and Marine Engineering* (Cambridge: Cambridge University Press, 1937), 129–30. The invention by Samuel Hall of the surface condenser in 1831 aimed toward a solution to the problem of providing "clean" feed water to the boilers. However, Hall's invention, while pointing the way, did not succeed. "It was not until 1860 that the increased boiler pressures made the surface condenser a necessity. Up to about this time the pressure carried did not exceed 30 pounds gage, and sea water was used for feed water. The amount of salt in the boiler water was tested from time to time by the salinometer, and when too concentrated the boiler was blown down and fresh sea water was added, the concentration always being kept below the point at which the calcium sulphate commenced to be deposited." George A. Orrok, "Development of the Surface Condenser," *Power and the Engineer*, June 1, 1909, 959–60.

13 Louis C. Hunter, *Steamboats on the Western Rivers* (Cambridge: Harvard University Press, 1949). High-pressure boilers were most often used on the western rivers. Their compact size and light weight made them preferable for shallow draft vessels, nor were they usually fitted with heavy condensers since they were operating in fresh water. Still, "Steam Navigation," 64.

14 John Laurence Busch, *Steam Coffin: Captain Moses Rogers and the Steamship Savannah Break the Barrier* (np: Hodes Historia, 2010).

15 Jacob Abbott, "The Novelty Works," *Harper's New Monthly Magazine* (May 1851), 725. For a complete description of iron manufacturing in this period see Frederick Overman, *The Manufacture of Iron in All Its Various Branches* (Philadelphia: Henry C. Baird, 1850).

16 Abbott, "The Novelty Works," 728–29.

17 My thanks to Professor Carey Rappaport, Distinguished Professor of Computer and Electrical Engineering, Northeastern University, for providing this calculation.

18 Busch, *Steam Coffin*, provides a detailed description of the building of *Savannah*, 128–212.

19 Busch, *Steam Coffin*, 156–57.

20 George A. Orrok, "Development of the Surface Condenser," *Power and the Engineer*, June 1, 1909, 959–60.

21 Busch, *Steam Coffin*, 162, 178.

22 Busch, *Steam Coffin*, 266.

23 The weight of ninety tons for the engine is taken from an estimate given by Robert Napier in 1833. He stated that "one ton per horsepower" was the calculation. "Quantity of Work done by Robert Napier," Napier Papers DC90/2/6/7, University of Glasgow Archives.

24 Busch, *Steam Coffin*, 272. Even given the gross inefficiency of *Savannah*'s engines it is surprising that in only three and a half days of steaming she consumed all her fuel. When not steaming *Savannah*'s crew took in the paddles to reduce drag. This was a time-consuming process matched only by the effort needed to deploy the paddles. It is possible that even when not using the engine for propulsion Rogers might have kept up fires, which would account for the heavy fuel consumption.

25 Cedric Ridgely-Nevitt, *American Steamships on the Atlantic* (Newark: University of Delaware Press, 1981), 57; See also David Budlong Tyler, *Steam Conquers the Atlantic* (New York: D. Appleton-Century Company, 1939), 1–17.

26 Between the voyages of *Savannah* and *Great Western* and *Sirius* (1838), at least four vessels made transatlantic steam passages: *Curacao* (1826), *Cape Breton* (1833), *Rhahdamthus* (1832), and *Royal William* (1833). All of these voyages, however, were one-way.

27 For an overview of the development of the port of Glasgow see William Forrest MacArthur, *History of Port Glasgow* (Glasgow: Jackson, Wylie and Co., 1932), 88–133.

28 James Deas, *The River Clyde* (Glasgow: James Maclehose, 1876), 1–2.

29 Smith, *A Short History of Naval and Marine Engineering*, 11–12.

30 G. N. Tunzelmann, *Steam Power and British Industrialization to 1860* (Oxford: Clarendon Press, 1978), 23. *Clermont* employed this type of engine.

31 Preble, *A Chronological History*, 44.

32 *Charlotte Dundas* was powered by a wheel mounted slightly forward of the stern. Although not economically successful she was a technical triumph, causing some to salute her as the first practical steamboat and herald Symington as the "father" of marine engineering. Preble, *A Chronological History*, 45; Smith, *A Short History*, 13.

33 J. Lawson to Matthew Boulton, February 5, 1803, in *The Selected Papers of Boulton and Watt*, ed. Jennifer Tann, 1:149. T. H. Beare, "William Symington," *Oxford Dictionary of National Biography*; this was a common and reasonable concern. For the same reason, steamboats were not allowed on the Erie Canal.

34 Smith, *A Short History*, 13.

35 Henry Bell to Edward Morris, October 1836, in Edward Morris, *Life of Henry Bell* (Glasgow: Printed for author, 1854), 17.

36 Morris, *Bell*, 42; Smith, *A Short History*, 14. In the fall of 1811 a "Great Comet" had swept across the skies of the Northern Hemisphere. Bell adopted the name. James Williamson, *The Clyde Passenger Steamer* (Glasgow: James Maclehose and Sons, 1904), 6.

37 George MacGregor, *The History of Glasgow* (Glasgow: Thomas Morrison, 1881), 395–96.

38 George Dodd, *An Historical and Explanatory Dissertation on Steam Engines and Steam Packets* (London: Printed for the author, 1818), xviii–xvix; John A. Kellett, *Glasgow: A Concise History* (London: Blond, 1967), 31.

39 Isaac Weld, "Passage From Dublin to London," in Dodd, *An Historical and Explanatory Dissertation*, 279.

40 Basil Greenhill, "Steam Before the Screw," in *Advent of Steam*, 13–14.

41 Edwin Hodder, *Sir George Burns, His Times and Friends* (London: Hodder and Stoughton, 1890), 122, 126; "James Burns," *Memoirs and Portraits of One Hundred Glasgow Men*, 61–63; http://gdl.cdlr.strath.ac.uk/mlemen/mlemen018.htm.

42 James Napier, *Life of Robert Napier* (London: William Blackwood and Sons, 1904), 49; "James Burns Memoirs."

43 Contract between David Napier and Robert Napier, February 3, 1836, Napier Papers DC90/2/5/4/1-9, University of Glasgow Archives; *Life of Robert Napier*, 29.

44 Napier, *Life of Robert Napier*, 32. *Leven*'s engine was working until 1877. It is now on display at the Scottish Maritime Museum in Glasgow.

45 Thomas Assheton Smith, *Oxford Dictionary of National Biography*.

46 Napier, *Life of Robert Napier*, 41.

47 Captain G. Grant to Robert Napier, June 24, 1837, Napier, *Life of Robert Napier*, 64.

48 Lords Commissioners to Napier, July 5, 1838, Napier, *Life of Robert Napier*, 71.

49 Erasmus Ommanney to Robert Napier, February 1843, Napier, *Life of Robert Napier*, 71–72.

50 Contract between David Napier and Robert Napier, February 3, 1836, Napier Papers DC90/2/5/4, University of Glasgow Archives. On July 28, 1835, one of David Napier's boilers blew up on the steamer *Earl Grey* quayside at Greenock, killing six people. Napier decided to take this moment to leave Glasgow, sell his Lancefield works to Robert, and move to London. "David Napier," *Oxford Dictionary of National Biography*.

51 Patrick Wallace to Robert Napier, March 26, 1833, Napier Papers DC90/2/4/10, University of Glasgow Archives.

52 Wallace to Napier, March 26, 1833.

53 Wallace to Napier, March 26, 1833.

54 Napier to Wallace, April 3, 1833, Napier, *Life of Robert Napier*, 101–13.

55 Quoted in W. S. Lindsay, *History of Merchant Shipping and Ancient Commerce*, (New York: AMS, 1965, repr.) 4:169; Tyler, *Steam Conquers the Atlantic*, 34.

56 See below Napier's advice to Cunard.

57 Napier recommended twelve seamen. Given that these were large full-rigged ships, twelve seamen seems a small number to manage the work on deck and aloft. Basil Greenhill and Peter Allington, "Sail Assist and the Steamship," in *Advent of Steam*, 146–51. Later owners preferred a schooner rig, which required a smaller crew for sail handling.

58 For purposes of converting to dollars I have used "Measuring Worth," https://www.measuringworth.com/datasets/exchangepound/result.php; Robert G. Albion, *Square-Riggers on Schedule* (Princeton: Princeton University Press, 1938), 100. Even construction of the famous, and overpriced, American clipper ships was less costly than steamships. Donna Souza, *The Persistence of Sail in the Age of Steam* (New York: Penguin, 1998), 109; Glenn A. Knoblock, *The American Clipper Ship, 1845–1920* (Jefferson, North Carolina: McFarland and Company, Inc., 2013), 107.

59 Albion estimates the fare for steerage on sailing packets at $20 (£5). He further estimates that each steerage passenger required "eighty cubic feet of space, the equivalent of two tons of freight." Napier calculated the revenue from "fine freight" at £3 per ton which roughly equates to nearly $15. Albion, *Square-Riggers on Schedule*, 247.

60 Napier, *Life of Robert Napier*, 113.

Chapter Seven: The British and North American Royal Mail Steam Packet Company

1 Francis B. C. Bradlee, *The First Steamer to Cross the Atlantic* (Salem: Essex Institute, 1925), 5.

2 In the years 1838–39 approximately thirty-seven steam crossings to New York were completed. The records, however, are sketchy and imprecise while the definition of a "steam crossing" is uncertain. The companies and their ships were as follows:

British and American Steam Navigation of London

Sirius (Owned by the St. George Steam Packet Company but chartered to British and American)

British Queen

President

Transatlantic Steamship Company of Liverpool

Liverpool

City of Dublin Steam Packet Company

Royal William (not the Canadian ship)

Great Western Steamship Company of Bristol

Great Western

Source: Edgar C. Smith, *A Short History of Naval and Marine Engineering* (Cambridge: Cambridge University Press, 1937), 38; Basil Greenhill, "Steam Before the Screw," in *The Advent of Steam*, ed. Robert Gardiner (Annapolis: Naval Institute Press, 1993), 19–20.

3 David MacIver to Samuel Cunard, April 16, 1841. Copy in Blakeley Papers MG 1 248, letter 43, Public Archives of Nova Scotia; Basil Greenhill, "Steam before Screw," *The Advent of Steam*, 21; *Baltimore Sun*, September 19, 1842.

4 John Armstrong and David Williams, "The Perceptions and Understanding of New Technology: A Failed Attempt to Establish Transatlantic Steamship Liner Service, 1824–1828," *Northern Mariner* 17, issue 4:41–56.

5 Greenhill, "Steam Before Screw," 20.

6 To address the remaining issues two agreements were reached between Great Britain and the United States. The Rush Bagot agreement of 1817 limited naval armament on the Great Lakes, and in the following year a Convention was approved that established the 49th parallel as the northern boundary between the United States and Canada, but only as far west as the Rocky Mountains. From there to the Pacific the two nations agreed to "joint occupation." The Maine/New Brunswick border was also left in contention. Neither Rush Bagot nor the Boundary Treaty settled permanently the issues between the United States and Great Britain. For nearly twenty years border disputes between the two nations persisted, and on some occasions turned violent. Julius W. Pratt, *A History of United States Foreign Policy*, 2nd ed. (New York: Prentice Hall, 1965), 70–71, 97–102, 105–13. Also bedeviling relations were questions over fishing rights. J. Bartlett Brebner, *Canada: A Modern History* (Ann Arbor: University of Michigan Press, 1960), 116–19.

7 "Memorandum on the Defense of Canada, to Lord Bathurst, March 1, 1819," in *Dispatches, Correspondence and Memoranda of Field Marshall Arthur Wellesley* (London: John Murray, 1867) 1:36–44. For an overview of American conflicts with Canada see Reginald Stuart, *United States Expansion and British North America, 1775–1871* (Chapel Hill: University of North Carolina Press, 1988), 77–105.

8 Between 1826 and 1832 the Royal Government built a canal linking Kingston on the St. Lawrence west to Ottawa (Bytown). The canal was constructed to provide a water route safe from American attack. Margaret Conrad, Alvin Finkel, and Cornelius Jaenen, *History of the Canadian Peoples* (Toronto: Longman Co., 1993), 1:411.

9 Presidential Proclamation, January 5, 1838. American Presidency Project, http://www.presidency.ucsb.edu/ws/?pid=67317.

10 Sir John Colborne to Lieutenant Colonel Turner, November 1, 1838, in J. A. MacDonell, *Sketches Glengarry in Canada* (Montreal: Wm. Foster Brown, 1893), 294.

11 Pratt, *A History of United States Foreign Policy*, 97–100.

12 Brebner, *Canada: A Modern History*, 240; *Baltimore Sun*, April 22, 1841; *New Hampshire Gazette*, August 18, 1841.

13 At this time the term Canada included two separate provinces: Upper Canada (Ontario) and Lower Canada (Quebec).

14 *Lord Durham's Report on the Affairs of British North America*. Edited with an Introduction by Sir C. P. Lucas, K. C. B., K. C. M. G, 3 vols. (Oxford: Clarendon Press, 1912). http://www.archive.org/stream/lorddurhamsrepor01durhiala/lorddurhamsrepor01durhiala_djvu.txt.

15 For examples see reports published in the *Times*, November 16, 1837, and December 6, 1837.

16 J. C. Arnell, *Atlantic Mails: A History of the Mail Service between Great Britain and Canada to 1889* (Ottawa: National Postal Museum, 1980), 62. Ann Parry, *Parry of the Arctic* (London: Chatto and Windus, 1963), 189.

17 Parry, *Parry*, 193.

18 Pierre Berton, *The Arctic Grail: The Quest for the North West Passage and the North Pole, 1818–1909* (Toronto: Anchor, 2001), 46.

19 Parry, *Parry*, 191; Edward Parry, *Memoirs of Sir W. Edward Parry* (London: Longman, Brown, Green, Longmans and Roberts, 1857), 254.

20 Quoted in John G. Langley, *Steam Lion*, (Halifax: Nimbus Press, 2006), 67.

21 William Crane and Joseph Howe to Lord Gleneig, August 24, 1838, in *The Speeches and Public Letters of Joseph Howe*, ed. William Annard (Halifax: The Chronicle Publishing Co., 1909) 1:181.

22 William Crane and Joseph Howe to Lord Gleneig, August 24, 1838, in Annard, 1:182.

23 *Commons Sittings in the Nineteenth Century*, "Budget," http://hansard.millbank systems.com/commons/1838/may/18/the-budget.

24 Arnell, *Atlantic Mails*, 93.

25 *Times*, November 8, 1838.

26 Edwin Hodder, *Sir George Burns, His Times and Friends* (London: Hodder and Stoughton, 1890), 138.

27 Hodder, *Sir George Burns*, 192.

28 Francis E. Hyde, *Cunard and the North Atlantic 1840–1973* (London: MacMillan, 1975), 5.

29 David Budlong Tyler, *Steam Conquers the Atlantic* (New York: D. Appleton-Century Company, 1939), 78.

30 In the summer of 1838 during one of his visits to England Cunard made a side trip to Bristol to "look in on Great Western." Isaac Cooke to [?] June 15, 1838. Copy in Blakeley Papers, Public Archives of Nova Scotia 3019 F 11.

31 Campbell to Lord Gleneig (nd) quoted in T. E. Hughes, "The Cunard Story," *Sea Breezes* (July 1965), 506.

32 Hughes, "The Cunard Story," 506; Cunard later requested that during the winter months between November and February he be required to make only monthly passages. The Admiralty agreed and deducted £1,000 for each canceled voyage. Hughes, 518. The horsepower figures are for each engine rated at Nominal Horse Power (NHP).

33 Samuel Cunard to Messrs William Kidston and Sons, February 25, 1839, in James Napier, *Life of Robert Napier* (London: William Blackwood and Sons, 1904), 124.

34 Cunard to Kidston, February 25, 1839, in Napier, *Life of Robert Napier*, 125.

35 Hodder, *Sir George Burns*, 140.

36 Napier to Kidston, February 28, 1839, in Napier, *Life of Robert Napier*, 128.

37 Napier to Kidston, February 28, 1839, in Napier, *Life of Robert Napier*, 128–29.

38 The biographers of Sir George Burns and Robert Napier disagree in some details of chronology.

39 Robert Napier to Messrs J. and G. Burns, January 28, 1842, in Napier, *Life of Robert Napier*, 131.

40 Napier to Burns, January 28, 1841, in Napier, *Life of Robert Napier*, 129–34; Hodder, *Life of Sir George Burns*, 194–98; James Brown Fleming, *John Park Fleming* (Glasgow: James Maclehose and Sons, 1885), 31–32. Among the various sources there are slight discrepancies in chronology.

41 The agreement needed to provide access for additional investors while leaving management in the hands of Cunard, Burns and MacIver.

42 The name was not changed officially to The Cunard Steamship Line until 1878, when it was incorporated.

43 Hodder, *Life of Sir George Burns*, 198; Hyde, *Cunard and the North Atlantic*, 10–11.

44 Hodder, *Life of Sir George Burns*, 200.

45 Napier to James Melvill, March 19, 1839, in Napier, *Life of Robert Napier*, 134.

46 List of investors:

Samuel Cunard	£55,000
James Donaldson	16,000
James Browne	11,600
James Wright	11,600
Thomas Buchanan	11,600
William Brown	11,600
Robert Rodger	11,600
W. Leckie Ewing	11,600
William Connal	11,600
Alexander Fletcher	11,600
William Stirling	11,600
Robert Hinshaw	10,900
Alexander M'Aslan	10,800
Elias Gibb	6,400
Alexander Glasgow	6,400
Robert Napier	6,000
James Campbell	6,000
George Burns	5,500
Alexander Downie	5,000
William Campbell	5,500
James Burns	5,000
David MacIver	4,000
Charles MacIver	4,000
James Merry, Jun	3,700
Alexander Bannerman	2,100
John Bannerman	2,100
Henry Bannerman	2,100
Archibald MacConnell	2,000
David Scott	1,600
James Martin	1,500

James M'Call	1,300
Alexander Kerr	700
David Chapman	1,500

Napier, *Life of Robert Napier*, 141–42.

47 Cunard to Napier, March 21, 1839, in *Life of Robert Napier*, 135.

48 Royal Meeker, "History of British Shipping Subsidies," American Economic Association *Publications*, 3rd series, vol. 6 no. 3 (August 1905): 5.

49 The contract did not stipulate tonnage but rather set a price of £32,000 per ship. Contract between Samuel Cunard and Robert Napier, March 18, 1839, Napier Papers DC90/2/5/6, University of Glasgow Archives.

50 Other amendments were also added. See Hyde, *Cunard and the North Atlantic*, 7–8; Hughes, "Cunard Story," 508–9.

51 Hughes, "Cunard Story," 515.

52 MacArthur, *History of Port Glasgow*, 97, 110; Captain H. Parker and Frank C. Bowen, *Mail and Passenger Steamships of the Nineteenth Century* (London: Sampson, Low, Marston and Co., 1928), 38–39, 1, 45, 76.

53 Daniel Allen Butler, *The Age of Cunard* (Annapolis: Lighthouse Press, 2004), 42. Eric Flounders and Michael Gallagher, *The Story of Cunard's 175 Years* (Ramsey; Isle of Man: Ferry Publications, 2014), 14–15.

54 *Morning Herald*, August 8, 1839.

55 Edward Chase Kirkland, *Men, Cities and Transportation A Study in New England History 1820–1900* (Cambridge: Harvard University Press, 1948) 1:125.

56 Kirkland, *Men, Cities and Transportation*. 1:135, 198.

57 *Boston Evening Transcript*, June 6, 1840.

58 *Boston Atlas*, August 9, 1839.

59 Quoted in *New Bedford Mercury*, April 4, 1839.

60 Massachusetts General Laws, ch. 0186 1833. http://archives.lib.state.ma.us/handle/2452/112186. The Company held extensive tracts of land in East Boston. No Author, *Sketch of the Recent Improvements at East Boston* (Boston: J. T. Buckingham, 1836), 3–4.

61 *Newport Mercury*, August 17, 1839.

62 *New Hampshire Sentinel*, June 24, 1840; *New Bedford Mercury*, April 26, 1839.

63 Blakeley Papers, 3014 F. 20 Public Archives of Nova Scotia.

64 *Acadian Recorder*, August 31, 1839.

Chapter Eight: Liverpool—Halifax—Boston—New York

1 T. E. Hughes, "The Cunard Story," *Sea Breezes* (July 1965): 506; After leaving the Saint Lawrence River the water route between Quebec and Halifax required taking a course to clear Cape Breton Island and then a long coastal sail along nearly the entire coast of Nova Scotia. The voyage was dangerous and long.

2 P. H. Watson, "The Two Hundredth anniversary of the Halifax Dockyard" (Halifax 1959 Occasional papers No. 5, Maritime Museum of Canada), 21.

3 John G. Langley, *Steam Lion* (Halifax: Nimbus Press, 2006), 74.

4 *Acadian Recorder*, September 21, 1839.

5 *Historical Atlas of Canada*, ed. R. Louis Gentilcore (Toronto: University of Toronto Press, 1987), 2: plate 25.

6 Cunard to William Maberly, November 28, 1840, Cunard to Maberly, May 29, 1841, MG 1, vol. 3014 F. 23, Public Archives of Nova Scotia. "William Maberly," *Oxford Dictionary of National Biography*.

7 Contract between Samuel Cunard and John Howe, December 14, 1841. "High Speed Stage Coach Line," http://ns1758.ca/cunard/cunard01.html. Seventeen hours was less than half the time it took the "waggons" to make the same trip. The ocean passage, Pictou to Halifax, was likely to be at least three days. James Douglas, "The Steamship 'Unicorn,' on the St. Lawrence Branch of the Cunard Company in 1840," *Transactions of the Literary and Historical Society of Quebec*, Sessions of 1908–09, no. 28 (Quebec: Chronicle Printing, 1910), 107.

8 Cunard to Maberly, November 28, 1840. MG1 vol. 3014 F. 23, Public Archives of Nova Scotia. At this moment the Provincial Treasury was running a surplus.

9 J. C. Arnell, *Atlantic Mails: A History of the Mail Service Between Great Britain and Canada* (Ottawa: National Postal Museum, 1980), 101.

10 Contract, December 14, 1841, http://ns1758.ca/cunard/cunard01.html.

11 *Boston Daily Advertiser*, May 11, 1840; *Southern Patriot*, March 16, 1840; *Times*, February 8, 1840.

12 *Baltimore Sun*, May 4, 1840.

13 *Connecticut Courant*, June 6, 1840.

14 Douglas, "The Steamship 'Unicorn,'" 101.

15 *Acadian Recorder*, June 6, 1840.

16 *Connecticut Current*, June 6, 1840; *Richmond Inquirer*, June 9, 1840.

17 *Connecticut Current*, June 6, 1840.

18 *Baltimore Sun*, June 8, 9, 1840.

19 *Times-Picayune*, April 24, 1839; *New Hampshire Sentinel*, June 6, 1840.

20 *Liverpool Mercury*, June 12, 1840, July 3, 1840.

21 *Liverpool Mercury*, July 3, 1840; *Liverpool Mercury*, July 10, 1840. The arrival of steamships presented new challenges to the dock system. Concerned about the threat of fire, dock operators first tried to segregate steamers, but eventually had to abandon the idea. An additional issue involved schedules. Steamers, such as *Britannia*, unlike most sailing vessels, were on a strict schedule. In order to maximize profit dock operators saw it to their advantage to crowd as many vessels as possible into a dock. "Steamship owners objected to vessels being boxed in or made to wait for berths. Each steamer therefore required a greater area of the dock than its dimensions would necessarily suggest, because other ships could not be parked in the space between it and the dock exit." Graeme J. Milne, *Trade and Traders in Mid-Victorian Liverpool* (Liverpool: Liverpool University press, 2000), 73. Size too was an issue. The normal beam of vessels was greatly enlarged by the "rapid increase in the width of paddle steamers," making it difficult for them to pass through narrow gates. Adrian Jarvis,

Liverpool Central Docks: 1799–1905: An Illustrated History (Liverpool: National Museums and Galleries, 1991), 9.

22 Woodruff was a last-moment replacement. Robert Ewing was her original commander. Woodruff was slated originally for *Columbia*. *Acadian Recorder*, July 18, 1840; Arthur J. Maginnis, *The Atlantic Ferry* (London: Whittaker and Co., 1893), 20–21.

23 *Acadian Recorder*, July 18, 1849; *New Hampshire Patriot and State Gazette*, July 27, 1840.

24 *New Hampshire Patriot and State Gazette*, July 27, 1840.

25 William H. Sumner, *History of East Boston with Biographical Sketches of the Early Proprietors and An Appendix* (Boston: J.E. Tilton, 1858), 623.

26 Sumner, *History of East Boston*, 478.

27 Among the toasts:

> "Cunard's Line of Steam Packets—the pendulum of a large clock, which is to tick once a fortnight."
>
> "The memory of Time and Space—famous in their day and generation—They have been annihilated by the steam engine."

Baltimore Sun, July 25, 1840.

28 *Connecticut Current*, July 25, 1840.

29 *Log Cabin*, August 8, 1840. To add to the luster of the event a committee was appointed "to procure and present a silver vase" to Cunard. Jones, Low and Ball, ancestor to the present Boston firm of Shreve Crump and Low, assigned the task, to the silversmith Obadiah Rich. It took Rich more than a year to complete the "Rich Vase," and it was not until the summer of 1842 that it was finished and shipped, with a "suitable letter," to Cunard aboard *Britannia*. Described as "a very splendid specimen of workmanship," for more than 150 years the "Vase" disappeared from sight until its 1967 discovery in a Maryland antique shop. The cup was purchased by the Cunard Company and today is on display aboard *Queen Mary 2*. *Southern Patriot*, July 11, 1842, *Times-Picayune*, July 14, 1842; http://cunardsteamshipsociety.com/2010/01/08/cunard-heritage/.

30 *Farmer's Cabinet*, July 24, 1840.

31 *New Hampshire Sentinel*, July 22, 1840; David Budlong Tyler, *Steam Conquers the Atlantic* (New York: D. Appleton-Century Company, 1939), 106–8.

32 *Rhode Island Republican*, November 4, 1840; *Portsmouth Journal of Literature and Politics*, January 23, 1841.

33 *New Hampshire Sentinel*, December 7, 1842.

34 *New Hampshire Patriot*, January 8, 1841.

35 *Baltimore Sun*, July 23, 1841.

36 *Baltimore Sun*, July 22, 1840.

37 *Southern Patriot*, October 27, 1841, reported a "demand for additional hotels" in Boston.

38 *Salem Gazette*, June 29, 1841.

39 *Southern Patriot*, October 27, 1841.

40 James Grant Wilson and John Fiske, eds., *Appleton's Cyclopedia* (New York: D. Appleton and Co., 1889) 6:43; Gilbert Haven and Thomas Russell, *Incidents and*

Anecdotes of Rev. Edward T. Taylor (Boston: The Boston Port and Seamen's Society, 1871), passim.

41 *Boston Journal*, August 13, 1841.

42 *Madisonian* (Washington, D.C.), February 9, 1841; Lemuel Shattuck, *Report to the City of Boston for the Year 1845. Embracing Collateral and Statistical Researches Illustrating the History and Condition of the Population and Their Means of Progress and Prosperity* (Boston: John H. Eastburn, City Printer, 1846), 38.

43 *Madisonian*, February 9, 1841.

44 Shattuck, *Report to the City of Boston for the Year 1845*, 38, Appendix AA, 50, Appendix FF, 54. In his analysis of Boston's prosperity Shattuck described the Cunard steamers as "intimately connected," 87.

45 While it is difficult to estimate income, at \$135 (£25) per passenger Cunard grossed approximately \$200,000. The income earned by vessels bringing the others varies. Albion gives an estimate of \$20 (£4) fare for steerage. It is quite likely that Cunard's income from passengers, although fewer in number, exceeded that of the sailing vessels. Robert G. Albion, *Square-Riggers on Schedule* (Princeton: Princeton University Press, 1938), 247.

46 *Madisonian*, February 9, 1841.

47 Letter from the Postmaster General, March 10, 1846.

48 *Britannia* could load 225 tons of cargo. Collins's *Roscius* had a capacity for at least 1,000 tons. *Roscius*, Certificate of Registration, April 25, 1840 NARA RG 41 Bureau of Marine Inspection and Navigation. Because of their lower costs (construction and operation) in cargo trades, particularly long distance, sailing vessels remained competitive for many decades. F. E. Chadwick and Others, *Ocean Steamships: A Popular Account of Their Construction Development, Management and Appliances* (New York: Charles Scribner's Sons, 1891), 22. Gerald S. Graham, "The Ascendancy of the Sailing Ship, 1850–1885," *Economic History Review* 9, issue 1 (August 1956): 74–88.

49 *Pittsfield Sun*, July 7, 1841.

50 *Salem Gazette*, June 29, 1841; *Boston Daily Atlas*, September 30, 1841.

51 *The Madisonian*, February 9, 1841.

52 Robert Napier to Patrick Wallace, April 3, 1833, James Napier, *Life of Robert Napier* (Edinburgh: William Blackwood and Sons, 1894), 101–13. The crew numbers for *Britannia* are actually taken from *Hibernia* (1843). *Hibernia*'s gross tonnage was 1,422, *Britannia*'s 1,154. James Douglas, "The Steamship 'Unicorn,'" 28:101; Francis E. Hyde, *Cunard and the North Atlantic 1840–1973* (London: Macmillan, 1975), 326–27.

53 Napier estimated gross revenues of each trip at nearly £5,000. Of that freight earnings accounted for only £300 per trip.

54 Robert G. Albion, *Square-Riggers on Schedule* (Princeton: Princeton University Press, 1938), 233–35.

55 David MacIver to Samuel Cunard, April 16, 1841, MG 1 vol. 248 letter 2, Public Archives of Nova Scotia.

56 During this period ocean freight rates were in decline. See Douglass North, "Ocean Freight Rates and Economic Development, 1750–1913," *The Journal of Economic*

History 18, no. 4 (December 1958): 537–55, and a revised view C. Knick Harley, "Ocean Freight Rates and Productivity, 1740–1913: The Primacy of Mechanical Invention Reaffirmed," *The Journal of Economic History* 48, no. 4 (December 1988): 851–76. For comments on passenger fares, mostly dealing with a later period but having some pertinent information, see Brandon DuPont, Drew Keeling and Thomas Weiss, "Passenger Fares for Overseas Travel in the 19th and 20th Centuries" (Paper Prepared for the Annual Meeting of the Economic History Association, September 21–23, 2012), 3, 32. http://eh.net/eha/wp-content/uploads/2013/11/Weissetal.pdf. In the spring of 1842 *British Queen* adopted a continental plan, that is, food and wine extra. Shortly thereafter the line gave up the New York service. *New York Herald*, April 23, 1842.

57 "Ship's Husband," http://legal-dictionary.thefreedictionary.com/Ship's+husband.

58 In modern times little has changed. In a current guide for merchant marine officers in the section "Ship's Business," Captain James Aragon comments, with obvious exaggeration, that "the weight of all the reports required aboard [are] approximately equal to the ship's tonnage." William B. Hayler, ed., *Merchant Marine Officer's Handbook* (Centreville: Cornell Maritime Press, 1990), 447.

59 MacIver to Cunard, April 16, 1841; George Burns to Cunard, April 17, 1841, MG 1 vol. 3017 F. 23 Public Archives of Nova Scotia.

60 A destructive fire at the Bay of Chaleurs added to Joseph's losses. *Weekly Herald*, September 18, 1841; Langley, *Steam Lion*, 99–106.

61 Quoted in Langley, *Steam Lion*, 101.

62 Quoted in Langley, *Steam Lion*, 124.

63 Quoted in Margaret Conrad, Alvin Finkel, and Cornelius Jaenen, *History of the Canadian Peoples Beginnings to 1867* (Toronto: Copp Clark Pitman, 1993), 325; Blakely, "Cunard," *Dictionary of Canadian Biography*; Rusty Bitterman, *Rural Protest on Prince Edward Island: From British Colonization to the Escheat Movement* (Toronto: University of Toronto Press, 2006), 167, 117n.

64 William Oland Bourne, *Gems From Fable Land: A Collection of Fables Illustrated by Facts* (New York: Charles Scribner, 1853), 318.

65 David and Charles MacIver to Leyland and Bullins, March 23, 1842, D.138/1/1, Cunard Papers, University of Liverpool Archives; John Rankin, *A History of Our Firm* (Liverpool: University of Liverpool, 1908), 205–6; *Memoirs and Portraits of One Hundred Glasgow Men*, 67. http://gdl.cdlr.strath.ac.uk/mlemen/mlemen018.htm.

66 David and Charles MacIver to Leyland and Bullins, March 23, 1842.

67 *Baltimore Sun*, March 30, 1842.

68 Langley, *Steam Lion*, 102.

69 Langley, *Steam Lion*, 103–04.

70 *Baltimore Sun*, July 20, 1843.

71 *Baltimore Sun*, July 20, 1843; *Times-Picayune*, October 13, 1843; Meeting of the Partners British and North American Royal Mail, January 25, 1844. MG 1 vol. 248 no. 42, Public Archives of Nova Scotia; Hamilton Andrews Hill, *Memoir of Abbott Lawrence* (Boston: Privately Printed, 1883), 69–72. Ninety percent of the loss was carried by

underwriters. The remaining 10 percent was insured by the company itself. Francis Hyde, *Cunard and the North Atlantic*, 16.

72 Arnell, *Atlantic Mails*, 181.

73 Hyde, *Cunard and the North Atlantic*, 326.

74 Arnell, *Atlantic Mails*, 149.

75 James Campbell to Cunard, June 2, 1841 RG 1, No. 248, 3014 F. 20. PANS

76 *Times*, July 20, 1846.

77 *Daily Atlas*, August 24, 1846.

78 "History of Shipping Subsidies," Part 1, p. 7; Walter Hubbard and Richard F. Winter, *North Atlantic Mail Sailings 1840–1875* (Canton, OH: U.S. Philatelic Society Classics Society, 1988), 12.

Chapter Nine: Collins and Congress

1 David Budlong Tyler, *Steam Conquers the Atlantic* (New York: D. Appleton-Century Company, 1939), 130.

2 George E. Hargest, *History of Letter Post Communication between the United States and Europe, 1845–1875* (Washington: Smithsonian Institution Press, 1971), 1.

3 *New London Morning News*, July 8, 1847.

4 John L. O'Sullivan, *United States Democratic Review* 1, no. 1 (1837): 15.

5 John L. O'Sullivan, "The Great Nation of Futurity," *United States Democratic Review* 6, issue 23 (1839): 427.

6 Chester G. Hearn, *Tracks in the Sea: Matthew Fontaine Maury and the Mapping of the Oceans* (Camden: International Marine, 2002), 81–94; See also Helen M. Rozwad-owski, "Introduction: Reconsidering Matthew Fontaine Maury," *International Journal of Maritime History* 28, no. 8 (May–June 2016): 388–93 and essays following 394–420.

7 Matthew Fontaine Maury, "Scraps from the Lucky Bag, No. II," *Southern Literary Messenger* 6, issue 5 (May 1840): 306. The "lucky bag" was a canvas sack carried aboard ship into which sailors threw lost articles. Hearn, *Tracks in the Sea*, 82.

8 Quoted in *Daily Atlas*, May 13, 1841. Although he is not specifically identified as the proposer, the evidence seems clear that it was he. The 1841 plan is almost identical to what he later proposed and executed. Thomas K. Bullard, *Sails, Steam and Subsidies: The Career of Edward Knight Collins* (Oak Park: Privately Printed, 1990), 17.

9 *Salem Gazette*, May 11, 1841.

10 *Pittsfield Sun*, April 29, 1841; In 1842 *Garrick* was valued at $70,000. Robert G. Albion, *Square-Riggers on Schedule* (Princeton: Princeton University Press, 1938), 101.

11 Mark W. Summers, *The Plundering Generation: Corruption and the Crisis of the Union, 1849–1861* (New York: Oxford University Press, 1987), 99.

12 Bullard, *Sails, Steam and Subsidies*, 17.

13 Until the adoption of the 22nd Amendment, the president took office on March 4.

14 Bullard, *Sails, Steam and Subsidies*, 17.

15 *Daily Atlas*, May 13, 1841. A modern container ship (4000–5000 TEUs) at eighteen knots consumes approximately fifty tons of fuel per day. At twenty knots this same

ship would consume nearly seventy-five tons. Speed is very expensive. https://people
.hofstra.edu/geotrans/eng/ch8en/conc8en/fuel_consumption_containerships.html.

16 *Daily Atlas*, May 13, 1841.

17 Secretary of State Daniel Webster remained in office only long enough to complete
negotiations on the pending Webster-Ashburton Treaty.

18 Bullard, *Sails, Steam and Subsidies*, 17.

19 Edward M. Steel, *T. Butler King of Georgia* (Athens: University of Georgia Press,
1964), 17.

20 The Bill called for appropriation of $789,310 for the support of a Home Squadron
consisting of two frigates, two sloops, two small vessels, and two armed steamers."
H.R.10, 27th Cong. 1st Sess. (1841).

21 Report on the Home Squadron Bill; printed congressional report (27th Cong., 1st
Sess., Report No. 3, House of Representatives.), July 7, 1841.

22 Report on the Home Squadron.

23 President John Tyler, Fourth Annual Message, December 3, 1844, http://www.pre
sidency.ucsb.edu/ws/?pid=29485.

24 *Senate Journal*, 28th Cong., 2nd Sess. (March 1, 1845); U.S. *House Journal*, 1845; 28th
Cong. 2nd Sess. (March 1, 1845).

25 *Statutes at Large*, Act of March 3, 1845, ch. 69.

26 C. L. Grant, "Cave Johnson: Postmaster General," *Tennessee Historical Quarterly*
20, no. 4 (December 1961): 324–25.

27 Grant, "Cave Johnson," 323.

28 Grant, "Cave Johnson," 325.

29 *Baltimore Sun*, October 23, 1845.

30 Brown Shipley and Co. to Brown Brothers, September 2, 1844, Records Brown
Brothers Harriman. NYHS Box 40, Folder 3; Bullard, *Sails, Steam and Subsidies*, 17.

31 Investors were cautious about steam. Torsten Feys, *The Battle for the Migrants: The
Introduction of Steamshipping on the North Atlantic and Its Impact on the European
Exodus* (St. John's: International Maritime Economic Association, 2013), 48–49.

32 Letter from the Postmaster General, March 10, 1846, 29th Cong., 1st Sess., H. Doc
162.

33 Tyler, *Steam Conquers the Atlantic*, 143.

34 Cedric Ridgely-Nevitt, *American Steamships on the Atlantic* (Newark: University of
Delaware Press, 1981), 128; Lars Maischak, *German Merchants in the Nineteenth
Century* (Cambridge: Cambridge University Press, 2013), 141.

35 Quoted in Tyler, *Steam Conquers the Atlantic*, 144.

36 Letter from Postmaster General, March 10, 1846.

37 Bullard, *Sails, Steam and Subsidies*, 17.

38 Collins to Postmaster General, March 6, 1846, quoted in John G. Dow, "The Collins
Line" (MA Thesis, Columbia University, 1937), 8–9.

39 Cong. Globe, 29th Cong., 1st Sess., (June 16, 1846).

40 *Journal of the Senate of the United States* (June 15, 1846).

41 Quoted in Henry Fry, *The History of North Atlantic Steam Navigation* (London: Sampson. Low, Marston and Company, 1896), 65.

42 Cong. Globe, 29th Cong. 1st Sess. (June 17, 1846).

43 *New York Tribune*, December 29, 1847.

44 S. 128 29th Cong. 2nd Sess. (Feb. 17, 1847).

45 Cong. Globe, 29th Cong., 2nd Sess. (March 3, 1847). Act of March 3, 1847, ch 62.

46 *New York Tribune*, March 24, 1847.

47 *New York Herald*, October 1, 1847; Ridgely-Nevitt, *American Steamships*, 128.

48 Another steamer—*United States*, built by a group of New Yorkers—proved equally unsuccessful. She spent most of her time "at anchor awaiting an opportunity to earn her keep." Ridgely-Nevitt, *American Steamers*, 148.

49 Date is from diary of Philip Hone. Newspaper accounts give the 29th. Bayard Tuckerman, ed., *The Diary of Philip Hone* (New York: Dodd, Mead and Company, 1889) 2:334–35.

50 *New York Herald*, January 15, 1858.

51 *Times-Picayune*, January 11, 1848.

52 *Trenton State Gazette*, December 9, 1847.

53 In his *Diary* Philip Hone mentions a "meeting of merchants," with no elaboration that welcomed Captain Ryrie. Bayard, ed. *Hone Diary*, 335. Newspapers as well were reserved and laconic in their accounts of the event.

54 *Times-Picayune*, January 11, 1848.

55 Cunard's home is now part of the campus of Wagner College. Wagner College website, http://wagner.edu/about/visit/campus_facilities/.

56 *Baltimore Sun*, January 1, 1848; *New York Herald*, January 3, 1848.

57 *New York Herald*, January 29, 1848.

Chapter Ten: Competition Begins: Collins versus Cunard

1 Frances Williams, "The Heritage and Preparation of a Statesman, John Y. Mason," *Virginia Magazine of History and Biography* 75, no. 3 (July 1967): 330.

2 K. Jack Bauer, "John Young Mason," in *American Secretaries of the Navy*, ed. Paolo Coletta (Annapolis: Naval Institute Press, 1980) 1:233; William B. Preston, Secretary of the Navy to Senator Thomas Rusk, Chair, Committee on Post Office and Post Roads, June 21, 1850, in Senate Committee Report 202, September 18, 1850, 31st Cong., 1st Sess., p. 42; Harold D. Langley, "William Ballard Preston," in Coletta, ed., *American Secretaries of the Navy*, 1:245–46.

3 Samuel Cunard to Viscount Canning, March 11, 1853. Copy in Blakely Papers, Public Archives of Nova Scotia.

4 "Circular Announcing Establishment of New York House, October 1825," in John Crosby Brown, *A Hundred Years of Merchant Banking* (New York: Privately Printed, 1909), 190.

5 J. R. Killick, "Sir William Brown," *Oxford Dictionary of National Biography*; the early years of Brown Brothers can be followed in Edwin J. Perkins, *Financing Anglo-American Trade: The House of Brown, 1800–1880* (Cambridge: Harvard University

Press, 1975), 17–82; John A. Kouwenhoven, *Partners in Banking: An Historical Portrait of a Great Private Bank, Brown Brothers Harriman and Co., 1818–1968* (Garden City: Doubleday, 1968) provides a more general overview. Perkins, *Financing Anglo-American Trade*, 40; Killick, "Sir William Brown," *Oxford Dictionary of National Biography.* The American consul in Liverpool Nathaniel Hawthorne met Brown at the cornerstone laying of the Liverpool library, to which Brown had made a large gift. He described him as "the plainest and simplest man of all—an exceeding unpretending gentleman in black; small, white-haired, pale, quiet and respectable." Entry for April 19, 1857, in Nathaniel Hawthorne, *English Notebooks*, ed. Randall Stewart (New York: Russell and Russell, 1962), 458.

 6 Perkins, *Financing Anglo-American Trade*, 121.

 7 Perkins, *Financing Anglo-American Trade*, 48–49, 122.

 8 William Bowen to Joseph Shipley, November 29, 1845, quoted in Perkins, 46.

 9 Perkins, *Financing Anglo-American Trade*, 48–49.

10 Perkins, *Financing Anglo-American Trade*, 48.

11 William to James Brown, October 18, 1847, quoted in Killick, "Sir William Brown," *Oxford Dictionary of National Biography.*

12 Collet and Hamilton to William Brown, June 4, 1852, quoted in Perkins, *Financing Anglo-American Trade*, 52.

13 Perkins, *Financing Anglo-American Trade*, 48.

14 William Brown to James Brown, January 23, 1848. Quoted in Killick, "Sir William Brown," *Oxford Dictionary of National Biography.*

15 United States Mail Contract New York and Liverpool (with documents A and B), November 1, 1847. Senate Report 202, 60–66.

16 "Indenture," February 6, 1849, Senate Document 202, 66–68.

17 James Carnahan Wetmore, *The Wetmore Family of America* (Albany: Munsell and Rowland, 1861), 359. Wetmore may well be best remembered for his Italianate-style villa, Chateau-sur-mere, that he built in Newport, Rhode Island. The Preservation Society of Newport County, http://www.newportmansions.org/explore/chateau -sur-mer.

18 Perkins, *Financing Anglo-American Trade*, 56.

19 Cedric Ridgely-Nevitt, *American Steamships on the Atlantic* (Newark: University of Delaware Press, 1981), 130–33.

20 Charles B. Stuart, *The Naval and Mail Steamers of the United States* (New York: Charles B. Norton, Irving House, 1853), 122–23. Stuart began his work with a dedication: "Dedicated with Sentiments of Respect and Esteem to Edward K. Collins To Whose Genius and Untiring Efforts Our Country is Greatly Indebted for one of the Proudest Achievements of Science and Enterprise."

21 Description in Nevitt, *American Steamships*, 99–100.

22 The contract for the *Baltic* and *Arctic* signed April 18, 1849, called for 95-inch diameter cylinders. Stuart, *The Naval and Mail Steamers*, 123.

23 W. S. Lindsay, *History of Merchant Shipping and Ancient Commerce* (New York: AMS repr., 1965), 4:205–8; and John G. Dow, "The Collins Line" (MA Thesis, Department

of Political Science, Columbia University, 1937), 21, gives the diameter at 96 inches. Stuart, *The Naval and Mail Steamers*, 123, reports 95 inches.

24 Frank M. Bennett, *The Steam Navy of the United States* 1:87.

25 Cong Globe, 32nd Cong., 1st Sess. (May 6, 1852).

26 Collins's contract called for five ships. The first four were to be ready within eighteen months and the fifth, later named *Adriatic*, was to come later. Dow, "Collins Line," 8.

27 This may not have been a wise choice. Cunard selected a black top to mask soot. Collins's red would need constant repainting.

28 Samuel Eliot Morison, *"Old Bruin": Commodore Matthew Calbraith Perry* (Boston: Little, Brown and Co., 1967), 253.

29 John H. Schroeder, *Matthew Calbraith Perry: Antebellum Sailor and Diplomat* (Annapolis: Naval Institute Press, 2001), 42, 187.

30 Quoted in Morison, *Old Bruin*, 257.

31 See, for example, Perry to Secretary, August 8, 1850, Matthew Calbraith Perry, Letter book, 1849–1850, misc. manuscripts, Yale University Library, microfilm.

32 William Skiddy, "The Ups and Downs of Sea Life From 1805," transcript of manuscript in William Skiddy Papers, Mystic Seaport Library.

33 Morison, *"Old Bruin,"* 257. Quoting letters.

34 Erastus Smith to President and Directors U.S. Mail Steamer New York and Liverpool Line, May 15, 1851. Erastus Smith Papers Mariners Museum B 1, F 18.

35 William Skiddy to Perry, January 21, 1849, quoted in Cong. Globe, 32nd Cong., 1st Sess. (May 6, 1852).

36 Dow, "The Collins Line," 26.

37 In 1841 Collins had estimated the cost of four 2,500-ton steamers at $750,000 each and had proposed an operating subsidy of only $15,000 per round trip. For political reasons he may have decided that it was easier to obtain a larger operating subsidy and forego the loan. Ironically, by taking the subsidy in advance he was using it as a construction loan. See above.

38 *Laws of New York Passed at the Second Session of the Legislature* (Toy: Albert W. Scribner and Albert West printers, 1849), ch. 407, 564–66.

39 Original Stockholders of the Collins Line. David B. Tyler, *Steam Conquers the Atlantic* (New York: D. Appleton-Century Company, 1939), 391.

James Brown	100 shares
Stewart Brown	15 shares
Samuel Nicholson	15 shares
James N. Brown	5 shares
J. Adger Co.	5 shares
A. Brown and Sons	50 shares
W. Wilson and Sons	10 shares
R. P. Brown	3 shares

Capt. Graham	5 shares
Capt. West	5 shares
De Lancey Kane	15 shares
J. A. Brown	15 shares
W. S. Wetmore	25 shares
E. Riggs	50 shares
E. K. Collins	90 shares
W. H. Brown	15 shares
J. M. Geery	10 shares
Capt. E. Nye	10 shares
E. B. Cobb	10 shares
J. C. Luce	15 shares
T. T. Woodruff	10 shares
J. H. Coley	5 shares
Stillman Allen Co.	10 shares
W. Redman	5 shares
Rowland Redmond	15 shares
Henry Dangerfield	5 shares
Susan A. Winson	5 shares
T. D. Stewart	5 shares
S. Coley	5 shares
Geo. Peabody	5 shares

40 United States Attorney's Office, November 29, 1847, Senate Report 202, 63.

41 Stuart, *The Naval and Mail Steamers*, 90.

42 Dow, "The Collins Line," 23. Collins gave an estimate of over $600,000. Collins to Senator Rusk, June 6, 1850, in Senate Doc. 202, 118.

43 Allaire Works to Collins, June 1, 1850, Erastus Smith Papers, Mariners Museum B 1 F 12.

44 Dow, "Collins Line," 26.

45 Collins to Rusk, June 6, 1850, Senate Report 202, p. 119.

46 G. W. Sheldon, "Old Shipbuilders of New York," *Harpers New Monthly Magazine* 65, issue 386 (July 1882): 235.

47 *New York Herald*, February 3, 1849.

48 "The Building of the Ship," *Complete Poetical Works of Henry Wadsworth Longfellow* (Boston: Houghton Mifflin, 1902).

49 *Senate Journal*, 31st Cong. 1st Sess. (May 28, 1850).

50 Senate Report 202.

51 Senate Report 202, 6.

52 Senate Report 202, 6.

53 *Pittsfield Sun*, May 9, 1850.

54 *Savannah Republican*, April 26, 1850.

55 *Daily Missouri Republican*, May 4, 1850.

56 Benjamin Silliman and C. R. Goodrich, *The World of Art and Industry* (New York: G. P. Putnam, 1854), 107.

57 *Edinburgh Journal* quoted in *Harpers* 1, issue 3:412.

58 *Illustrated London News*, May 25, 1850.

59 *Chambers Edinburgh Journal* quoted in *Harpers*, 411; designed by Isambard Kingdom Brunel, *Great Britain* was a marvel for her time. Launched in 1843, she was built of iron and powered by a screw propeller. In 1846 she ran aground on the coast of Ireland. After nearly a year she was freed and brought to Liverpool and laid up. Nicholas Fogg, *The Voyages of the Great Britain* (London: Chatham Publishing, 2002), 21–26.

60 Dow, "Collins Line," 32.

61 Adrian Jarvis, *Liverpool Central Docks: 1799–1905: An Illustrated History* (Liverpool: National Museums and Galleries, 1991), 9.

62 Graeme J. Milne, *Trade and Traders in Mid-Victorian Liverpool: Mercantile Business and the Making of a World Port* (Liverpool: Liverpool University Press, 2000), 86.

63 Description is from *Chamber's Edinburgh Journal* as quoted in *Harpers* 1, issue 3: 411–14.

64 This is the origin of the modern term "bridge," describing the place from which a vessel is commanded. John G. Rogers, *Origin of Sea Terms* (Mystic, CT: Mystic Seaport Museum, 1985), 25.

65 Cunard to Charles MacIver, May 1, 1847, quoted in Edward P. Sloan, "Collins vs. Cunard: The Realities of a North Atlantic Steamship Rivalry, 1850–1858," *International Journal of Maritime History*, vol. 4, no. 1 (June 1992), 90.

66 Killick, "Sir William Brown," *Oxford Dictionary of National Biography*.

67 This arrangement remained hidden from the public until 1975, when Francis Hyde discovered the evidence in the Cunard corporate papers and published it in his history *Cunard and the North Atlantic*. Francis Hyde, *Cunard and the North Atlantic, 1840–1975* (Liverpool: University of Liverpool, 1975): 39–45.

Chapter Eleven: Crossing the Atlantic: Life Aboard

1 John G. Dow, "The Collins Line" (MA Thesis, Columbia University, 1937), 43. *Atlantic*'s registered tonnage 2845, RG 41, Bureau of Marine Inspection and Navigation Custom House Documentation, National Archives; *Pacific*'s registered tonnage 2707, RG 41, National Archives;

  Baltic's registered tonnage 2552, RG 41, National Archives;

  Arctic's registered tonnage 2654, RG 41, National Archives;

  Adriatic's registered tonnage, 4154, RG 41, National Archives.

2 Quoted in Dow, "The Collins Line," 37.

3 Dow, "The Collins Line," 44. British and American figures do differ, but the general comparison remains much in favor of Collins. Quoted in Carl Cutler, *Greyhounds of the Sea* (New York: G.P. Putnam, 1930), 201.

4 This was the same summer that American yacht *America* won the Royal Regatta at Cowes.

5 The Bremen Line carried 2,053 and the Havre Line passengers numbered 1,645. Dow, "The Collins Line," 45.

6 Royal Meeker, *History of Shipping Subsidies, Part I* (New York: Published for the American Economic Association by the Macmillan Co., 1905), 9; *London Daily News*, Nov. 11, 1850.

7 Brandon DuPont and Thomas Weiss, "Overseas Travel by Americans, 1820–1860," *Cliometrica* (2013) 7:322, Table 1.

8 Doug Hart, "The Grand Saloon and Victorian Propriety," *Powerships* no. 298 (Summer 2016): 215–26. After accounting for machinery, coal, stores, and crew accommodations there was little space left for passengers. In 1851 Collins did introduce a lower cost "second-class cabin" at a rate of $70 compared to $120 for first class. This would seem to be an end run around his contract with Cunard. *Daily Atlas*, Dec. 12, 1851.

9 Abbott, a graduate of Bowdoin College, wrote more than 180 books. Among them was a ten-book series, *Rollo in Europe*.

10 Abbott, *Rollo on the Atlantic* (Boston: Brown and Taggard, 1853), ch. 5.

11 Philip Sutton and Stephen A. Schwarzman, Milstein Division of United States History, Local History and Genealogy, "Maury and the Menu: A Brief History of the Cunard Steamship Company," http://www.nypl.org/blog/2011/06/30/maury-menu -brief-history-cunard-steamship-company.

12 For the advice given on how women ought to behave on a crossing see Eliza Leslie, *Miss Leslie's Behaviour Book: A Guide and Manual for Ladies* (Philadelphia: T. B. Peterson, 1859), 143–49.

13 Abbott, *Rollo on the Atlantic*, ch. 9.

14 John S. C. Abbott, "Ocean Life," *Harpers Monthly Magazine* 5, issue 25 (June–November, 1852): 64–65.

15 This does not include groundings or collisions at sea with other vessels or icebergs.

16 September 7, 1851, Journal of the *Baltic*, Comstock Family Papers, Rhode Island Historical Society.

17 March 10, 1854, Journal of the *Baltic*.

18 March 10, 1854, Journal of the *Baltic*. Since ships lost by collision with icebergs were likely to disappear without notice, the records concerning such events are sketchy. Institute for Ocean Technology Ice Database, http://www.icedata.ca/index.php.

19 Charles Dickens, *American Notes* (London: Chapman and Hall, 1852) 1:39–40.

20 Sutton and Schwarzman, "Maury and the Menu."

21 Thurlow Weed, *Letters from Europe and the West Indies* (Albany: Weed, Parsons and Co., 1866), 408.

22 Bullard, *Sails, Steams and Subsidy*, 22–23.

23 Abbott, "Ocean Life," 62; Sutton and Schwarzman, "Maury and the Menu."

24 Catherine Hooper Voorsanger and John K. Howat, *Art and the Empire City, New York 1825–1861* (New York: Metropolitan Museum, 2000), 366. The flatware was square-tipped, narrowing down to the neck. It was likely manufactured at the Oneida Community in upstate New York.

25 Horace Greeley, *Glances at Europe* (New York: DeWitt and Davenport, 1851), 16.

26 Eliza Leslie, *Miss Leslie's Behaviour Book*, 143–49. Douglas Hart, "Sociability and 'Separate Spheres' on the North Atlantic: The Interior Architecture of British Atlantic Liners, 1840–1930," *Journal of Social History* 44, no. 1 (Fall 2010): 189–212.

27 *New York Times*, June 21, 1861.

28 Douglass's birth date is uncertain. Frederick Douglass, *Narrative of the Life of Frederick Douglass: An American Slave* (London: H. G. Collins, 1851), 1.

29 John R. McKitigan, ed., *Frederick Douglass Papers, Series Three, Correspondence* (New Haven: Yale University Press, 2009), 1:xlviii.

30 John W. Blassingame, ed., *The Frederick Douglass Papers, Series One, Speeches, Debates, Interviews* (New Haven: Yale University Press, 1979), 1:63–65.

31 Blassingame, *Frederick Douglass*, 63–65.

32 Douglass to *Times*, April 6, 1847. The *Liberator*, May 14, 1847, carried a number of articles about the incident.

33 *Times*, April 8, 1847.

34 Cunard to *Times*, April 13, 1847.

35 *Baltimore Sun*, July 20, 1860; *Macon [GA] Gazette*, July 31, 1860; and *Trenton State Gazette*, September 17, 1860.

36 The custom of a ship's officer, often the master, conducting religious services following the Anglican tradition, remains today aboard Cunard ships. Other denominational services are also held.

37 The ensuing events are described in *Brooklyn Eagle*, September 23, 1850.

38 Henry Fry, *The History of North Atlantic Steam Navigation* (London: Sampson, Low, Marston and Company, 1896), 81.

39 Fry, *The History of North Atlantic Steam Navigation*, 81.

40 *Punch* 21 (1851), 117.

41 *Boston Daily Atlas*, June 6, 1851.

42 *Times*, August 9, 1852 quoted in Middletown (CT) *Constitution*, September 1, 1852.

Chapter Twelve: A Rising Storm in Congress

1 President Andrew Jackson's Veto Message, July 10, 1832, http://avalon.law.yale.edu/19th_century/ajveto01.asp.

2 Cong Globe, 32nd Cong., 1st Sess. (April 21, 1852).

3 *Baltimore Sun*, September 23, 1850.

4 P. T. Barnum, *Forty Years' Recollections* (New York: American News Company, 1871), 282.

5 Certificate of Registry Atlantic, April 26, 1850; Bureau of Marine Inspection and Navigation, RG 41 National Archives. RG 41.

6 *Liverpool Mercury*, August 6, 1850.

7 "To Captain West," in Anne Charlotte Lynch Botta, *Poems* (New York: Putnam, 1849).

8 *New York Weekly Herald*, September 7, 1850.

9 *Herald*, September 7, 1850.

10 *Herald*, September 7, 1850.

11 *Herald*, September 7, 1850

12 *Herald*, September 7, 1850.

13 *Herald*, September 7, 1850.

14 *Herald*, September 2, 1850.

15 *Herald*, September 7, 1850; *New Hampshire Gazette*, September 10, 1850.

16 *Barre Gazette*, June 15, 1849; *Boston Emancipator and Republican*, June 28, 1849; *Liverpool Mercury*, May 2, 1848. In 1856 *Ashburton* set the record for slowest crossing of the Atlantic by any packet—eighty-nine days. Robert G. Albion, *Square-Riggers on Schedule* (Princeton: Princeton University Press, 1938), 197.

17 John F. Maguire, *Father Mathew: A Biography* (London: Longman, Green, Longman, Roberts and Green, 1863), 462.

18 *Baltimore Sun*, November 10, 1851; *Trenton State Gazette*, November 11, 1851; "Theobald Mathew," in *Oxford Dictionary of National Biography*.

19 Robert F. Dalzell, *American Participation in the Great Exhibition of 1851* (Amherst: Amherst College Press, 1960), 7–12.

20 *Trenton State Gazette*, July 23, 1851.

21 *London Illustrated News*, December 6, 1851.

22 Quoted in Fry, *History of North Atlantic Steam Navigation*, 73.

23 "Ocean Steam Navigation,' *North American Review*, October 1864, 505, 494.

24 "Ocean Steam Navigation," 493.

25 *Ohio State Journal*, November 26, 1850.

26 *Baltimore Sun*, January 27, 1851.

27 Cong. Globe, 32nd Cong., 1st Sess. (May 8, 1852).

28 Cong. Globe, 29th Cong., 1st Sess. (August 12, 1846).

29 "Bitter Feelings in the Senate Chamber" http://www.senate.gov/artandhistory/history/minute/Bitter_Feelings_In_the_Senate_Chamber.htm.

30 Daniel Webster to Robert Cumming Schenck, February 17, 1851. Charles Wiltse and Michael J. Birkner, eds., *The Papers of Daniel Webster*. Ser. 1 (Dartmouth: University Press of New England, 1986), 7:204; Webster to Collins, July 29, 1851, 7:497.

31 John G. Dow, "Collins Line," (MA Thesis, Columbia University, 1937), 49. By this time Cunard was offering weekly service to New York.

32 Quoted in Ari Hoogenboom, *Gustavus Vasa Fox* (Baltimore: Johns Hopkins Press, 2008), 47.

33 *Baltimore Sun*, January 26, 1851; Gustavus Vasa Fox *Journal*, June 1851–December 1855, quoted in Edward W. Sloan, "The Baltic Goes to Washington: Lobbying for a Congressional Steamship Subsidy, 1852, *Northern Mariner*, no. 1 (January 1995): 21.

34 *Baltimore Sun*, February 27, 1852.

35 *Baltimore Sun*, February 27, 1852.

36 Cong. Globe, 32nd Cong. 1st Sess. (March 5, 1852).

37 Cong. Globe, 32nd Cong., 1st Sess., 657.

38 For an analysis of the period see Mark W. Summers, *The Plundering Generation: Corruption and the Crisis of the Union, 1849–1861* (New York: Oxford University Press, 1987).

39 Jeffrey L. Pasky, "Democracy, Gentility, and Lobbying in the Early U.S. Congress," in *The American Congress: The Building of Democracy*, ed. E. Zeilzer (Boston: Houghton Mifflin, 2004), 44.

40 Cong. Globe, 32nd Cong., 1st Sess. (March 5, 1852); *Trenton State Gazette*, March 3, 1852.

41 *Baltimore Sun*, March 3, 1852.

42 *Baltimore Sun*, March 3, 4, 1852.

43 *Trenton State Gazette*, March 2, 1852.

44 *New York Herald*, March 7, 1852, quoted in Sloan, "The Baltic Goes to Washington," 24.

45 *Richmond Enquirer*, March 26, 1852.

46 *Baltimore Sun*, March 3, 1852.

47 Cong. Globe, 32nd Cong., 1st Sess. (March 27, 1852).

48 Cong. Globe, 32nd Cong., 1st Sess. (April 21, 1852). This was a state-chartered railroad intended to link Erie, Pennsylvania, on Lake Erie with Sunbury in northeastern Pennsylvania on the Susquehanna River. *Poor's Manual of Railroads in the United States* (New York: Poor's Publications, 1903), 722.

49 Cong. Globe, 32nd Cong., 1st Sess. (April 21, 1852).

50 Cong. Globe, 32nd Cong., 1st Sess., 1146.

51 Act of July 21, 1852, ch. 66; Dow, "The Collins Line," 58–59.

52 As is often the case in long debates speakers repeated information. The debates are recorded in the Journal of the Senate 32nd Cong., 1st Sess., passim.

53 *New York Evening Post*, May 8, 1852, as cited in Dow, "The Collins Line," 59.

54 Cong. Globe, 32nd Cong., 1st Sess. (May 17, 1852).

55 Bullard, *Sails, Steam and Subsidies*, 37.

56 William Bowen to Brown Brothers, June 12, 1852, Box 40, f. 3 Records of Brown Brothers Harriman, NYHS.

57 *Baltimore Sun*, July 3, 1852.

58 *Boston Daily Atlas*, July 1, 1852.

59 Act of July 21, 1852, ch. 66; Dow, "Collins Line," 63.

60 William Bowen to Brown Brothers, June 12, 1852.

61 Bowen to Brown (New York) July 15, 1852, Box 40, F. 3, Records Brown Brothers Harriman, New York Historical Society.

Chapter Thirteen: Vesta

1 *Boston Daily Atlas*, July 1, 1852.

2 *Times*, August 2, 1852; *Illustrated London News*, May 31, 1851.

3 Edwin Hodder, *Sir George Burns* (London: Hodder and Stoughton, 1890), 297.

4 Royal Meeker, "History of Shipping Subsidies," *Publications of the American Economic Association*, 3rd series, no. 3 (August 1905), 8. The British and North American Royal Mail Steam Packet Company (Cunard) remained a partnership until incorporated in 1878. Eric Flounders and Michael Gallagher, *The Story of Cunard's 175 Years* (Ramsey, Isle of Man: Ferry Publications, 2014), 27.

5 Screw propulsion made its appearance between 1833 and 1836. The first iron-hulled screw-propulsion vessel in the Cunard fleet was *British Queen*, which he purchased in 1851. She served in the Mediterranean. Collins never adopted either iron hulls or screw propulsion. For him, and Cunard to a point, paddle wheels and wood were "fool proof." Carl Cutler, *Greyhounds of the Sea* (New York: G.P. Putnam, 1940), 147. See also David Budlong Tyler, *Steam Conquers the Atlantic* (New York: D. Appleton-Century Company, 1939), 169–72, 184–85; in 1863, before a Parliamentary Committee Cunard testified that he was reluctant to adopt screw propulsion because he feared that it would force him to carry steerage passengers, which he thought would be uneconomical. "Note," Blakely Papers, Public Archives of Nova Scotia F 28. For a discussion of carrying steerage passengers in the age of steamers see Raymond L. Cohn, *Mass Migration under Sail* (Cambridge: Cambridge University Press, 2009), 223–25.

6 *Times-Picayune*, October 18, 1853.

7 *Washington Daily Globe*, April 7, 1858.

8 *New York Herald*, March 12, 1853; *Middletown Connecticut Constitution*, May 5, 1852.

9 Emery R. Johnson, *History of Domestic and Foreign Commerce of the United States* (New York: Burt Franklin, repr., 1964), 2:46.

10 The first transatlantic cable linking Newfoundland to Ireland was completed in 1858.

11 *New Hampshire Patriot*, October 24, 1850.

12 *New York Times*, October 3, 1851.

13 *Harper's New Monthly Magazine* 7, issue 38 (July 1853): 273; Harry Sinclair Drago, *The Steamboaters* (New York: Bramhall House, 1967), 17.

14 While steamships made a dramatic impact, for some time the sailing ship remained dominant, particularly on long ocean voyages. The adoption of the iron hull and screw propulsion, the development of improved engines, and the opening of the Suez Canal would eventually prove decisive. Gerald S. Graham, "The Ascendancy of the Sailing Ship, 1850–1885," *Economic History Review* 9, no. 1 (1956): 74–88.

15 In 1856 Nathaniel Currier joined in partnership with James Ives to form Currier and Ives. Because of the high cost of construction and operation, clippers eventually proved uneconomical. Carl Cutler, *Greyhounds of the Sea: The Story of the American Clipper Ship* (New York: G. P. Putnam's Sons, 1930), 353–76; Glenn A. Knoblock, *The American Clipper Ship, 1845–1920* (Jefferson: McFarland and Company, 2013), 232–54.

16 *Harper's Magazine* 7, issue 38, (July 1853): 273.

17 *Times-Picayune*, July 23, 1853.

18 *Times-Picayune*, July 26, 1854. The prize for the fastest crossing became known as the "Blue Riband."

19 *Times-Picayune*, July 26, 1854.

20 Robert G. Albion, *Square-Riggers on Schedule* (Princeton: Princeton University Press, 1938), 170–71.

21 No Author, *Ships and Shipmasters of Old Providence* (Providence: Providence Insti-
    tution for Savings, 1919), 48–49.

22 Steam whistles were not in general use aboard ocean liners. William Henry Flay-
    hart, *Disaster at Sea* (New York: W.W. Norton, 2003), 38.

23 "Frightful Collisions at Sea," *Scientific American* 10, issue 6 (Oct 21, 1854): 45.

24 Journal of U.S. mail steamer *Baltic*, 1850–1855, Comstock Family Papers, Rhode
    Island Historical Society; *Honolulu Friend*, April 1, 1854.

25 John A. Butler, *Atlantic Kingdom: America's Contest with Cunard in the Age of Sail and
    Steam* (Washington: Brassey, 2001), 202.

26 *Times-Picayune*, April 27, 1853.

27 *Baltimore Sun*, August 4, 1854.

28 Numbers vary. These numbers are taken from the *Liverpool Mercury*, quoting
    Collins's Liverpool agent Brown, Shipley. *Liverpool Mercury*, October 13, 1854.

29 These numbers are calculated from the *Liverpool Mercury* list. Entries such as "friends"
    and "servants" make it impossible to calculate precisely the gender of those aboard,
    nor are the terms "children" and "infant" well defined. *Liverpool Mercury*, October
    13, 1854.

30 Seamen working aboard steamships generally received higher wages than those on
    sailing vessels. Arthur L. Bowley, *Wages in the United Kingdom in the Nineteenth
    Century* (Cambridge: University Press, 1900), 79.

31 Bullard, *Sails, Steam and Subsidies*, 23. These numbers varied from voyage to
    voyage, as the number of crew employed aboard depended upon the number of
    passengers being served. The numbers here reflect a "full ship."

32 The shift from sail to steam and its impact on life at sea has long been a favorite topic
    for historians as well as novelists. See, for example, John Stilgoe, *Lifeboat* (Char-
    lottesville: University of Virginia Press, 2003), 20–39; as well as works by William
    McPhee, Rudyard Kipling, and Joseph Conrad.

33 A steamer of 2,500 tons traveling at 10 knots burned 41.2 tons of coal per day. The
    same ship traveling at 12 knots burned 71.2 tons per day. Bullard, *Sails, Steam and
    Subsidies*, 49.

34 Tyler, *Steam Conquers the Atlantic*, 188; *Brooklyn Eagle*, December 31, 1850.

35 While freely admitting that the data is incomplete and often conflicting, Bullard,
    Sails, Steam and Subsidies, 48, drawing from congressional documents, offers the
    following figures. Data is arranged by round trips:

Category	December 1851	February 1855
Expenses	$8,845	$83,210 (combining expense, fuel, engine repairs, extra engine work, other expenses)
Fuel	8,612*	
Engine repairs	4,572	
Extra engine work	4,643	

Other expenses	12,762	
Insurance	8,904	19,493
Interest on above	8,438	5,000
Depreciation	8,438	5,000

*This number seems suspiciously low.

The large increase in expenses (not itemized) for 1855 likely reflects repairs and replacement on worn-out machinery. The estimate for crew costs, likely included in "expenses" and "other expenses," was approximately $10,500. Collins paid considerably more than Cunard. Cunard captains earned $2,500 per year. Collins paid his masters $6,000 per year. Dow, "The Collins Line," 59.

36 For his steamers at the Jersey pier Cunard imported coal from his own Cape Breton mines. *Scientific American* 8, issue 34 (May 7, 1853): 268.

37 William J. Tenney, ed., *Mining Magazine* 3 (New York: John F. Trow, printer, 1854), 442–44.

38 *Inventions and Designs Issued by the United States from 1790 to 1847* (Washington: J. and G. S. Gideon, 1847), 160.

39 "Wethered's Steam and Stame Apparatus," *Scientific American* 10, issue 6 (October 21, 1854): 45; *Trenton State Gazette*, December 6, 1850.

40 *Scientific American* 10, issue 6 (October 21, 1854): 45.

41 *Pittsfield Sun*, August 3, 1854; *Times-Picayune*, August 26, 1854.

42 New Orleans *Daily Picayune*, September 2, 1854.

43 New Orleans *Daily Picayune*, September 1, 2, 1854: On the other hand, the *Missouri Republican*, September 9, 1854, reported that the machinery had been installed "successfully."

44 Graeme J. Milne, *Trade and Traders in Mid-Victorian Liverpool* (Liverpool: Liverpool University Press, 2000): 72–75.

45 *Report of Commissioners Relative to Encroachment and Preservation of the Harbor of New York* (Albany: C. Van Benthuysen, 1856), 8.

46 *Trenton State Gazette*, August 7, 1851.

47 Thomas Baines, *History of the Commerce and Town of Liverpool* (London: Longman, Brown, Green and Longman 1852), 769–70.

48 Given the complications and expense of remaining in a dock, Collins's ships left as soon as possible and moored in the river to await passengers and mail. *New York Herald*, March 12, 1853.

49 Alexander Crosby Brown, *Women and Children Last* (New York: G.P. Putnam's Sons, 1961), 32–37. Brown notes that the ship was so full that a group of eighteen Roman Catholic Nuns bound for California who had planned to sail on *Arctic* had to remain in Liverpool when accommodations could not be found on the ship. Brown, 37.

50 Brandon DuPont and Thomas Weiss, "Variability in Overseas Travel by Americans, 1820–2000," *Cliometrica* (2013): 322.

51 David W. Shaw, *The Sea Shall Embrace Them: The Tragic Story of the Steamship Arctic* (New York; The Free Press, 2002), 78–80; "M. Woodruff and Lady" are also listed, *New York Times*, October 7, 1854.

52 Passenger and crew lists appeared in a number of newspapers. Not all agree. The most reliable is the list provided by the agent in Liverpool. *Liverpool Mercury*, October 13, 1854.

53 *Liverpool Mercury*, October 31, 1854.

54 *Vesta* has also been described rigged as a schooner.

55 In 1536 Jacques Cartier claimed the islands of St. Pierre and Miquelon for France. As a result of the wars between France and England the islands changed hands several times until finally after the second abdication of Napoleon (1815) they were returned to the possession of France. They quickly became an important base for French fishing on the Grand Banks. "St Pierre and Miquelon," in Norah Story, *The Oxford Companion to Canadian History and Literature* (Toronto: Oxford University Press, 1967), 743. See also "Histoire des Iles St. Pierre et Miquelon," http://grandcolombier .com/category/english/.

56 Alexander Crosby Brown, "The Steamer *Vesta:* Neglected Partner in a Fatal Collision," *American Neptune* 20 (1960): 177–78, 180.

57 Flayhart, *Disaster at Sea*, 25.

58 *Washington Sentinel*, October 20, 1854.

59 *Times*, October 31, 1854.

60 *Baltimore Sun*, October 12, 1854.

61 The custom of sitting at individual tables aboard passenger ships did not arrive until some years later.

62 *Liverpool Mercury*, November 10, 1854.

63 *Liverpool Mercury*, November 10, 1854.

Chapter Fourteen: The Arctic *Disaster*

1 Several firsthand accounts of *Arctic*'s collision with *Vesta*, and her subsequent sinking, were published in both the United States and Great Britain. Crew who wrote included Captain James Luce, third mate Francis Dorian, assistant storekeeper Peter McCabe, and fireman Patrick Tobin. Passengers James Smith and George Burns also left accounts. Captain James Russell, master of the *Cambria*, left an account of his role in the rescue. *Vesta*'s captain Alphonse Duchesne's comments have also been published. For an overview of these accounts and links to them see Alexander Crosby Brown, *Women and Children Last*; Brown, "The Steamer *Vesta*: Neglected Partner in a Fatal Collision," *American Neptune Magazine* 20 (July 1960): 177–84; Henry Howe, "Destruction of the Ocean Steamer *Arctic*, by Collision with the *Vesta*, a French Propeller on the Banks of Newfoundland," reprinted in Rainer K. Baehre, ed., *Outrageous Seas: Shipwreck and Survival in the Waters Off Newfoundland 1583–1893* (Montreal: McGill–Queen's University Press, 1999), 281–308; and "Loss of the Steamer *Arctic*," http://steamerarctic.blogspot.com/.

2 *St. John's Public Ledger*, October 3, 1854. Quoted in "Loss of the Steamer *Arctic*," http://steamerarctic.blogspot.com/.

3 This observation was made in a letter from Charles C. Nott written in 1912 recalling events. Alexander Crosby Brown, "A Footnote to the Loss of the *Arctic*," *American Neptune Magazine* 19 (April 1959): 129.

4 *Statutes at Large*, 32nd Cong., 1st Sess., Act of August 30, 1852, ch. 106.

5 John R. Stilgoe, *Lifeboat* (Charlottesville: University of Virginia Press, 2003), 148.

6 "Every such vessel, carrying passengers, shall have at least two good and suitable boats, supplied with oars, in good condition at all times for service, one of which boats shall be a life-boat made of metal, fire proof, and in all respects a good, substantial, safe sea boat, capable of sustaining inside and outside, fifty persons, with life-lines attached to the gunwale, at suitable distances. And every such vessel of more than five hundred tons, and not exceeding eight hundred tons measurement, shall have three life-boats; and every such vessel of more than eight hundred tons, and not exceeding fifteen hundred tons measurement, shall have four life-boats; and every such vessel of more than fifteen hundred tons measurement, shall have six life-boats—all of which boats shall be furnished with oars and other necessary apparatus." *Statutes at Large*, 32nd Cong., 1st Sess., Act of August 30, 1852, ch. 106. The law did not apply to sailing vessels. The lack of concern for lifeboats and the requirement for life preservers suggests that in its actions Congress was more concerned with coastal, lake, and river steamers than those on the high seas.

7 *Boston Daily Atlas*, October 16, 1854.

8 *Times*, November 3, 1854.

9 *Times*, November 3, 1854.

10 Brown, "A Footnote," 130.

11 *Times*, November 3, 1854.

12 *Times*, October 27, 1854.

13 *Sacramento Daily Union*, November 15, 1854. In "Heads of the Colored People: The Schoolmaster," *Frederick Douglass' Newspaper*, November 3, 1854, the black abolitionist and New York physician James McCune Smith celebrated the heroism of Holland and Downer. He expected a monument to be erected to Holland but not to Downer because she was "a woman and colored." John Stauffer, ed., *The Works of James McCune Smith* (New York: Oxford University Press, 2006), 227–28.

14 *Delaware State Reporter*, October 13, 1854.

15 *Delaware State Reporter*, October 13, 1854.

16 *Delaware State Reporter*, October 13, 1854.

17 "4 Phases of Cold Water Immersion," http://beyondcoldwaterbootcamp.com/4 -phases-of-cold-water-immersion; "Hypothermia," http://www.seagrant.umn.edu /coastal_communities/hypothermia#time; Luce noted that the water temperature was 45 degrees. *Boston Daily Atlas*, October 16, 1854. The average fall temperature at this location today (2016) is 50–55° Fahrenheit. Communication with Captain Albert E. Theberge, NOAA, July 15, 2016.

18 *Washington Daily Globe*, October 13, 1854.

19 *Boston Daily Atlas*, October 16, 1854.

20 Since *Arctic*'s exact resting place is uncertain the precise depth of the water in which she lies cannot be known. In the area where she went down, however, the waters are fairly shallow at less than 100 fathoms. Communication with Captain Albert E. Theberge. With her heavy iron boilers, furnaces, and engines pulling her down, it would not have taken long for her to strike bottom.

21 Allen's company Stillman, Allen, better known as the Novelty Iron Works, had built engines for *Arctic* and *Atlantic*. Allen himself was an investor in the Collins Line.

22 *Washington Daily Globe*, October 13, 1854.

23 *Washington Daily Globe*, October 13, 1854.

24 Howe, "Destruction of the Ocean Steamer *Arctic*," in Baehre, ed., *Outrageous Seas: Shipwreck and Survival*, 301.

25 *Boston Daily Atlas*, October 12, 1854.

26 It may have been that the others who stayed aboard *Huron* did so to avoid encountering a public likely to condemn their actions.

27 Report of Captain Russell, *Sacramento Daily Union*, November 15, 1854.

28 *St John's Public Ledger and General Advertiser*, October 3, 1854, http://steamerarctic.blogspot.com/.

29 http://steamerarctic.blogspot.com/.

30 *Trenton State Gazette*, October 5, 1854.

31 New Orleans *Daily Picayune*, October 10, 1854.

32 *The Diary of George Templeton Strong*, eds. Allan Nevins and Milton Halsey Thomas (New York: Octagon Books, 1974, repr.), 2:186.

33 Brown, *Women and Children Last*, 159.

34 *Weekly Herald*, October 21, 1854.

35 Howe, "Destruction of the Ocean Steamer *Arctic*," in Baehre, 303.

36 Strong, *Diary*, 2: 188.

37 Cortlandt Van Rensselaer, "God's Way in the Deep; A Discourse on the Occasion of the Wreck of the *Arctic*" (Delivered in the Presbyterian Church, Burlington, New Jersey, October 15, 1854); Robin Miskolcze, *Women and Children First: Nineteenth-Century Sea Narratives and American Identity* (Lincoln: University of Nebraska Press, 2007), 53.

38 David Bevan, *Drums of the Birkenhead* (Aylesbury, Bucks: A. Larson, 1972), 37.

39 Bevan, *Drums*, 41.

40 Bevan, *Drums*, 45.

41 Bevan, *Drums*, 49.

42 Bevan, *Drums*, 49.

43 Miskolcze, *Women and Children First*, xx.

44 *Times*, November 1, 1854; November 14, 1854.

45 *Times*, October 27, 1854.

46 Beecher, October 15, 1854 quoted in Dow, "The Collins Line," 71.

47 *Middletown Constitution*, December 27, 1854.

48 Strong, *Diary*, 2:192.

49 *Times*, October 28, 1854.

50 *Times*, October 28, 1854.

51 July 1849 Colonization Circular no. 9, 23, https://www.nla.gov.au/ferguson/14614 278/18490731/00000009/17–24.pdf.

52 *Times-Picayune*, October 17, 1854. The company also ordered the use of the steam whistle and bells during reduced visibility. *Boston Daily Atlas*, October 24, 1854.

53 *Boston Daily Atlas*, October 24, 1854. Matthew Fontaine Maury also chimed in and suggested that lanes be established for ships crossing the Atlantic. Maury, *Lanes for Steamers Crossing the Atlantic* (New York: The Underwriters, 1855).

54 *Boston Daily Atlas*, October 24, 1854. In July 1853 Luce's friend Samuel Colt, following *Arctic*'s record passage, presented the captain with a "cased, etched, engraved and gold washed navy revolver contained within a deluxe rosewood-veneered brass-bound case." Sotheby's auction catalogue, *Heal Cali Collection of Fine American Percussion Revolvers and Civil War Carbines*, May 12, 2014.

55 Franklin Pierce, *Second Annual Message*, December 4, 1854, http://www.presi dency.ucsb.edu/ws/?pid=29495.

Chapter Fifteen: Commodore Vanderbilt

1 John G. Langley, *Steam Lion: A Biography of Samuel Cunard* (Halifax: Brick Tower Press, 2006), 119.

2 *Times*, October 30, 1854.

3 Quoted in Langley, *Steam Lion*, 112.

4 *Wealth and Biography of the Wealthy Citizens of New York City* (New York: Published at the Sun Office, 1845), 30.

5 Wheaton Lane, *Commodore Vanderbilt: An Epic of the Steam Age* (New York: Alfred A. Knopf, 1942), 11.

6 Lane, *Commodore Vanderbilt*, 13; T. J. Stiles, *The First Tycoon: The Epic Life of Cornelius Vanderbilt* (New York: Alfred A. Knopf, 2009), 23.

7 Quoted in Lane, *Commodore Vanderbilt*, 14.

8 Lane, *Commodore Vanderbilt*, 71.

9 Richard Barry, "The Four Hundred," *Pearson's Magazine*, 26, no. 6 (December 1911): 715; Vanderbilt had very little formal education. He generally spelled phonetically or, as he called it, "according to common sense." Lane, *Commodore Vanderbilt*, 12, 109.

10 Lane, *Commodore Vanderbilt*, 137.

11 Lane, *Commodore Vanderbilt*, 109, 137.

12 J.J. Colledge, *Ships of the Royal Navy* (New York: Augustus Kelley, 1969), 1:591.

13 Lane, *Commodore Vanderbilt*, 107.

14 For an overview of the voyage see John O. Choules, *The Cruise of the Steam Yacht North Star* (Boston: Gould and Lincoln, 1854), 36, 50.

15 Mark Summers, *The Plundering Generation* (New York: Oxford University Press, 1987), 104–6; Stiles, *The First Tycoon*, 258.

16 "Jeremiah Simonson," http://www.shipbuildinghistory.com/shipyards/19thcentury/simonson.htm; "Smaller Transatlantic Steamship Lines, 1853–1926," http://siegelauctions.com/ph/pdf/052.pdf.

17 Stiles, *The First Tycoon*, 257; *Times*, January 1, 1855.

18 *New York Times*, March 9, 1855, January 5, 1877; *Times-Picayune*, February 24, 1855; Stiles, *First Tycoon*, 258.

19 Cong. Globe, 33rd Cong., 1st Sess. (August 4, 1854); *Times-Picayune*, January 1, 1855.

20 *Times-Picayune*, January 23, 1855.

21 H.R.595, "Making Appropriations for the Transportation of United States Mail," 33rd Cong., 2nd Sess.

22 *Times-Picayune*, January 23, 1855.

23 *Sails, Steam and Subsidies*, 38.

24 Olds's long and tedious remarks are contained in Cong. Globe, 33rd Cong., 2nd Sess., Appendix (February 15, 1855), 178–86.

25 Cong. Globe 33rd Cong., 1st Sess. (July 29, 1854); John G. Dow, "The Collins Line," 73.

26 *New York Times*, February 16, 1855; Cong. Globe, 33rd Cong., 2nd Sess., Appendix, February 15, 1855; Bynne wrote his letter in June 1854. It may be presumed that it was addressed to Olds, although this is not certain. The other materials culled by Olds were all at least three years old.

27 Quoted in Daniel Allen Butler, *The Age of Cunard* (Annapolis: Lighthouse Press, 2003), 77; Cong. Globe, 33rd Cong., 2nd Sess., Appendix, February 15, 1855.

28 Alvin A. Fahrner, "William 'Extra Billy' Smith, Governor of Virginia 1864–1865: A Pillar of the Confederacy," *Virginia Magazine of History and Biography* 74, no. 1 (January 1966): 68.

29 W. H. Graham to James Brown, February 13, 1855, Brown Papers, Box 40, F 7.

30 Cong. Globe, 33rd Cong., 2nd Sess. (February 16, 1855).

31 *Journal of the Senate*, February 17, 1855; *Journal of the Senate*, February 28, 1855.

32 *New York Daily Tribune*, March 3, 1855.

33 Gustavus Myers, *History of the Great American Fortunes* (Chicago: C.H. Kerr Co., 1909–10), 2:115.

34 "An Act to Supply Deficiencies." *United States Statutes at Large*, Act of July 21, 1852, ch. 66.

35 Collins to Postmaster James Campbell, January 27, 1854; Cong. Globe, 33rd Cong., 2nd Sess., Appendix, 185.

36 Franklin Pierce Veto Message, March 3, 1855. http://www.presidency.ucsb.edu/ws/index.php?pid=67624.

37 Cong. Globe, 33rd Cong., 2nd Sess. (March 3, 1855).

38 Quoted in Stiles, *The First Tycoon*, 261.

39 *New York Daily Tribune*, March 8, 1855.

40 Cong. Globe, 33rd Cong., 2nd Sess. (March 3, 1855).

41 The act provided funding for the deficiencies ending June 30, 1855, and complete funding for the year ending June 30, 1856. "An Act for Making Appropriations for the Naval Service," *United States Statutes at Large*, March 3, 1855, ch. 198.

42 *Boston Daily Atlas*, March 6, 1855; *Texas State Gazette*, March 24, 1855; *New Hampshire Patriot*, March 21, 1855; *New York Evening Post*, March 8, 1855.

43 *New York Daily Tribune*, March 8, 1855.

44 *Boston Daily Atlas*, March 17, 1855.

45 Within a few years, however, competition from newly formed foreign lines, including the British Inman Line as well as the North German Lloyd Line, cut deeply into his revenue. Vanderbilt gradually abandoned the Atlantic run, and by the early years of the American Civil War, taking advantage of the high prices offered for his vessels, he sold his ships and left the sea to concentrate on railroads. Stiles, *The First Tycoon*, 267–68; Lane, *Commodore Vanderbilt*, 153–56.

46 Cedric Ridgely-Nevitt, *American Steamships on the Atlantic* (Newark: University of Delaware Press, 1981), 164.

47 *New York Herald*, April 12, 1856.

48 David Budlong Tyler, *Steam Conquers the Atlantic* (New York: D. Appleton-Century Company, 1939), 237.

49 Brown, Shipley to Brown Brothers (New York), March 30, 1855 Box 40, F. 7; Brown, Shipley to Brown Brothers (New York), October 9–10, 1857, Box 40, F. 7. Brown Brothers Harriman Papers, New York Historical Society; Bullard, *Sails, Steam and Subsidies*, 28.

50 *New Hampshire Packet*, October 17, 1855.

51 Eldridge's career is well described in Vincent Miles, *The Lost Hero of Cape Cod* (Yarmouth Port: Historical Society of Old Yarmouth, 2015).

52 Henry C. Kittredge, *Shipmasters of Old Cape Cod* (Boston: Houghton Mifflin Company, 1935), 194.

53 *Washington Daily Globe*, February 7, 1856.

54 *Baltimore Sun*, February 9, 1856; *Liverpool Mercury*, January 25, 1856.

55 *Boston Daily Atlas*, February 9, 1856.

56 *Boston Daily Atlas*, February 11, 1856.

57 *Liverpool Mercury*, March 1, 1856.

58 *Weekly Raleigh Register*, March 26, 1856.

59 *Frank Leslie's Illustrated Newspaper*, April 5, 1856.

60 *Middletown, Connecticut Constitution*, March 19, 1856.

61 *San Joaquin Republican*, March 22, 1856. On August 7, 1861, the *New York Times* reported that a bottle had washed up "on the western shore of Uls, in the Hebrides." According to the newspaper account the bottle contained a note signed by a crewman of the doomed *Pacific*. "On board the Pacific, from L'pool to N. York. Ship going down. [Great] confusion on board. Icebergs around us on every side. I know I cannot

escape. I write the cause of our loss, that friends may not live in suspense. The finder of this will please get it published."

62 *Georgia Telegraph*, March 18, 1856.

63 Bullard, *Sails, Steam and Subsidies*, 54; Robert G. Albion, *Square-Riggers on Schedule* (Princeton: Princeton University Press, 1938), 170.

64 *Charleston Mercury*, March 13, 1856.

65 *Chicago Times*, April 3, 1856.

66 *Times-Picayune*, August 1, 1856.

67 Collins to Thurlow Weed, February 12, 1856, Seward Correspondence, University of Rochester.

68 *Baltimore Sun*, January 8, 1856.

Chapter Sixteen: *End of the Line*

1 Campbell, until recently a Whig, identified himself as being in "opposition." He was part of the emerging Republican Party that had begun to take form since an 1854 meeting at Ripon, Wisconsin, attended by Conscience Whigs and Free Soil Democrats. Bills and Resolutions of the House H.R.316. 34th Cong., 1st Sess., 1 (1856); *Biographical Directory of the American Congress, 1774–Present*, http://bioguide.congress .gov/scripts/biodisplay.pl?index=C000096.

2 Thomas R. Bullard, *Sails, Steam and Subsidies*, 40; Dow, "The Collins Line" (MA Thesis, Columbia University, 1837), 8.

3 Cong. Globe, 34 Cong., 1st Sess. (August 15, 1856); Bullard, *Sails, Steam and Subsidies*, 68–69.

4 Debate in the House can be followed in Cong. Globe, 34th Cong. 1st Sess. (August 16–18, 1856) and *Senate Journal*, 34th Cong., 1st Sess. (August 16, 1856).

5 *New York Herald*, February 7, 1858.

6 The Act authorized $819,500 but then instructed the Secretary of the Navy "to terminate the arrangements for the additional allowance." Act of August 18, 1856, ch. 162.

7 *New York Herald*, August 19, 1856.

8 *New York Herald*, August 23, 1856.

9 In the spring of 1856 *Persia* took the record from *Baltic*, beating her by thirty-six minutes.

10 *Charleston Mercury*, April 9, 1856; *Boston Daily Atlas*, April 8, 1856; *Trenton State Gazette*, April 8, 1856; *New York Weekly Herald*, April 12, 1856.

11 *New York Weekly Herald*, April 12, 1856.

12 *Baltimore Sun*, April 10, 1856.

13 *New York Tribune*, October 7, 1856.

14 A detailed description of *Adriatic* can be found in *New York Tribune*, October 7, 1856. At her launching (1853) Donald McKay's clipper *Great Republic* was larger than *Adriatic*. After a fire, however, she was rebuilt, resulting in a smaller vessel. Carl C. Cutler, *Greyhounds of the Sea* (New York: G. P. Putnam's Sons, 1930), 275, 428.

15 *Brooklyn Eagle*, September 26, 1856.

16 Guide to Allen Family Papers, Hagley Museum and Library, http://findingaids
.hagley.org/xtf/view?docId=ead/1978.xml.

17 A detailed description of the engine appears in Cedric Ridgely-Nevitt, *American Steamships on the Atlantic* (Newark: University of Delaware Press, 1981), 167–69.

18 *New York Tribune*, October 7, 1856.

19 *New York Tribune*, October 7, 1856.

20 *Times*, December 7, 1857.

21 *New York Tribune*, October 7, 1856.

22 *Times*, December 30, 1856.

23 "Frederick Elsworth Sickels," Find A Grave, http://www.findagrave.com/cgi-bin
/fg.cgi?page=gr&GRid=39684214.

24 "The Steamships of the Collins Line," *Scientific American* 13, issue 13 (April 24, 1858): 261.

25 Ridgeley-Nevitt, *American Steamships*, 168–69; *New York Herald*, January 1, 1858; *New York Times*, April 8, 1895; Sickels, "Find A Grave."

26 *Baltimore Sun*, November 25, 1857; *Webb* went on to serve in the Confederate States Navy. *Dictionary of American Naval Fighting Ships* (Washington: Navy Department, 1963), 2:581.

27 *Baltimore Sun*, November 25, 1857.

28 Taken from the Old Testament, Jonah is a person who brings ill fortune to a ship. "Jonah," Peter Kemp, ed., *The Oxford Companion to Ships and the Sea* (Oxford: Oxford University Press, 1993), 434.

29 Ridgely-Nevitt, *American Steamships*, 169; *New York Times*, April 14, 1860.

30 *Illustrated London News*, December 19, 1857; *Liverpool Mercury*, December 7, 1857; *Persia*'s record time was nine days, sixteen hours.

31 *Illustrated London News*, December 19, 1857.

32 *Liverpool Mercury*, December 7, 1857.

33 Both were more than halfway through their expected service life of ten years. *Charleston Mercury*, January 11, 1858.

34 Dow, "The Collins Line," 100.

35 Dow, "Collins Line," 45. The total number of passengers carried by Collins:

    1850–1,899
    1851–4,097
    1852–4,567
    1853–6,249
    1854–6,218
    1855–7,113
    1856–3,374
    1857–1,490
    1858–78

Bullard, *Sails, Steam and Subsidies*, 63–66.

36 *Acadia* was the only one of the original quartet remaining in service. She was scrapped in 1858. Cunard had also expanded service to the Mediterranean. Francis

E. Hyde, *Cunard and the North Atlantic 1840–1873* (London: Macmillan, 1975), 1–58.

37 *Sacramento Daily State Journal*, April 1, 1858.

38 Cunard built an elegant Italianate-style house on Staten Island, Westwood, which is now part of the campus of Wagner College. http://wagner.edu/wagnermagazine/?p=176.

39 Hyde, *Cunard and the North Atlantic*, 45; John G. Langley, *Steam Lion: A Biography of Samuel Cunard* (Halifax: Nimbus, 2006), 142. *Arabia*, built in 1852, was wood-and-paddle-driven. *Persia*, built 1856, was iron-hulled and paddle-driven. Hyde, *Cunard and the North Atlantic*, 326. For a full list see "Shipwrecks of the Cunard Line," http://www.cunardshipwrecks.com/fleet.html.

40 Not until 1878 did the name appear officially as the Cunard Steamship Line. Hyde, *Cunard and the North Atlantic*, 24. In 1859 George Burns retired from the company, followed by his brother James.

41 Quoted in Hyde, *Cunard and the North Atlantic*, 48.

42 *New Hampshire Patriot*, November 30, 1859.

43 Sam Warwick and Mike Roussel, *Shipwrecks of the Cunard Line* (The Mill: The History Press, 2012), 128.

44 *Charleston Mercury*, August 5, 1857.

45 *Macon Weekly Telegraph*, August 31, 1858.

46 *Middletown* [CT] *Constitution*, September 28, 1859.

47 Quoted in Lindsay Lord, *Nautical Etiquette and Customs* (Centreville, MD: Cornell Maritime Press, 1987), 41. See also "Mark Twain on the Cunard Line," http://paperspast.natlib.govt.nz/cgi-bin/paperspast?a=d&d=MIC18730509.2.19.

48 *Times-Picayune*, July 23, 1858; *Pittsfield Sun*, June 26, 1857.

49 Among the casualties was Cunard's agent in Boston, Edward Bates. His failure was attributed to "speculation in sugar." *Times-Picayune*, August 22, 1857.

50 Edwin J. Perkins, *Financing Anglo-American Trade: The House of Brown, 1800–1880* (Cambridge: Harvard University Press, 1975), 35, 55–56.

51 *Charleston Mercury*, February 5, 1858.

52 *Washington Daily Globe*, February 17, 1858.

53 *Times-Picayune*, August 1, 1856.

54 *New York Herald*, March 29, 1858.

55 The details of the auction are taken from *New York Herald*, April 2, 1858.

56 *New York Herald*, April 1, 2, 1858.

57 *San Francisco Daily Bulletin*, March 20, 1858.

58 *Houston Telegraph*, June 30, 1858.

59 *Senate Journal*, 36th Cong., 1st Sess. (June 10, 1858).

60 *Statutes at Large*, June 14, 1858, ch. 164.

61 *Baltimore Sun*, July 28, 1859.

62 Bullard, *Sails, Steam and Subsidies*, 44; *Daily National Intelligencer*, May 10, 1858.

63 Bullard, *Sails, Steam and Subsidies*, 44; Cedric Ridgely-Nevitt, *American Steamships*, 250.

64 Collins to Seward, May 19, 1860. Correspondence of William Henry Seward, University of Rochester Rare Books and Special Collections.

65 "Statement" of the Wellsville Coal and Land Company, 1853; *New York Times*, August 16, 1852.

66 This quote is taken from *Before the Memory Fades* (Wellsville: Wellsville Historical Society, 1950), which is a summary of articles from the local newspaper, *The Wellsville Patriot*. It is difficult to separate direct quotes from comments made by the compiler. I am therefore placing quotation marks around the entire quote.

67 *Before the Memory Fades*, 34–35.

68 The house still stands on State Route 213 in Wellsville, Ohio. Conversation with present owner Mr. William Iddings, January 9, 2016: *Steubenville Herald Star*, November 1, 1999.

69 *New York Times*, December 27, 1860; *Before the Memory Fades*, 38.

70 By this he most likely meant an outside bowling green.

71 *New York Herald*, January 3, 1863.

72 This includes Manhattan, the Bronx, Staten Island, Brooklyn, and Queens.

73 Francis R. Kowski, *Country, Park and City: The Architecture and Life of Calvert Vaux* (New York: Oxford University Press, 1998), 150.

74 Frederick Law Olmsted to his father, July 22, 1860. *The Papers of Frederick Law Olmsted*, edited by Charles C. McLaughlin (Baltimore: Johns Hopkins Press, 1977–2015) 7:256; Judith Doolin Spikes, *Larchmont, New York People and Places* (Larchmont: Fountain Square Books, 1991), 65 suggests that it is unlikely that Olmsted and Vaux themselves executed the design, leaving it to others in his firm.

75 The editors of the Olmsted Papers make the point that "no surviving document illustrates the Olmsted-Faux plan, which may have been their first collaborative design for a major estate. *Papers of Frederick Law Olmsted*, 3; 257n. Spikes, in *Images of Larchmont* (Charleston: Acadia Press, 2003), 36, provides an illustration of a map drawn in 1862 laying out the lots. This may be the original Olmsted-Vaux plan.

76 *New York Herald*, January 3, 1863.

77 *New York Herald*, February 4. 1863.

78 *New York Herald*, June 20, 1865.

79 *New York Herald*, April 15, 1867; Edward Knight Collins Probate Documents, February 7, 1878, Liber 1165, New York County Surrogate's Court, New York, NY (New England Historic Genealogical Society Case Number M103013A-2 Addendum).

80 By this time Mrs. Tucker had left to be replaced by Mrs. E. A. Barney, *New York Herald*, June 3, 1869; United States Census Mamaroneck, Westchester County, New York 1870.

81 *New York Herald*, January 27, 1873.

82 *New York Herald*, April 30, 1872, June 6, 1872; Spikes, *Larchmont, New York People and Places*, 59–69.

83 *New York Herald*, January 29, 1873.

84 The exact movement of the family is uncertain. From the Probate file it is clear that he went to Wellsville early in 1867. The 1870 U.S. Census puts him back in Larchmont.

January 1873 newspaper accounts put him in Ohio. He died on January 23, 1878, but was home many months before his death.

85 *New York Times*, January 23, 1878; *Philadelphia Inquirer*, January 24, 1878.

86 Edward Knight Collins Probate File.

87 The properties were at Madison Avenue and 133rd Street, 78th Street, and 135th Street. *New York Tribune*, January 24, 1889.

88 *New York Tribune*, May 3, 1889.

89 Woodlawn Cemetery, Lot I, Range 2.

Epilogue

1 H. David Bess and Martin T. Farris, *U.S. Maritime Policy: History and Prospects* (New York: Praeger, 1981), 20, estimates that Cunard's subsidy was 25 percent of total operating costs.

2 William Henry Flayhart, *The American Line (1871–1902)* (New York: W.W. Norton, 2000), 7.

3 *Historical Statistics of the United States Colonial Times to 1970 Part 2* (Washington: Department of Commerce, 1975), 750. Vessels engaged in international trade are registered by country and fly the flag of that nation. Historically, for the most part the main prerequisite for American registry is that the ship must have been built in the United States and crewed by American seamen. Kenneth J. Blume, *Historical Dictionary of the U.S. Maritime Industry* (Lanham: Scarecrow Press, 2012).

4 "Go west, young man, go west," by John Babsone Lane Soule first appeared in the *Terre Haute Express* in 1851. Greeley rephrased it slightly but did give credit to Soule. J. W. Ellison, "Go West, Young Man, Go West," *Dictionary of American History* (Farmington: Gale Group, 2003), http://www.encyclopedia.com/doc/1G2-3401801733.html.

5 Maury Klein, "Financing the Transcontinental Railroad," *History Now Journal of the Gilder Lehrman Institute*, https://www.gilderlehrman.org/history-by-era/develop ment-west/essays/financing-transcontinental-railroad.

6 Bess and Farris, *U.S. Maritime Policy*, 28.

7 *Historical Statistics*, 749–50, 760–61; John R. Spears, *The Story of the American Merchant Marine* (New York: The Macmillan Company, 1919), xiii–xvii, 298.

8 By a special exemption Norwegian Cruise Lines operates a foreign-built vessel, *Pride of America*, under American registry. The ship is confined to service in the Hawaiian Islands.

9 John Frittelli, *Cargo Preference for U.S. Flag Shipping* (Washington: Congressional Research Service, 2015), 7; United Nations Conference on Trade and Development, *Review of Maritime Transport 2015* (New York: United Nations, 2016), 42.

INDEX

A NOTE ON THE AUTHOR

William M. Fowler Jr. is Distinguished Professor of History Emeritus at Northeastern University in Boston.